SPIRITUAL RESOURCES IN FAMILY THERAPY

SPIRITUAL RESOURCES

IN

FAMILY THERAPY

Edited by

FROMA WALSH

THE GUILFORD PRESS
New York   London

© 1999 The Guilford Press
A Division of Guilford Publications, Inc.
72 Spring Street, New York, NY 10012
http://www.guilford.com

Printed in the United States of America

This book is printed on acid-free paper.

Last digit is print number: 9 8 7 6 5 4 3 2 1

Library of Congress Cataloging-in-Publication Data

Spiritual resources in family therapy / edited by Froma Walsh.
   p. cm.
  Includes bibliographical references and index.
  ISBN 1-57230-508-8
  1. Family psychotherapy—Religious aspects. 2. Spirituality. 3. Religion and psychology. I. Walsh, Froma.
  RC488.5.S69 1999
  616.89′156—dc21   99-38031
                                                CIP

About the Editor

Froma Walsh, MSW, PhD, is a professor in the School of Social Service Administration and the Department of Psychiatry at the University of Chicago. She is also a codirector of the University-affiliated family therapy training institute, the Chicago Center for Family Health. She is the editor of the *Journal of Marital and Family Therapy,* past-president of the American Family Therapy Academy, a recipient of AFTA's Award for Distinguished Contribution to Family Therapy Theory and Practice, and an Approved Supervisor of the American Association for Marriage and Family Therapy. She is author of *Strengthening Family Resilience* and editor or coeditor of *Normal Family Processes, Living Beyond Loss,* and *Women in Families.*

97954

Contributors

Herbert Anderson, PhD, Catholic Theological Union, Graduate School of Ministry, Chicago, Illinois

Harry J. Aponte, ACSW, private practice, Philadelphia, Pennsylvania

Mary Jo Barrett, MSW, Center for Contextual Change, Evanston, Illinois

Nancy Boyd-Franklin, PhD, Graduate School of Applied and Professional Psychology, Rutgers University, Piscataway, New Jersey

William J. Doherty, PhD, Department of Family Social Science, University of Minnesota, St. Paul, Minnesota

Celia Jaes Falicov, PhD, Department of Psychiatry, University of California at San Diego, San Diego, California

Mona DeKoven Fishbane, PhD, Chicago Center for Family Health, Chicago, Illinois

Melissa Elliott Griffith, MSN, Church St. Center, Vienna, Virginia

Tonya Walker Lockwood, PsyD, Graduate School of Applied and Professional Psychology, Rutgers University, Piscataway, New Jersey

Wayne Muller, MDiv, Bread for the Journey, Santa Fe, New Mexico

Alice de V. Perry, DMin, Andover Newton Theological School, Newton, Massachusetts; Milford Pastoral Counseling Center, Milford, Connecticut

Janine Roberts, EdD, School of Education, University of Massachusetts, Amherst, Massachusetts

John S. Rolland, MD, Chicago Center for Family Health, Chicago, Illinois; Department of Psychiatry, University of Chicago, Chicago, Illinois

Richard C. Schwartz, PhD, Family Institute at Northwestern University, Evanston, Illinois

Fred Taylor, MDiv, ThM, FLOC Inc., Washington, DC

Froma Walsh, MSW, PhD, School of Social Service Administration and Department of Psychiatry, University of Chicago, Chicago, Illinois; Chicago Center for Family Health, Chicago, Illinois

Kathy Weingarten, PhD, Program in Narrative Therapies, Family Institute of Cambridge, Cambridge, Massachusetts; Department of Psychology, Harvard Medical School, Cambridge, Massachusetts

Steven J. Wolin, MD, George Washington University, Washington, DC; Project Resilience, Washington, DC

Sybil Wolin, PhD, Project Resilience, Washington, DC

Lorraine M. Wright, RN, PhD, Family Nursing Unit and Faculty of Nursing, University of Calgary, Calgary, Alberta, Canada

Preface

Spirituality is a powerful dimension of human experience, with growing importance and diversity in today's changing world. Yet it has long been regarded as off-limits in clinical training and practice, leaving most therapists and counselors blind to its significance and reluctant to approach it. Many have regarded clients' spirituality as a private matter not to be intruded on and best left to clergy, pastoral counselors, or faith healers. Some have worried that therapists might impose their own convictions on vulnerable clients. Others fear the intensity of feelings and conflicts that can be aroused by delving into spiritual issues. Therapists who do not consider themselves to be especially religious, or those who lack training in this area, may underestimate the powerful influence of spirituality in the lives of most clients and in the very process of therapy.

This volume is intended as a sourcebook to inform and inspire mental health, health care, pastoral, and human service professionals of all disciplines about this vital dimension in clinical work with couples and families. The aim of this book is to open family therapy practice to spirituality: to explore clients' spiritual beliefs and practices, to understand those that have constrained clients' growth, and to tap resources for resilience and transformation.

Rather than presenting a particular spiritual approach to therapy based on an author's own religious convictions, this volume presents a broad and pluralistic view of spirituality, offering an ecumenical wellspring for therapists and clients of diverse faith orientations. With varied spiritual orientations and therapeutic approaches, the authors each examine spirituality in families and family therapy from a unique vantage point. All are grounded in a systemic orientation, a strengths perspective, and a collaborative partnership with clients.

As Chapter 1 reveals, the vast majority of families regard religion as important in their lives and adopt some form of expression for their spirituality. Many who seek help for physical, emotional, or interpersonal problems are also in spiritual distress. Most importantly, research has begun to document the benefits of faith and congregational support in well-being and longevity, as well as recovery from illness, loss, substance abuse, and trauma. If we are to understand our clients and assist in their healing and growth, it is crucial to explore their spiritual beliefs and practices, attend to spiritual sources of their distress, and encourage them to draw on spiritual resources.

Moreover, as our world rapidly changes and our society becomes increasingly diverse, we therapists need to develop a spiritual pluralism, with understanding and respect for the varied faith perspectives of our clients, which are intertwined with other aspects of culture and life circumstances. There is growing religious diversity within families, as well, through conversion, intermarriage, and the blending of varied faith orientations. It is important to understand how such differences may contribute to conflict or estrangement so that we can foster greater understanding, acceptance, and relational healing.

This volume also encourages us as clinicians to examine our own ethical and spiritual positions, since the therapeutic process and goals involve the interaction of core beliefs of therapists and clients. Faulty assumptions or inattention to spiritual influences may undermine therapeutic efforts or lead to inappropriate aims. Just as we have recognized that therapists cannot be neutral and must attend to larger cultural influences, so must we be aware of our own values and biases as we attend to the spiritual dimension of our clients' experience. My work on family resilience sparked my interest in exploring spirituality more deeply and bringing it into my therapeutic work. Adversity and suffering open us to the spiritual domain. Studies of resilient individuals and families have documented the power of spirituality in surmounting life challenges and in transcending painful experience. No clinical sourcebook on spirituality yet existed, so I envisioned one that would bring together some of the most creative family therapists at the forefront of our field, who were expanding their vision and practice to include this vital dimension.

This volume approaches spirituality not simply as a special topic, but rather as streams of experience that flow through all aspects of people's lives, from family heritage to belief systems and practices, intimate relationships, and congregational affiliations. These streams ebb and flow and often alter their courses over the family life cycle and across generations. It is important to explore the spiritual meaning of experience with *all* clients, not just with those who initially present spiritual concerns. Spiritual belief systems influence how people define problems, view causes and solutions, and make meaning of adversity and suffering. They also influence how families approach coping, acceptance, and change, and where members turn for help. We need to understand how trauma or persistent hardship has wounded the soul; how constraining beliefs, negative religious experiences, or a spiritual void may contribute to distress and block healing.

In Part I of this volume, Chapter 1 presents an overview that examines the growing importance and diversity of religion and spirituality for individuals and their families. Spirituality is broadly defined as beliefs and practices that are both deeply personal and transcendent, and can be experienced either within or outside formal religious institutions. Chapter 2 explores ways to open therapeutic practice to this vital dimension in order to understand spiritual sources of distress and foster resilience, healing, and growth. In it I share my own experience and reflections, so as to encourage therapists to explore their own religious upbringing, complex family and cultural legacies, and ongoing spiritual journeys.

In Part II, chapter authors explore spiritual resources in families and the ways therapists can tap those potential wellsprings. The authors examine such topics as illness, healing, and resilience; spiritual concerns and resources of poor, minority, and immigrant families; and ways to draw on spiritual resources in intergenerational relations and everyday family life.

In Part III, contributors focus on spiritual aspects of the therapeutic process itself, bridging the longstanding divide that has separated clinical and faith-based approaches to practice. Chapters consider the integration of moral and ethical issues in therapy; spiritual aspects in recovery from trauma; and ways of approaching clients' personal relationships with God. Several authors describe the essence of healing and growth as a profoundly spiritual experience for both client and therapist. The volume concludes with chapters addressing ways to bring spirituality into family therapy training and ways for clients and therapists alike to express spirituality through social action.

Buddhism counsels one to assume a beginner's mind when embarking on a spiritual journey. The authors in this volume offer their experiences and reflections not from a position of authority, but more tentatively, as explorers in unfamiliar territory, with humility and respect for the power and potential of the spiritual in therapeutic practice. Readers will not find detailed maps for how to navigate this territory, since we are only beginning this journey in our field. Perhaps of greater value, the contributors have tried to share their beliefs, experiences, and reflections with integrity and openheartedness. I hope this volume will inspire others to open the therapeutic door to spirituality and, as many of us have found, that it will enrich therapy and foster greater meaning, wholeness, and connection.

In this way, the ramifications of our practice extend beyond those who come to us in distress, rippling out to kin, communities, and beyond. As Albert Einstein wrote,

> A human being is part of the whole, called by us "Universe"; a part limited in time and space. He experiences himself, his thoughts, and feelings as something separated from the rest—a kind of optical delusion of his consciousness. This delusion is a kind of prison for us, restricting us to our personal desires and for affection for a few persons nearest to us. Our task must be to free ourselves from this prison by widening our circle of compassion to embrace all living creatures, and the whole of nature in its beauty.

FROMA WALSH
Chicago, IL

Acknowledgments

On behalf of all the authors who have contributed to this book, I would like to express our appreciation to our families, our colleagues, and, most of all, to the students and clients with whom we have been privileged to work. We have all found that the spirit is nourished and grows through such meaningful connections.

As editor of this volume, it has been gratifying to create a space for cherished colleagues to share, each in our own ways, our deepening awareness of the importance of the spiritual dimension in our therapeutic efforts. I thank all the contributors for the wonderful and inspiring chapters that make this a truly extraordinary sourcebook.

I would like to acknowledge the valuable assistance of Carmen Crosser, a family therapist and doctoral student, who has worked enthusiastically with me over the past year in the preparation of this volume. I am especially grateful for her help in searching through the vast literature on religion and spirituality for the introductory chapter, particularly in tracking down and making meaning of elusive statistics. I would also like to thank the responsive staff at The Guilford Press, with special appreciation to Kitty Moore, Senior Editor, for her valuable feedback on chapters; to Paul Gordon, for a truly inspired cover design; and to Anna Brackett, for her attentive oversight of production.

Finally, I would like to express my love and appreciation for my family. My husband, John, had not thought of his deep roots and dedication to social justice as "spiritual" until he began looking at them in this light, as he collaborated on a chapter with his close friend, Alice Perry. (I also value our special bond with Allie, who participated in our marriage ceremony, alongside a rabbi, and offered a feminist perspective on Adam and Eve.) This year I have been so proud of my daughter, Claire, as she has blossomed into a young woman of uncommon depth and compassion. She, too, has developed a burning interest in the study of ethics and world religions and has become passionate about social justice. (This summer she is taking part in a community service project in a small village in Guadeloupe.)

I feel that my own calling to do this book and more actively pursue my own spiritual journey is guided by the loving spirit of my parents. My mother and my father each suffered painful adversity and losses in their lives; yet through their darkest hours, their deeply personal spirituality was an ever-burning flame that sustained their resilience. This book is dedicated to their spirit; I never stop missing them, and yet they are always there for me, deep within my soul and in the stars in the night sky.

Contents

PART III
Spirituality and Family Therapy: Bridging the Divide

SPIRITUAL RESOURCES IN FAMILY THERAPY

PART I

Overview

CHAPTER 1

Religion and Spirituality
Wellsprings for Healing and Resilience

FROMA WALSH

We are not human beings having a spiritual experience;
we are spiritual beings having a human experience.
—PIERRE TEILHARD DE CHARDIN

Over the centuries, people have lit candles, prayed together, meditated, and quietly turned to faith for solace, strength, and connectedness in their lives. At times of crisis and adversity, spiritual beliefs and practices have fostered resilience and recovery from loss, trauma, and suffering. Today, the vast majority of families adopt some form of expression for their spirituality. Many who seek help for physical, emotional, or interpersonal problems are also in spiritual distress. Therefore, as therapists and human service professionals, we need to attend to the spiritual beliefs and practices of our clients if we are to understand them and assist in their healing and growth.

Spirituality is not simply a special topic, although some clients may present particular spiritual concerns. Rather, it involves streams of experience that flow through all aspects of our lives, from family heritage to personal belief systems, rituals and practices, and congregational affiliations. Spiritual beliefs influence ways of coping with adversity, the experience of pain and suffering, what is labeled as a problem, and the meaning of symptoms. They also influence how people communicate about their pain; their beliefs about its causes and future course; their attitudes toward helpers—clergy, physicians, therapists, faith healers; the treatment they seek; and their preferred approaches to acceptance or change. Moreover, psychotherapy itself, long considered a healing art, can be a profoundly spiritual experience for both clients and therapists, yet this has been a hidden aspect of our work. The very essence of the therapeutic relationship and meaningful change are ultimately spiritual in nature, fostering personal transformation, wholeness, and relational connection with others.

Family therapists and trainees are beginning to show keen interest in exploring and developing the spiritual dimensions of our practice. Yet most of us are groping in the dark as we approach such unfamiliar terrain. This overview chapter examines the growing importance and diversity of religion and spirituality for individuals and families today. Chapter 2 then explores ways to surmount barriers to the integration of spirituality and family therapy so that we may tap into this wellspring for resilience, healing, and growth.

RELIGION AND SPIRITUALITY IN A CHANGING WORLD

There has been a resurging interest in religion and spirituality at the close of the 20th century as people have sought greater meaning, harmony, and connection in their lives. Over recent decades, families worldwide have experienced tumultuous social and economic dislocations, generating a spiritual malaise (Lerner, 1994). As the world around us changes at an accelerated pace, daily lives seem on the brink of chaos. Harried, fragmented schedules undermine the very sense of identity, well-being, and purpose we desperately seek (Hochschild, 1997). Job security, health care coverage, and future retirement benefits are increasingly uncertain. Our consumer-based economy consumes us without yielding fulfillment. Image-focused media and political "spin" saturate our lives, leaving a hunger for substance and moral integrity. Beseiged parents are unsure how to raise their children well in a hazardous world and counter destructive pressures of the wider pop culture (Pipher, 1997).

The cultural ethos of the "rugged individual" and self-oriented decades of "looking out for number one" have contributed to the breakdown of communities and the fraying of our social fabric, accompanied by a widespread sense of isolation, powerlessness, and despair (Bellah, Madsen, Sullivan, Swidler, & Tipton, 1983). As Lifton (1993) observes, many feel adrift on their own fragile life rafts in a turbulent sea.

Marriage and family life have become especially precarious. With divorce and remarriage increasingly common, families tend to break up and recombine with ever greater complexity. With the growing diversity of family forms and cultural values, changing gender roles, and varied life cycle course, no single model fits all. Instead, families are having to reinvent themselves, many times over, to fit the challenges of our times (Walsh, 1993, 1998a). A widespread sense of disruption and confusion accompany changes in the structure of family relationships. Family members struggle to deal with real and symbolic losses as they redefine their values, practices, and living arrangements.

Moreover, as aging baby boomers experience the deaths of parents and other loved ones and begin to face their own mortality, there is growing impetus to explore the meaning of life and the mystery of an afterlife, as evidenced in the recent burst of films and best-selling books on these subjects. The AIDS epidemic has heightened consciousness of life and death issues.

It may be only an illusion that life was ever more secure in earlier times or distant places, as seen through the rose-colored lens of nostalgia (Walsh, 1993). Yet, in the relativism of our postmodern era, many are alarmed by a seeming collapse of universal moral values. The rise in religious fundamentalism in many parts of the world can be seen as one expression of a need to return to traditions that provide structure and absolute certainties in reaction to rapid social change. Buffeted by societal and global forces seemingly beyond control or comprehension, we yearn for inner peace, for a sense of wholeness and coherence in our fragmented lives, and for more meaningful connection with others beyond ourselves. It is no wonder that so many dispirited people have been turning to spiritual sources of resilience, which over the centuries have anchored and nourished families and their communities.

DEFINING RELIGION AND SPIRITUALITY

It is helpful to clarify our understanding of religion and spirituality, since the terms are often used interchangeably. Wright, Watson, and Bell (1996) offer some useful distinctions between religion, as extrinsic, organized faith systems, and spirituality, as more intrinsic personal beliefs and practices.

Religion: Organized Belief System and Affiliation

Religion can be defined as an organized belief system that includes shared, and usually institutionalized, moral values, beliefs about God or a Higher Power, and involvement in a faith community. Religions provide standards and prescriptions for individual virtue and family life grounded in core beliefs. Particular ideas and practices are often considered to be right or true and go unquestioned. Congregational affiliation provides social and health benefits as well as support in times of crisis.

Rituals and ceremonies offer participants a sense of collective self and, as Taggart (1994) so aptly puts it, "a place in the chaos of reality" (p. 32). The family is central in rites that mark the birth of a new member, entry into the adult community, marriage vows, and the death of a loved one. For instance, the practice of Judaism is centered on the family observance of rituals, from weekly Shabbat (Sabbath) candle lighting to the major holidays in the Jewish calendar year and rites of passage across the life cycle. Each ritual carries significant meaning connecting family members with their larger community and with the history of the Jewish people, their covenant with God, and their survival over adversity.

Spirituality: Transcendent Beliefs and Practices

Spirituality, an overarching construct, refers more generally to transcendent beliefs and practices (Walsh, 1998). Spirituality can be experienced either within or outside formal religious structures, and is both broader and more personal (Elkins, 1990). James and Melissa Griffith have offered a simple yet profound definition of spirituality as "that which connects one to all there is" (Griffith & Griffith, 1999). Spirituality concerns an active investment in an internal set of values. It fosters a sense of meaning, inner wholeness, harmony, and connection with others—a unity with all life, nature, and the universe (Stander, Piercy, MacKinnon, & Helmeke, 1994). One's spirituality may (or may not) involve belief in a supreme being or an ultimate human condition toward which we strive. Spiritual resources might range from congregational affiliations to personal practices of meditation; they might include the use of traditional faith healing rituals, crystals, or special potions. They might also include numinous experiences, which are holy or mystical and difficult to define or explain in ordinary language and imagery. Spiritual and religious belief systems provide faith explanations of past history and present experiences; for many, they predict the future and offer pathways toward understanding the ultimate meanings of life and existence (Campbell & Moyers, 1988).

A moral awareness often evolves out of such spiritual belief systems (Coles, 1990, 1997). Morality involves the activity of informed conscience—judging right and wrong based on principles of fairness, decency, and compassion (Doherty, 1995). Moral or ethical values spur us to go beyond repair to improve conditions; to respond to the suffering of others; to feel an obligation to dedicate efforts to help others; to alleviate pain or injustice. At their best, they promote humanity. Spirituality invites an expansion of consciousness, along with personal responsibility for and beyond oneself, from local to global concerns.

Spirit; Soul

Universally, the spirit is seen as our vital essence, the source of life and power. In many languages the word for "spirit" and "breath" are the same: in Greek, *pneuma*; in Hebrew, *reach* ("ray-akh"); in Latin, *spiritus*; and in Sanskrit, *prana* (Weil, 1994). The soul, similarly, has been seen over the ages as the source of human genuineness, depth, joy, sorrow, and mystery. Herbert Anderson, a leading theological educator on marriage and the family, notes that the literal translation of Proverbs 23:16 is "my kidneys will rejoice when your lips speak what is right" (Anderson, 1994, p. 209).

Similarly, we sense something as true or profound in our "gut." Yet, Anderson adds that because the human being is a unity, soul or liver or kidney may also refer to the individual as a whole. He defines the soul as something like the visualizing center of life, the quality of living with ourselves and others. The soul, in many religions, is also a metaphor expressing the relationship between human beings and God: to tend to the soul is to restore and strengthen that connection (Becvar, 1996).

Taking a double view, Anderson (1994) describes soul as being everywhere but nowhere—not something we can take out and look at. Rather, it is in every cell of the body and also capable of self-transcendence. In this view, we are both soul-filled bodies and embodied souls, linked to earth and sky. As Thomas Moore (1992) affirms, "It takes a broad vision to know that a piece of sky and a chunk of the earth lie lodged in the heart of every human being, and if we are to care for that heart we will have to know the sky and earth as well as human behavior" (p. 20).

These perspectives are strikingly akin to those of Native American spirituality. Black Elk, a Holy Man of the Lakota tribe, recounted the story of his people during the tragic decades of the Custer battle and the Wounded Knee Massacre, revealing the spiritual source of resilience that sustained Native American tribes. In his eloquent and profound narrative, he described the system of beliefs based in a vision of the unity of all creation: "All living things that have legs, wings, or roots are children of one mother, Mother Earth, and their father is one Spirit. We are related to all things: the stars in the universe and the grasses of the earth" (Neihardt, 1932/1979, p. 5).

Many think of the spirit as living on after the death of the body. Native Americans, for instance, abhorred the common Yankee practice of hanging wrongdoers, believing that it blocked the ability of the soul to be released from the body in its last breaths (Deloria, 1994). Some people believe that the soul resides in a spirit world for all eternity; many believe that they can be in contact or receive visits from spirits, particularly in times of need, to offer reassurance to the bereft or when a serious wrong has not been attended to. For most people the spirits of the deceased live on in the minds, hearts, and stories of their loved ones. They can become guiding spirits, inspiring the best efforts and actions of the living.

Moore (1992) contends that the "loss of soul" has been the primary source of the maladies of our century, afflicting us individually and socially: "When soul is neglected, it doesn't just go away; it appears symptomatically in obsessions, addictions, violence, and loss of meaning. Our temptation is to isolate these symptoms or to try to eradicate them one by one; but the root problem is that we have lost our wisdom about the soul, even our interest in it" (p. xi). The result is a deficit of human spirit. We often refer to someone in despair (i.e., dispirited) as a "lost soul," without purpose or community, struggling to survive. Many of the challenges that are given pathological labels in therapeutic settings may also be understood as maladies of the modern soul. We are searching for soul—for meaning and connection in our lives, in our world, and in the universe.

In Moore's view, the recovery of the soul begins with acknowledgment of its mystery. We can only glimpse it in part and cannot penetrate its essence. More process and substance, the language of soul is not technical or scientific but rather embodied in poetry, art, and music. Imagination is the expression of soul; it involves the making of meaningful memory, linking the past, present, and future; the individual with the community and all that is beyond.

Soul also involves purposeful activity and restful replenishing. When we lose ourselves in a multitude of activities and petty concerns, we endanger the soul. Soul also involves vulnerability and uncertainty. As humans we are all susceptible to being wounded. Resilience is not invulnerability; rather, it is forged through fully experiencing a crisis and integrating it into the fabric of our lives. We nourish the soul by living without pretense or armor, able to move toward all experience with openness, courage, and compassion.

SPIRITUAL BELIEFS AND PRACTICES: GROWING IMPORTANCE AND DIVERSITY

The United States is one of the most religious nations in the industrialized world in the level of attested spiritual beliefs and practices. Gallup Surveys have been polling Americans since 1939 about their spiritual/religious beliefs and affiliations, tracking the ebbs and flows.[1] Religious interest and church attendance surged following World War II, through the 1950s, with such leaders as the Rev. Billy Graham and Bishop Fulton J. Sheen reaching into the home via the new television medium. In the 1960s, the Rev. Martin Luther King, Jr., galvanized the spirit and activism of the civil rights movement with his rallying call for social justice. A more militant and separatist Black Muslim movement also emerged at that time. Religious involvement declined somewhat from the late 1960s through the 1980s, in the midst of societal upheaval. In the 1990s there has been renewed vitality in organized religion and an expanding landscape of faiths. Today 90% of all adults say religion is important in their lives. Nearly 60% consider it very important and for one-third it is the most important part of their lives (Gallup, 1996). (One in three persons report watching some religious television each week; there are more than 250 religious TV stations!)

Importance of Religion and Spirituality in Families

For most people, religion and family life are deeply intertwined (Burton, 1992; Cornwall & Thomas, 1990; D'Antonio, Newman, & Wright, 1982).

Family process research has found that transcendent spiritual beliefs and practices are key ingredients in healthy family functioning (Beavers & Hampson, 1990; Stinnett & DeFrain, 1985). A system of values and shared beliefs that transcend the limits of their experience and knowledge enables family members to better accept the inevitable risks and losses in living and loving fully. Gallup Surveys (1996) support these findings: Nearly 75% of respondents report that their family relationships have been strengthened by religion in the home. More than 80% say that religion was important in their family of origin when they were growing up; notably, they were significantly more likely to report that religion is strengthening current family relationships a great deal.

Family Values

In recent political discourse, family values has been a hotly debated topic. Some on the conservative Christian right (as well as Orthodox Jews and fundamentalist Muslims) have asserted that the changing family forms and gender roles over recent decades have led to the demise of the family and the decay of "family values." In an era of growing family diversity and a rich variety of kinship patterns, it is crucial to move beyond the myth that one family standard must be the paragon of virtue for all families to emulate and that all others are inherently damaging (Stacey, 1996; Walsh, 1993). Family form has been confused with family substance. Family processes and community connections that strengthen the quality of relationships have far more impact on the ability of families and their members to survive and thrive (Walsh, 1998c).

All families have values—even those who have difficulty attaining their aims, often for reasons beyond their control. Some values break with tradition, as in the increasingly prevalent belief that men and women should be equal partners in marriage and family life. Most values maintain continuity with the past in terms of commitment, personal responsibility, and the strong desire to raise children to be healthy and have a good life. Of interest, in recent surveys (Gallup, 1996) "moral and spiritual values based on the Bible" far outranked "family counseling," "parent training classes," and "government laws and policies" as the main factor thought to strengthen the family, superseded only by "family ties, loyalty, and traditions."

Religion and Spirituality across the Family Life Cycle

Religion and spirituality involve dynamic processes that ebb and flow and that change in meaning over the life course and across the generations (Worthington, 1989). Frank McCourt, the author of *Angela's Ashes*, looked back on his childhood rearing as a Catholic in Ireland:

> When the altar boy rang the bell we slid from the pew seats to our knees. We kept our heads down. . . . Older people would groan and grumble over the stiffness in their bones but this was the high moment of the Mass, the Consecration, and God Himself was up there on the altar.
>
> He wasn't there metaphorically or symbolically. He was there in person or all three persons, the Father, the Son, and the Holy Ghost. The wine was His blood, the wafer His body and if we sneaked a peek we saw the priest raise the wafer, the Host, to the sky and we heard all around us the sighs of the grown-ups, their quiet rejoicing in the presence of the Lord. We might have been small, barely past First Communion and heading for Confirmation, but we knew we knelt in the presence of great mystery and we asked no questions. Not yet.
>
> In our adolescent years we might have discovered some inconsistencies and contradictions in Catholic teaching but if we asked questions they were brushed aside. If we didn't understand the Trinity, the Immaculate Conception, the Assumption of the Virgin Mary body and soul into heaven we were told it was a matter of faith so drink your tea and shut up. (McCourt, 1998, p. 63)

For most religions, marriage and procreation are the most important events in the family life cycle. Marriage often brings religious considerations to the fore. Decisions about the wedding itself set the course of the couple's relationship. Conflict may arise over whether to have a religious or civil ceremony. Partners of the same faith may differ in their particular sect or degree of observance. Conflict may arise, for instance, as to whether a rabbi and marital vows should be Orthodox, Conservative, or Reform. Families of origin may weigh in to steer wedding plans in line with their own convictions, often fueling intergenerational conflicts and in-law triangles that can reverberate over the years. The desire for a religious commitment ceremony by gay and lesbian couples may be met with opposition by family members who believe it violates their religious doctrine limiting marriage to heterosexual couples (Laird & Green, 1996).

Intermarriage greatly complicates the issues couples ordinarily bring to any relationship (Falicov, 1995; McGoldrick & Preto, 1984). Under stress, tolerance for differences can erode, particularly if one way is believed to be right and morally superior while the other is viewed as wrong or even immoral. In cases of interfaith marriage, it is important to ask couples whether both families of origin approved of the marriage and whether they attended the wedding. The choice of a spouse from a different religious background may express rebellion against parental values and authority (Friedman, 1985). Parental acceptance or disapproval can have long-lasting ramifications for the success or failure of the marriage and for intergenerational relations.

Remarriage can be fraught with religious complications. For Orthodox Jews, a woman wishing to remarry after divorce must obtain a "get," or written permission from her ex-spouse (Rosen & Weltman, 1996). (Men wishing to remarry are not required to do so.) The Catholic church allows divorce but only sanctions remarriage in cases of annulment. This strict ruling has led many Catholics to leave the church at remarriage. Other couples may decide to live together without legal remarriage or religious rites. It has also led a growing number of Catholics to petition the church for annulment of a former marriage when they wish to remarry. Such annulments are commonly granted, especially to influential men, even when the marriage had lasted many years, and over the objection of a former wife and children who may be deeply wounded that an annulment invalidates their prior family life and legitimacy. It is crucial to explore such conflict-laden religious issues in working with divorced and remarried families.

The vast majority of adults want their children to have religious training. Most teens say it is important for parents and children aged 12 and younger to attend church together (Gallup, 1996). With the birth of the first child, couples who may have viewed religion as unimportant in their lives are often startled to find that one or both care deeply about the religious upbringing of their children. Conflicts may arise over decisions about such rituals as christening, baptism, confirmation, or Bar/Bat Mitzvah. Here again, the older generation, now as grandparents, may make their religious preferences strongly known. Previous acceptance of their children's choice of a nontraditional wedding or an interfaith marriage may shift when they consider the moral development and religious identification of their grandchildren. This is an especially agonizing issue in the Jewish community, where there is deep concern about the future of Judaism, with high rates of interfaith marriage in recent decades (Foster & Tabachnik, 1993). Studies have found that when the gentile partner converts to Judaism, children tend to grow up with a Jewish identity and practice their faith, but when the spouse does not convert, children are likely not to develop a sense of themselves as Jewish.

Yet, sometimes it is the children who draw parents back to religious roots. Musician Bob Dylan (born Robert Zimmerman) broke away from his Jewish upbringing in the 1960s and then became an ardent born-again Christian in the early 1970s, but he was brought back to Judaism by his son who, when approaching the age of 13, requested a Bar Mitzvah.

It may surprise some that 95% of teenagers believe in God; 93% say God loves them; 91% believe in heaven; 76% believe in angels; 76% believe in hell. Three in four teens pray when they are alone. More than 60% say they have a great deal of interest in discussing the existence of God; over half express interest in discussing life's meaning and how to make moral decisions (Gallup, 1996). Like their parents, more than 8 in 10 teenagers follow one of the Judeo-Christian faiths. Nearly half say they went to church or synagogue in the past week. Just 9% state they have no religious preference, and only a fraction say they are either agnostic or atheist.

Young adults, particularly those in college, often distance themselves from their religious upbringing (Elkind, 1971). Of note, 15% of college freshmen report no religious preference (Gallup, 1996). Some young adults simply become less involved and lose faith, while others more actively question their religion or cut off altogether from their family's traditions. Many explore other spiritual paths in search of meaning, faith, and commitment (Parks, 1986).

Middle to later life is a time of growing saliency of spiritual values, as people grapple with questions about the meaning of life and face the death of loved ones and their own mortality (Erikson, Erikson, & Kivnick, 1986; Walsh, 1998b). Active congregational participation as well as prayer tend to become increasingly important over adulthood. Whereas only 35% of young adults aged 18–29 attend their place of worship weekly, 41% of persons aged 30–49, 46% of those aged 50–64, and 56% of those over 65 attend weekly. Over half of all adults expect religion to become even more important to them with aging. Surely the wisdom of elders is deepened by their growing spirituality.

Growing Religious Pluralism

The United States was founded by religious dissidents on the principle of respect and tolerance for such diversity (Gaustad, 1966). The culture was largely shaped by a Christian revival in the 19th century but has grown increasingly diverse in spiritual beliefs and practices in recent decades (Greeley, 1969). The religious landscape has changed dramatically, as people are seeking spiritual expression and connection in varied ways.

More than 90% of Americans identify with a specific religion.[2] The country remains predominantly Christian (85%), although membership in various denominations has been shifting (Gallup, 1996, 1998). Fifty-seven percent consider themselves Protestant. (The largest Protestant denominational affiliations are as follows: Baptist, 19% of all adults; Methodist, 9%; Lutheran, 6%; Presbyterian, 4%; Episcopalian, 2%; and Pentecostal, 1%.) Twenty-six percent of all adults are Roman Catholic. An additional 2% are Mormon (Church of Jesus Christ of Latter-Day Saints) and 1% are Eastern Orthodox (such as Greek or Russian). Many denominations are hard to distinguish; terms such as fundamentalist, evangelical, and charismatic are blurred, overlapping, and in flux.

There is much confusion about the Christian right. The so-called religious right has become a strong political coalition in recent years; however, it is unclear just who belongs to this movement. Some see it as a revival of the "moral majority"; others view it as a broad-based interracial, interfaith coalition combining fundamentalist visions of religion with a politically and socially conservative agenda. Actually, 18% of adults think of themselves as members of the religious right (Gallup, 1996), with the highest identification for women, Southerners, Blacks, seniors, and those who did not attend college. One-third of those who say they are "born-again" Christians also identify with the religious right, but two-thirds do not. Therefore, we must be careful not to assume that those who consider themselves "born again" or "evangelical" necessarily hold conservative social and political ideologies. (For instance, President Bill Clinton and Vice President Albert Gore, as well as former Vice President Dan Quayle, have all attested that they were born again.)

The non-Christian proportion of the U.S. population has been rapidly increasing: From 3.6% in 1900, non-Christians rose to 9.9% in 1970 and to 14.6% by 1995 (Gallup, 1996). Two percent of Americans identify as Jewish (down from 5% at midcentury, but stable since 1972). Five percent follow other religions: Islam, Hinduism, and Buddhism, each currently at 1%, are growing rapidly. (Worldwide, Muslims—followers of Islam—will soon outnumber Christians.) Buddhism is the fastest-growing Eastern religion in the United States, including many converts to Tibetan Buddhism. Still others identify with the Sikh, Bahai, Shinto, and Tao faiths. Some combine faith traditions, as do Bahais and Unitarian/Universalists. Some are drawn to mysticism from ancient religious sects, such as Sufism. A strong revival of Native American spiritual traditions has been occurring, especially among young people.

The New Age movement, while it may have some misguided prophets (like other religions), offers a range of approaches to people whose spiritual longings have not been met by conventional religions. Many New Age seekers are attempting to reinvigorate Christianity on their own terms (e.g., "A Course in Miracles" [Schucman and Thetford, 1996], a self-study program of spiritual psychotherapy).

Religious militants and extremist groups are small in number but pose a growing threat of violence. Although people commonly link terrorism with Muslim fundamentalists, the vast majority of Muslims abhor such militancy. Violence in the United States has more often been sparked by right-wing White militia groups, or others associated with extremist religious movements that espouse creeds of racism and religious intolerance (as in the recent shooting spree of Orthodox Jews, Blacks, and Asians by a member of the World Church of the Creator).

Others are drawn to religious cults, cutting off from their families and communities to live communally and follow the ideology of a charismatic leader, who may be seen as a prophet (Galanter, 1989). Anguished families may seek help to recover and "deprogram" a family member lost to such groups. The approach of the millennium has seen an upsurge in apocalyptic prophesies of the end of the world, "doomsday cults," and survivalist communes.

The wide spectrum of faiths today has been called a "supermarket" of religions, attesting to the strength and vitality of spiritual beliefs and practices. A multicultural perspective is required to understand the compexity and diversity of religious experiences.

Religion and Multicultural Influences

Religion and culture are interwoven in all aspects of our spiritual experience. Frank McCourt (1998) describes the image of God he formed in his Irish Catholic upbringing:

> We didn't hear much about a loving God. We were told God is good and that was supposed to be enough. Otherwise the Irish Catholic God of my memory is one the tribes of Israel would have recognized, an angry God, a vengeful God, a God who'd let you have it upside your head if you strayed, transgressed, coveted. Our God had a stern face. When he wasn't writhing up there on the cross in the shape of His son, He had His priests preaching hellfire and damnation from the pulpit and scaring us to death. We were told that the Roman Catholic Church was the One True Church, that outside the Church there was no salvation. (p. 64)

McCourt (1998) developed two different versions of God in his head—Irish and Italian:

> Our faith was mean, scrimped, life-denying. We were told this was a vale of tears, transitory, that we'd get our reward in heaven. If, that is, we'd stop asking those dumb questions. . . . Statues and pictures of the Virgin Mary in the Irish churches seemed disembodied and she seemed to be saying, "Who is this kid?" In contrast Italian art portrayed a voluptuous, maternal Mary with a happy infant Jesus at her bosom. (p. 64)

McCourt wondered: "Was it the weather? Did God change His aspect as He moved from the chilly north to the vineyards of Italy?" (p. 64). He thought that, all in all, he'd prefer the Italian expression of Catholicism to the Irish.

Religious adherence and more personal spiritual beliefs and practices vary greatly across and within cultures. For instance, U.S. Muslims include African Americans and immigrants from South Asia, the Middle East, North and sub-Saharan Africa, Pakistan, China, and Indonesia. All Muslims perform the same daily prayers and share a set of precepts from the Holy Koran that guide their life. Yet each family places a distinct cultural stamp on its practices (Mahmoud, 1996). Differences are also found between those from rural, traditional backgrounds and those from urban settings with more education and middle-class values. Religion is also intertwined with such influences as race, recent immigration, and the degree of fit vis-à-vis the dominant culture or local community. Religious prejudice or outright discrimination leads some people to suppress identification with a religion or its expression.

Ethnicity influences religious preference, yet it is crucial that we not reflexively link religion with ethnicity. Contrary to popular belief, only one-third of Arab Americans are Muslim; many are Christian. Although most Irish Americans are Catholic, those from Northern Ireland may well be Protestant. Streams of recent immigrants from Southeast Asia may be Christian or bring Eastern religious traditions. Some, such as Russian Jews, come, as many immigrants did historically, fleeing religious persecution in their country of origin. Refugees from the former Yugoslavia are not only Serbian, Croatian, Bosnian, or Kosovar, they are also Orthodox Christian, Catholic, or Muslim—differences that carry heavy historical meaning (i.e., the imposition of Islam by invading Turks) and have fueled hatred and bloodshed across the generations. (Our Chicago Center for Family Health is currently working with Bosnian refugee families; we keep mindful of the religious aspect of their scarring trauma.)

Among African Americans, 73% are Protestant, 10% are Catholic, and a growing number are Muslim (Gallup, 1996). Blacks of all faiths are far more likely than others to consider religion important: Religious experience starts young and continues throughout their lives. Most African Americans participate actively in their local church congregation and choir. They take religion seriously, practice it fervently, and look to it for strength in dealing with adversity (see Boyd-Franklin & Lockwood, Chapter 5, this volume).

Although Hispanics are commonly assumed to be Catholic, in fact, 60% are Catholic and 25% are Protestant, with a growing number turning to Pentacostal churches. Alongside their Christianity, they commonly follow traditional spiritual beliefs and practices, comingling African and indigenous tribal influences, as in *santería* and *espiritismo*. Most turn to the church for weddings, christenings, and funerals, yet tend to personalize their relationship with God through special relationships with saints, and show faith and gratitude through promises and offerings, prayers, and lighting of candles (Garcia-Preto, 1996). Many also believe in spiritualism, an invisible world inhabited by good and evil spirits who influence human behavior. Spirits can either protect or harm, as well as prevent or cause illness, and can be influenced by good or evil deeds. Incense, candles, and powders, alleged to have mystical properties, are used to cure illness and ward off the "evil eye" (see Falicov, Chapter 6, this volume).

We must be cautious not to judge diverse faith orientations, particularly those of non-European and indigenous tribal cultures, as inferior when they differ from predominant Euro-Christian standards. Throughout history and across the globe, imposition of the dogmatic belief that there is only one "true religion" has led to catastrophic consequences, as in holy wars to convert, subjugate, or annihilate nonbelievers, be they Jewish and Moslem "infidels" in the Spanish Inquisition or "pagan savages" in the "New World." Native Americans were viewed by early European conquerers as primitive heathens, uncivilized and un-Christian. Their deepest spiritual beliefs and practices were feared and loathed as witchcraft. These persistent attitudes led to government and Catholic missionary programs to educate and acculturate Indians, eradicating their tribal

language, religion, and customs and forcing them to adopt Christianity
and Western (i.e., Eurocentric) ways. Children, forcibly taken from their
families and tribes, were locked up in boarding schools, where they were
stripped of their cultural identity and religious heritage. Today, native
youth are returning in large numbers to the spiritual roots of their ancestors seeking identity and worth in their spiritual community (DeLoria,
1994).

Many thoughtful and useful systems of ancient peoples have been
viewed as primitive by Western religious thinkers (even implicitly, in
ethnocentric models of spiritual development, see, e.g., Fowler, 1981). Native American scholar Deloria (1994) cautions us not to assume that people spent centuries in a state of delusion because their experience of
God—or many gods—could not be described or understood in Christian
terms. As he sees it, "The problem of contemporary people, whatever
their ethnic or cultural background, lies in finding the means by which
they can once again pierce the veil of unreality to grasp the essential
meaning of their existence" (p. 284).

Religious Congregations

The liberty Americans cherish has enabled organized religion to flourish
in many forms. There are more than 2,000 denominations, nearly half
founded since the mid-1960s, as well as countless independent churches
and faith communities (Gallup, 1996; Lindner, 1998). There are nearly
500,000 churches, temples, and other places of worship—from small store-
front congregations to huge amphitheaters drawing tens of thousands of
worshippers. Membership in a church, synagogue, or other religious body
has been consistently high—nearly 7 in 10 persons—over the past 50 years.
Nearly 6 in 10 respondents report that they attend services monthly; 4 in
10 attend weekly (including half of all women, compared to 37% of men).

Most religious congregations encourage small-group participation.
Members sing in the choir and meet to pray together, discuss religious
topics, and study scriptures. Virtually every religion teaches a gospel of
service and charity, in one form or another. In religious support groups,
members find strength in one another, and as they learn to help each
other and those outside their group, their own feelings of self-esteem are
heightened and they enhance their understanding of themselves and feel
drawn closer to God.

The clergy are thought by most Americans to be dealing well with the
needs of their parishioners and the problems of their communities (Gallup, 1996). Religious leaders are generally held in high esteem: Clergy are
ranked second to pharmacists as the profession most respected in terms
of honesty and ethical standards—slightly ahead of doctors, dentists, engi-
neers, and college professors. (Ranked lowest are members of Congress
and car salesmen!)

Common Beliefs and Practices

Prayer

Prayer has strong meaning for a great many Americans: 90% say they pray in some fashion at least weekly; three-fourths pray daily (Gallup, 1996). For most, prayer originates in the family, is centered in the home, and grows in importance over the life course. Saying grace or giving thanks to God before meals is a common practice. Some pray most often at bedtime. Yet, most report that prayer can occur whenever they feel the need.

Some pray with an emphasis on asking, or petition, whereas others pray in thanksgiving, adoration, intercession, or forgiveness. Almost all (98%) pray for their family's health and happiness. Few (5%) pray for bad tidings for others. Prayer generates feelings of hope and peace. Most who pray (86%) believe it makes them better persons. Nearly all report their prayers have been heard and answered. Most (62%) say they got what they hoped for, and most (62%) have received divine inspiration or a feeling of being led by God. One in four reports a voice or vision as a result of prayer. Yet, one in five has been angered or disappointed on at least one occasion when it was felt prayers had not been answered. Some (30%) have had long periods of time when they stopped praying, most because they got out of the habit. A few (10%) stopped because they had lost their faith, were angry with God or the church, or felt their prayers had not been answered.

Every religion values some form of prayer or meditation. Most Americans say they pray to a Supreme Being, such as God, Jehovah, or Jesus Christ. Very few (2%) report that their prayers are in a "New Age" mode to a transcendent or cosmic force, or to "the god within." Because Hinduism does not require regular worship at a temple, mediation and offerings to various gods take place most often in the home, where small statues and shrines are placed (Almeida, 1996). One of the five pillars of Islam is observance of ritual prayer, facing Mecca, five times daily (where possible at the call of the muezzin from the minaret of the local mosque). For Muslims, one reason to pray is to express praise and gratitude for life itself. A deeper reason is to keep life in perspective, considered the most difficult lesson people must learn. Human beings keep living as if they were the centers of the world, with laws unto themselves. Prayer reorients them toward God, acknowledging that they are but creatures before the Creator (Smith, 1991).

Common Spiritual Beliefs

It may surprise many secular therapists that 96% of Americans believe in God or a universal spirit, although these conceptions vary widely. Only 3% are atheists (those who do not believe in the existence of God), and 1% are agnostic (those uncertain about whether God exists) (Gallup,

1996; "God in America," 1998). Some think of God as a "force" that maintains a balance in nature, but most people believe in a personal God who watches over and judges people. Of these, 8 in 10 feel that God has helped them to make decisions. Most believe that God performs miracles today. Many say they have felt the presence of God at various points in their lifetime and believe that God has a plan for their lives. The closer people feel to God, the better they tend to feel about themselves and others.

Most Americans believe that they will be called before God on Judgment Day to answer for their sins (Gallup, 1996). Eighty percent report that they believe in an afterlife: 72% believe in heaven and most believe in angels; only 56% believe in hell and half believe in the devil; yet three-fourths rate their own chances of going to heaven as excellent or good. (A keen eye will notice that this includes a few nonbelievers, who are perhaps hedging their bets!)

Since the vast majority of Americans are Christian or Jewish, it is not surprising that they believe the Bible was either the literal or inspired Word of God and regard the Ten Commandments as valid rules for living. For Muslims, the Koran builds on those foundations and provides specific guidelines and prohibitions for individual, family, and community life (Armstrong, 1993).

Religious beliefs profoundly influence character development: 8 in 10 respondents say that their religious convictions help them to respect themselves and other people and to assist those in need; 6 in 10 say that religion answers their questions and helps them to solve their problems. Further, for most, their beliefs keep them from doing things they know they shouldn't do. One-third report a profound spiritual experience, either sudden or gradual, that dramatically altered their lives. Those who say religion is the most important influence in their lives and those who receive a great deal of comfort from their faith are far more likely to feel close to their families, to find their jobs fulfilling, and to be hopeful about the future (Chamberlain & Zika, 1992).

Patriarchy, Sexism, and Heterosexism

Patriarchy, an ancient and enduring cultural pattern embedded in most religious traditions, has been a dominant force and powerful legacy. Over the centuries, it has sanctioned the subordination and abuse of women and children (Bottoms, Shaver, Goodman, & Qin, 1995; Bowman, 1983; Bridges & Spilka, 1992). In Genesis 3:16 Eve was admonished, "In pain you shall bring forth children; yet your desire shall be for your husband, and he shall rule over you." The traditional daily prayers of Orthodox Jewish men, as well as Muslim males reciting the Koran, have included thankfulness to God (Allah) for not having been born a woman (Fernea & Bezirgan, 1976). In Islamic law, the failure of a wife to produce a male offspring is grounds for divorce (Brook, 1995). Christianity, as well, has preached a doctrine of separate and unequal sexes. St. Paul told women, "You must lean and adapt yourselves to your husbands" (Colossians 3:18) and "The husband is the head of the wife" (Corinthians 11:3). In Timothy (2:11–15) he pronounced, "Let a woman learn in silence with all submissiveness. I permit no woman to teach or to have authority over men; she is to keep silent." Confucius (551–479 B.C.) boldly proclaimed, "One hundred women are not worth a single testicle." A legacy of this devaluation in China is the still common practice of infanticide and abandonment of daughters. The Hindu Code of Manu (c. 100 A.D.) declared, "In childhood a woman must be subject to her father; in youth to her husband; and when her husband is dead, to her sons. A woman must never be free of subjugation." Following the ancient Hindu custom of Sati a widow is expected to immolate herself on the funeral pyre of her husband to show her devotion to him, a practice that persists in some parts of India (Almeida, 1996). Paradoxically, *shakti* is the female generative force critical to all action and being in the Hindu universe.

Today, voices across the religious spectrum have been calling for women's rights and equality. Still, within more conservative religious denominations, many women continue to support traditional role relations, adhering to their deep faith convictions and valuing the respect—and even reverence—they receive for their centrality in family life as mothers, caregivers, and keepers of the hearth. However, the denigration and marginalization of women have alienated others from their religious roots. Many have found new sources of meaning and esteem through nontraditional expressions of spirituality; some have turned to ancient goddess-centered religions. Feminist scholars have challenged androcentric standards of moral development (Gilligan, 1982) and have sought to reinterpret and lay claim to their rightful place in religious traditions (Fishbane, 1994; see also Chapter 8, this volume). Historians are finding that much of the folk wisdom and stories in the Bible as well as the poetry in Islam originated with women. There is evidence that early Jewish and Christian women became leaders of synagogues and assumed clerical roles in the church. Over the centuries, worldwide cultural norms supported religious dogma and institutions in rigidifying more patriarchal gender roles. The theologian Tikva Frymer-Kensky (in Murphy, 1998) asserts that the complex, multifaceted nature of the one God of the Bible, combining all the attributes that went into the making of humankind, set a standard of unity without sex or class division that should be an inspiration to all.

Religious doctrine condemning homosexuality has been a source of deep anguish for gay men and lesbians, who have felt exiled from most traditional faith communities (Fortunato, 1982). Within the Catholic church, some have spoken out denouncing this hypocritical stance, when many nuns and priests themselves are homosexual (Curb & Manahan, 1985). Some denominations have adopted a loving acceptance of homosexual persons as human beings created by God yet continue to abhor homosexual practices as unnatural and sinful. Such a dualistic position unfortunately perpetuates stigma and shame, producing a deep schism in an individual's sexual identity and affiliative orientation that wounds the soul. Many gay men and lesbians have shown resilience in forging their own spiritual pathways (O'Neil & Ritter, 1992) and new ministries are springing up in many communities to meet their spiritual needs.

Long-standing religious opposition to same-sex unions is currently being challenged. In a confrontation reverberating through the Protestant churches, Methodist pastors who have conducted marriage ceremonies for gay couples face trial in cases testing a prohibition against homosexual unions as binding church law. Similar debates have produced deep chasms in other denominations. Gallup (1996) surveys find that most parishioners are far more tolerant than is official church doctrine. In a 1993 poll, 47% of Catholics stated their belief that people who engage in homosexual acts are still good Catholics and 44% disagreed with the church position that homosexual behavior is always wrong. Increasingly, the treatment of women and the rights of lesbians and gay men are being viewed as ethical issues concerning basic human rights and dignity.

Interfaith Boundaries, Tolerance, and Marriage

Through the first half of the 20th century, most Americans were acutely aware of differences between religious faiths and denominations, often with sharp divisions along social class and ethnic lines (Browning, Miller-McLemor, Couture, Lyon, & Franklin, 1977; Gallup, 1996). In recent years, 25% have changed faiths or denominations from the one in which they were raised. Most reported changing because they preferred the religious stance. Interfaith marriage led to change for one in four cases.

Many religions traditionally had prohibitions against intermarriage. Young people were strongly discouraged from marrying or even dating someone of even another denomination. Before 1970, the Catholic church did not recognize out-marriages unless the non-Catholic spouse vowed to raise the couple's children in the Catholic faith. In recent decades, intermarriage has increased dramatically: Currently 52% of Jews, 32% of Catholics, and 57% of Buddhists marry outside their faith. Although Blacks are only half as likely as Whites to oppose interracial marriages, they are more opposed than Whites to interfaith marriages (Gallup, 1996).

Yet, in general, acceptance of interfaith marriages has grown with the support of ecumenical and interfaith movements and the blurring of racial and ethnic barriers. Most parents and children show increasing religious tolerance and favor courses in public schools to provide non-devotional instruction about various world religions. Most agree that all religions are essentially good and also believe that people can be ethical even if they don't believe in God.

Discontinuities and New Connections

Discontinuities often exist between religious teachings and personal spiritual beliefs and practices. Some adhere to religious rituals without finding spiritual meaning in them. Others disavow formal institutionalized religion yet lead deeply spiritual lives. Congruence between religious/spiritual beliefs and practices yields a general sense of well-being and wholeness, whereas a dissonance can induce shame, guilt, or spiritual malaise.

Even though religion has again become very popular, it doesn't necessarily change people's lives. There is often a gap between their faith and knowledge of their religion, its core tenets, and family religious roots. Many revere their holy scriptures, but few read or study them. One survey found that although 93% of homes contain a Bible, 58% of respondents couldn't name five of the ten commandments; 10% thought Joan of Arc was Noah's wife (reported in *New York Times Magazine*, December 7, 1997, p. 61).

It's important to distinguish surface religion, such as attending church for social reasons, from deep transforming faith that is lived out in daily life, relationships, and service to others. It is the level of spiritual commitment that makes a significant difference in personal well-being and concern for others. Those with a deeply integrated and lived-out faith gain personal strength from their religious convictions and often spend significant time helping those in need. They are more likely to be tolerant of other faiths and more giving and forgiving in their personal relationships.

There is another gap between believers and belongers, as well as between faith and practice. Millions of people of all religions are strong believers but do not actively participate in congregational life. Most view their faith as a matter between them and God. While Orthodox Jews center their lives on observance of traditional laws and practices, 62% of American Jews believe they can be "religious" without being "particularly observant" (Jewish Theological Seminary, New York, cited by R. Shorto, *New York Times Magazine*, December 7, 1997, p. 61). Catholics are among the most devout worshippers, yet 64% agree that one can be a good Catholic without going to Mass and 82% say that using birth control is "entirely up to the individual" (Gallup, 1996). The vast majority (78%) of American Catholics disagree with the Church's refusal to sanction remarriage after divorce; 62% believe that those who have abortions are still good Catholics and 58% believe the Church should relax its standards prohibiting abortions. Younger Catholics tend to be more liberal in these beliefs than their elders, often generating intergenerational tensions within Catholic families. Personal attitudes about abortion, euthanasia, and the death penalty are strongly polarized within and across religions. In sum, Americans are highly independent in their spiritual lives.

Religion and spirituality are expected to grow in significance over the coming decades, shaped less by institutions and more by the people who are seeking meaning. In our rapidly changing world, religion is less often a given that they are born into and accept unquestioningly. Instead, people commonly pick and choose among beliefs and practices to fit their lives. Canadian sociologist Reginald Bibby calls this "religion à la carte" (in Gallup, 1996, p. 8). Deloria (1994) sees the combining of elements of varied faiths more like a platter of "religious linguini." As religious diversity within families increases, many are creating their own recipes, blending Christianity and Native American spirituality, Judaism and Zen Buddhism. Most are taking a broader ecumenical view. As Monica McGoldrick and Joe Giordano observe, "We are all migrants, moving between our ancestors' traditions, the worlds we inhabit, and the world we will leave to those who come after us" (1996, p. 8).

SPIRITUALITY AND CONNECTEDNESS

Faith is inherently relational, from our earliest years, when the most fundamental convictions about life are shaped within caregiving relationships. We experience deep bonds with "kindred spirits" and "soul mates" (Moore, 1994). Relationships offer pathways for spiritual growth (Levine & Levine, 1995) as they strengthen resilience, as in the Quaker adage, "I lift thee and thou lifts me." Caring bonds with partners, family members, and close friends nourish spiritual well-being; in turn spirituality deepens and expands our connections with others. It can be a spiritual experience to share physical and emotional intimacy, to give birth, to care for a frail elder, to befriend strangers, or to receive the loving-kindness of others. For many, belief in a personal relationship with God strengthens them through their darkest hours (see Griffith, Chapter 12, this volume).

The transcendent sense of family and community is forged through shared values, commitment, and mutual support through adversity. Banding together in activism for such concerns as environmental protection or social justice can be a powerful expression of spirituality (see Perry & Rolland, Chapter 15, this volume). In contrast to the highly individualized concept of human autonomy centered on the "self" in Western societies, most cultures in the world consider the person as embedded within the family and larger community. The African theologian John Mbiti (1970) describes this sociocentric view of human experience with the dictum, "I am because we are."

We can find spiritual connection and renewal in nature, as in mountain vistas, a walk in the woods, or the rhythm of waves on the seashore.

Such experiences can be uplifting, take us beyond ourselves, and make us feel at one with other life and the universe. Many are attracted to people and places with high spiritual energy—gurus, pilgrimages to Mecca; sacred shrines, cathedrals, and temples; or healing waters, places of wonder. Beauty in many forms can have a spiritual, healing effect. We can be inspired by great art, literature, and drama that communicates our common humanity. Music offers a powerful transcendent experience. African American gospel "spirituals," blues, jazz, and "soul" music have been creative expressions forged out of the cauldron of slavery, racism, and impoverished conditions, transcending those scarring experiences through the resilience of the human spirit. As Native Americans say, "to watch us dance is to hear our hearts speak."

For me, music has a deep spiritual resonance as well as a bond with both my mother and my daughter. When I was growing up, my mother was not only the organist at our Jewish temple but, with an ecumenical command of the great hymns and religious music, she was also in demand to play at holidays for congregations of various Christian denominations in our town. Music, whether secular or religious, was a transcendent spiritual experience for her—as it became for me, accompanying her on those many occasions, and inheriting her passion for all forms of music. My teenage daughter and I also share that bond; when stressed out, we close our eyes and listen together to Celtic songs, Moroccan Gnaoua rhythms, or other deeply moving world music.

Faith, intimacy, and resilience are intertwined (Higgins, 1994). Love sustains us and infuses our lives with meaning. Victor Frankl (1946/1984), in recounting his experiences in Nazi prison camps, came to the realization that salvation is found through love. As he visualized the image of his wife, a thought occurred: "I didn't even know if she were still alive. I knew only one thing—which I have learned well by now: Love goes very far beyond the physical person of the beloved. It finds its deepest meaning in his spiritual being, his inner self."

Often, people who have had negative experiences of religion in childhood find ways of expressing their spirituality through communion with nature, creative writing, and activism. The author Alice Walker combined all three. In her recent collection of essays, *Anything We Love Can Be Saved* (1997), Walker wrote about her life as an activist and her faith in the human heart. She described her beloved mother, who was devoted to her rural church, as someone who took action, brought children in need into her home, and looked out for the welfare of others in her struggling, isolated community. Walker notes that her mother wouldn't have thought of herself as an activist; she would have called it just being a person.

Walker's own spiritual journey began in a childhood subjected to "White orthodox Christianity" which her parents followed. She dropped out at age 13, feeling that the preacher and the way the church was set up reinforced the gender inequality she saw everywhere. She found that instead of church attendance, nature nourished her through long country walks, being out in the rain, and running with the wind. She became what she calls a "born-again pagan" experiencing spirituality through the land, as a country dweller, a peasant. Her activist spirit found powerful expression in her writing, as well as her work in movements for social justice. She believes that if you just accept conditions and do nothing, nothing changes and you become someone who shuts down. She's found, instead, that activism transforms; it's almost impossible to stay depressed about anything if you act to change it. Her optimism is rooted in her nature-derived spirituality.

Faith fuels the resilient spirit. Research has found that faith in surmounting adversity is intertwined with faith in the power of human relationships (Higgins, 1994). Most people who come for therapeutic help today are seeking more than symptom reduction, problem solving, or communication skills; they yearn for greater meaning and deeper connections with others in their lives. Many are in spiritual distress at the core of physical, emotional, and relational problems. As family therapists develop ways to successfully integrate this vital dimension in our practice, we can begin by making space for spirituality in our therapeutic work and encouraging spiritual connections in family and community life. The healing art of therapy has much in common with a spiritual journey. The Native American scholar Vine Deloria, Jr., urges us to follow this spiritual path not only for our own well-being but for the sake of the generations to come: "The future of humankind lies waiting for those who will come to understand their lives and take up their responsibilities to all living things."

NOTES

1. It is difficult to find reliable data on religious beliefs and practices. Nearly all reported statistics, from *Life* magazine's special issue on God, December 1998, to reference volumes such as the *Encyclopedia Britannica* and the *World Almanac*, are obtained from a single source, Gallup Surveys, conducted for more than 50 years and disseminated by the Princeton Religion Research Center, headed by George Gallup, Jr. The latest full report of decade trends and particular surveys conducted 1990–1995 can be found in *Religion in America 1996* edited by Gallup. Quarterly newsletters reporting more recent polls on particular topics can be obtained by contacting the Center at 1-609-921-8112.

   Actual membership data reported by Christian church denominations throughout North America are gathered by the National Council of Churches of Christ and are presented most recently in the *Yearbook of American and Canadian Churches 1998*, edited by Eileen W. Lindner. The numbers of people who consider themselves to be religious (or spiritual) are obviously far larger than those who belong to a congregation and are counted as members of a particular religious denomination.

2. Interestingly, while social scientists have been reluctant to ask about religion, survey respondents seem not to be hesitant to reveal their beliefs and affiliations. Survey response rates are high and only about 8% state no religious preference.

REFERENCES

Almeida, R. (1996). Hindu, Christian, and Muslim families. In M. McGoldrick, J. Giordano, & J. Pearce (Eds.), *Ethnicity and family therapy* (2nd ed., pp. 395–423). New York: Guilford Press.

Anderson, H. (1994). The recovery of the soul. In B. Childs & D. Waanders (Eds.), *The treasure in earthen vessels: Explorations in theological anthropology* (pp. 208–223). Louisville, KY: Westminster Press/John Knox Press.

Armstrong, K. (1993). *A history of God: The 4,000 year quest of Judaism, Christianity, and Islam.* New York: Ballantine Books.

Beavers, W. R., & Hampson, R. B. (1990). *Successful families: Assessment and intervention.* New York: Norton.

Becvar, D. (1996). *Soul healing: A spiritual orientation in counseling and therapy.* New York: Basic Books.

Bellah, R. N., Madsen, R., Sullivan, W., Swidler, A., & Tipton, S. (1985). *Habits of the heart.* Berkeley: University of California Press.

Bottoms, B. L., Shaver, P. R., Goodman, G. S., & Qin, J. (1995). In the name of God: A profile of religion-related child abuse. *Journal of Social Issues, 51,* 85–111.

Bowman, M. (1983, November/December). Why we burn: Sexism exorcised. *The Humanist,* pp. 28–29.

Bridges, R. A., & Spilka, B. (1992). Religion and the mental health of women. In J. F. Schumaker (Ed.), *Religion and mental health* (pp. 43–53). New York: Oxford University Press.

Brook, G. (1995). *Nine parts of desire: The hidden world of Islamic women.* New York: Anchor Books.

Browning, D., Miller-McLemore, B., Couture, P., Lyon, K., & Franklin, R. (1977). *From culture wars to common ground: Religion and the American family.* Louisville, KY: Westminster Press/John Knox Press.

Burton, L. A. (1992). *Religion and the family: When God helps.* New York: Haworth Press.

Campbell, J., & Moyers, B. (1988). *The power of myth.* New York: Doubleday.

Chamberlain, K., & Zika, S. (1992). Religiosity, meaning in life, and psychological well-being. In J. F. Schumaker (Ed.), *Religion and mental health* (pp. 138–148). New York: Oxford University Press.

Coles, R. (1990). *The spiritual life of children.* Boston: Houghton Mifflin.

Coles, R. (1997). *The moral intelligence of children.* New York: Random House.

Cornwall, M., & Thomas, D. L. (1990). Family, religion, and personal communities: Examples from Mormonism. *Marriage and Family Review, 15,* 229–252.

Curb, R., & Manahan, N. (1985). *Lesbian nuns: Breaking silence.* Tallahassee, FL: Naiad Press.

D'Antonio, W. V., Newman, W. M., & Wright, S. A. (1982). Religion and family life: How social scientists view the relationship. *Journal for the Scientific Study of Religion, 21,* 218–225.

Deloria, V., Jr. (1994). *God is red: A native view of religion* (2nd ed.). Golden, CO: Fulcrum.

Doherty, W. J. (1995). *Soul searching: Why psychotherapy must promote moral responsibility.* New York: Basic Books.

Elkind, D. (1971). The development of religious understanding in children and adolescents. In M. P. Strommen (Ed.), *Research of religious development* (pp. 655–685). New York: Hawthorn Books.

Elkins, D. (1990, June). On being spiritual without necessarily being religious. *Association for Humanistic Psychology Perspective,* pp. 4–6.

Erikson, E. H., Erikson, J. M., & Kivnick, H. Q. (1986). *Vital involvement in old age.* New York: Norton.

Falicov, C. (1995). Cross-cultural marriages. In N. S. Jacobson & A. S. Gurman (Eds.), *Clinical handbook of couple therapy* (pp. 231–246). New York: Guilford Press.

Fernea, E. W., & Bezirgan, B. Q. (1976). The Koran on the subject of women. In E. W. Fernea &

B. Q. Bezirgan (Eds.), *Middle Eastern Muslim women speak*. Austin: University of Texas Press.

Fishbane, M. D. (1994). Ruth: Dilemmas of loyalty and connection. In J. Kates & G. Reimer (Ed.), *Reading Ruth: Contemporary women reclaim a sacred story* (pp. 298–308). New York: Ballantine Books.

Fortunato, J. (1982). *Embracing the exile: Healing journeys of gay Christians*. San Francisco: HarperCollins.

Fowler, J. (1981). *Stages of faith: The psychology of human development and the quest for meaning*. San Francisco: Harper & Row.

Frankl, V. (1984). *Man's search for meaning*. New York: Simon & Schuster. (Original work published 1946)

Friedman, E. H. (1985). *Generation to generation: Family process in church and synagogue*. New York: Guilford Press.

Galanter, M. (1989). *Cults and new religious movements*. Washington, DC: American Psychological Association.

Gallup, G., Jr. (1996). *Religion in America: 1996 Report*. Princeton, NJ: Princeton Religion Research Center.

Gallup, G., Jr. (1998). *Newsletter of the Princeton Religion Research Center*. Princeton, NJ: Princeton Religion Research Center.

Garcia-Preto, N. (1996). Puerto Rican families. In M. McGoldrick, J. Giordano, & J. K. Pearce (Eds.), *Ethnicity and family therapy* (2nd ed., pp. 183–199). New York: Guilford Press.

Gaustad, E. S. (1966). *A religious history of America* (rev. ed.). San Francisco: Harper & Row.

Gilligan, C. (1982). *In a different voice: Psychological theory and women's development*. Cambridge, MA: Harvard University Press.

God in America [Special issue]. *Life, 21*(13).

Greeley, A. (1969). *Why can't they be all like us?* New York: American Jewish Committee.

Griffith, J. L., & Griffith, M. E. (1999). *Sacred encounters*. New York: Guilford Press.

Higgins, G. O. (1994). *Resilient adults: Overcoming a cruel past*. San Francisco: Jossey-Bass.

Hochschild, A. (1997). *Time bind*. New York: Holt.

Laird, J., & Green, R.-J. (Eds.). (1996). *Lesbians and gays in families and family therapy*. San Francisco: Jossey-Bass.

Lerner, M. (1994). *Jewish renewal: A path to healing and transformation*. New York: G. P. Putnam's Sons.

Levine, S., & Levine, O. (1995). *Embracing the beloved: Relationship as a path of spiritual awakening*. New York: Anchor Books.

Lifton, R. S. (1993). *The protean self: Human resilience in an age of fragmentation*. New York: Basic Books.

Lindner, E. W. (1998). *Yearbook of American and Canadian churches 1998* (66th ed.). Nashville, TN: Abingdon Press.

Mahmoud, V. (1996). African American Muslim families. In M. McGoldrick, J.Giordano, & J. K. Pearce (Eds.), *Ethnicity and family therapy* (2nd ed., pp. 112–128). New York: Guilford Press.

Mbiti, J. S. (1970). *African religions and philosophy*. Garden City, NY: Anchor Books.

McCourt, F. (1998, December). God in America: When you think of God—What do you see? *Life 21*(13), 60–74.

McGoldrick, M., & Giordano, J. (1996). Overview: Ethnicity and family therapy. In M. McGoldrick, J. Giordano, & J. K. Pearce (Eds.), *Ethnicity and family therapy* (2nd ed., pp. 1–27). New York: Guilford Press.

McGoldrick, M., & Preto, N. G. (1984). Ethnic intermarriage: Implications for therapy. *Family Process, 23*, 347–364.

Moore, T. (1992). *Care of the soul: A guide for cultivating depth and sacredness in everyday life*. New York: HarperCollins.

Moore, T. (1994). *Soul mates: Honoring the mysteries of love and relationship*. New York: Harper/Perennial Library.

Murphy, C. (1998). *The word according to Eve: Women and the Bible in ancient times*. Boston: Houghton Mifflin.

Neihardt, J. (1979). *Black Elk speaks: Being the life story of a Holy Man of the Oglala Sioux.* Lincoln: University of Nebraska Press. (Original work published 1932)

O'Neil, C., & Ritter, K. (1992). *Coming out within: Stages of spiritual awakening for lesbians and gay men.* New York: HarperCollins.

Parks, S. (1986). *The critical years: Young adults and the search for meaning, faith, and commitment.* San Francisco: HarperCollins.

Pipher, M. (1997). *The shelter of each other: Rebuilding our families.* New York: Ballantine Books.

Rosen, E. J., & Weltman, S. F. (1996). Jewish families: An overview. In M. McGoldrick, J. Giordano, & J. K. Pearce (Eds.), *Ethnicity and family therapy* (2nd ed., pp. 611–630). New York: Guilford Press.

Schucman, H., & Thatford, W. (1996). *A course in miracles: Foundation for inner peace* (2nd ed.). New York: Viking/Penguin.

Smith, H. (1991). *The world's religions: Our great wisdom traditions* (rev. ed.). New York: HarperCollins.

Stacey, J. (1996). *In the name of the family: Rethinking family values in the postmodern age.* Boston: Beacon Press.

Stander, V., Piercy, F. P., MacKinnon, D., & Helmeke, K. (1994). Spirituality, religion, and family therapy: Competing or complementary worlds? *American Journal of Family Therapy, 22,* 27–41.

Stinnett, N., & DeFrain, J. (1985). *Secrets of strong families.* Boston: Little, Brown.

Taggart, S. (1994). *Living as if: Belief systems in mental health practice.* San Francisco: Jossey-Bass.

Walker, A. (1997). *Anything we love can be saved: A writer's activism.* New York: Random House.

Walsh, F. (1993). Conceptualization of normal family processes. In F. Walsh (Ed.), *Normal family processes* (2nd ed., pp. 3–69). New York: Guilford Press.

Walsh, F. (1998a). Beliefs, spirituality, and transcendence: Keys to family resilience. In M. McGoldrick (Ed.), *Re-Visioning family therapy: Race, culture, and gender in clinical practice* (pp. 62–77). New York: Guilford Press.

Walsh, F. (1998b). Families in later life: Challenges and opportunities. In B. Carter & M. McGoldrick (Eds.), *The expanded family life cycle* (3rd ed., pp. 307–326). Needham Heights, MA: Allyn & Bacon.

Walsh, F. (1998c). *Strengthening family resilience.* New York: Guilford Press.

Weil, A. (1994). *Spontaneous healing.* New York: Knopf.

Worthington, E. L., Jr. (1989). Religious faith across the lifespan: Implications for counseling and research. *Counseling Psychologist, 17,* 555–612.

Wright, L., Watson, W. L., & Bell, J. M. (1996). *Beliefs: The heart of healing in families and illness.* New York: Basic Books.

CHAPTER 2

Opening Family Therapy to Spirituality

FROMA WALSH

> May we see not only with our two eyes but with the one eye which is our heart.
>
> —BLACK ELK

Several years ago, I worked with a family in the aftermath of the father's sudden death in an auto accident. The father had been a minister, beloved by his congregation as he was by his family. Within months of the death, the mother had moved with three of her four children to a new community to start a new life. When they came to me for therapy a while later, we worked together for several months to address the many ramifications of their painful unresolved loss. I wrote about our "successful" work (Walsh & McGoldrick, 1991) and included it in many presentations on loss. Then, one day a divinity student attending my class asked a simple question about the family: "What happened to their spirituality after the father's death?" I was stunned. I replied honestly that I didn't know. I had no idea because I had never asked. And no family member ever mentioned it.

Moreover, the oldest daughter, age 17 at the death, had run off to live on a commune with a cult leader, severing all contact with her family and former life. Although the mother and I worked successfully over time to restore contact with that daughter, never did we explore the possible spiritual meaning of the daughter's attachment to the cult and its charismatic leader, as a replacement for her father (the spiritual leader of her family and community).

I couldn't believe that I had not considered the spiritual dimension of family loss, especially in a case in which the father had been a Christian minister and the family's life had been centered on their church community. In many presentations of the case, no clinical colleague or student had ever raised the subject. It was as if all consciousness of spirituality had been erased by our clinical training. Even when it was right in front of me, I was blind to its significance. It was a divinity student, trained to attend to the spiritual, who could see this dimension hidden to us all.

Throughout the mental health professions, spirituality has been regarded as a taboo subject to be checked at the office door by both the client and the therapist. When I became interested in working on a book on spirituality in clinical practice, one academic colleague remarked that it was a good thing that I already have tenure. Some clinicians looked appalled, and others worried that I might have gone off the deep end, possibly into some fringe group. For most psychotherapists, opening conversation on spirituality has been even more taboo than broaching such topics as sex, money, or death. Spirituality and religion have been purposefully left out of clinical training, practice, and research. The unspoken assumption has been that religion is not our proper domain and we should not "intrude" into it. This has translated into an implicit understanding between professionals and clients of "Don't ask; don't tell." Therapists have been reluctant to raise the subject and uncomfortable in dealing with it when it does arise. Clients sense that spirituality doesn't belong in the clinical context and censor themselves from bringing this dimension of their lives into the therapeutic conversation.

There is a growing surge of interest in spirituality by family therapists and other mental health professionals. Yet, most feel ill equipped from their training, constrained from broaching the subject with clients, and uncomfortable in thinking about the spiritual dimension of their therapeutic practice. We are just beginning to explore this most significant dimension of human experience in our field. This chapter explores ways to move beyond constraints and suggests a variety of ways to incorporate spirituality in clinical assessment and intervention to understand spiritual sources of distress and tap resources in healing, recovery, and resilience.

OVERCOMING CONSTRAINTS

In the field of family therapy, Prest and Keller (1993) found a glaring lack of professional literature addressing spirituality and religious frameworks, as in the broader field of mental health. Several influences have contributed to this omission.

Sacred and Secular

Our nation's founding principle of separation of religion from the secular has fostered a dualism in our culture, contributing to the segregation of religious beliefs and practices from professional psychotherapy. Like the larger society, secular therapists adopted a hands-off attitude, attempting to be value free so as not to intrude into clients' spirituality or impose their own religious views.

Rigid boundaries were drawn. Spiritual beliefs and practices became regarded as "off limits" for psychotherapy, viewed as a "private" matter or personal relationship between individuals and their God. Spiritual issues were seen as existing in a separate realm from physical and psychosocial distress, restricted to the domain of clergy or pastoral counselors. Likewise, spiritual healing practices were deemed outside the province of psychotherapy. It was expected that faith healers and professional helpers should each tend to their own issues and stay in their own territory.

Reinforcing these boundaries, professionals were trained to adopt a stance of neutrality as a way to remain objective and unbiased. However, there has been growing recognition that therapists cannot be neutral (Walsh, 1993). Inescapably, the practice of therapy involves the interaction of therapists' and clients' value systems. Just as other aspects of culture (such as ethnicity, social class, and gender) influence client and therapist constructions of norms, problems, and solutions, so too does the spiritual dimension of experience. What we ask and pursue—or do not—influences the therapeutic relationship, course, and outcome. We best respect our clients not by avoiding discussion of spirituality altogether but by demonstrating active interest in exploring and understanding their values and practices. It is most crucial to understand constraining beliefs and to affirm and encourage those that foster well-being. At times, specific beliefs or practices are to be challenged where they contribute to distress or are harmful to others, as when violence toward wives is rationalized by citing fundamentalist religious precepts (see Chapter 1, this volume).

Power and Proselytizing

A related barrier separating psychotherapy and spirituality concerns the potential abuse of power in the therapeutic relationship if therapists actively or subtly influence clients to adopt their own religious views. Therapists were trained to be cautious not to reveal their own values or practices in order to protect clients from even the appearance of proselytizing. Concern about therapists' persuasion and clients' susceptibility stems largely from recognition of the power of the therapist and the dependent position of clients. In many ways, psychotherapists have assumed the roles of shamans and priests in more traditional cultures but have lacked training in how to use such power constructively (Harner, 1980). Most therapists are uncomfortable with this power differential; many deny their influence. Nevertheless, power is projected onto therapists by clients, who are vulnerable, in distress, to adopting their therapist's beliefs and practices.

As therapists, it is best if we recognize these influences and work collaboratively, reflecting power back in ways that foster resilience and empowerment in clients, their family relationships, and their communities (Walsh, 1998b). At times we can benefit clients therapeutically by sharing aspects of our own spiritual journey, such as a strengthening of faith (or a questioning of it), at a time of crisis in our lives. Such disclosure must be done with exquisite sensitivity to its appropriateness and potential value in our work toward client aims. When shared in this spirit, the healing relationship itself is profoundly deepened (see Weingarten, Chapter 14, this volume).

Science and Faith

Despite psychotherapy's roots in spiritual healing traditions, developments in the mental health field produced a schism between faith-based and scientific paradigms. Historically, there was not a clear distinction between the psychological and the spiritual—*psyche* was the Greek word for spirit. Mental disorders, such as schizophrenia, are still seen and treated as possession by spirits in many traditional cultures (Comas-Díaz, 1981; Falicov, 1998; see also Falicov, Chapter 6, this volume). Over the centuries, shamanic healers have held highly influential roles as therapists in their communities, taking a holistic approach to human distress, involving physical, emotional, and spiritual healing (Butler, 1988; Eliade, 1972; Somé, 1994). Likewise, priests, ministers, rabbis, and other religious advisers have attended to the emotional suffering and relational problems of members of their congregation.

However, in 20th-century America, religion and psychotherapy generally became separate and distinct domains. Freud's (1927/1961) scorn for religion as offering no more than comforting illusions strongly influenced the exclusion of spirituality from psychotherapy theory and practice. Jung (1933, 1958) was one of the few leading therapists and theorists who believed that healing the psyche necessitated a reconnection to spirit and a religious outlook. (See Simpkinson and Simpkinson, 1999, for an annotated bibliography of leading voices in psychology, from William James to Karen Horney, Victor Frank, and Jerome Frank, who maintained a strong spiritual perspective in their work.) The scientific paradigm emerged as the dominant epistemology in the new field of mental health, along with skepticism toward faith-based belief systems. Although many marriage and family therapists/counselors came out of pastoral traditions, most mainline mental health professionals have been trained to uphold firm boundaries between the "helping professions" and faith-based healing.

With the professionalization of psychotherapy, faith-based healers and clergy became viewed as less skilled and knowledgeable (at best) or as dangerous or misguided prophets (at worst) compared to mental health experts trained to deal with psychological/psychiatric conditions in "clinical practice" based in the medical model. Marital and family therapists, along with other professionals, sought to gain scientific credibility and status through empirically based practice, distancing from aspects of client experience and therapeutic processes that presumably could not be observed and measured. If the spirit or soul is deep within every cell and is also transpersonal, how can it be quantified and verified? How are spiritual distress and recovery to be investigated?

Some see the growing interest in spirituality as a shift of the pendulum away from empirical science. Yet, increasingly we are seeing possibilities for integration of science and spirituality (e.g., see Capra, 1975; Johnson, 1998). As qualitative studies are gaining credence as methods to explore the meaning of experiences, we are learning more about the role of faith beliefs and practices in problem construction and solution (Wright, Watson, & Bell, 1996). Quantitative studies have begun to find empirical support for spiritual influences in mental health (Gartner, Larson, & Allen, 1991; Hood, Spilka, Hunsberger, & Gorsuch, 1996) and physical well-being (e.g., Koenig et al., 1998), as well as for the healing power of prayer (Dossey, 1993). Studies of meditation document its influence in reducing stress and blood pressure, improving sleep and mental alertness, and managing chronic pain; it even raises self-esteem and lowers reactivity in relationships (Carrington, 1986). The mental health disciplines are beginning to reopen practice to religion and spirituality (Kelly, 1995; Shafranske, 1996; Steere, 1997; Woolfolk, 1998).

The inclusion of spiritual issues in the latest revision of the *Diagnostic and Statistical Manual of Mental Disorders* (DSM-IV) is indicative of a growing recognition of their importance in mental health assessment and treatment. In DSM-IV, the Religion or Spiritual Problem category (V code 62.89) can be used "when the focus of clinical attention is a religious or spiritual problem. Examples include distressing experiences that involve loss or questioning of faith, or questioning of spiritual values that may not necessarily be related to an organized church or religious institution" (American Psychiatric Association, 1994, p. 685).

To further this integration, Wright and her colleagues (1996) urge systems-oriented professionals to conceptualize persons as bio-psycho-social-spiritual beings. As we dissolve the barriers constructed between spirituality and other aspects of our experience, we can advance a truly holistic view of families, their suffering, and their healing potential. Gregory Bateson, our most visionary systems theorist, taught us to look for the "patterns that connect" and to see mind and nature as a necessary unity (Bateson, 1979). Albert Einstein, considered the greatest scientist of the 20th century, was also proudly spiritual. Looking ahead, he envisioned a form of spirituality providing complementarity rather than contradiction between the two domains of science and religion: "The religion of the future will be a cosmic religion. It should transcend a personal God and avoid dogma and theology. . . . [I]t should be based on a religious sense arising from the experience of all things natural and spiritual as a meaningful unity" (Einstein, 1931, p. 355).

Healing and Treatment

Although psychotherapists are considered specialists in the healing art, many are uncomfortable with the notion of healing. In part, it carries spiritual connotations of the therapist as healer, with divinely inspired power to cure others or alleviate their pain, much like faith healers and the laying on of hands. Yet, therapists nonetheless assumed a science-based position of power over their "patients" by virtue of their special knowledge, treatment models, and professional status. Medical and psychoanalytic treatment paradigms influenced early focus on therapist skills and strategies to alter family pathology.

Increasingly, family therapists have re-envisioned healing in terms of a therapeutic relationship that encourages clients' own inherent healing potential. This collaborative approach is at the core of strength-based and resilience-oriented models of practice (Walsh, 1998c). Distinct from curing or problem resolution, healing is seen as a natural process in response to injury or trauma. Sometimes people heal physically but don't heal emotionally, mentally, or spiritually; or badly strained relationships remain unhealed. Some may recover from an illness but not regain a spirit to live and love fully. Yet, we are able to heal psychosocially even when we do not heal physically or when a traumatic event cannot be reversed. Similarly, resilience can be fostered even when problems can't be solved or when they may recur. The literal meaning of healing is becoming whole—and, when necessary, adapting and compensating for losses of structure or function.

Healing and treatment are quite different concepts. Whereas healing involves a gathering of resources within the person, the family, and the community, and is fostered through the therapeutic relationship, treatment is externally administered by experts. Western scientific medicine has been focused on identifying external agents of disease and developing technological weapons to defeat them. Metaphors of war are prominent: fighting germs; combating illness; aggressive treatments to destroy disease. An unbalanced focus on pathology rather than health contributes to despair (Weil, 1994). In contrast, medicine grounded in Eastern religious and philosophical traditions is based on a set of beliefs about healing processes and the importance of mind–body interactions. The healing system is a functional system, not an assemblage of structures. Chinese medicine, for instance, explores ways of increasing our internal resilience as resistance to disease so that whatever harmful influences we are exposed to we can remain healthy. This belief in strengthening protective processes assumes that the body has a natural ability to heal and grow stronger. A number of recently developed "alternative" approaches to medicine and psychotherapy draw on these beliefs to decrease pain and foster greater well-being (e.g., Kabat-Zinn, 1990, 1994); noninvasive touch therapies such as craniosacral therapy and *qigong* can free restrictions in energy flow.

Resources for diagnosis, self-repair, and regeneration exist in all of us and can be activated as need arises. Knowledge about the healing system enables clinicians to enhance these processes as the best hope for recovery when illness occurs. Such efforts are more effective than interventions that simply suppress symptoms, like reducing a fever.

Strength-based approaches to practice encourage a family's own healing resources and reduce vulnerability. Emphasis has shifted from earlier focus on therapist techniques to see that the fundamental power for change resides within the family, encouraging clinicians to tap into the family's own healing forces (Minuchin, 1992). In strengthening resilience, we inspire people to believe in their own possibilities for regeneration. Therapy best fosters this resilience in two ways: (1) through a healing therapeutic relationship that is a collaborative partnership with clients, and (2) by activating relationship networks as a healing environment for the relief of suffering and renewal of life passage. Our faith in each client's desire to be healthy and potential for healing and growth can encourage their best efforts.

LETTING IN THE SPIRIT

The general public is clearly indicating a need for mental health and health care professionals to attend to the spiritual dimension in their practice. A recent survey found that 81% of respondents preferred to have their own spiritual practices and beliefs integrated into any counseling process; 75% wanted physicians as well as therapists to address spiritual issues as part of their care. Yet, therapists tend to be less religious than most clients (Bergin & Jensen, 1990) and may underestimate the importance of spirituality in their work. Bergin (1991) notes that therapists who neglect the potential relevance of clients' spiritual beliefs and practices are likely to be at odds with those they work with. Moreover, when clients hold back spiritual concerns, therapy leaves them feeling fragmented (Griffith & Griffith, in press).

Among family therapy pioneers, Viriginal Satir stands out as one of the few who openly embraced a transcendent spirituality in her practice (Satir, 1972/1988). More recently, a number of family therapists, most from a Christian orientation, have begun to break down barriers to explore ways to bring spirituality into therapeutic work (Anderson & Worthen, 1997; Becvar, 1996, 1998; Gutsche, 1994; Holmes, 1994; Kramer, 1995; Kudlac, 1991; Pittman, 1988, 1990; Prest & Keller, 1993; Ross, 1994; Stander, Piercy, MacKinnon, & Helmeke, 1994). Weaver, Koenig, and Larson (1997) have called for greater collaboration with clergy in family therapy training, practice, and research. Several offer approaches with very religious families (Butler & Harper, 1994; Griffith, 1986; Joanides, 1996; Nakhaima & Dicks, 1995; Rotz, Russell, & Wright, 1993;

Stewart & Gale, 1994). We are starting to address such issues as violence in fundamentalist marriages (Whipple, 1987) and the painful spiritual challenges of gay men and lesbians (Laird & Green, 1996; Markowitz, 1998; O'Neil & Ritter, 1992). In *Soul Searching*, William Doherty (1995) criticized psychotherapy's overemphasis on self-interest and called for greater sensitivity in therapy to the moral responsibilities we have in loving relationships and in our community (see Chapter 10, this volume). Doherty's message resonates with pioneer family therapist Ivan Boszormenyi-Nagy's (1987) emphasis on the ethical dimension of intergenerational relationships, as well as Viktor Frankl's (1955) belief that both therapist and client ethical convictions are powerful resources to be drawn upon in the therapeutic process. Dorothy Becvar (1996) relates how she brings her own spiritual orientation into her practice to tap into clients' yearning for meaning and purpose and facilitate a holistic sense of wellness. She stresses the need to walk a path with heart, following hopes and dreams while enriching the soul.

Incorporating Spirituality in Family Assessment

Just as family therapists have recognized the importance of inquiring about ethnicity and other aspects of culture, assessment should routinely explore the spiritual dimension of clients' lives. Therapists should not only note specific religions on the genogram (McGoldrick, Gerson, & Shellenberger, 1999) but also explore their significance for clients. It is important to clarify whether identifying as Catholic is based in deeply held convictions or a family background that has not been followed meaningfully. Is it associated with a loving Christ or rigid church doctrine? Is God seen as benevolent or vengeful? The following questions suggest some lines of inquiry that can be fruitful:

- How important are faith, religious practice, and congregational support in clients' lives?
- To what extent do various family members identify with a religion or spiritual orientation? How are differences handled and accepted?
- How might religious differences within a marriage/family fuel tension, conflict, or estrangement?
- Where there has been intermarriage and/or conversion, how was the decision made? Has it been supported by the families of origin? Has it been regretted?
- What is the clients' concept of the "ideal" marriage and family of their faith? How do they judge themselves by comparison? What is their own vision for desired future spirituality?
- How do past or present spiritual beliefs and practices contribute to presenting problems or block healing and growth?

- How has adversity or trauma wounded the spirit?
- Have sexist or heterosexist religious precepts contributed to client suffering or abuse?
- How might a spiritual void or cutoff from religious roots exacerbate suffering or alienation?
- How can past, current, or potential spiritual resources be identified and drawn on to ease distress, support problem solving, enable clients to accept what cannot be changed, and foster healing and transformation? Explore the following:

  - The role of faith, prayer, meditation, rituals
  - Congregational affiliation and support
  - Turning to clergy for religious guidance or support

In working with clients, it is important to learn how family members, from their own distinct sociocultural background, blend the core principles of their faith with varied aspects of their lives. For many, traditional religious beliefs and practices can be a positive sustaining resource in weathering crisis. For others, they have become outmoded and fail to serve as a foundation for psychosocial and spiritual well-being. We can help clients who feel oppressed by religious dogma to find alternate constructions and practices consonant with transcendent spiritual beliefs and ethical values without rejecting spirituality altogether.

Religious precepts may be used to justify abusive patterns in couple and family relationships (Whipple, 1987). A husband's controlling, demeaning, or violent behavior toward his spouse may be grounded in religious tenets that a wife should be submissive. One fundamentalist Christian woman told me that her husband was right to beat her because she had challenged his authority over her. In exploring this, she expressed her belief that to be "a woman of God" required her to be submissive, and that this was hard for her but she was working on it. Her husband concurred that this was her probem. As family therapists, we have an ethical responsibility to challenge abuses of power and harmful behavior, even where it is supported by cultural or religious traditions. Above all, every religion upholds the core principles of respect for others and the dignity and worth of all human beings.

Even when presenting problems do not ostensibly involve spirituality, often a spiritual component will become apparent as the therapist explores this dimension. One client, Theresa, was referred for therapy by her mother-in-law because of her inconsolable grief many months after her second child was stillborn. Comingling with her depression, she admitted to me, was a profound sense of guilt. She had immigrated from Poland, leaving her devout Catholic family behind. She fell in love with a Jewish man; they married in a civil ceremony, neither feeling very religious at that time in their lives. When their first child, a son, was born, they decided to avoid conflict over their differences by not bringing him up in either faith. When she lost her second child, she became convinced that this was God's punishment for not having baptized her son. It was important to include couples' sessions in therapeutic work to repair the growing estrangement in their relationship and discuss how to handle faith differences for rearing their son and any future children.

TAPPING INTO SPIRITUAL RESOURCES FOR HEALING, RECOVERY, AND RESILIENCE

Suffering, and often the injustice or senselessness of it, are ultimately spiritual issues (Wright et al., 1996). Adversity and suffering have vastly different meanings in various religious traditions. For instance, Jews believe that it was through their suffering that they became God's chosen people. The biblical story of the Exodus, in which the Jewish people were led by Moses out of bondage in Egypt, is retold at family Passover seders to reconnect with that common history. Christians share the belief that Christ suffered and was crucified for our sins and that one's redemption is found through acceptance of Christ as Lord and Savior. Buddhists believe that life is filled with suffering, rooted in cravings for power, pleasure, or other worldly things. In turn, such cravings condemn us to a cycle of death and rebirth in which our actions (Karma) may prolong our suffering (Smith, 1991). Religious texts and traditions also offer solace and guidance through dark and difficult times, as in the biblical Song of David: "Yea, though I walk through the valley of the shadow of death, I will fear no evil for thou art with me; thy rod and staff they comfort me . . . " (Psalm 23). Each faith, in its own ways, fortifies resilience (see Wolin et al., Chapter 7, this volume).

Resilience is the capacity to rebound from adversity strengthened and more resourceful (Walsh, 1998c). It is an active process of endurance, self-righting, and growth out of crisis or persistent life challenges. Survivors of traumatic experiences may become trapped in a victim position, blocked from growth by anger or blame. In contrast, the qualities of resilience enable people to heal from painful wounds, take charge of their lives, and go on to live and love fully.

Family resilience involves key transactional processes that enable the family system to rally in times of crisis, buffering stress, reducing the risk of dysfunction, and supporting optimal adaptation for all members, from small children to frail elders. As family members pull together and support one another, relationships are strengthened and the family is better able to meet future challenges (Walsh, 1998c). Family belief systems are powerful influences in making meaning of adversity and suffering; they can facilitate or constrain change (Dallos, 1991; Wright et al., 1996), as well as acceptance of what cannot be changed.

The paradox of resilience is that the worst of times can also bring out our best. A crisis can lead to transformation and growth in unforeseen directions. It can be a "wake-up call" alerting us to the importance of loved ones or jolting us to reorder life priorities. In the midst of suffering, as we dig deeply within ourselves and reach out to others, the hardship endured opens ways for the spirit to grow. In turn, spiritual beliefs and practices strengthen the ability to withstand and transcend adversity. Such keys to resilience as meaning-making, hope, courage, perseverance, and connectedness are all enhanced by spirituality (Walsh, 1998a).

Faith supports the belief that we can overcome adversity. This involves more than simply being religious; studies suggest that what matters most is being able to give meaning to a precarious situation, having faith that there is some greater purpose or force at work, and finding solace and strength in these outlooks (Walsh, 1998c). In therapy, contemplative questions can facilitate such positive views or respectfully question constraining beliefs.

Robert Coles (1990) coined the term "moral energy" as a source of courage, a life-sustaining force of conviction that lifts us above adversity. In studying children in hardship or brutalizing conditions, Coles found many who transcended their experience and valued compassion, fairness, and decency. They showed a generous spirit in their capacity to give despite having received very little. The healing power of compassion and forgiveness is central to the teachings of all major religions, as well as to many approaches to therapy (Hargrave, 1994).

In their longitudinal study of resilience in poor multiethnic families on the Hawaiian island of Kauai, Werner and Smith (1992) found that faith was an important protective factor from childhood through adulthood. Religion—including Buddhism, Catholicism, Mormonism, Jehovah's Witnesses, and others—strengthened these families through times of adversity by providing a sense of purpose, mission, and salvation. Many resilient individuals credited involvement in a highly structured religious group. One woman described her deep involvement in the Mormon church since adolescence and her abiding faith in God: "When I felt like life wasn't worth living, there was a God who loved me and would help me come through." Follow-up studies found that resilience could be developed and lives could be transformed at any point in the life cycle. A crisis often became an epiphany, opening lives to a spiritual dimension previously untapped.

Spiritual distress, an inability to invest life with meaning, impedes coping and mastery in the face of life challenges. Clients who seek our help need not only to solve immediate problems but also to reach for meaning and purpose in life. It is crucial to explore how religious ideations or experiences may have had a destructive or dispiriting effect, fostering guilt, shame, or worthlessness. From sources in family history, culture, and spirituality, we can help clients invest in traditions, rituals, and spiritual communities that link them to one another and to life in more positive ways. For others, new spiritual wellsprings can be tapped to offer a larger vision of humanity and meaningful connections that inspire their best potential. Even empirically oriented behavioral scientists have begun to recognize this positive power of spirituality. Martin Seligman (1990), who introduced the concepts of "learned helplessness" and "learned optimism," believes that the soul—that which is deep within the personality—is the key to change and that our change efforts need to take into account the human spirit.

Health Benefits of Faith

Our beliefs are powerful influences in health and illness. The ability to bring a sense of coherence to an illness experience fosters resilience (Antonovsky, 1987). Medical studies find increasing evidence that faith, prayer, and spiritual rituals can strengthen health and healing by triggering emotions which influence physiological systems (Ellison & Levin, 1998). Older persons with strong religious beliefs are more likely to be satisfied with their lives and to have lower blood pressure, reducing the risk of heart disease (Koenig et al., 1998). Both depression and alcohol abuse are reduced by prayer. Those who find strength and comfort in religious beliefs often survive at a higher rate than those lacking faith. For instance, Yale epidemiologists (Oxman, Freeman, & Manheimer, 1995) studied 232 elderly patients who had undergone open heart surgery. Those who found strength and comfort in their religious outlook had a survival rate *three times* higher than those who did not. Most deaths were from cardiac arrhythmia. Having faith appeared to translate into being more soothed physiologically; a calmer mind lowered the risk of irregularity in the rhythm of the heart. Faith was even more important in this resilience than were frequency of participation in religious services, overall religious activity, or simply a feeling of being deeply religious. The solace and hopefulness in the religious outlook made the difference.

A review of medical studies on the efficacy of prayer (Dossey, 1993) found that the most effective prayers are not directly petitionary but rather "Thy will be done" prayers. The ritual of prayer triggers emotions that, in turn, positively impact the immune and cardiovascular systems, thereby improving health. Such religious rituals as the laying on of hands may stimulate endocrine or immune responses to facilitate healing. Many clinicians, like Dossey, have adopted the practice of praying for their own family members and, at times, for clients who are suffering.

Although faith can make a difference, we must be cautious not to attribute failures to recover to a lack of personal spiritual purity. Some holistic health practitioners, emphasizing mental influences over physical states, at times have implied blaming attributions for failure to recover, such as not having had a positive enough attitude. Those who are tempted

to believe that enlightenment and transcendence of negative emotions offer immunity to illness and death should bear in mind that studies of the
relationship between prayer and healing have compiled an impressive list
of saints who have died of cancer (Weil, 1994).

Facing Death and Recovering from Loss

Family therapy pioneer Norman Paul (in Walsh & McGoldrick, 1991)
noted the paradox that although a constant shadow of death exists in all
lives, we each entertain notions of our own immortality. We spend an inordinate amount of energy maintaining character armor as a shield
against the reality of human finitude, as Ernest Becker (1973) has noted.
In attempting to flee from the anxiety of death, we may hide from life itself. Western Judeo-Christian belief systems heighten this dilemma in
their emphasis on mastery and control over our destiny. The end of life is
approached in terms of loss of control and the failure of treatments—or of
will. In contrast, Eastern and tribal spiritual traditions approach death as
a natural part of the human life cycle. Buddhism teaches that in accepting
death, we discover life (Levine, 1987).

Facing death and the loss of a loved one are the most painful of all life's
challenges. Family and community bonds are central in easing this passage
in all faith traditions, although religious rites vary widely (see, e.g., the importance of the family support system in the Amish way of dealing with
death in Bryer, 1979). Spiritual distress can be profound when proper
funeral and burial rituals are not observed. Religion influences family
response to loss (Bohannon, 1991), especially with complicated deaths. Religious condemnation of suicide fosters shame and secrecy (Domino &
Miller, 1992) and can contribute to the anguish of family members around
end-of-life decisions. Yet faith can also facilitate adaptation (Gilbert, 1992).
The end of life offers gifts to those who face it openly with courage and compassion, as Cardinal Joseph Bernardin, Archbishop of Chicago, demonstrated in the last months of his life (Bernardin, 1997). More than any other
human experience, death and loss put us in touch with what most matters in
our lives. One man who lost his partner to AIDS was both devastated and
transformed by this experience. As he wrote to his family, "Words like 'soul'
or 'spirit' disappeared with medical training and are absent from our culture. This is what I've been given by the illness and the death: An appreciation of the soul, an understanding of the spirit. How great is our
responsibility to restore those words!"

It is important to understand varying conceptions of death and afterlife. It is in the face of death that Native American tribal religions have
their magnificence (Deloria, 1994). While death is truly saddening, it is
viewed as an event that faces every person and tribe, not as an arbitrary,
capricious exercise of divine wrath. The ability of tribespeople to deal
with death flows from the larger context in which Native Americans un-

derstand life. Human beings are an integral part of the natural world; in death they contribute their bodies to become the dust that nourishes the plants and animals, which, in turn, feed people during their lifetime. Moreover, because Native Americans see the family and tribal community as a continuing unity, death is simply another transitional event in a much larger and longer human life cycle.

Therapists can help family members to face death and loss by encouraging their full presence and participation in the dying process, drawing on their spiritual beliefs and practices to assist them. Those with a Western orientation have difficulty when there is no more that can be done to *stop* death; a sense of helplessness and despair contributes to conflict or avoidance of contact and blocks soulful communication. When my father was dying, I was extremely uncomfortable simply being with him; I kept wanting to *do* something, preferably to run an errand. By calming my anxieties, I became better able to be fully present with him, sitting quietly at his bedside, stroking his arm, taking his hand, contemplating the sunlight passing through the mimosa tree just outside the window from dawn to dusk. Those last few weeks of his life became the most precious and intimate times in our relationship, a profoundly spiritual experience that eased his suffering and passage as it forever deepened our bond.

Some losses can be devastating, especially the death of a child. An Italian Catholic couple came for counseling after their first baby was stillborn. When I asked if they were able to find solace in their faith, the wife said they hadn't been able to return to their church and looked to her husband to explain. The husband shouted, "I'm mad at God!" He began sobbing. I asked him to help me understand. He replied, "I believe that when something happens there's always a reason. And I just can't fathom what the reason is here. We did everything right; by the book. I don't blame the doctors or the hospital; I'm angry at God. He took our son. And it's not fair. I don't mean for me—but for my son. He never had a chance at life."

As therapists trained to help families solve problems, we may feel helpless at such times; there is no way we can bring back a loved one. What is most important is to be fully present with our clients' suffering, to offer compassion for expression of the full range of feelings in their despair, and to help them comfort each other. Often, encouraging clients' contact with clergy, or consulting with clergy ourselves, can be helpful in finding ways for them to reconnect with their spiritual moorings.

Recovery from Addictions

In attempts to understand what contributes to successful recovery from substance abuse, researchers and clinicians have often overlooked the role of spiritual beliefs and practices in preventing use and relapse (Gorsuch, 1995; Miller, 1998). An emphasis on spirituality has been a key component in 12-step programs of recovery from addictions, such as Alcoholics

Anonymous (Minnick, 1997), which can be a valuable adjunct to couple or family therapy (Berenson, 1990). In addition to offering fellowship and group support, these programs address spiritual issues concerning identity, integrity, an inner life, and interdependence (Peteet, 1993). The steps are designed to promote a spiritual awakening that prepares individuals and family members to practice the principles for abstinence and greater well-being in all aspects of their lives. A recent study of African American and Latino inner-city participants in a 12-step program for drug addiction (Green, Fullilove, & Fullilove, 1998) found that persons in drug recovery often undergo intense spiritual journeys as they embrace a Higher Power through the program. Often, this spiritual awakening sparks life-altering transformations along with abstinence. The ability to connect with a Higher Power through prayer and meditation also facilitates reflection that sustains them through times of trouble.

The Alcoholics Anonymous serenity prayer can be very helpful to anyone facing difficult circumstances: "May I have the serenity to accept the things I cannot change, the courage to change the things I can, and the wisdom to know the difference." This position, a key to resilience, helps us to "master the possible" and accept things beyond our control.

Barriers of Poverty and Racism

Religious faith and congregational support help people to survive and transcend impoverished conditions, barriers of racism, and other adversity (Billingsley, 1992; see Boyd-Franklin & Lockwood, Chapter 5, this volume). In *Bread and Spirit*, Harry Aponte (1994) urges therapists to attend to spiritual as well as practical needs of poor families. Many have become *dispirited*, losing hope and faith in their chances for a better life. At the core, they suffer a poverty of despair, a destruction of soul, with a pervasive sense of injustice, helplessness, and rage at the inequalities surrounding them. Aponte (1994) encourages therapists to go beyond theory and technique to reach for meaning and purpose in people's lives:

> Therapy can be an enemy or a friend to spirit. The technology of therapy has attempted to replace tradition, ritual, and customs. Therapy has also masqueraded as spirit. However, just as medication can only succeed when it cooperates with the healing powers of the body, therapy only works when it joins with the indigenous forces of culture and faith in people's lives. (p. 8)

In the midst of despair, there still survives a spirit of love, courage, and hope, although often muted. Aponte believes that we, as therapists, can make a difference by recognizing that potential and joining in a revitalization of family and community spirit (see Aponte, Chapter 4, this volume).

Searching out Religious Roots

Trained to look to family-of-origin history for problems and conflicts that may be sources of current difficulties, therapists need to rebalance focus to search for strengths. Faith was often a powerful source of resilience in weathering the losses and adaptive challenges of immigration or in withstanding the brutal and dehumanizing effects of racism. Discovering such connections and the strength of religious roots can be an invaluable part of therapeutic work, particularly with clients where experiences of oppression or forced migration have shattered a coherent sense of identity and severed vital linkages with ancestors and cultural heritage.

For instance, many African Americans are descendants of Muslims brought from West Africa as slaves, but they often are unaware of this heritage (Mahmoud, 1996). Because the practice of African religions and the speaking or writing of Arabic were suppressed and punished by slave holders, the practice of Islam was often done in secret and passed down surreptitiously in oral history or by family members imitating behaviors without attributing their source. Mahmoud (1996) has found that often, in doing a genogram with African Americans in clinical practice, a story might surface of a distant relative who always prayed facing east, refused to eat pork, gave their children "funny" (non-Christian) names, and didn't allow them to be baptized. Restoring vital bonds with a family's religious heritage is healing and empowering.

Use of Meditation

Meditation is becoming widely used to support the work of therapy (Bogart, 1991). It offers a way for the mind to seek clarity and the heart to find tranquillity (Bell, 1998); meditation can empty the mind of "noise," ease suffering, and rid the body of tension and pain. Becoming mindful in still and focused concentration can lead to more deliberate action as Being infuses Doing. Meditation can enhance therapy in various ways, used as a resource to the therapist and as a resource to clients as part of the therapeutic process.

First, therapists' own practice of meditation outside therapy can increase therapeutic rapport and effectiveness. It can free therapists to be more open, attentive, and responsive to clients, and to remain focused and clearheaded even in the midst of their turmoil (Rosenthal, 1990). It also heightens our own keen thinking and creative processes, helping therapists, as Rosenthal observes, "avoid locking into preconceptions and fixed ideas that can close off the new possibilities arising in the therapeutic encounter" (1990, pp. 40–41). Where therapists have felt that they had to push for change, they report greater ease and success as the process flows more naturally.

Second, therapists can encourage clients to practice meditation in a variety of forms, in or between sessions. It may be especially helpful when clients are anxious, depressed, or dispirited by mental or physical suffering. Zen meditation and other Eastern relaxation methods are often introduced by contemporary therapists (see Nhat Hahn, 1975/1987, for an excellent manual). Even clients who may not seem "the type" may be familiar with such techniques as deep breathing and guided imagery. They may have tried them in the past and found them beneficial but may have gotten "out of the habit" or had not thought to tap into these resources in their current distress. The form of meditation used should fit with each client's spiritual beliefs, preferences, and comfort. All religions value some form of meditation or contemplation. It may involve reading scriptures, chanting, or rituals, such as lighting candles, reciting a rosary, or—for Muslims—observing the call to prayer five times daily. Quietly listening to music can be deeply spiritual in a contemplative atmosphere. An inner serenity and communion with nature can be experienced simply by an early morning walk or watching a sunset. Shared meditative experiences foster authentic and empathic communication, reduce defensive reactivity, and can deepen couple and family bonds.

Meditation can be brought directly into therapy, either by providing a quiet place for a client's contemplation before or after sessions or by devoting several minutes of a session to meditation led by the therapist (Kabat-Zinn, 1994). Contrary to concerns that vulnerable clients might experience dissociation, Bell (1998) contends that meditation supports integration and wholeness: a clearer knowledge and acceptance of themselves and a deeper connection with others. Deep breathing exercises connect mind, body, and spirit, as they reduce anxiety and tension. At the same time therapists are cautioned to proceed slowly and prepare clients for whom difficult or painful memories and feelings may emerge, such as survivors of trauma, helping them to hold such experiences in a safe, bounded, and centered way that fosters their transformation (Nhat Hanh, 1991; see Barrett, Chapter 11, this volume). A therapist might have a client visualize a caring person and interaction from childhood, hold that moment in mind, and then describe that experience, such as being cradled in the arms of a grandmother in her rocking chair, and how comforting and secure that felt.

Use of Rituals

Through sacred ceremonies and rituals, stories and music, meditation and communion, we find connection with our deepest spiritual core and with all that is outside ourselves. As a Hopi proverb goes: "Work hard, keep the ceremonies, live peaceably, and unite your hearts." In every culture, religious and spiritual rituals serve valuable functions in dealing with adversity (Imber-Black & Roberts, 1992). Rituals can summon courage through the darkest hours. They can ease us through uncertain transitions and unfamiliar situations. In times of crisis or profound sorrow, they can script our actions and responses, as funeral rites do. Rituals also connect a particular tragedy with all human experience, a death and loss with all others. To symbolize and ease the transition of death and loss, some Native American tribes traditionally made medicine bundles containing bits of hair and other intimate things of the deceased along with skin or claws of animals and birds closely related to the family. This bundle was kept in the family dwelling for a year after the death and treated as if the person were still present. In that way, the trauma of loss was extended over a period of time, fostering gradual acceptance, and family members could be comforted that the deceased, although not visible, was spiritually and emotionally present.

Therapists can ask about and encourage spiritual rituals that have been meaningful in a family's past or a return to their heritage. We can also help clients transform empty rituals into meaningful ones, create new rites, or bridge formal religious differences in an expression of spirituality that is both more personal and transcendent.

Encouraging Faith-Based Activism

The Rev. Martin Luther King, Jr., a guiding spirit to so many oppressed people throughout the world, maintained an abiding faith that social justice will prevail. Yet, his was not a passive faith in waiting for a better world to happen. Rather, it was a rallying call to individual and collective action to bring about change. Similarly, James Comer (1997) urges us to take action if we are to improve the condition of public schools rather than sit by helplessly, waiting for a miracle.

Studies of resilient people have found that they gain strength in overcoming adversity and find healing from trauma through collaborative efforts to right a wrong or to bring about needed change in larger systems (Walsh, 1998c). Following her daughter's brutal murder, one mother was consumed by rage and helplessness, not wanting to go on living. Her therapist encouraged her to visit her daughter's grave and seek inspiration for the path ahead. The night after her visit to the cemetery, she slept deeply for the first time and awoke "knowing" that her daughter's spirit would want her to forge a larger purpose and benefit to others out of the tragedy. She turned self-destructive feelings into concerted action with other families and community leaders to reduce neighborhood violence. Such activism requires courage, initiative, and perseverance, which therapists can encourage. Perry and Rolland (see Chapter 16, this volume) bring this important dimension of faith-based activism into clinical practice.

Experiencing Others' Spiritual Beliefs and Practices

Experiences that acquaint us with religious/spiritual beliefs and practices that differ from our own traditions can deepen our understanding of others, spark new perspectives on our own spirituality, and strengthen our sense of connectedness. My daughter's friend Jodie participated in a community service project on the Shoshone reservation in Wyoming. Her multicultural group of teenagers worked at the Boys and Girls Club and helped start a Big Sister/Big Brother program. They were invited to help prepare, witness, and participate in the annual sun dance ceremony. Jodie shared with us her extraordinary experience:

> "I had the amazing opportunity to be in a sweatlodge. First we crawled in counter clockwise. Lorenna, a medicine man, poured cedar over burning lava rocks, which formed a solar system of burning circles. We all blessed ourselves. As he poured water over the rocks, the room filled with steam. My hair clung to me, my clothes were drenched, and sweat poured out of me. We began to pray out loud, each in our own tribal languages: Shoshone, Samoan, Hebrew, Serbo-Croatian, and English. Then we chanted Shoshone songs together.
>
> "The ceremony took place for four days from sunrise to sunset. We helped make prayer sticks and build an arbor of logs and brush. Dancers, who had to be Native American, danced around a tree in the center, praying. At the end, we were offered prayer sticks to bring home. A month later, the ceremonial tree is burned and the smoke carries people's prayers up to the Creator."

Jodie returned home feeling transformed by the experience: "I was introduced to a culture unknown to so many and I feel blessed that I had this life-altering opportunity."

Creative Uses of Spirituality to Foster Community and Bring out the Best

When thinking about ways to bring our own spirituality into family therapy for personal and relational growth, we need only look around us for creative models. Phil Jackson, who coached the Chicago Bulls to six National Basketball Association championships, drew on his own blend of Christian, Zen Buddhist, and Native American spirituality to build teamwork and extraordinary success (Jackson, 1995; Simon, 1997). Jackson's unique coaching philosophy transformed the Bulls from a one-man show, known as "Michael Jordan and the Jordanaires," to develop an extraordinary team. Jackson grew up in the pews of his father's Pentecostal church in Montana. He left his parents' fundamentalist faith to become an All-American basketball player and discovered Zen meditation.

As coach he used his strong spiritual convictions to help players handle overwhelming stress, build confidence, rebound from setbacks, and deal with group conflict. Above all, they helped establish the conditions to bring out the best in each player and in the team as a whole. To prepare them to achieve such a high degree of harmony and success, Jackson started with the question, "What's our goal going to be as a group?" He believed that the players needed to envision a larger goal, beyond a championship, or fame, or money, which he saw as hollow in themselves. Jackson agreed with historian Joseph Campbell about the need for mythic symbols to get beyond just thinking in material terms and get a team to work together as a community (Simon, 1997, p. 51). He took a Native American group he was familiar with, the Lakota nation, and drew upon the symbols that had meaning for them, starting with the team's name—bulls are one of the most traditional images of Native Americans. In the team meeting room he hung symbols and made sure team members understood their meanings. An arrow placed above their TV set symbolized a prayer or a thought that is targeted and sent. He would ask the players to hear his message as an arrow that strikes home to their hearts. Jackson wasn't sure how much the players actually believed in the symbols, but if they didn't, that was fine: "I ask them to just pretend they believe and we go from there" (quoted in Simon, 1997, p. 51). At stressful times, he would bring in a spiritual consultant for group meditation sessions. Afterward, they would talk together about the team as a community and about ways to bring out the best in one another; invariably the team would then go on a winning streak.

Jackson contrasted his spiritually infused coaching with a more conventional approach:

> Most leaders tend to view teamwork as a social engineering problem: take x group, add y motivational technique, and get z results. But . . . I've learned that the most effective way to forge a winning team is to call on the players' need to connect with something larger than themselves . . . to surrender their self-interest for the greater good so that the whole adds up to more than the sum of its parts. (1995)

Responsiveness to Spiritual Diversity

As our world is changing and our own society becomes increasingly diverse, therapists will have more contact with different faiths and the need to develop a spiritual pluralism, with knowledge and respect for varied beliefs and practices. Therapeutic approaches and services need to be sensitive and responsive to this spiritual diversity. As therapists, particularly when from the dominant cultural group, we must be cautious not to take our own values as the norm or be judgmental toward differences, especially when they seem "foreign" to us. Instead, we must seek to understand their meaning and function in our clients' lives.

48 OVERVIEW

Deloria (1994) tells of attending a burial of a Sioux Indian in a Christian cemetery:

> After the body was in the grave . . . an old woman stepped forward and put an orange on the grave. The Episcopal priest who had conducted the service rushed over and took the orange away, saying, "When do you think the departed will come and eat this orange?" One of the Sioux men standing there said, "When the soul comes to smell the flowers!" No one said anything after that. (p. 171)

Cultural traditions and spiritual beliefs need to be integrated in a holistic approach to mental health and health care. When one Hmong family from Southeast Asia brought their young daughter to a California hospital emergency room for treatment of a seizure, a cross-cultural crisis ensued (Fadiman, 1997). The family members wanted the daughter's distress alleviated, but they didn't want to stop her seizures, which they believed to be sacred trance states signifying positive connection with the spirit world. As they put it, "The spirit catches you and you fall down." The well-intentioned medical staff gained a court-ordered removal of the girl from her parents so that they could control her seizures. However, this only heightened her distress and alienated the family, who refused further treatment after her return home. If the health care professionals had tried to understand and work with the spiritual beliefs of the family instead of taking an adversarial approach, the tragedy might well have been averted (Walsh, 1998c).

With growing religious diversity *within* families, therapists may need to take a role somewhat like a culture broker, as McGoldrick and Giordano (1996) suggest. A family member who chooses to convert or "marry out" may be seeking to rebalance the family's ethnic or religious orientation, moving away from some values and toward others. In some cases, this may express an attempt to separate and differentiate from one's family of origin (Friedman, 1985). Parents may experience such a choice as a rejection of them. Indeed, some may wish to cut off from religious or parental upbringing that was experienced as oppressive. In interfaith marriages, differences that initially attracted partners may over time become contentious, especially in raising children. Where there is conflict or estrangement, therapists can help partners, parents, or extended family members to better understand and respect one another's beliefs and practices. To resolve conflicts, we can help them avoid polarization or shift from a stance of "moral superiority" to an acceptance of different spiritual pathways.

When therapists are of the same religion as clients, it can be easier to form a natural rapport. However, one can easily overidentify with the client, see only positive or negative influences of religion, or be hesitant to question beliefs that are assumed to be fundamental. If we share the same religious orientation, clients may assume we judge them according to official religious doctrine. We may not be knowledgeable about the many varied religious orientations of our clients, and we are not trained to offer religious counseling. Yet our practice can be informed by the emerging literature on common patterns in families of various religious orientations (see, e.g., Butler & Harper, 1994, on religious Christian couples; Comas-Díaz, 1981, on Puerto Rican *espiritismo*; Cornwall & Thomas, 1990, on Mormon families and communities; Daneshpour, 1998, on Muslim families). McGoldrick and Giordano (1996) stress that culturally sensitive practice begins with awareness of the profound influence of core beliefs and an openness to learn from our clients. As in dealing with issues of ethnicity, we need to be openhearted in listening to and exploring religious and spiritual questions and beliefs that have profound implications for their lives.

A Leap of Faith: The Spiritual Essence of Therapy

At its best, the very process of psychotherapy becomes a spiritual wellspring for healing and resilience. As the family therapy field has matured, we have increasingly come to see that the value of our endeavor is found less in therapist strategies and techniques, and more in the quality of our collaborative relationship with clients. Yet as we have moved from cybernetic metaphors and clever interventions for rapid change, we must now counter managed care constraints to meet our client's needs for more soulful conversations about life and death, love and loss, trauma and recovery, meaning and purpose. In being fully present, open, respectful, curious, and compassionate, we deepen our connection and the process of transformation and growth.

A resilience-oriented approach to therapy is forged through this "courageous engagement" of therapist and clients—a wonderfully apt description offered by Waters and Lawrence (1993). We seek to understand our clients as heroes who have been challenged on their own life journeys. As therapists, we, as well as our clients, need courage to question constraining beliefs or destructive actions; to support clients' attempts to move from despair and reach for their hopes and dreams; to learn from their mistakes and act on their best intentions. When our clients lose hope, our faith in their potential can restore their faith. When we believe in the worth of our clients, they are better able to rise to meet their challenges with confidence and competence. Valuing human connection, we help our clients to seek reconciliation to heal wounded relationships and encourage them to forge more meaningful personal and spiritual bonds (Walsh, 1998c). These are essentially spiritual endeavors.

As I've come to work less from my head and more from my soul, I know less than I used to but I trust more my leap of faith and believe it's made me a better therapist. As Mary Jo Barrett found in her work with trauma survivors (see Chapter 11, this volume), this deeper level of work is not only transformative for our clients but can also be restorative for therapists (see also Schwartz, Chapter 13, and Weingarten, Chapter 14, this volume).

EXPLORING OUR OWN SPIRITUAL ROOTS AND BRANCHES

As therapists, we also need to be aware of our own spiritual beliefs (including atheist, agnostic, or secular humanist perspectives) and their influence in our therapeutic work. Our current beliefs and practices, as well as our family traditions and their legacies, operate in many ways, whether intentionally or unwittingly. If we hold a narrow, rigid view of spirituality as limited to formal, institutionalized, religion, we may not appreciate the many possibilities for spiritual experience. If our own childhood exposure to religion was largely negative or devoid of spiritual meaning, it may block us from realizing its potential source of strength and comfort for clients to draw upon in current distress. Therapists and trainees benefit from deepening knowledge of their family traditions and reflection on their own spiritual journeys (see Roberts, Chapter 15, this volume). Such self-awareness increases comfort in tapping into clients' spirituality for healing and growth.

It is not surprising for me to find myself drawn to explore spirituality since it was a core issue in my family of origin. In fact, my name, Froma, means spiritual or pious. Yet, as for many families, religion was a complicated matter in our lives, rife with secret keeping, conflict, and cutoffs.

My mother had been cut off (as in excommunicated) from her family after leaving the Catholic church and then converting to Judaism when she married my father. Just before my mother's death, when I was 27 and eager to know her better, she shared the secret she had held from even my father: She had been a nun for 17 years. She died before I could ask her the many questions I was left with. Through my own family-of-origin work I reconnected with her family and learned more about my Catholic roots.

Naming is often a way of making connections across the generations and in the joining of families by marriage. In my own family, naming became a way for my mother to weave together the disparate threads of her life and identity. Her mother, a devout French Canadian Catholic, named her and her brother Mary and Joseph. She had hoped that her favored son would become a priest, but Joe left the seminary after a year to marry his sweetheart. Hoping to win her mother's approval, my mother not only took his place, entering the convent, she even took his name: Sister Josephine. When she eventually left the religious order to lead a "normal" life, she held on to that part of her identity by becoming Mary Jo. When she married my father, she converted to Judaism (at his mother's request), and became known as Jo. To bridge the cultural and religious divide and to win the approval of her new mother-in-law, she named me after my father's maternal grandmother, Frimid. (Ironically, my Jewish grandmother turned to Christian Science readings in her last years of life.)

Only when I reached adulthood did I learn that my name, Froma (like Frimid), derives from the Jewish name "Fruma," meaning pious or spiritual. (No one had ever mentioned the meaning to me.) My name would have had significance for my mother. Although she chose a secular life, she remained a deeply spiritual person. She found it easy to convert to Judaism, and as she made sure I went through Sunday school to Confirmation, she herself became a Sunday school teacher and the temple organist. Later, she even became B'nai Brith president.

However, that year, someone in the congregation spoke out against her, contending that it was not proper for her to hold such a position—that she was not *really* a Jew. (Actually, by Jewish law, she was.) She was devastated and withdrew from formal religion altogether for the rest of her life. I left for college and disengaged from Judaism myself for many years, feeling I didn't quite belong anywhere, much as my mother must have felt. My father found spiritual connection through the Masonic lodge, yet true to his Jewish faith, only read the Old Testament, and never took a Christian vow.

I experienced a further jolt at college with my first experience of anti-Semitism. After my freshman year in the dorms, I decided to go through rush for a sorority along with several close friends. I knew there were Jewish houses, but I didn't want to be segregated; I just wanted to be in a "regular" sorority. We all went around to the initial open houses. My (Christian) friends all went on to pledge. I received not a single invitation back. I was stunned. No one had warned me, but I learned I had been blackballed. Although I hadn't identified as Jewish, my name, Froma Weisberg, was a giveaway. But, as resilience is forged through crisis, my devastating experience became transformative. Dazed, I found an apartment on my own and refocused from my social life to my studies. This deep concentration awakened my passion for learning. Moreover, I gained a perspective on my social world that I would not have otherwise. I became involved in the growing civil rights movement and, at graduation, went into the Peace Corps. Interestingly, I chose to go to Morocco, an Arab Islamic culture blended with ancient Berber spiritual traditions. Morocco became a spiritual home for me, and I return often for nourishment.

In groups that have experienced the stigma of bias and discrimination, such as Jews, we may absorb the larger society's prejudices and become conflicted about our own religious identity. Such fear and conflict led me to hide my Jewish identity. Blue eyed and fair, I could "pass" easily in gentile circles. I gladly took (and kept) the family name of my first husband, Walsh. (Actually, they were Jewish too; like many others, their Eastern European immigrant parents' name had been simplified to Walsh at Ellis Island.) Strangers, on meeting me, often comment that my name,

Froma, is "interesting" or unusual and ask where it comes from. I learned to discern in each situation whether it seemed "safe" to reveal its Jewish origin and meaning. If I thought the person was probably not Jewish (and might be anti-Semitic), I would simply say it was an old family name. If pressed further, I might say I was named after a great-grandmother who had come from Hungary. If I thought the person asking was Jewish, I would respond openly. If I wasn't sure, I might say that I was named for a great-grandmother and watch for a knowing smile, a twinkle in the eye. Older and more traditional Jews often reply, "Ah, you're a Frum!" and we share a moment of communion.

Now I do at times reveal my religious roots in therapy; at other times I don't, depending on the situation. If asked, I no longer hesitate to be open. If I think that sharing some aspect of my spiritual journey might be helpful to clients, I may tell a part of my story as it relates to their dilemma or might inspire them to pursue their own spiritual paths.

In reflecting on my therapeutic work over a decade ago with the family who lost their husband/father, a minister (described at the opening of this chapter), I believe that my unease at that time with my own complicated spiritual identity contributed, out of awareness, to my blindness to the family's spiritual pain. As I have gained awareness and acceptance of my own spiritual complexities, I find my sight and hearing greatly improved, with comfort in exploring the spiritual dimension of my clients' lives.

I see my own spiritual journey as a lifelong process of exploration, hopefully with deepening and expanding awareness and connection. My ecumenical bookshelf is chock full of books calling out to be read and re-read. Although I don't fit neatly into any one religious category, I identify most strongly with my Jewish religious and cultural roots. Yet, like both my parents, I've stitched together strands of many faith traditions into a deeply personal spirituality. I've gained an appreciation and an affinity toward many aspects of Christian, Buddhist, Islamic, and Native American traditions. Rather than seeing these in conflict, I experience each as offering many valuable ways of approaching the spirit. Common across faiths is a version of the Golden Rule ("Do unto others as you would have them do unto you"). Each helps us grapple with such universal questions as "Where have we come from, why are we here, and where are we going?" We may turn to different faiths to seek answers. What matters most is the journey itself; we find meaning in the quest, even when the answers prove to be elusive and when each answer opens a new mystery.

Buddhism counsels us to assume a beginner's mind. This chapter, like the others in this volume, is offered not from a position of expertise but in an ecumenical spirit of opening our therapeutic door to this vital dimension of experience. Following this chapter, a list of suggested readings is offered to broaden acquaintance with the many diverse spiritual beliefs and practices clients may bring. A beginning understanding of core convictions can serve to prevent ignorance, faulty assumptions, or stereotyped views from interfering with therapeutic rapport. I hope it will also inspire deeper exploration of our own faith traditions as well as new spiritual possibilities for resilience and growth in our practices and our personal lives. As the Shawnee proverb affirms, "We are all one child spinning through Mother sky."

REFERENCES

American Psychiatric Association. (1994). *Diagnostic and statistical manual of mental disorders* (4th ed.). Washington, DC: Author.

Anderson, D. A., & Worthen, D. (1997). Exploring a fourth dimension: Spirituality as a resource for the couple therapist. *Journal of Marital and Family Therapy, 23,* 2–12.

Antonovsky, A. (1987). *Unraveling the mystery of health.* San Francisco: Jossey-Bass.

Aponte, H. (1994). *Bread and spirit: Therapy with the new poor.* New York: Norton.

Bateson, G. (1979). *Mind and nature: A necessary unity.* New York: Dutton.

Becker, E. (1973). *The denial of death.* New York: Free Press.

Becvar, D. (1996). *Soul healing: A spiritual orientation in counseling and therapy.* New York: Basic Books.

Becvar, D. (Ed.). (1998). *The family, spirituality, and social work.* Binghamton, NY: Haworth Press.

Bell, L. G. (1998). Start with meditation. In T. Nelson & T. Trepper (Eds.), *101 interventions in family therapy* (Vol. 2, pp. 52–56). New York: Haworth Press.

Berenson, D. (1990). A systemic view of spirituality: God and twelve-step programs as resources in family therapy. *Journal of Strategic and Systemic Therapies, 9,* 59–70.

Bergin, A. E. (1991). Values and religious issues in psychotherapy and mental health. *American Psychologist, 46,* 394–403.

Bergin, A. E., & Jensen, J. P. (1990). Religiosity of psychotherapists: A national survey. *Psychotherapy, 27,* 3–7.

Bernardin, J. (1997). *The gift of peace.* Chicago: Loyola Press.

Billingsley, A. (1992). *Climbing Jacob's ladder: The enduring legacy of African-American families.* New York: Simon & Schuster.

Bogart, G. (1991). The use of meditation in psychotherapy: A review of the literature. *American Journal of Psychotherapy, 45,* 383–412.

Bohannon, J. R. (1991). Religiosity related to grief levels of bereaved mothers and fathers. *Omega, 23,* 153–159.

Boszormenyi-Nagy, I. (1987). *Foundations of contextual family therapy.* New York: Brunner/Mazel.

Bryer, K. B. (1979). The Amish way of death: A study of family support systems. *American Psychologist, 34,* 255–261.

Butler, K. (1990). Spirituality reconsidered. *Family Therapy Networker, 14,* 26–37.

Butler, M. H., & Harper, J. M. (1994). The divine triangle: God in the marital system of religious couples. *Family Process, 33,* 277–286.

Capra, F. (1975). *The Tao of physics: An exploration of the parallels between modern physics and Eastern mysticism.* London: Wildwood House.

Carrington, P. (1986). Meditation as an access to altered states of consciousness. In B. Wolman & M. Ullman (Eds.), *Handbook of states of consciousness.* New York: Van Nostrand Reinhold.

Coles, R. (1990). *The spiritual life of children.* Boston: Houghton Mifflin.

Comas-Díaz, L. (1981). Puerto Rican *espiritismo* and psychotherapy. *American Journal of Orthopsychiatry, 51,* 636–645.

Comer, J. (1997). *Waiting for a miracle.* New York: Viking.

Cornwall, M., & Thomas, D. L. (1990). Family, religion, and personal communities: Examples from Mormonism. *Marriage and Family Review, 15,* 229–252.

Dallos, R. (1991). *Family belief systems, therapy, and change.* Philadelphia: Open University Press.

Daneshpour, M. (1998). Muslim families and family therapy. *Journal of Marital and Family Therapy, 24,* 355–368.

Deloria, V., Jr. (1994). *God is red: A native view of religion* (2nd ed.). Golden, CO: Fulcrum.

Doherty, W. J. (1995). *Soul searching: Why psychotherapy must promote moral responsibility.* New York: Basic Books.

Domino, G., & Miller, K. (1992). Religiosity and attitudes toward suicide. *Omega, 25,* 271–282.

Dossey, L. (1993). *Healing words: The power of prayer and the practice of medicine.* San Francisco: Harper.

Einstein, A. (1931). Religion and science. In A. M. Drummond & R. H. Wagner (Eds.), *Problems and opinions* (pp. 355–358). New York: Century.

Eliade, M. (1972). *Shamanism: Archaic techniques of ecstasy.* New York: Harper Torchbooks.

Ellison, C. G., & Levin, J. S. (1998). The religion-health connection: Evidence, theory, and future directions. *Health Education and Behavior, 25,* 700–720.

Fadiman, A. (1997). *The spirit catches you and you fall down.* San Francisco: Ferrer.

Falicov, C. (1995). Training to think culturally: A multidimensional comparative framework. *Family Process, 34,* 373–388.

Falicov, C. (1998). *Latino families in therapy.* New York: Guilford Press.

Frankl, V. (1955). *The doctor and the soul.* New York: Knopf.

Freud, S. (1961). The future of an illusion. In J. Strachey (Ed. and Trans.), *The standard edition of the complete psychological works of Sigmund Freud* (Vol. 21, pp. 1–56). London: Hogarth Press. (Original work published 1927)

Friedman, E. H. (1985). *Generation to generation: Family process in church and synagogue.* New York: Guilford Press.

Gartner, J., Larson, D. B., & Allen, G. D. (1991). Religious commitment and mental health: A review of the empirical literature. *Journal of Psychology and Theology, 19,* 6–25.

Gilbert, K. (1992). Religion as a resource for bereaved parents. *Journal of Religion and Health, 31,* 19–30.

Gorsuch, R. L. (1995). Religious aspects of substance abuse and recovery. *Journal of Social Issues, 51,* 65–83.

Green, L. L., Fullilove, M. T., & Fullilove, R. E. (1998). Stories of spiritual awakening: The nature of spirituality in recovery. *Journal of Substance Abuse Treatment, 15,* 325–331.

Griffith, J. L. (1986). Employing the God-family relationship with religious families. *Family Process, 25,* 609–618.

Griffith, J. L., & Griffith, M. E. (in press). *Sacred encounters.* New York: Guilford Press.

Gutsche, S. (1994). Voices of healing: Therapists and clients journey towards spirituality. *Journal of Systemic Family Therapies, 13,* 7–15.

Hargrave, T. (1994). *Families and forgiveness.* New York: Brunner/Mazel.

Harner, M. (1980). *The way of the shaman: A guide to power and healing.* San Francisco: Harper & Row.

Holmes, T. (1994). Spirituality in systemic practice: An internal family systems perspective. *Journal of Systemic Therapies, 13,* 26–35.

Hood, R. W., Spilka, B., Hunsberger, B., & Gorsuch, R. (1996). *The psychology of religion: An empirical approach* (2nd ed.). New York: Guilford Press.

Imber-Black, E., & Roberts, J. (1992). *Rituals for our times: Celebrating, healing, and changing our lives and our relationships.* New York: HarperCollins.

Jackson, P., with Delehanty, H. (1995). *Sacred hoops: Spiritual lessons of a hardwood warrior.* New York: Hyperion Books.

Joanides, C. J. (1996). Collaborative family therapy with religious family systems. *Journal of Family Psychotherapy, 7,* 19–35.

Johnson, G. (1998, June 30). Science and religion: Bridging the great divide. *New York Times,* p. F4.

Jung, C. G. (1933). *Modern man in search of a soul.* New York: Harcourt, Brace.

Jung, C. G. (1958). *Psychology and religion: West and East.* New York: Pantheon.

Kabat-Zinn, J. (1990). *Full catastrophe living: Using the wisdom of your mind and body to face stress, pain, and illness.* New York: Dell.

Kabat-Zinn, J. (1994). *Wherever you go, there you are: Mindfulness meditation in everyday life.* New York: Hyperion Press.

Kelly, E. W. (1995). *Religion and spirituality in counseling and psychotherapy.* Alexandria, VA: American Counseling Association.

Koenig, H., George, L., Hays, J., Larson, D., Cohen, H., & Blazer, D. (1998). The relationship between religious activities and blood pressure in older adults. *International Journal of Psychiatry, 28,* 189–213.

Kramer, S. Z. (1995). *Transforming the inner and outer family: Humanistic and spiritual approaches to mind–body systems therapy.* New York: Haworth Press.

Kudlac, K. E. (1991). Including God in the conversation: The influence of religious beliefs on the problem-organized system. *Family Therapy, 18,* 277–285.

Laird, J., & Green, R.-J. (Eds.). (1996). *Lesbians and gays in families and family therapy.* San Francisco: Jossey-Bass.

Levine, S. (1987). *Healing into life and death.* New York: Doubleday.

Mahmoud, V. (1996). African American Muslim families. In M. McGoldrick, J. Giordano, & J. K. Pearce (Eds.), *Ethnicity and family therapy* (2nd ed., pp. 112–128). New York: Guilford Press.

Markowitz, L. (1998). Essential conversations: Raising the sacred in therapy. *In the Family, 3*(3), 7–13.

McGoldrick, M., Gerson, R., & Shellenberger, S. (1999). *Genograms: Assessment and intervention* (2nd ed.). New York: Norton.

McGoldrick, M., & Giordano, J. (1996). Overview: Ethnicity and family therapy. In M. McGoldrick, J. Giordano, & J. K. Pearce (Eds.), *Ethnicity and family therapy* (pp. 1–28). New York: Guilford Press.

McGoldrick, M., & Preto, N. G. (1984). Ethnic intermarriage: Implications for therapy. *Family Process, 23,* 347–364.

Miller, W. R. (1998). Researching the spiritual dimensions of alcohol and other drug problems. *Addiction, 93,* 979–990.

Minnick, A. M. (1997). *Twelve-step programs: Contemporary American quest for meaning and spiritual renewal.* New York: Praeger.

Minuchin, S. (1992). *Family healing: Strategies for hope and understanding.* New York: Macmillan.

Nakhaima, J. M., & Dicks, B. H. (1995). Social work practice with religious families. *Families in Society: Journal of Contemporary Human Services, 76,* 360–368.

Nhat Hahn, T. (1987). *The miracle of mindfulness: A manual on meditation.* Boston: Beacon Press. (Original work published 1975)

Nhat Hahn, T. (1991). *Peace is every step: The path of mindfulness in everyday life* (A. Kotler, Ed.). New York: Bantam Books.

O'Neil, C., & Ritter, K. (1992). *Coming out within: Stages of spiritual awakening for lesbians and gay men.* New York: HarperCollins.

Oxman, T. E., Freeman, D. H., & Manheimer, E. D. (1995). Lack of social participation or religious strength and comfort as risk factors for death after cardiac surgery in the elderly. *Psychosomatic Medicine, 57,* 5–15.

Peteet, J. R. (1993). A closer look at a spiritual approach in addictions treatment. *Journal of Substance Abuse Treatment, 10,* 263–267.

Pittman, F. (1988). Lead us not: Capturing the essence of religious experience. *Family Therapy Networker, 12*(6), 73–75.

Pittman, F. (1990). The rattle of God. *Family Therapy Networker, 14*(5), 42–46.

Prest, L. A., & Keller, J. F. (1993). Spirituality and family therapy: Spiritual beliefs, myths, and metaphors. *Journal of Marital and Family Therapy, 19,* 137–148.

Rosenthal, J. (1990). The meditative therapist. *Family Therapy Networker, 14,* 38–41, 70–71.

Ross, J. L. (1994). Working with patients within their religious contexts: Religion, spirituality, and the secular therapist. *Journal of Systemic Therapies, 13,* 7–15.

Rotz, E., Russell, C. S., & Wright, D. W. (1993). The therapist who is perceived as "spiritually correct": Strategies for avoiding collusion with the "spiritually one-up" spouse. *Journal of Marital and Family Therapy, 19*, 369–375.

Satir, V. (1988). *Peoplemaking.* Palo Alto, CA: Science & Behavior. (Original work published 1972)

Seligman, M. (1990). *Learned optimism.* New York: Random House.

Shafranske, E. P. (Ed.). (1996). *Religion and the clinical practice of psychology.* Washington, DC: American Psychological Association Press.

Simon, R. (1997, March–April). Systems therapy NBA style. *Family Therapy Networker, 21*, 49–61.

Simpkinson, C., & Simpkinson, A. (1999). Simply the best. *Common Boundary: Exploring Psychology, Spirituality, and Creativity, 17*(1), 32–37.

Smith, H. (1991). *The world's religious: Our great wisdom traditions* (rev. ed.). New York: HarperCollins.

Somé, M. P. (1994). *The healing wisdom of Africa.* New York: Tarcher/Putnam.

Stander, V., Piercy, F. P., MacKinnon, D., & Helmeke, K. (1994). Spirituality, religion, and family therapy: Competing or complementary worlds? *American Journal of Family Therapy, 22*, 27–41.

Steere, D. A. (1997). *Spiritual practice in psychotherapy: A guide for caregivers.* New York: Brunner/Mazel.

Stewart, S. P., & Gale, J. E. (1994). On hallowed ground: Marital therapy with couples on the religious right. *Journal of Systemic Therapies, 13*, 16–25.

Walsh, F. (1993). Conceptualization of normal family processes. In F. Walsh (Ed.), *Normal family processes* (pp. 3–69). New York: Guilford Press.

Walsh, F. (1998a). Beliefs, spirituality, and transcendence: Keys to family resilience. In M. McGoldrick (Ed.), *Re-visioning family therapy: Race, culture, and gender in clinical practice* (pp. 62–77). New York: Guilford Press.

Walsh, F. (1998b). Families in later life: Challenges and opportunities. In B. Carter & M. McGoldrick (Eds.), *The expanded family life cycle* (3rd ed., pp. 307–326). Needham Heights, MA: Allyn & Bacon.

Walsh, F. (1998c). *Strengthening family resilience.* New York: Guilford Press.

Walsh, F., & McGoldrick, M. (Eds.). (1991). *Living beyond loss: Death in the family.* New York: Norton.

Waters, D., & Lawrence, E. (1993). *Competence, courage, and change.* New York: Norton.

Weaver, A. J., Koenig, H. G., & Larson, D. B. (1997). Marriage and family therapists and the clergy: A need for clinical collaboration, training, and research. *Journal of Marital and Family Therapy, 23*, 13–25.

Weil, A. (1994). *Spontaneous healing.* New York: Knopf.

Werner, E. E., & Smith, R. S. (1992). *Overcoming the odds: High risk children from birth to adulthood.* Ithaca, NY: Cornell University Press.

Whipple, V. (1987). Counseling battered women from fundamentalist churches. *Journal of Marital and Family Therapy, 13*, 251–258.

Woolfolk, R. (1998). *The cure of souls: Science, values, and psychotherapy.* San Francisco: Jossey-Bass.

Wright, L., Watson, W. L., & Bell, J. M. (1996). *Beliefs: The heart of healing in families and illness.* New York: Basic Books.

SUGGESTED READINGS ON RELIGION AND SPIRITUALITY: RESOURCES FOR A SPIRITUAL JOURNEY

Angelou, M. (1986). *All God's children need traveling shoes.* New York: Vintage.

Armstrong, K. (1994). *A history of God: The 4,000-year quest of Judaism, Christianity, and Islam.* New York: Ballantine Books.

Becvar, D. (1996). *Soul healing: A spiritual orientation in counseling and therapy.* New York: Basic Books.

Bellah, R. N., & Hammond, P. E. (1980). *Varieties of civil religion.* New York: Harper & Row.

Bridges, H. (1970). *American mysticism from William James to Zen.* New York: Harper & Row.

Brook, G. (1995). *Nine parts of desire: The hidden world of Islamic women.* New York: Anchor.

Brown, J. E. (1953). *The sacred pipe: Black Elk's account of the seven rites of the Oglala Sioux.* Norman, OK: University of Oklahoma Press.

Campbell, J. (1964). *The masks of God.* New York: Viking.

Campbell, J., & Moyers, B. (1988). *The power of myth.* New York: Doubleday.

Das, S. (1997). *Awakening the Buddha within: Tibetan wisdom for the Western world.* New York: Broadway.

Deloria, V., Jr. (1994). *God is red: A native view of religion* (2nd ed.). Golden, CO: Fulcrum.

Dewey, J. (1929). *The quest for certainty.* New York: Minton, Balch.

Durkheim, E. (1915). *The elementary forms of religious life: A study in religious sociology* (J. W. Swain, Trans.). London: Allen & Unwin.

Eliade, M. (1961). *The sacred and the profane: The nature of religion.* New York: Harper Torchbooks.

Epstein, M. (1995). *Thoughts without a thinker: Psychotherapy from a Buddhist perspective.* New York: Basic Books.

Four Winds Development Project. (1984/1989). *The sacred tree: Reflections on Native American spirituality* (3rd ed.). Wilmot, WI: Lotus Light.

Frank, J. (1974). *Persuasion and healing* (rev. ed.). New York: Schocken Books.

Frankl, V. (1955). *The doctor and the soul.* New York: Knopf.

Frankl, V. (1984). *Man's search for meaning.* New York: Simon & Schuster. (Original work published 1946)

Friedman, E. H. (1985). *Generation to generation: Family process in church and synagogue.* New York: Guilford Press.

Fromm, E. (1959). *Psychoanalysis and religion.* New Haven, CT: Yale University Press.

Galanter, M. (1989). *Cults and new religious movements.* Washington, DC: American Psychological Association.

Gallup, G., Jr. (1996). *Religion in America: 1996 report.* Princeton, NJ: Princeton Religion Research Center.

Gibran, K. (1961). *The prophet.* New York: Knopf.

James, W. (1985). *The varieties of religious experience.* New York: Mentor. (Original work published 1902)

Jung, C. G. (1933). *Modern man in search of a soul.* New York: Harcourt, Brace.

Jung, C. G. (1958). *Psychology and religion: West and East.* New York: Pantheon.

Kabat-Zinn, J. (1990). *Full catastrophe living: Using the wisdom of your mind and body to face stress, pain, and illness.* New York: Dell.

Kabat-Zinn, J. (1994). *Wherever you go, there you are: Mindfulness meditation in everyday life.* New York: Hyperion Press.

Kertzer, M. N., & Hoffman, L. H. (1996). *What is a Jew? A guide to the beliefs, traditions, and practices of Judaism* (rev. ed.). New York: Touchstone.

Kornfield, J. (1993). *A path with heart: A guide through the promises and perils of spiritual life.* New York: Bantam.

Law, E. H. F. (1993). *The wolf shall dwell with the lamb: A spirituality for leadership in multicultural communities.* St. Louis, MO: Chalica Press.

Lerner, M. (1994). *Jewish renewal: A path to healing and transformation.* New York: Harper Perennial.

Levine, S. (1987). *Healing into life and death.* New York: Doubleday.

Levine, S., & Levine, O. (1995). *Embracing the beloved: Relationship as a path of spiritual awakening.* New York: Anchor.

Maslow, A. (1976). *Religions, values, and peak experiences.* New York: Penguin. (Original work published 1940)

May, R. (1953). *Man's search for himself.* New York: Norton.

Mbiti, J. S. (1970). *African religions and philosophy.* Garden City, NY: Anchor.

Miles, J. (1995). *God: A biography.* New York: Knopf.

Momaday, N. S. (1968). *House made of dawn.* New York: Harper & Row.

Moody, H. (1997). *The five stages of the soul: Charting the spiritual passages that shape our lives.* New York: Anchor.

Moore, T. (1992). *Care of the soul: A guide for cultivating depth and sacredness in everyday life.* New York: HarperCollins.

Moore, T. (1994). *Soul mates: Honoring the mysteries of love and relationship.* New York: Harper Perennial.

Murphy, C. (1998). *The word according to Eve: Women and the Bible in ancient times.* Boston: Houghton Mifflin.

Myss, C. (1996). *Anatomy of the spirit.* New York: Three Rivers Press.

Neihardt, J. (1979). *Black Elk speaks: Being the life story of a Holy Man of the Oglala Sioux.* Lincoln, NE: University of Nebraska Press. (Original work published 1932)

Nhat Hahn, T. (1987). *The miracle of mindfulness: A manual on meditation.* Boston: Beacon Press. (Original work published 1975)

Nhat Hahn, T. (1991). *Peace is every step: The path of mindfulness in everyday life* (A. Kotler, Ed.). New York: Bantam.

Nhat Hahn, T. (1999). *The heart of the Buddha's teaching.* New York: Broadway.

Peck, M. S. (1978). *The road less travelled: A new psychology of love, traditional values, and spiritual growth.* New York: Simon & Schuster.

Perrone, B., Stockel, H. H., & Krueger, V. (1989). *Medicine women, curanderas, and women doctors.* Norman, OK: University of Oklahoma Press.

Plaskow, J., & Christ, C. P. (Eds.). (1989). *Weaving the visions: New patterns in feminist spirituality.* San Francisco: HarperSanFrancisco.

Rashad, A. (1991). *The history of Islam and black nationalism in the Americas.* Beltsville, MD: Writers.

Rinpoche, S. (1992). *The Tibetan book of living and dying.* San Francisco: HarperSanFrancisco.

Rosten, L. (1975). *Religions of America: Ferment and faith in an age of crisis.* New York: Simon & Schuster/Touchstone.

Satir, V. (1988). *People making.* Palo Alto, CA: Science & Behavior. (Original work published 1972)

Schucman, H., & Thetford, W. (1996). *A course in miracles: Foundation for inner peace* (2nd ed.). New York: Viking, Penguin.

Sewell, M. (Ed.). (1991). *Cries of the spirit: A celebration of women's spirituality.* Boston: Beacon Press.

Simpkinson, A., & Simpkinson, C. (1998). *Soul work: A field guide for spiritual seekers.* New York: HarperCollins.

Singer, J. (1994). *Boundaries of the soul: The practice of Jung's psychology.* New York: Anchor. (Original work published 1972)

Smith, H. (1991). *The world's religions: Our great wisdom traditions* (rev. ed.). New York: HarperCollins.

Somé, M. P. (1994). *Of water and the spirit: Ritual, magic, and initiation in the life of an African shaman.* New York: Penguin.

Somé, M. P. (1998). *The healing wisdom of Africa.* New York: Tarcher/Putnam.

Vardey, L. (Ed.). (1996). *God in all worlds: An anthology of contemporary spiritual writing.* New York: Vintage.

Watts, A. (1961). *Psychotherapy east and west.* New York: New American Library.

Weil, A. (1994). *Spontaneous healing.* New York: Knopf.

Williamson, M. (1997). *The healing of America.* New York: Simon & Schuster.

Zukov, G. (1989). *The seat of the soul.* New York: Fireside.

PART II

Spiritual Resources in Families

Tapping into the Wellsprings

CHAPTER 3

Spirituality, Suffering, and Beliefs

The Soul of Healing with Families

LORRAINE M. WRIGHT

I first experienced suffering from illness in my childhood. My grandmother, who lived with us, suffered chronic pain from rheumatoid arthritis. I felt the demoralizing effects of suffering, whether it was observing my grandmother's suffering or as I suffered emotionally with her. I also learned that this chronic pain controlled all of our lives, how well my brother and I would behave on any given day, how much my grandmother was able to "mother," and how we children became more compassionate because of having a pain sufferer in the family. My grandmother was the center of our family, but the chronic pain she suffered ultimately ruled all our lives. The disease severely disfigured her hands, caused her knees to be swollen much of the time, resulted in her walking with a severe limp, and dictated how well she was able to live her life on any given day. But those disfigured hands made us apple pie, weeded our garden, and lifted numerous cups of tea while we exchanged stories of our lives with her. However, I do not recall as a child hearing *her* stories of suffering with chronic pain. Perhaps I did not listen. Perhaps these stories were not told.

Now, however, I have several questions that I would eagerly ask of her. What meaning did my grandmother give to this life of chronic pain? What did she believe was the best treatment or healing for her pain? What did she believe helped to alleviate or diminish some of her suffering? What made it worse? What made it better? What help or hindrance were her spiritual/religious beliefs? What invited her to reconnect with her Roman Catholic church in her later years? Did she pray for relief of pain or to endure the pain? Did she pray at all? What did she believe health professionals did to help or hinder her healing? Which was worse: the emotional, physical, or spiritual suffering? I wonder if these kinds of conversations would have been healing for both my grandmother and me.

As a family therapist/nurse educator working predominantly with families experiencing illness, I have the privilege of engaging in numerous therapeutic conversations about illness. These conversations invariably include family members' descriptions of suffering, the meaning they give to their suffering from spiritual domains, and their beliefs about their illness experience. I have become a passionate observer of and participant in the healing effect and changes that occur in the bio-psycho-social-spiritual structure of family members and myself.

SPIRITUALITY, SUFFERING, AND BELIEFS: A NEW TRINITY

I have come to believe that a new trinity is emerging in my practice of family therapy: spirituality, suffering, and beliefs. I find it impossible to think about spirituality without thinking about suffering and beliefs. And I find it as equally impossible to think about suffering without talking about spirituality and beliefs. These three notions are thoroughly intertwined and closely related. However, I will initially discuss each of these concepts separately in order to justifiably bring them together later.

Spirituality

The influence of family members' spiritual and religious beliefs on their illness experiences has been one of the most neglected areas in family work. However, there is evidence that family therapists are waking up to this neglected aspect of spirit in human experience. Increasing numbers of articles have appeared in professional journals, and entire issues of newsletters have been devoted to spirituality and couples and family therapy. The book in which this chapter appears is perhaps the beacon light signaling this awakening of the ever-present spiritual aspects of our privileged work with families.

My own clinical experience with families has taught me that the experience of suffering from illness becomes transposed to one of spirituality as family members try to make meaning out of their suffering and distress. To understand how family members offer compassion and what efforts are made to alleviate suffering, it is imperative that therapists explore religious and spiritual beliefs in clinical work with families. It is through the medium of therapeutic conversations about beliefs concerning spirituality and religion that a manner of understanding, explaining, conversing, and creating changes and healing with families becomes possible.

The most significant learning about suffering that I have gleaned in my clinical work with families over 25 years is that a discourse of suffering invariably opens up a discourse of spirituality if we, families and therapists, are open to it. Suffering invites and leads us into the spiritual domain. A shift to and emphasis on spirituality is frequently the most profound response to suffering from illness. If family therapists are to be helpful, we must acknowledge that suffering and often the senselessness of it are ultimately spiritual issues (Patterson, 1994).

I have had one recurring piece of feedback about my clinical work with families in recent years that has guided me in becoming more cognizant and appreciative of the spiritual dimension of therapeutic work. Colleagues and students alike have been offering their unsolicited observations on the "spiritual" aspects of my therapy for several years. I have found this observation fascinating, as I had not put any direct or intended emphasis about spiritual issues in family work. Only rarely did I mention my own spiritual and religious beliefs as a Christian and specifically as a practicing Mormon. I reflected that somehow I must have changed from my early years as a therapist, as this feedback was news of a difference. One very curious observation came about 8 years ago when a valued colleague told me that he would describe my clinical work as "secular theology." This comment perturbed me for some time. He elaborated and suggested what he believed to be the most powerful aspect of my clinical work with families: the notion of "reverencing" that occurred between families/clients and myself. In those moments of reverencing, there is a profound awe and respect for the individuals seated in front of you. It is not a linear phenomenon in these moments. I feel that same reverencing from family members being given back to me. In those moments of reverencing in clinical work something very special happens between the therapist and the family; it is something felt by all—a deep emotional connection. I know and have felt these moments in therapy, both in the therapy room and from behind the one-way mirror as a supervisor or team member. During these times, I have witnessed the most profound changes in family members' thinking, behavior, illness experience, and most importantly, in their suffering. In these instances, I have felt an emotion that seems to arise only when there is reverencing. This emotion I submit is pure love. I have come to understand and recognize moments of reverencing as the spiritual nature of my clinical work with families that perhaps invites colleagues and students to comment that they observe a "spiritual" aspect to my work with families. I hope this is so, as I believe it makes a quantum difference to the healing process when reverencing occurs.

The quiet intervention of prayer is also receiving more attention in clinical work with families and in my own practice. Dossey (1993) reviewed numerous medical studies examining the efficacy of prayer in producing physical changes. For example, he suggested that the ritual of prayer may trigger emotions that, in turn, may lead to changes in health by positively impacting the immune and cardiovascular systems. Thomas (1997) also conducted a fascinating review of doctors who pray for or with their patients, and who encourage their patients to pray for themselves and within their religious community. From this review, he offered his belief that some prayer is better than no prayer.

Dossey (1993) and Cousins (1989) summoned health professionals to recognize that there are many nonphysiological reasons persons and families heal from illness. Over the past few years, I have on occasion independently adopted Dossey's (1993) practice of praying for, although not with, the clients and families with whom I work. As Dossey (1993) suggested, if a health professional believes that prayer works, not to use it is analogous to withholding a potent medication or surgical procedure: "Both prayer and belief are nonlocal manifestation of consciousness, because both can operate at a distance, sometimes outside the patient's awareness. Both affirm that, 'it's not all physical,' and both can be used adjunctively with other forms of therapy" (p. 141). In praying for our clients, we perhaps also heighten our connection with them and our investment in their recovery and well-being.

Beliefs

In daily life, the best medium for hearing our own and others' beliefs is in the stories we exchange through our conversations. Beliefs are the blueprints from which we construct our lives and proceed to intermingle them with the lives of others. At no time are family and individual beliefs more affirmed, challenged, or threatened than when illness emerges (Wright, Watson, & Bell, 1996). What one believes about illness contributes dramatically to how one experiences an illnesses. No two people and no two families have the same experience with the same disease, whether it be the common cold or multiple sclerosis. Some families view illness as a sign that they are sinful and disease as a punishment for ungodly living. Other families believe that being ill is a natural physical sign that the ill member should slow down and take care of him- or herself, that no longer can his or her health be neglected. There are also many beliefs about how family members should behave when illness enters a family.

Consequently, how families adapt, manage, and cope with illness arises from their beliefs about the illness that is confronting them. Rolland (1994) suggests these beliefs may be influenced by the stage in the family life cycle of the individual, the family, and the illness. How family members experience an illness depends on the beliefs that they have embraced prior to the illness experience as well as the beliefs that evolve through the experience of the illness. The beliefs that family members hold are often reconstructed after the experience of an illness (i.e., blueprints are revised); conversely, family member beliefs influence and shape the processes and outcomes of illness. For example, how family members treat even the common cold depends on their beliefs concerning how they "caught" the cold in the first place. If one believes that colds are related to experiences of loss, one will probably treat one's cold differently than if one believes a cold is due to inadequate rest and working long hours. If a person believes the best remedy for a cold is to rest, drink plenty of fluid, and take vitamin C, that regime will probably be followed. If the treatment remedy does not work, will the belief about the etiology be maintained? Will there be more openness to other treatment remedies? Many factors influence what people consider treatment options when their original beliefs about the etiology and the cure of an illness have been challenged. Of course, there are circumstances when beliefs may have little or no influence over the reaction of the body. For example, if a person is given an injection of a thousand units of quick-acting insulin, no matter what the belief, the chances are overwhelming that the person will become unconscious as the blood sugar plunges (Dossey, 1993).

Not all beliefs matter to the experience of an illness. The core beliefs that I have found most useful to uncover and explore with families about their illness experience are the following: beliefs about etiology/cause of illness; beliefs about diagnosis of illness; beliefs about healing and treatment; beliefs about prognosis/outcome; beliefs about mastery/control and influence on illness; beliefs about the place of illness in our lives and relationships; beliefs about spirituality and religion; beliefs about the role of family members; and, finally, beliefs about the role of health care professionals (Wright, Watson, & Bell, 1996).

Family therapists bring their own strong personal and professional beliefs about families and illness to the clinical domain. Their beliefs influence how they view, assess, and—most importantly—care for and intervene with families. For example, family therapists' beliefs about etiology may influence how a family is received, perceived, and treated. A therapist who believes alcoholism is a consequence of irresponsibility and personal weakness will likely respond differently to a family experiencing alcoholism than to a family experiencing the effects of a congenital heart defect, an illness over which a health professional may believe the individual or family has no control. The core beliefs of family therapists that will affect relationships with families are their beliefs about illness, about families, about change, and about their own role as therapists in the lives of families.

Suffering

The alleviation of suffering has always been the cornerstone of caring. "Suffering gives caring its own character and identity, and all forms of caring aim, in one way or another, to alleviate suffering" (Lindholm & Eriksson, 1993, p. 1354). What *is* suffering? One description of suffering that I have found useful is by Morse and Johnson (1991). They offer the idea that suffering is a comprehensive concept that includes the experience of both acute and chronic pain, the strain of trying to endure, the alienation of forced exclusion from everyday life, the shock of institutionalization, and the uncertainty of anticipating the ramifications of illness. Other descriptions of suffering include despair, lack of strength, longing for love, something that hurts, and a breakdown in relationships.

In a study by Hinds (1992), the suffering of family caregivers of noninstitutionalized cancer patients revealed descriptions such as fear of loneliness, uncertainty about the future, communication breakdown, and lack of support. It can be seen that suffering from illness manifests itself in many ways. While I concur with these efforts to define and describe suffering, I most readily resonate with a patient who once described his suffering to me as "just feeling awful and heavy most of the time."

Individual beliefs of patients and family members are involved in both the experience of suffering and in making inferences of suffering. Certain beliefs may conserve or maintain an illness; others may exacerbate symptoms; others alleviate or diminish suffering (Wright et al., 1996). When therapists can invite persons to reflect on their beliefs, those persons often become more open to consider other possibilities.

In an eloquent and illuminating description of his illness experiences, Frank (1995) offers his idea of how persons make meaning of their suffering. He asserts that people tell stories of their illnesses to make sense of their suffering; and when they turn their diseases into stories, they find healing. From my own clinical practice and research with families, I have come to strongly believe that talking about one's experience with illness can often alleviate or diminish emotional, physical, and/or spiritual suffering (Wright et al., 1996). To me, this talking about and listening to illness stories in therapeutic conversations becomes the context from which suffering can first be acknowledged and then alleviated when healing begins.

I believe my goal and my obligation when working with families is to diminish, alleviate or heal emotional, physical, and spiritual suffering. With my colleagues Wendy L. Watson and Janice M. Bell, I have evolved a clinical approach (the Illness Beliefs Model) emphasizing the altering, challenging, or modifying constraining beliefs to assist with alleviating or diminishing suffering in families (Wright et al., 1996). Some of the ways we have found useful in alleviating suffering are acknowledging suffering; inviting, listening to, and witnessing suffering; connecting suffering and spirituality; recognizing and challenging our own constraining beliefs; creating a healing environment; and inviting reflections about suffering.

Acknowledging Suffering

One beginning effort to alleviate suffering is to acknowledge that suffering exists. Suffering *is* the illness experience, whether it is short and in-

tense or prolonged and pervasive. Suffering is part of our human existence—from stories of Job to stories of holocaust victims to stories of
illness.

Inviting, Listening To, and Witnessing Stories of Suffering

The inviting, listening to, and witnessing illness stories provides a powerful validation of a profound human experience. Health professionals are
in a privileged position to hear and affirm illness narratives. By acknowledging illness narratives, we engage in the essential, ethical practice of
recognizing the ill person as the "suffering other" (Frank, 1994). The deliberate and clear acknowledgment of suffering frequently opens the door
for the disclosure of other fears or worries not previously expressed, for
example, the fear by a caregiver that if her health fails, then who will care
for her spouse? In my clinical practice, I also want to open possibilities,
through therapeutic conversations, for recognizing the ill person and
other family members as the heroic other, the joyful other, the giving
other, the receiving other, the compassionate other, the passionate other,
and the strengthened other.

Positive responses and reduction in emotional and physical suffering
have convinced me of the necessity to invite family members to tell their
illness stories. In our professional encounters with families, we move beyond social conversations about the illness to purposeful therapeutic conversations (Tapp, 1997). We direct the conversation in a manner that we
hope will give voice to the human experiences of suffering and symptoms
as well as to the experiences of courage, hope, growth, and love. Through
the telling of the story, "the patient can interpret her own suffering [and,
we would add, strength]; the role of witness is to provide moral affirmation of the struggle to find that interpretation. Thus the patient's voice
must be cultivated, not cut off" (Frank, 1994, p. 14).

By providing a context for the sharing among family members of
their illness experiences, intense emotions are legitimized. By inviting
family members to share their illness narratives, which include stories of
sickness and suffering, we allow them, as Frank (1994) suggests, to reclaim their right to tell what are their own experiences and to reclaim a
voice over the medical voice and a life beyond illness. I have had many
families tell me that having someone listen to their illness stories, ask
questions about their stories, and commend them for their courage in the
face of suffering has enabled them to gain a new and sometimes renewed
appreciation of their ability to cope. Through this witnessing, listening,
and commending, the family's resilience is often rediscovered with very
positive outcomes. In many instances, these positive outcomes have been
the alleviation of physical symptoms and familial conflict as well as the diminishing or alleviating of emotional and/or spiritual suffering:

68 SPIRITUAL RESOURCES IN FAMILIES

One of our most difficult duties as human beings is to listen to the voices of those who suffer. The voices of the ill are easy to ignore, because these voices are often faltering in tone and mixed in message. . . . Listening is hard, but it is also a fundamental moral act; to realize the best potential in postmodern times requires an ethics of listening. The moment of witness in the story crystallizes a mutuality of need, when each is *for* the other. (Frank, 1995, p. 25)

Recognizing and Challenging Our Own Constraining Beliefs

Health professionals' beliefs can hinder or enhance the possibilities for alleviating suffering (Levac et al., 1998; Wright, Bell, Watson, & Tapp, 1995). One belief frequently offered to those suffering with illness is that "life could be worse." This belief is offered to provide comfort and encouragement. One woman suffering from endometriosis did not find this belief useful. She responded: "I know life could be worse. I could have only one eye or leg, and I am very fortunate to have all I do have. . . . But those philosophies do not solve the disease, do not get rid of the pain, the tears, the frustrations, or the heartaches that come with the problems" (Donoghue & Siegel, 1992, p. 55). This example highlights the need for health professionals to recognize that each person's suffering with illness is unique and that attempting to have persons "count their blessings" can inadvertently trivialize suffering from illness.

Creating a Healing Environment

The ultimate desired outcome is to create a healing environment for family members for the relief of suffering from their illness experiences. Remen (1993) eloquently offered the notion that healing is different from curing: "Healing is a process we're all involved in all the time. . . . Sometimes people heal physically, and they don't heal emotionally, or mentally, or spiritually. And sometimes people heal emotionally, and they don't heal physically" (p. 244).

Frank (1995) offers the powerful metaphor that ill people are more than victims of disease or patients of medicine—they are wounded storytellers. He argues that people tell stories to make sense of their suffering; when they turn their diseases into stories, they find healing. This coincides with a strong belief that exists in our North American health care culture that eliciting, discussing, and expressing one's illness story and accompanying emotions can be very healing. Families have often remarked in my clinical practice how they appreciated the opportunity to talk about their illness experiences and the healing effect these conversations had on their lives and relationships.

The capacity of health professionals to be "witnesses" to the stories of suffering of patients and families is central to providing care; it is frequently the genesis of healing, if not curing (Frank, 1994; Kleinman, 1988).

Inviting Reflections about Suffering

To alter existing beliefs, family therapists need to invite family members to a reflection about their constraining beliefs (Wright et al., 1996). Through these reflections, a person begins to entertain different or alternative beliefs in order to get out of a state of confusion, struggle, or suffering. For example, beliefs about hope and optimism in the illness experience have generally not been addressed by the dominant medical system. Consequently, the appeal of alternative or complementary healing approaches becomes very understandable. Many persons suffering with illness find these approaches more positive than the conventional medical approach because complementary healing approaches do not shy away from some of the big questions surrounding illness: Why has this illness happened to me? Why do people get sick despite living well? Why do some people die "before their time"?

CLINICAL EXAMPLE: "WHERE WILL I GO *AFTER* I DIE?"

I offer the following clinical example to illustrate the interrelatedness of the trinity of spirituality, suffering, and beliefs.

This family consists of a 63-year-old English Canadian husband and his 62-year-old French Canadian wife. They have two grown children living elsewhere. The husband had experienced a myocardial infarction 6 months prior to this session. The family had been seen for two sessions prior to my being invited for a consultation. The couple had made good progress in these two sessions and reported to me that talking in therapy about how the illness had impacted on their marriage had helped to bring forth a lot of worries and fears that each were experiencing. Consequently, the couple reported that they were now talking more at home, having breakfast together for the first time in many years, and feeling understood by each other.

When I work with families where one spouse has experienced a heart attack, I routinely ask the nonaffected partners if they worry about their spouses having another heart attack. In this case, the wife responded, "Yes, all the time." When I asked the husband if he worried about having another coronary, he confirmed that he *does not* worry about dying from a heart attack. The most fascinating aspect of this therapeutic inquiry occurred when the wife disclosed her belief that *she* is going to have a heart attack. She also disclosed that she has been on antidepressant medication for 20 years because of her fear of dying. In this verbatim transcript of my clinical work with this family, a significant distinction is made. (LMW indicates Dr. Lorraine Wright; W indicates wife; H indicates husband.)

LMW: So when you say (*addresses wife*) that you have a fear of dying, what do you mean by that?

W: I don't know where I'm going to go, that's the fear. I'm afraid. I don't know where I'm going to go, I don't know why, I mean. I don't know if it's the religion, or the school, I mean it's the way I was brought up.

LMW: So, you're saying that the biggest worry around that for you is not how you're going to die, is it? But, where you're going to go after you die?

W: Exactly.

LMW: I see.

W: Exactly.

This is a fascinating and most important distinction and self-disclosure. This dear woman clarifies that it's not her fear of dying that is most troublesome but rather her fear of where she's going to go *after* she dies. Further clarification of this belief then ensues.

W: If you're good, then you're going to heaven, and if you're bad, you're going to hell. So it was always on my mind, everything was a sin, so I grew up like that and I was afraid of everything and it's still on my mind today.

LMW: Hmmm.

W: So to me, I always see the clock (*gestures a pendulum*) and if you're good (*gestures to one side*) and if you're bad (*gestures to the other side*) and there's no middle. I don't know where I'm going to go.

LMW: So when you evaluate your life today, [wife's name], would you say . . .

W: Well, I was bad sometimes, like everybody else . . .

LMW: Sure . . .

W: But then many times or most of the times, but uh . . .

LMW: But when you evaluate your life now and you look at your life, do you feel good about how you've lived your life?

W: Yes, sure . . .

LMW: Do you think, uh . . .

W: Sure, I wouldn't change my life, even though we went through a lot, I mean, with family and everything, but I wouldn't change my life anyway.

LMW: I wonder, I mean, I know quite a bit about Catholicism, but maybe you can help me more. Do you believe that you will be judged for the way you've lived your life here?

W: By God, you mean?

LMW: By God.

W: Exactly, yes.

LMW: And so, if God were to judge you today, do you think He would be happy with you . . .

W: I don't know.

LMW: . . . or not happy?

W: This is what I'm asking myself, you see.

LMW: Ah . . . and what do you say to yourself?

W: We all know in my family I'm afraid to die, even my children. I kept telling them really so many times a month, I'm afraid, I'm afraid not to be sick or something, it's to die . . .

LMW: It's to die being fearful how you will be judged.

After this significant disclosure and further clarification of her beliefs, I make a beginning effort to challenge this constraining belief. I do this by asking a question that I routinely ask in my practice: a hypothetical facilitating belief question (Wright et al., 1996). This question offers or embeds a facilitating belief and is an indirect way of challenging or altering a constraining belief. The question always begins with, "If you were to believe . . . " This question invites this woman to consider an alternative facilitating belief, one that suggests altering her beliefs may give rise to new stories and new behaviors.

LMW: This might seem like a very strange question, but I'm going to ask it anyway. If you were to believe, eh, if you were to believe for even ten minutes today that God was very pleased with you, at how you've lived your life as a wife, as a mother, as a person . . .

W: That would change everything.

LMW: . . . what difference would that make in your life?

W: It would change everything for me.

LMW: Can you tell me what it would change? What would be a couple of things that would change for you?

W: First of all, I wouldn't be scared anymore, and then, I would say, well, if I die tomorrow, well, I die tomorrow, then I know where I would go. God knows when.

LMW: And if you weren't scared anymore, how would you live your life differently do you think? What would be different for you?

W: Well, I would be more, um, calm . . .

LMW: More calm . . .

W: Definitely, because it's all inside, it's working on me all the time and, uh, I wouldn't live that stress that I live all the time and . . . if you understand what I mean?

LMW: Yes, I do—if you could believe, I just want to really make sure I've got this—if you could believe even just for 10 minutes that God was pleased with you, that you had lived a good life, that He would judge you, eh, very well, that you said that would make all the difference in the world for you . . .

W: Exactly, yes, definitely.

LMW: . . . that you would be more calm, and you would be more . . .

W: I wouldn't be on anybody's nerves like I am on account of death—something to do with it, too.

LMW: Yes. Wow, that's incredible, eh?

Here is a woman who has suffered terribly for many years with the belief that she will have a heart attack *and* an even more troubling belief that she doesn't know how she will be judged when she dies. Consequently, she does not know where she will go after death.

In this next transcript, an amazing revelation comes forth. This woman is considering discontinuing all of her antidepressant medication. Of course I'm curious to learn if she were to believe she was going to heaven, would she need less medication? Her responses are astonishing, and her beliefs begin to change right in front of me within our evolving therapeutic conversation. Her response is even more amazing as she completes my sentence for me and knows exactly the connection that I am hypothesizing.

LMW: I don't know, maybe this is a crazy idea, but I'm wondering, um, do you think that if you could believe that you were going to heaven, do you think there's any connection there; that you would need . . .

W: . . . less pills?

LMW: That you need less pills, yes.

W: Sure, definitely.

LMW: Wow. So maybe this idea, eh, that if you have the courage, and are more positive . . .

W: Yes, just like a lightning (*points to head, light bulb?*), hey?

LMW: You start thinking that "yes, I am a good person, I will, eh, probably be judged very well, eh, by God, and, um, be able to go to heaven." And I want you to know I have those same religious beliefs about heaven . . .

W: You do?

LMW: . . . and hell, and that will we be judged, and I hope I do okay too, eh, but I don't worry about it all the time like you do. That must be a terrible thing.

W: Oh, it is terrible, sometimes I used to say to [her husband], it's terrible, you don't know what I feel inside, it's like I could scream.

LMW: Yes . . .

W: Some days I used to say, I would prefer to die, but still I said, I don't want to die.

LMW: So you think there could be a connection there. So, as you would come off the pills, maybe then you would be getting more courage about believing, eh, more positively about yourself.

W: Exactly.

At the end of this session, I offer my impressions and commendations to this family. I offer what I believe that I have learned from this couple, particularly from this open, courageous woman. I also relate to her how I would like to tell her story to others.

LMW: I want to tell you a couple of my impressions and a couple of things that I've learned from you today. The first thing I have learned that is that you've been married 38 years, and the thing that you've really taught me today is that even after 38 years of marriage, marriages can get better, it doesn't have to get worse, eh?

W and H: Yes, yes.

W: I'm so happy about that.

LMW: That you would probably say, I'm guessing, that you would say your marriage maybe is perhaps the best it has ever been, would you go that far?

W: Exactly, yes.

LMW: One of the best . . .

W: For me, yes.

LMW: . . . one of the best periods in your marriage . . .

H: Oh, the best periods for us.

LMW: . . . periods in your marriage.

H and W: Definitely, yes.

LMW: See, that is incredible, I think. After 38 years, it's even getting better. This is one thing I've really learned today that we should never give up hope on marriages. That they can even get better, even after many, many years of marriage. The other thing that I've learned today that was very helpful to me is this notion that illness doesn't have to always be a terrible thing in a family, that illness sometimes can be scary, it can be a terrible thing but some very good positive things can come out of it. Your marriage is stronger, you've come together, you've united more, and that's a very wonderful thing. The other thing (*addresses wife*), when I go back to Calgary, my students will be asking me, "What did you learn?" I'm going to think about you, and you know the story I would like to tell, can I tell you? . . . is: the story about a woman who believed for many, many years—eh, I feel very touched by this story . . . but—a woman who believed for many years that she was going to maybe be judged very harshly by God, eh? That she wasn't sure if she would go to heaven or hell, and yet through her own courage, eh, she made a connection that maybe if she could give up this medication, there was connection there that maybe she didn't have to be on medication any more, if she could begin to have more ideas and better beliefs about herself. That she was a good person and a good wife, and a good mother. And as she started to just think about that a little bit, and allow herself that idea, she also came up with the idea that maybe she could give up her antidepressant medication of 20 years! That is a remarkable story that I would like to be able to tell.

I trust that this piece of clinical work also illustrates the phenomenon of reverencing between this courageous woman and me. As our conversation evolved, I believe that we experienced increasing awe, respect, and a deep emotional and spiritual connection. As we said goodbye to one another, she told me that she had not wanted to come to the session that day but was very grateful that she did. She also spontaneously hugged me as we bid each other goodbye. And I hugged her back.

CONCLUDING REFLECTIONS

The depth of one person's suffering is distinguished from others by each person's unique experience. I have ached, cried, and lamented when I have suffered for others, but it is only my own suffering that I have experienced first hand. Suffering experiences cannot be compared, but unfortunately comparisons *are* made about which sufferings we believe are the most horrific. The most important role we have as therapists is to be listeners and witnesses to others' sufferings. We must acknowledge suffering and ask questions that will challenge any constraining beliefs that may be exacerbating their suffering and encourage more facilitating beliefs, possibilities, and opportunities for change and growth. Through this exchange between family members and therapists about suffering, a domain of spirituality is encountered. This journey into spirituality manifests itself in the offering of reverencing, compassion, and love between and among family members and therapists. Likewise, these efforts to alleviate suffering cross the border into healing—a healing that is not reserved only for family members but also for therapists. As Frank (1995) suggests, the primary lesson that the ill have to offer us is the "pedagogy of suffering." Through this highly privileged exchange, spirituality, suffering, and beliefs become the new trinity and the soul of healing in our clinical work with families.

REFERENCES

Cousins, N. (1989). *Beliefs become biology* [Videotape]. Victoria, British Columbia, Canada: University of Victoria.

Donoghue, P. J., & Siegel, M. E. (1992). *Sick and tired of being sick and tired: Living with invisible chronic illness.* New York: Norton.

Dossey, L. (1993). *Healing words: The power of prayer and the practice of medicine.* San Francisco: Harper.

Frank, A. W. (1994). Interrupted stories, interrupted lives. *Second Opinion, 20*(1), 11–18.

Frank, A. W. (1995). *The wounded storyteller: Body, illness and ethics.* Chicago: University of Chicago Press.

Hinds, C. (1992). Suffering: A relatively unexplored phenomenon among family caregivers of non-institutionalized patients with cancer. *Journal of Advanced Nursing, 17,* 918–925.

Kleinman, A. (1988). *The illness narratives.* New York: Basic Books.

Levac, A. M., McLean, S., Wright, L. M., Bell, J. M., "Ann," & "Fred." (1998). A "Reader's Theatre" intervention to managing grief: Post-therapy reflections by a family and a clinical team. *Journal of Marital and Family Therapy, 24*(1), 81–94.

Lindholm, L., & Eriksson, K. (1993). To understand and alleviate suffering in a caring culture. *Journal of Advanced Nursing, 18,* 1354–1361.

Morse, J. M., & Johnson, J. L. (1991). Toward a theory of illness: The Illness-Constellation Model. In J. M. Morse & J. L. Johnson (Eds.), *The illness experience: Dimensions of suffering* (pp. 315–342). Newbury Park, CA: Sage.

Patterson, R. B. (1994, June). Learning from suffering. *Family Therapy News,* pp. 11–12.

Remen, R. N. (1993). Wholeness. In B. Moyers (Ed.), *Healing and the mind* (pp. 343–363). New York: Doubleday.

Tapp, D. M. (1997). *Exploring therapeutic conversations between nurses and families experiencing ischemic heart disease.* Unpublished doctoral dissertation, University of Calgary, Alberta, Canada.

Thomas, G. (1997, January 6). Doctors who pray: How the medical community is discovering the healing power of prayer. *Christianity Today,* pp. 20–28.

Wright, L. M., Bell, J. M., Watson, W. L., & Tapp, D. (1995). The influence of the beliefs of nurses: A clinical example of a post-myocardial-infarction couple. *Journal of Family Nursing, 1,* 238–256.

Wright, L. M., Watson, W. L., & Bell, J. M. (1996). *Beliefs: The heart of healing in families and illness.* New York: Basic Books.

CHAPTER 4

The Stresses of Poverty and the Comfort of Spirituality

HARRY J. APONTE

Theodora, twice widowed, lived poor. A son had been killed attempting a robbery. Both her twin daughters, Jeannie and Jeannette, had sickle cell anemia, with Jeannette also ravaged by a cocaine habit. Theodora was raising Jeannette's first child. Every weekend she also helped Jeannie with her neurologically impaired son. On top of all that, she personally cared for the godfather of the twins, a widowed, elderly man whose health was fading. Theodora did not deny the difficulties of her life, but she had hope. Her support was the local African American Baptist church. She loved her family, and had her church and her God.

When asked about all her troubles, Theodora answered, "All this goes along with making me stronger" (Aponte, 1994, p. 226). She saw purpose in her personal sacrifice for her family. She now faced a moral dilemma of whether to support Jeannie's caring for her addicted sister's youngest daughter. Theodora knew Jeannie was not taking care of her own health and her sickly son, and could not also care for her sister's child. She reluctantly but firmly said, "Let [the child] go into the system." For her, Jeannie's health and her obligation to her own children came first. Theodora had her recourse; "We'll pray about it" (Aponte, 1994, p. 236).

THE CHALLENGE OF POVERTY

Theodora was poor by this society's economic standards and conscious of the racial stresses. She had more than the ordinary share of personal troubles. Yet, she did not feel defeated or bitter. Her self-esteem and emotional strength drew from her spiritual beliefs.

The Theodoras of this world suffer life's trials and challenges with the added burdens of their poverty and minority status, often contributing to the following:

1. Loss of a sense of identity and self-worth
2. Diminished power over everyday living and their future destiny
3. Separateness from the larger society, and a loss of stable relationships in their personal lives and communities

Jeannette had surrendered to her addiction. Theodora and Jeannie, facing the same personal, social, and economic circumstances, held onto their hope through their church and faith.

In treating poor minority clients, therapists find daunting social and environmental circumstances that undermine clients' physical and emotional health as well as family relationships. They encounter the consequent personal "underorganization" of the families (Aponte, 1994, pp. 13–31) that resists the usual psychological interventions. Therapists are left looking for new ways to help with the effects of society's troubles on the most undervalued of our citizens. An underutilized resource with the poor and all our clients is their spirituality.

Spirituality speaks to the very heart of people's existence, the essential meaning, purpose, and value of life itself. It gives a transcendent significance to every pilgrim's personal and social circumstances (see John Bunyan, 1976). For the disadvantaged, spirituality is a resource that can transcend their personal discouragement, the deprivation of poverty, and oppression by society. In an impersonal environment it can enhance identity and self-worth by giving meaning to a person's struggles. In a disempowering society, it can generate autonomy through the internal gyroscope of a person's convictions. In a disconnected society, it can offer relationship through church community and spiritual connection with God, all of special importance to the most disadvantaged and marginalized of our society.

Spirituality is a fundamental life resource, offering therapists a source of strength, connection, and direction for their clients. It is for therapists to learn how to recognize, speak to, and work with spirituality.

What Is Spirituality?

St. Paul discovered an altar in Athens that the Greeks had dedicated to the "Unknown God" (Acts 17:23). He believed he knew who that God was, but he spoke to the Greeks' pursuit as to a universal human impulse. Consciously or unconsciously, everyone is searching for an overarching meaning and purpose to pain and pleasure, life and death. Everyone has a spirituality. Everyone's life draws on some aspect of spirituality, which in its fullness is composed of morality, a belief system, and often a communal ritual that relates to a personal God.

Those who live with pain, deprivation, and death are often the closest to their spirituality. However, they can also plunge to the depths of hopelessness. The impoverished and peripheral of society need a therapy that recognizes that *their* lives are worth living and contending for even in the face of the greatest losses, deprivation, and oppression. Our therapy can address the spiritual in their lives—their morals, beliefs, and religious communities, *enfin* their God within or without a formal religious affiliation, which Pargament speaks of (1996, p. 216) as the "search for significance" taken explicitly to the level of the "sacred."

As important as it is, spirituality in people is not easily grasped. It comes as a complex and often conflicted bundle of legacies from parents, culture, television, and church that often do not match and even contradict each other (Aponte, 1998). Yet, that spirituality is hidden in all people's hearts, secretly influencing their lives while publicly manifested in society under many names and guises.

While the core of people's spirituality is hidden in their souls, their spirituality is reflected in the degrees of importance that they give to things in their lives, whether it be professional success, the ecology of the planet, or the selfless love of others. Their spirituality is evidenced in their national character, whether it values personal wealth and power or commitment to family and community. Spirituality is found in religious outlooks, whether of Zen's "universal within" (Wulff, 1991, p. 348), focusing on the self and the now, or the Christians' looking "above self" (St. Bonaventure, 1996, p. 10) to a personal God and the hereafter. Character and outlooks are shaped by the spiritual elements in life experiences, families, communities, and ethnic and racial identities. When those spiritual influences are diluted or negated, people may disconnect from their personal sense of identity and lose the direction and social support that comes from their own roots. The human soul suffers. The effects may show up in troubles with family relationships, school performance, work stability, and the law.

The Loss of Spirituality among Poor Minorities

America's poorest and most troubled minorities suffered the greatest loss of their spiritual roots. Many lost their cultural and religious traditions in the historical turmoil of this country (Aponte, 1994). The vitality of their families and communities was sapped when roots of their spiritual values were weakened or cut off. Today, in the United States we see a country becoming more materialistic and secular. Psychotherapists are not alone saying we need something spiritual to give significance to our lives. A review in *Business Week* of Lester C. Thurow's *The Future of Capitalism: How Today's Economic Forces Shape Tomorrow's World* observes:

In *The Future of Capitalism,* Thurow concedes that no other system [than the capitalist system] provides such gobs of efficiency and technology. But with no guiding ideology other than avarice, these very strengths could become the system's undoing—it operates in and often contributes to a world of growing economic imbalances. Missing is a set of common goals and values that citizens could rally behind. (Baker, 1996, p. 15)

In this social environment, neighborhoods are vulnerable to whatever socially opportunistic virus is out there. The Wall Street broker has his line of cocaine, while the inner-city kid does crack. The Hollywood celebrity faces another paternity suit, and the corner dealer contends with his girlfriend's caseworker. The suburban housewife with a gun license legally arms herself, while the gang member deals for his weapons in the street.

About the effects on the poor, Wilson (1996) observes: "In the more socially isolated ghetto neighborhoods, networks of kin, friends and associates are more likely to include a higher proportion of individuals who . . . tend to doubt that they can achieve approved societal goals" (p. 76). Under these socially unhealthy conditions, poor communities have little defense against the devaluing of law and morality (Bellah, Madsen, Sullivan, Swidler, & Tipton, 1991, p. 3) and of love and commitment (Wilson, 1996, p. 76) that is plaguing society in general. In light of these social conditions Wilson would "expect lower levels of perceived self-efficacy in ghetto neighborhoods—which feature underemployment, unemployment and labor-force-dropouts, weak marriages, and single-parent households" (p. 76). Wilson looks for economic solutions, but that is not enough. A bullish stock market has not made for a more virtuous society. The deprived and disadvantaged need a renewal of spirit not dependent upon economic conditions. In this social crucible spirituality offers hope—the ability of the most deprived to transcend the turbulence of life and find meaning in their every personal struggle. Spirituality provides supports, motivation, and a transcendent means of coping with the stress of life.

SPIRITUALITY IN ACTION

To more effectively address the loss of self-worth, personal power, and community among poor minorities, therapists need to better bridge psychology with the spiritual. Clinicians should strive to do the following:

1. Work consciously with the spirituality in people's lives.
2. Build a value base (platform) for their clients' therapy.
3. Pivot the therapy on their clients' life (moral) choices.

Working Consciously with Spirituality

To work deliberately with the spirituality of the disadvantaged means attending to the spiritual aspects of their personal struggles. Among poor minority families, we may find their spirituality affected by the culture of their social conditions. Wilson (1996) talks about "the cultural experiences . . . [that communities] have accumulated as a consequence of historical and existing economic and political arrangements" (p. 66). He is referring to the cultural effects on people living with the legacy of poverty and discrimination. The oppressiveness of the inner city can foster a mentality of hopelessness and anger, undermining morality. For people to transcend the social, physical, and economic limits of their life circumstances, they must have within themselves and their communities belief systems that motivate them. They also need the family and social structures that reflect their spirituality and support their values.

However, for therapists, understanding and working with spirituality must happen within the borders of good clinical diagnostics and technical intervention. The therapist's task is to treat spirituality as a facilitator of therapeutic outcome. For therapists, spirituality makes possible a deeper understanding of the human spirit. It potentially strengthens the will of people to strive and offers the possibility of the support in their community of shared belief and the relationship with the transcendent.

The seat of spirituality is in the heart. That also happens to be where therapists are toiling when they touch on clients' attitudes and feelings about themselves and their problems. Helping them reach within for self-acceptance, a loving feeling toward a family member, or an optimistic outlook about the solution of a problem is to find hope from within. For those with a belief in a personal God, that source of hope may also lie in the Presence that abides in the soul. That hope can overcome discouragement from the world outside and the battered spirit within.

To work consciously with spirituality also calls for working actively with both the people and institutions in which clients' spirituality finds its nurturance. There will be families who are potential sources of love and encouragement even if at the moment clients have difficult relationships with them. Even with families that appear fragmented and depleted, the challenge for therapists is to mine the spiritual strength, shared values, and religious practices existing among family members.

Religion may also provide "family" in the form of a church community, which can be especially important when people have little family to support them. They may discover among fellow worshippers guidance from the clergy, personal support from the brotherhood or sisterhood, and a safe social milieu for their children. Church may be the only community that cares about them and is prepared to embrace them just where they are.

There are those who believe that "the only institution with the spiritual message and physical presence to offer" the values poor minority families need is the church (Leland, 1998, p. 22). However, religion may also hold some deeply hidden conflict for some people. In their histories, church and God may come with both positive and negative experiences. They may report memories of solace and support, as well as of disappointment and betrayal. Sadly, they often have done little to resolve and heal the relationship with their church. Therapists can help them revisit, reengage, and rework earlier personal stories to liberate their spirituality.

Building the Spiritual Platform of Therapy

Attending to the spiritual aspects of clients' personal struggles calls for awareness by clinicians of the spiritual environment they create in their therapy. All therapy rests on a spiritual platform of values and philosophical outlook that reflects the spirituality of the clinician, that is, his or her moral standards, sociopolitical convictions, and religious outlook. Therapists judge what is sick or healthy and worthy or unworthy goals. They determine the merits of a solution not just by whether it works but also by whether it is right or wrong. The spiritual platform they construct will support or undermine, contribute to or detract from the spirituality of their clients. The therapy will help shape people's solutions to their problems and thereby the spiritual quality of their lives.

Therapists have values ingrained from their respective professions and orientations to therapy. They are not value neutral. Even when it comes to diagnostic exploration, "There is no way of asking neutral questions," says Michael White (in Wylie, 1994, p. 46). Particularly in today's world, therapists come with pretty well-formed preconvictions about the roles of men and women in marriage, sexual mores in and out of marriage, and Eastern versus Western spirituality. However, they often are not even aware of the spirituality they bring to bear on clients' issues. Yet, their biases have real influence over clients' spirituality (Aponte, 1996).

Therapists also carry inside themselves their own *personal* spirituality. That spirituality influences basic attitudes about therapy that depend on one's spiritual outlook about life. Therapists' beliefs about people's ability to change themselves, the potential of adversity to promote change, and the healing power of personal relationships all profoundly affect their therapy with our society's most defeated members.

Do therapists believe that people can change themselves even if they cannot change life's circumstances? The conviction that people can change their attitudes about themselves and about life even if they cannot alter what is happening to them can bring hope to the most hopeless. The belief that people can have self-respect and do the right thing no matter how bad their problems may be can affirm the worth of clients' lives and of those they love.

The belief that hard times can promote change means that, however unwelcome, adversity can be what people need to turn their lives around.

Hardship often prompts people to consider changes that they had never thought they could make. Peck (1978, p. 16) says, "It is only because of problems that we grow mentally and spiritually." Socioeconomically disadvantaged people may discover a new hope in their difficulties that can overcome despair about themselves and their lives.

Belief in the restorative potential of relationship means faith in the power of love. Ties to spouses, children, and relatives, as well as to the neighborhood and society, however flawed and complicated, offer the strength and support of the human family. Religion with its community of the faithful and the relationship with God offers the power of the spiritual family. Therapists' beliefs in the healing power of love, whether in their clients' relationships with family or God, can make possible what seemed otherwise impossible.

However, therapists' beliefs are only half of the spiritual equation in the therapeutic relationship. The other half belongs to even the least powerful client. In therapy, clinicians are in a position to lend importance and power to clients' values and religious convictions. With poor minorities in particular, it is critical to negotiate equitably (Aponte, 1985) the spiritual base of the therapy, that is, the morality, worldview, and religious beliefs by which clients engage in solving their particular personal issues. When clients can assert their personal worth and identities, it is easier for them to acknowledge flaws and hardships. They feel more personally secure and self-confident when they sense their values are recognized and respected. They have greater control over the solutions to their problems. In sum, when clients' spirituality is an active part of the therapy's spiritual platform, they can express their souls—who they are and aspire to be. The spiritual beliefs clinicians and clients bring to their co-construction of a spiritual platform gives direction and meaning to the therapy.

Therapy That Pivots on the Clients' Life Choices

Therapy that pivots on clients' free will is a work grounded in clients' belief that they can direct their own lives. The freedom to choose is where people convert their personal uniqueness into their personal action. It is where they decide issue by issue how they will live their lives. For the powerless and invisible, acting on the freedom to choose is to claim their potential and importance in the face of daunting circumstances.

The power and freedom to make life choices ultimately flow from people's essential moral nature to choose good over bad, better over worse. Free will lends spiritual wings to the psychological effort to overcome personal distress. The exercise of choosing can be action that is an internal decision about attitude or an external one about behavior. The act itself of choosing lends people ownership of themselves at the very moment their decision can change or affirm the course of their lives.

The choices that patients make about their lives in treatment are steeped in their values, ethics, and beliefs—in a word, in the *morality* of their spirituality. For the poor and marginal, these moral decisions are an exercise in human freedom and self-determination. They can choose reality or denial, fighting or being passive, betterment or defeat. In that personal exercise of free will lies the mystery of their essential worth and independence even in the face of oppression and scarcity. By supporting their values, therapy can support clients' personal identity and power. Therapy based on the freedom of clients to choose calls for helping clients identify options and rationale for the choices they face. By offering the technical resources of the intervention and providing the support of the relationship, therapists bolster their clients' motivation and will to choose. When therapists help them make choices that are theirs, clients are better able to accept responsibility for the consequences of their decisions.

Therapists' consciousness of spirituality, building of a spiritual value platform, and working from their clients' free will lays the groundwork for a therapy grounded in their clients' spirituality. The approach to spirituality lends support to clients' freedom and power while recognizing that, like everyone else's spirituality, clients' spiritual life is ultimately a mystery, their mystery. Spirituality with all its power and mystique is a rich and fertile environment for those otherwise impoverished, to grow and change.

AN ILLUSTRATION

The following is an example of a young woman who overcame the worst of life with a boost from her spirituality. A clinician built the following therapeutic effort on her religious experiences.

The spiritual strength of families lives within their hearts as well as in their community life. The spiritual potential for our work with the poor in particular lies first in our ability to reach deeply for the personal *significance* of what troubles them, even to the spiritual dimension of their struggles; secondly, our therapy's efficacy depends on accessing the sources of their spirituality lying within them, their families, or churches. In today's environment of brief therapy and managed care, it is especially urgent to tap into the deepest sources of strength of clients. The *spiritual* offers a powerful and at the same time uniquely intimate and private hope for transcending personal failure and socioeconomic hardship.

For five months, a therapist had been working with Tess, a 29-year-old African American woman, and Grace, her 9-year-old daughter. Progress in therapy was slow in coming. This was a family on food stamps, with a mother recovering from years of abusing cocaine. She came for help with her daughter, who in the last year had been violent at home and disruptive in school. The therapist requested a consultation.

At the time the consultant met with the family and the therapist, the therapist had not seen the family for a few weeks. In their last session, Tess had been upset and ready to give up on her daughter. Instead, Tess without Grace in the room opened up to the therapist about a secret pain inside herself. She revealed that when she was Grace's age, she had been repeatedly abused sexually by her father. To her continued distress, her mother had not acknowledged the abuse even after Tess's revelation of it to her. Tess had been living with this secret shame. Early in life she had smothered the pain with cocaine, but even now she held the hurt hidden within herself. In the therapy she had refused any work on herself, and after this talk with her therapist was still undecided about getting help for herself.

In response to the consultant's question, Tess stated that what she wanted help with at that moment was to recapture the love that she and Grace had lost in the last year. However, in talking about Grace she added that they have gotten along better in the last few weeks since she, Tess, had returned to church. Her church attendance was news to the therapist. The consultant asked her to expand on what happened with church. Tess described a powerful spiritual experience, with a history.

The story that unfolded was that coming off of her molestation by her father, she gradually sank into cocaine abuse. She subsequently became pregnant and gave birth to Grace. She raised Grace alone, but with difficulty because she was strung out so much of the time. A few years ago, she became pregnant again and gave birth to a "cocaine baby." Three months later, while Tess was high, the child died of sudden infant death syndrome. Tess became distraught with guilt. At the funeral, a Baptist minister whom an aunt had brought to the services sought out Tess. At the minister's invitation, she commenced praying at home and attending church. It was enough to motivate her to stop her addiction cold turkey. She became more attentive to Grace, and life improved for both her and Grace.

However, over the last year she had stopped going to church, although she did not stop her prayers. She and Grace began to battle again, and Grace's behavior deteriorated. Several times, Grace hit her grandmother when corrected by her. Grace's anger carried over into school, and she became unmanageable in class. School insisted Tess get help for Grace, and Tess began work with her present therapist. However, the therapy was not bringing about the change they sought. Nor had Tess trusted her therapist with her secret until their last meeting.

Since that last session with the therapist, the situation with Grace had continued to decline. Tess became desperate, and she again returned to church. She spoke of a renewed connection with God. She awakened to how she was being hurtful to Grace—yelling, at, hitting, and not listening to her. She then stopped hurting Grace and was able to connect emotionally with her. Grace responded, and her behavior improved rapidly.

The consultant acknowledged the significance of Tess's spiritual experience. He then asked where she now wanted to go with therapy. Tess believed she had to decide whether to explore the history and the pain of the incest. For Tess, the ability to face the issue rested on the strength and security she had discovered in her spirituality. With that, Tess agreed to bring her personal hurt to therapy even as she continued to work on her relationship with Grace.

How to explain this spiritual experience of Tess? Whatever the mystery of what happened to her spiritually, its psychological effect appeared to be everything her therapist could have wished for. Tess holds herself accountable for her behavior with Grace. Also, she who had been shut down, isolated, and angry in her secret shame can open herself to help from her therapist. Because of her renewed church involvement, she no longer thinks of herself as alone but rather as cared about by her God. Consequently she regards herself as worthy of help. She matters.

Therapy has had and will have a critical place in Tess's change, but the impetus for the depth of this change has come from life outside therapy, from Tess's church and prayer life. Her religion has become one of those healing life forces which Duncan (1997) calls "extratherapeutic factors" and which he considers so influential on the outcome of therapy. Her spirituality has given Tess a sense of belonging and being loved, which allows her to trust and be vulnerable in therapy. In her spirituality, she has found the motivation and courage to face her demons. The pain of her baby's death gave Tess the original opportunity to discover her spirituality. The recent trouble with Grace has been the goad that now urged her back to church. Her therapist discovered Tess's spirituality, the new source of hope in this woman's life.

WHOSE SPIRITUALITY?

Now, as a professional, how would the therapist relate to Tess's spirituality? Yes, she would need to stretch herself to understand and get a feeling for the thinking, direction, and energy that Tess's spirituality lent to her life. However, what about the therapist's values and belief system that would interface with Tess's spirituality?

The relevant question here is how to support the spirituality of the disadvantaged who are particularly vulnerable to therapists' influence. Past self-proclaimed "neutral" therapists wanted to believe that they did not communicate political, moral, and religious values. However, therapists today, in their honest desire to help, increasingly feel entitled to promote their values and belief systems.

Many therapists now view their roles as experts on spirituality and values. W. J. Doherty (1995) states that his book *Soul Searching* "calls for the inclusion of moral discourse in the practice of psychotherapy and the cultivation in therapists of the virtues and skills needed to be moral consultants to their clients in a pluralistic and morally opaque world" (pp. 7–8). Like Sigmund Freud, his source of moral authority seems to be science and the field of psychotherapy. Doherty argues that psychotherapists "saw the oppressiveness of cultural norms dressed up as moral principles and could see themselves as agents of emancipation who deconstructed clients' unexamined but powerful moral codes and helped them to make their own decisions" (1995, p. 11). Does he see therapists as liberating clients from the "oppressiveness" of unquestioning faith? His thinking is in line with that of Michael White, who, according to Wylie (1994, p. 44), "deconstructs the dominant authority . . . [and its] culturally determined prescription for the way people *should be*," and in White's own words he is "about opening up possibilities for people to become *other* than who they are" (Wylie, 1994, p. 44; emphasis his). Wylie continues: "For White, the personal is, and must be, deeply embedded in the political" (p. 44). By Wylie's account, White's therapy rests on his political values.

Emilio Santa Rita (1996) sounds like just such a psychotherapeutic "emancipator" when talking about the "cultural baggage" (p. 325) of an ethnic group in modern America whose heritage stems from the Catholicism of the Philippines. He sees as emotionally pathogenic their adherence to their traditional religion's "beliefs on abortion, contraception, and homosexuality [which] contribute to a self-righteous, judgmental stance that is out of place in a pluralistic society with alternative lifestyles" (p. 326). These therapists assert through their therapy philosophical attitudes with serious implications about how people should think about and live life.

To what extent does psychotherapy place itself between people and their spiritual roots? To what extent do we as its representatives so place ourselves? For ethnic and racial minorities whose cultural heritage and family values are often steeped in their religious beliefs, does therapy assume the posture of critic to their very spiritual identity and religious values? For the power-poor disadvantaged, does therapy become a place to remake their values and religious faith according to the beliefs of the professional psychotherapist?

The Clinical Implications of Our Various Belief Systems

Poor underorganized families often find themselves in therapy under some kind of control from courts, schools, and departments of social welfare. They even face control from state-sponsored medical services for welfare clients. They may be ordered into treatment, but even when they voluntarily seek therapy, their health plans usually choose the therapist for them. Many underorganized families come into therapy on unsteady cultural and moral foundations and weakly supported community values. Counselors have an inordinate influence and power over disadvantaged families that depend on the system for survival.

The varieties of philosophies therapists bring to their work insinuate morality and worldviews that in practical ways affect therapy's goals, assessment, and interventions. Whether it is ensconced within their politics, therapeutic philosophy, or personal religion, therapists' spirituality skews how they look at their clients' lives. The approach to a client's issues, for example, may reflect a Buddhist outlook that doubts "all fixed assumptions about the nature of things" (Epstein, 1995, p. 62) or, in contrast, by the spirituality of a St. Francis of Assisi that says, "realness is whatever corresponds to truth and fact" (Foley, 1949, p. 34). For a victim confronting the denial by his or her family of sexual abuse, does the objectivity of reality matter? Therapists' views about morality will also influence how they handle accountability for the abuse and the role of forgiveness in healing (Aponte, 1998). Therapists' divergent philosophies about life translate into fundamentally different approaches to helping families in therapy.

Clinicians also face the challenge of detecting what values and philosophy are built into their own work. Is it therapy's responsibility to supply families with new and better belief systems? There are those who openly identify their therapy's system of values, as do the Christian therapists. Most therapists do not publicly acknowledge their belief systems. When clinicians let people know the value base of their therapy, their clients have a better chance to judge whether to buy into or reject a therapist's philosophy. Most clients do not get that chance.

Therapists in their unawareness of their therapy's spiritual values are seldom able to lend their clients a level of awareness that allows them to exercise control over the values that dominate the therapy. Therapists who know their value biases can choose whether to promote their beliefs with clients. Those working with poor minority clients can help them exercise their right of refusal about the values and belief systems by which the therapist attempts to solve problems. Ideally, with awareness and security about their own spirituality, therapists can empower clients to exercise their spirituality in the therapeutic relationship.

Training Therapists on Their Own and Their Clients' Spirituality

It is clear that if therapists are to work with spirituality, their training must include the study of spirituality in the treatment of emotional and relationship problems. Through their own spirituality, therapists need to learn how to relate to their client families' ethnic, cultural, and religious belief systems, all of which are "full of possibilities for misunderstanding" (Montalvo & Gutierrez, 1990, p. 35) in therapy.

Practitioners need to be comfortable as well as skillful in examining, talking about, and working with spirituality. They need to be able to see and work with the power and potential of clients' spirituality even where they confront ambiguity and conflict. They need to be able to share their own beliefs where necessary and appropriate—this only in ways that potentialize their most vulnerable clients' ability to choose the spirituality that will light paths of *their* own choosing to the solutions that are *their* own.

CONCLUSION

Poor and minority clients often bring to therapy the effects of their hurtful history and difficult socioeconomic circumstances. These realities are around them and inside them. A therapy that is sensitive to their lives will need to overcome those forces that would erase their identity, diminish their self-worth, or take away their power over their lives. Therapists will, I hope, offer a therapy that will connect the disadvantaged to the strength, guidance, and love that is congruent with and that exists within their own culture, belief systems and religions. At times, therapists will have to offer suggestions of values and perspectives on life that may influence their clients' work with them. They will, I hope, do so with some humility about the culture and beliefs of their clients, and always with respect for clients' right to choose their own values. Spirituality offers drive, direction, and structure to any clinical effort. Therapists can help their most disadvantaged clients reach into their spiritual resources for the hope to transcend their social and economic circumstances, and live with dignity and self-respect.

ACKNOWLEDGMENT

Theresa Romeo-Aponte deserves grateful acknowledgment for her contributions to all aspects of this chapter.

REFERENCES

Aponte, H. J. (1985, September). The negotiation of values in therapy. *Family Process, 24*(3), 323–338.
Aponte, H. J. (1994). *Bread and spirit: Therapy with the new poor.* New York: Norton.
Aponte, H. J. (1996, Fall). Political bias, moral values, and spirituality in the training of psychotherapists. *Bulletin of the Menninger Clinic, 60*(4), 488–502.
Aponte, H. J. (1998, February). Love, the spiritual wellspring of forgiveness: An example of spirituality in therapy. *Journal of Family Therapy, 20*(1), 37–58.
Baker, S. (1996, March 11). Is capitalism headed for a new Dark Age? *Business Week,* p. 15.
Bellah, R. N., Madsen, R., Sullivan, W. M., Swidler, A., & Tipton, S. M. (1991). *The good society.* New York: Knopf.
Bunyan, J. (1976). *The pilgrim's progress.* New York: Penguin.

Doherty, W. J. (1995). *Soul searching.* New York: Basic Books.

Duncan, B. L. (1997, July/August). Stepping off the throne. *Family Therapy Networker, 21*(4), 22–33.

Epstein, M. (1995). *Thoughts without a thinker.* New York: Basic Books.

Foley, T. (1949). *In the spirit of Saint Francis.* Paterson, NJ: St. Anthony Guild Press.

Leland, J. (1998, June 1). Savior of the streets. *Newsweek,* pp. 20–25.

Montalvo, B., & Gutierrez, M. J. (1990). Nine assumptions for work with ethnic minority families. In G. W. Saba, B. M. Karrer, & K. V. Hardy (Eds.), *Minorities and family therapy* (pp. 35–52). New York: Haworth Press.

Pargament, K. I. (1996). Religious methods of coping: Resources for the conservation and transformation of significance. In E. P. Shafranske (Ed.), *Religion and the clinical practice of psychology* (pp. 215–239). Washington, DC: American Psychological Association.

Peck, M. S. (1978). *The road less traveled.* New York: Simon & Schuster.

Santa Rita, E. (1996). Pilipino families. In M. McGoldrick, J. Giordano, & J. K. Pearce (Eds.), *Ethnicity and family therapy* (2nd ed., pp. 324–330). New York: Guilford Press.

St. Bonaventure. (1960). *The works of Bonaventure.* Quincy, IL: Franciscan Press.

Wilson, W. J. (1996). *When work disappears.* New York: Knopf.

Wulff, D. M. (1991). *Psychology of religion: Classic and contemporary views.* New York: Wiley.

Wylie, M. S. (1994, November/December). Panning for gold. *Family Therapy Networker, 18*(6), 40–48.

CHAPTER 5

Spirituality and Religion
Implications for Psychotherapy with African American Clients and Families

NANCY BOYD-FRANKLIN
TONYA WALKER LOCKWOOD

Spirituality and religion have been essential components of the cultural heritage of African Americans and a major source of strength and survival skills. This chapter addresses the incorporation of these issues into the treatment process with African American clients and families—an area that has often been neglected or ignored in the clinical literature. Clinical case examples are presented to illustrate the central concepts.

In recent years, the mental health field has begun to address the role of spirituality and religion in psychotherapy (Bergin, 1985, 1988, 1991; Bergin & Payne, 1991; Jones, 1994; Worthington, 1989). Gallup surveys have found that two-thirds of the American population views religion as important in their lives (Gallup Organization, 1985; Bergin, 1991). While 77% of clinicians surveyed indicated strong religious beliefs (Bergin, 1991), few therapists rated religious issues as important in treatment with their clients. Bergin's (1991) explanation is that "such matters have not been incorporated into clinical training as have other modern issues such as gender, ethnicity and race" (p. 396). A number of studies have indicated that this oversight may lead many clients to seek counseling from clergy rather than mental health professionals (Bergin, 1988, 1991; Veroff, Kulka, & Douvan, 1981). Bergin (1991) suggests that "perhaps this spiritual humanism would add a valuable dimension to the therapeutic repertoire if it were more clearly expressed and overtly translated into practice" (p. 396; see also Bergin & Jensen, 1990).

There have been few attempts to discuss the central role that these is-

sues can play in psychotherapy with specific populations, particularly with African Americans (Boyd-Franklin, 1989; Comas-Díaz & Greene, 1993; Comas-Díaz & Griffith, 1988; Stevenson, 1990). Spirituality and religion have long been acknowledged as major strengths within African American families and sources of resiliency and survival skills (Billingsley, 1968, 1992; Boyd, 1982; Boyd-Franklin, 1989, 1991; Stevenson, 1990; Brown & Walters, 1970; Hill, 1972; Knox, 1985; Comas-Díaz & Griffith, 1988). Baker, Williams, Bailey, and Jackson (1992) have documented the very powerful role of religion and spirituality in the lives of many African American women.

Spirituality and religion are interconnected but hold very different meaning in the lives of African Americans. Many African Americans have an internalized sense of spirituality but are often not part of an organized religion or church (Boyd-Franklin, 1989). Watts (1993) found through his research that religion and spirituality are two distinct entities for African American men. Spirituality refers to an outlook on life and a personal relationship with God, whereas religion refers to church doctrines. Brisbane and Womble (1985/86) stated that African Americans' spiritual power and a belief in something higher than themselves provide a reinforcing function of conviction and fulfillment. This can be a positive factor in the treatment of addictions and alcoholism and can help to counter resistance (Smith, Buxton, Bilal, & Seymour, 1993).

The African American community is diverse, and clinicians will encounter considerable variability on the issue of spirituality and religion. Spirituality or religion/religious orientation may manifest as a deeply ingrained personal belief system, as a formalized set of religious beliefs and institutional practice, or as a combination of both. It would be a serious error for clinicians to stereotype all African Americans as possessing a uniform set of beliefs.

THE ROLE OF SPIRITUALITY IN THERAPY WITH AFRICAN AMERICAN CLIENTS AND FAMILIES

It is important to recognize that for persons of African descent, the psyche and the spirit are often seen as one (Knox, 1985; Mbiti, 1970; Nobles, 1980). Psychological pain is frequently expressed in spiritual terms (Boyd-Franklin, 1989). Knox (1985) summarizes the most commonly expressed beliefs as "God will solve my problems" (p. 32), "God is punishing me for having sinned" (p. 32), and "God never gives you more than you can carry" (p. 2). These beliefs can be used as a part of "spiritual reframing" with African American clients in therapy (Boyd-Franklin, 1989; Mitchell & Lewter, 1986).

Spirituality often refers to a belief in a "Higher Power" or God. References to prayer and God are ingrained within African American culture:

even individuals who do not consider themselves to be religious incorporate these references into everyday life (Levin, 1984). For example, a parent told her therapist in a family session that she asked God for help in
dealing with her son's increasingly dangerous acting-out behavior. This
mother did not attend church, but she reported a deep spirituality and
prayed or "talked to God" when she was troubled. It is important that
therapists not assume that religious references imply institutional religious involvement.

It should also be noted that adolescents and young adults in a stage of
rebellion against families who are very religious may engender strong conflicts by forsaking religion and spirituality. These same individuals, however, are very likely to draw on these strong beliefs when they are in trouble, adopting a "crisis intervention" approach to spirituality. It is also not
unusual for once-rebellious men and women to return to the church when
they have children of their own. Once mental health practitioners are
aware of the role that spirituality and religion play in the lives of African
American clients, they can utilize this understanding in therapy. These issues become particularly important when one explores the responses to
treatment in the African American community.

RESPONSES TO TREATMENT
IN THE AFRICAN AMERICAN COMMUNITY

Many clinicians in the mental health field are unaware that attempts by
the therapeutic community to be neutral, secular, and "aspiritual" have
led to therapy being viewed as "antispiritual" by some members of the
African American community, particularly those with strong religious
beliefs (Hines & Boyd-Franklin, 1982; Boyd-Franklin, 1989). This is reinforced when therapists who do not know of the deep spiritual roots in African American culture ignore this key component of their clients' core
belief systems. In addition, ministers who would otherwise be powerful referral sources may be reluctant to refer troubled congregants to mental
health providers because of the profession's reputation for being narrowly secular. (This may be true also of other cultures with strong religious beliefs [Bergin, 1991; Bergin & Jensen, 1990].)

This issue has particular relevance when it is viewed in the broader
context of skepticism about therapy within the African American community. This skepticism has many historical roots within the culture. The legacy of racism and discrimination has compelled many African Americans
to view institutions (clinics, hospitals, schools, etc.) with "healthy cultural
suspicion" (Grier & Cobbs, 1968; Hines & Boyd-Franklin, 1982; Boyd-
Franklin, 1989), leading to a reluctance to discuss "family business in public." Therapy is considered very public within African American communities, particularly poor communities. Another confounding variable is

the view held by many African Americans that therapy is a shameful process and hence only for "sick or crazy" people. While these concerns are not held exclusively by African Americans, the strength of these beliefs within Black communities should not be underestimated.

Given these considerations, it is incumbent on therapists working with African American clients and families to maximize the joining process and facilitate the development of trust. This is particularly true in cross-racial therapy. Therapists who fail to inquire about religion and spirituality may be missing an opportunity to create a therapeutic alliance with African American clients who have a strong belief system.

In recent years, a number of authors have stressed the importance of incorporating spirituality and religion into the treatment of African American clients (Hines & Boyd-Franklin, 1982; Boyd-Franklin, 1987, 1989). Others have emphasized the role of Black churches within these communities (Billingsley, 1992). Therapists, however, may be frustrated in trying to incorporate these issues into treatment without training. This article addresses the need for clinical case material.

THE ROLE OF THE BLACK CHURCH AND THE "CHURCH FAMILY"

Within the Black community, many different denominations and religious groups are represented, including Baptist, African Methodist Episcopal, Jehovah's Witnesses, Church of God in Christ, Seventh-Day Adventist, Pentecostal churches, Apostolistic churches, Presbyterian, Lutheran, Episcopal, Roman Catholic, Nation of Islam, and numerous other Islamic sects (Boyd-Franklin, 1989). We will focus primarily on the Baptist and African Methodist Episcopal groups, which account for the largest percentage of Black members.

Black churches have long served a multitude of needs in African American communities (Boyd-Franklin, 1989). They have established their own schools and have historically served as the focal point of political activism since the days of slavery, when they were forbidden (Wilmore, 1973; Boyd-Franklin, 1989; Rabateau, 1987). During segregation, they provided what Frazier (1963) described as "a refuge in a hostile white world" (p. 44), and perhaps the only opportunity for Black men and women to feel respected for their abilities. To this day, they are a place where Black people irrespective of socioeconomic level can achieve status. In our view, "Black people have used this as a major coping mechanism in handling the often overwhelming pain of racism and discrimination" (Boyd-Franklin, 1989, p. 81). Frazier (1963) and Du Bois (1903) have shared this point of view.

It is important that therapists be aware of such meaningful concepts as "church home" and "church family" (Smith, 1985). The church home is one the family regularly attends, often for generations. Families who move to a new community often travel a long distance to attend services at their home church. This identification can be so strong that even when individuals go away to school or relocate for a job, they continue to support this church financially. The concept of a "church family" captures the fundamental role of a Black church as a support network. Often members of the church are considered non-blood-related, extended family members. "Church family" members often share meals and fellowship before and after services. "Church families" often resemble extended families, wherein the minister, the minister's spouse, deacons, deaconesses, prayer partners, and "sisters or brothers" in the church function as resources in times of need (Boyd-Franklin, 1989). These "church families" can be as highly cohesive as close-knit extended families.

When African American families move, some may be anxious to find a new "church home" and "church family," often carrying letters of introduction from their minister. This connection may be extremely important for African American clients isolated from natural support systems. Efforts can be made as a part of the therapeutic process to acquaint or reacquaint clients with these networks of support. This may be particularly useful for single mothers in that churches can serve valuable socialization and child-rearing functions. Many African American mothers who do not attend church themselves will send their children to services, Sunday school, or social and recreational activities at the church. For many poor families, the "vacation Bible school" substitutes for summer camp and provides constructive activities for children.

The minister is often sought out for counseling by people who would not choose to go for "treatment." Although this courtesy is rarely given, mental health and family service professionals would benefit greatly from meeting with ministers in the communities they serve, given the very powerful leadership position of ministers in the African American community. This is helpful from the point of view of community entry, organizational involvement, and as an equal partnership in the community referral network. This connection can counteract the "healthy cultural suspicion" discussed above.

One researcher who collected "life stories" from elderly African Americans residing in southwestern Virginia found that the role of the Black church and religion/spirituality were salient themes for those he interviewed (Nye, 1993). In expanding upon E. Franklin Frazier's work (1963), Nye (1993, p. 105) identified six subthemes of the function of the African American church:

1. An *expressive* function or as an outlet for one's deepest emotions. This was found in the way in which many respondents couched their deepest concerns in religious terms and references.
2. A *status* function, or religious participation confers recognition which may be lacking or denied in the wider, White-dominated world.

3. A *meaning* function, or a source of order and understanding for one's life. This function is particularly important in maintaining continuity.
4. A *refuge* function as a haven in an oftentimes hostile world.
5. A *cathartic* function or as an avenue for the release of pent-up emotions and frustrations felt by an oppressed minority.
6. An *other worldly* orientation function, which guides the person to see eventual fulfillment in the next life.

There are at least two other valuable functions:

7. A *social function*, that is, the opportunity to meet, socialize, and share fellowship with others who share a similar background and interests. This peer involvement can be especially important for adolescents vulnerable to pressures to join gangs, use drugs, or become sexually active.
8. A *child-rearing and socialization function*, which is especially important for single parents. Often churches provide baby-sitting during services in addition to the youth activities discussed above.

The following case illustrates the process of incorporating spirituality and religion into treatment with an African American family.

Martha was referred by her pastor for home-based family treatment. She is a 44-year-old African American single parent who has six children. Martha resides in a housing project with three of her children: Dominique (age 17), Daniel (age 13), and Roshanda (age 9). The three oldest children (ages 24, 22, and 21) live within walking distance. Martha is a recovering addict who has been drug free for 10 years and still attends Narcotics Anonymous meetings regularly.

Martha has a strong spiritual identity: she proclaims that God revealed himself to her 10 years ago when she got on her knees to pray that he rid her of her addiction. During the initial interview, she stated that God granted her sobriety in exchange for her service to him every day of her life and her willingness to spread the gospel of Jesus Christ.

Martha is currently a member of an influential Baptist church in her community. The church is a powerful agency in her life. The pastor also acts as a surrogate father to her children, particularly her daughter Dominique.

During the first 6 months of treatment, Martha repeatedly used religious metaphors for her life struggles. She was very receptive to spiritual or religious reframes from her two counselors, conveying her feeling that God had brought them to her because he knew that she needed help in making new strides in her life.

After the family had been in treatment for approximately 6 months, Martha revealed that she was in crisis and was considering having her children removed from her home because they were threatening her sobriety. Martha complained that the children were violating the rules of the home, such as not informing her where they were or when they would return, and engaging in physical violence with one another and verbal aggression toward her. She found their behavior so stressful it brought on intense migraine headaches.

Martha stated that she was not willing to allow her children to threaten her gift from God. She believed they must be put out of the house so that she might have the opportunity to become strong again in her commitment to sobriety that enabled her to function as a person and as a mother. She discussed contacting the child welfare agency and asking for their removal. Martha and her counselors brainstormed ideas on how to deal with the crisis in a less drastic manner.

Although Martha had a very supportive family network, they were consumed by their own interpersonal problems. Martha's support network was extensive and included her prayer partner, friends from church, her pastor, as well as God himself. With the support of her therapist, Martha called her friends from the church, who responded immediately. Her prayer partner and husband were willing to take the children in for as long as Martha needed. Martha's children were thus able to stay within the extended kin network, eliminating the threat of removal by a child welfare agency while she had an opportunity to regroup. This experience reaffirmed Martha's faith in God, as well as her trust in her counselors to assist her in her time of crisis. Moreover, Martha was encouraged to call her prayer partner to pray together several times a day. Martha was also encouraged to call her pastor, who knew of her family situation and had been supportive in the past, as well as to attend Narcotics Anonymous meetings daily so that she could once again feel safe in her sobriety.

This case demonstrates how crucial a client's spirituality and "church family" can be in a time of crisis. Martha was assisted in identifying a resource that she was already connected to that could offer support. The church also provided Martha with the six functions discussed above: expressive, status, meaning, refuge, cathartic, and other worldly orientation (Nye, 1993).

This case also underscores the value of contacting Black ministers in the community. When the home-based family therapy project began, the directors contacted this family's minister and a close working relationship subsequently developed. He therefore trusted the project and felt comfortable referring this family. Given the concerns about therapy in the Black community, it is unlikely that this would have occurred without initial outreach.

Integrating spirituality into clinical treatment is critical in working with many African American clients. This will minimize attrition as well as facilitate the joining process between client and clinician (Boyd-

Franklin, 1989). Furthermore, an understanding of spirituality, as well as the religious institutions themselves, can offer great insight into the lives of African American clients. Another life transition in which spirituality and/or religion becomes important is the loss of a loved one.

SPIRITUAL ISSUES OF DEATH AND DYING

For members of all cultures and religious groups, death and dying is a time when spiritual beliefs and rituals are utilized (Walsh & McGoldrick, 1991). This has been particularly true for African Americans given their historical vulnerability to sudden and often violent death. Within the African tradition, life and death are seen as part of a cycle of existence (Nobles, 1980; Mbiti, 1970). Because of the African philosophy of collective unity rather than individualism, times of loss bring the entire family, extended family, friends, members of the church family, and community together to mourn. Funerals are one of the most important rites of passage in the African American community and are often held many days after the death in order to allow extended family members who live at a distance to attend (Boyd-Franklin et al., 1995). Funerals in Black churches are frequently cathartic and very emotional experiences. In fact, many Black churches have a nursing corps to help mourners who faint or develop medical symptoms during the service.

The belief in a life after death is also a strong component of the African American tradition. Funeral services are often called a "Homegoing," a "Celebration of the Life," or a "Homecoming." Music is an active part of all Black church services and expresses these deeply held beliefs. Before and after the service and the burial, family and friends bring food and gather at the home of the deceased. These occasions offer spiritual fellowship, support, shared grief and mourning, as well the joy of a lifetime of memories.

It is striking, however, that after this brief period of mourning, family members are expected to "get on with life," "be strong," and "wipe away the tears." In contrast to the public spiritual catharsis of the church service, the period of mourning is often a very personal, private spiritual time. Because of the pressure to move on, there are often issues of unresolved mourning in African American families, particularly when a series of losses occur in rapid succession. African Americans experiencing this kind of pain will frequently express it in spiritual terms, such as "a pain in the soul." In many African American families when a much-loved family member is lost, a vacuum in the connectedness of family relationships may be experienced. This is particularly true when the deceased held the family together and served as a "switchboard" (Boyd-Franklin, 1989).

When this type of significant loss has occurred, family members are particularly vulnerable to depression, psychosomatic complaints, and—in children and adolescents—acting-out or conduct-disordered behavior. The following case illustrates how a therapist incorporated spirituality in helping the members of an African American family begin the healing process after multiple deaths and losses.

Jamar, a 14-year-old African American male, was brought for therapy by his aunt, Laverne Smith, on the recommendation of his school guidance counselor. In the last year, Jamar's school performance had declined drastically and he was now in danger of failing. His aunt was also concerned because he had been picked up by the police in an incident that was termed "gang violence."

The therapist learned that Jamar's behavioral problems had begun when his mother died from AIDS the previous year. Approximately 3 months later, his maternal grandmother—who had raised him, his four brothers and sisters, and cared for his mother when she was terminal—died of a heart attack. Jamar's aunt reported that he was devastated and withdrew from the family after these losses. In her words, he "went to the streets." Prior to this, Jamar had been a parental child and had helped to care for his mother and his younger siblings (ages 11, 9, 5, and 4). His aunt now had custody of all the children but was overwhelmed, particularly by Jamar's behavior. When asked how she coped, Ms. Smith replied that she "prayed to the Lord . . . from him comes my strength."

The therapist inquired about the family's spiritual and religious beliefs. Ms. Smith replied that the family's "church home" was a large, active Baptist church in the community. She reported that Jamar had been very involved, including participation in the choir and membership on the junior usher board, but had "fallen away from the church" since the deaths of his mother and grandmother. When the therapist attempted to explore these issues with Jamar, he became silent.

In a session about 3 months into therapy, after the therapist had visited the school with Jamar and his aunt and was able to help them develop a plan for addressing his school problems, the therapist met with Jamar alone and again explored his feelings about his losses. He told the therapist that he had been "very angry with God" for taking his mother and his grandmother and that he had turned away from the church and his family. His therapist empathized with his loss and helped him to see that his anger was a normal part of the grieving process. For the next few months, he was seen individually with bimonthly family meetings with his aunt and occasionally with his siblings. His individual sessions were very productive. He gradually opened up and talked more about his anger and how he felt that it was "eating him up."

In one session the therapist explored Jamar's anger at his mother and grandmother for dying and leaving him. An "empty chair" technique was used to allow him to express out loud his anger, sadness, and love to his mother and grandmother. As the anniversary of his mother's death approached, the empty chair was used and he expressed his anger, sadness, and hurt to God. After both sessions, he burst into tears.

In one family session, with his therapist's help, he told his aunt and brothers and sisters what he had been experiencing. Many reported that they had been feeling these mixed feelings also but had told no one. The therapist helped to normalize the feelings of anger, sadness, loss, and love. It was clear that there was a great deal of unresolved mourning in the family. Jamar, in an important moment of insight, shared with his aunt that that was why he had pulled away from his family and the church and was "running the streets."

The therapist suggested that the entire family might benefit from a ritual of mourning during this anniversary period. With the therapist's help, they designed a "memorial service." The aunt suggested inviting their minister and some members of their "church family." As the guest list of people important to the family grew, Jamar reluctantly agreed to have the service at the church. He picked the music and his mother and grandmother's favorite hymns, which he asked a cousin to sing. The therapist attended. The minister led the service, and each family member said something about their memories of the loved ones; Jamar talked about how he had felt many feelings of love, anger, and loss. When the hymn "Precious Lord" was sung, there was not a dry eye in the congregation.

This ritual, with Jamar and other family members' active involvement and with the therapist's participation, was very significant for the entire family. Jamar became less angry. Subsequent sessions focused on "healing." His aunt reported that he was home more and was studying again. His grades began to improve. Although Jamar still does not attend church, he reports that he has "made his peace with God."

This case illustrates many of the multigenerational issues concerning religion and spirituality in African American families. Jamar's "anger at God" and his rebellion against the family's religious beliefs are typical of many adolescents. The case also demonstrates the ways in which spirituality can be used as a therapeutic tool to help heal unresolved grief and mourning.

GUIDELINES FOR PSYCHOTHERAPEUTIC WORK
WITH AFRICAN AMERICAN CLIENTS AND FAMILIES

Mental health professionals can benefit from an understanding of the importance of spirituality in the process of change for all communities, but especially for the African American community in which it is, for many, an already existing strength/resource upon which to build. The following are guidelines for incorporating spirituality or religion into treatment with African American clients.

1. The decision to integrate spirituality into therapy should be contingent on a careful assessment and diagnosis of a client's spiritual or religious worldview and the role or impact that it has on the client's life (Boyd-Franklin, 1989; Comas-Díaz & Griffith, 1988; Knox, 1985). Clients frequently reveal such orientation by referring to God as either a source of strength (i.e., "God never gives you more than you can carry") or retribution (i.e., "God is punishing me for having sinned"). It is important not to impose a spiritual or religious orientation on clients for whom it is not relevant.

2. Clinicians should be aware of the risk of an African American client leaving therapy prematurely because the clinician failed to address a client's spirituality or belief system. It is key that the therapist be able to initiate this type of dialogue and empower clients to discuss their spirituality or belief system as they would any other area of relevance. Otherwise clients may become confused and doubt that the therapeutic relationship is the appropriate arena for spiritual concerns.

3. Clinicians should understand that being in therapy may generate spiritual conflict for African American clients (Boyd-Franklin, 1991). Clients may feel that being in treatment goes against their religion, particularly when religious leaders have communicated pejorative views of therapy, (i.e., that it is "atheistic"). In addition, individuals themselves may be suspicious of therapy, viewing it as antispiritual or antireligious. In our experience, women in therapy groups have revealed that they had never spoken of spiritual beliefs or conflicts with previous therapists, fearing they would not be interested in this part of their lives (Boyd-Franklin, 1991). In the event that psychological scarring results from shame and guilt originating in religion, therapists' sensitivity to these issues can help clients to experience a release from that pain.

4. Therapists should be aware that the church can be utilized in times of crisis and offer aid to an African American family in need. The family may be more receptive to help from a church that is a familiar community resource than to help from an outside agency. In addition, a church can help families who are socially isolated and emotionally cut off from their extended families to reconnect with their "home church," or find a new church that will provide a supportive network.

5. When doing genograms (family trees) or ecomaps (drawings of other social systems involved in the client's life), therapists should be careful to assess the role of the "church family" in the lives of African Americans who report a church affiliation (Boyd-Franklin, 1989).

6. Differences in spiritual or religious beliefs may trigger conflict or intergenerational disagreements in African American families. This commonly occurs when a conversion to another religion has taken place, such

as from Christianity to Islam, or from Baptist to Jehovah's Witness. In such cases, the therapist can bring key family members together to discuss issues in ways that foster mutual understanding and tolerance for different beliefs and practices.

7. Therapists should be aware that psychological symptoms such as depression, anxiety, psychosomatic illness, and acting-out or conduct-disordered behavior may mask issues of unresolved grief and loss. Often these losses involve psychological and spiritual pain. If a family member has a strong spiritual or religious orientation, the incorporation of these issues into therapy can help expedite the healing process.

8. As the first case illustrates, ministers are very powerful figures within Black communities. Clinics, hospitals, and therapists working in these communities should make a special effort to reach out to these leaders. This personal contact will help to build trust and credibility for therapeutic work.

IMPLICATIONS FOR TRAINING

It is imperative that client needs and dilemmas concerning strong religious or spiritual beliefs be given the same importance in training programs as issues of gender, ethnicity, and race (Bergin, 1991). Therapists must be trained to recognize, assess, and appreciate the diversity of spiritual or religious beliefs that exist within each family, and also be cautioned to not assume that certain beliefs are present.

This issue raises a number of ethical concerns in training and therapy. Professional organizations (e.g., American Psychological Association, 1992) have instructed therapists of their ethical obligation to understand the needs of their diverse clients. Religion and spiritual beliefs are a vital part of most cultures. When these issues are ignored in training, therapists are vulnerable to ethical abuses by intentionally or unwittingly imposing their own religious/spiritual values and beliefs on clients. Careful training and supervision are necessary to help psychotherapists learn to provide effective therapy with African Americans and clients from other cultural groups who hold strong religious or spiritual values.

CONCLUSION

In conclusion, it is essential that spirituality be integrated into the coping measures and theories of psychosocial competence (Watts, 1993) and into the theory and practice of psychotherapy (Bergin, 1991). Spirituality is one of the many powerful facets that make up a human life experience (Comas-Díaz & Griffith, 1988), and more than any other it has, throughout time, offered hope and solace to those who are suffering.

REFERENCES

American Psychological Association. (1992). Ethical principles of psychologists and code of conduct. *American Psychologist, 47,* 1597–1611.

Baker, F. M., Williams, L., Bailey, S., & Jackson, G. F. (1992). Black, middle class women in San Antonio, Texas. *Journal of the National Medical Association, 84*(6), 497–502.

Bergin, A. E. (1985). Proposed values for guiding and evaluating counseling and psychotherapy. *Counseling and Values, 29,* 99–116.

Bergin, A. E. (1988). Three contributions of a spiritual perspective to counseling, psychotherapy, and behavior change. *Counseling and Values, 33,* 21–31.

Bergin, A. E. (1991). Values and religious issues in psychotherapy and mental health. *American Psychologist, 46*(4), 394–403.

Bergin, A. E., & Jensen, J. P. (1990). Religiosity of psychotherapists: A national survey. *Psychotherapy, 27,* 3–7.

Bergin, A. E., & Payne, I. R. (1991). Proposed agenda for a spiritual strategy in personality and psychotherapy. *Journal of Psychology and Christianity, 10,* 197–210.

Billingsley, A. (1968). *Black families in White America.* Englewood Cliffs, NJ: Prentice Hall.

Billingsley, A. (1992). *Climbing Jacob's ladder: The enduring legacy of African-American families.* New York: Simon & Schuster.

Boyd, N. (1982). Family therapy with black families. In E. E. Jones & S. J. Korchin (Eds.), *Minority mental health* (pp. 227–249). New York: Praeger.

Boyd-Franklin, N. (1987). Group therapy for black women: A therapeutic support model. *American Journal of Orthopsychiatry, 57*(3), 394–401.

Boyd-Franklin, N. (1989). *Black families in therapy: A multisystems approach.* New York: Guilford Press.

Boyd-Franklin, N. (1991). Recurrent themes in the treatment of African-American women in group psychotherapy. *Women and Therapy, 11*(2), 25–40.

Boyd-Franklin, N., Steiner, G. L., & Boland, M. G. (Eds.). (1995). *Children, families, and AIDS/HIV: Psychosocial and therapeutic issues.* New York: Guilford Press.

Brisbane, F. L., & Womble, M. (1985/86). Treatment of black alcoholics. *Alcoholism Treatment Quarterly, 2*(3/4).

Brown, D. R., & Walters, R. B. (1970). *Exploring the role of the Black church in the community.* Washington, DC: Howard University, Mental Health Research and Development Center, Institute for Urban Affairs and Research.

Comas-Díaz, L., & Greene, B. (Eds.). (1993). *Women of color: Integrating ethnic and gender identities in psychotherapy.* New York: Guilford Press.

Comas-Díaz, L., & Griffith, E. (1988). *Clinical guidelines in cross cultural mental health.* New York: Wiley.

Du Bois, W. E. B. (1903). *The souls of Black folk.* Chicago: McCluig.

Frazier, E. F. (1963). *The Negro church in America.* New York: Schocken Books.

Gallup Organization. (1985). *Religion in America,* Report No. 236. Princeton, NJ: Author.

Grier, W. H., & Cobbs, M. (1968). *Black rage.* New York: Basic Books.

Hill, R. (1972). *The strengths of black families.* New York: Emerson-Hall.

Hines, P. M., & Boyd-Franklin, N. (1982). Black families. In M. McGoldrick, J. K. Pearce, & J. Giordano (Eds.), *Ethnicity and family therapy* (pp. 84–107). New York: Guilford Press.

Jones, S. L. (1994). A constructive relationship for religion with the science and profession of psychology. *American Psychologist, 49,* 184–199.

Knox, D. H. (1985). Spirituality: A tool in the assessment and treatment of Black alcoholics and their families. *Alcoholism Treatment Quarterly, 2*(3/4), 31–44.

Levin, J. S. (1984). The role of the black church in community medicine. *Journal of the National Medical Association, 76,* 477–483.

Mbiti, J. S. (1970). *African religions and philosophies.* Garden City, NY: Anchor Books (Doubleday).

Mitchell, M. M., & Lewter, N. C. (1986). *Soul theology: The heart of American Black culture.* San Francisco: Harper & Row.

Nobles, W. (1980). African philosophy: Foundations for Black psychology. In R. Jones (Ed.), *Black psychology* (2nd ed., pp. 23–36). New York: Harper & Row.

Nye, W. (1993). Amazing grace: Religion and identity among elderly Black individuals. *International Journal of Aging and Human Development, 36*(2), 103–114.

Rabateau, A. (1987). *Slave religion: The invisible institution in the "antebellum South."* New York: Oxford University Press.

Smith, D. E., Buxton, M. E., Bilal, R., & Seymour, R. B. (1993). *Cultural points of resistance to the 12-step recovery process.*

Smith, W. C. (1985). *The church in the life of the Black family.* Valley Forge, PA: Judson Press.

Stevenson, H. (1990). The role of the African-American church in education about teenage pregnancy. *Counseling and Values, 34,* 131–133.

Veroff, J., Kulka, R. A., & Douvan, E. (1981). *Mental health in America.* New York: Basic Books.

Walsh, F., & McGoldrick, M. (1991). *Living beyond loss: Death in the family.* New York: Norton.

Watts, R. (1993). Community action through manhood development: A look at concepts and concerns from the frontline. *American Journal of Community Psychology, 21*(3), 333–359.

Wilmore, G. (1973). *Black religion and Black radicalism.* Maryknoll, NY: Orbis.

Worthington, E. L. (1989). Religious faith across the life span: Implications for counseling and research. *The Counseling Psychologist, 17,* 555–612.

CHAPTER 6

Religion and Spiritual Folk Traditions in Immigrant Families
Therapeutic Resources with Latinos

CELIA JAES FALICOV

> When it comes to our work, however, spirituality is an arena
> where we need our clients. It will require that we see
> ourselves not as proprietary experts on the subject, but as
> companions on a journey, *their* journey. We do not own the
> expertise about the spirit. As therapists, we are not the new
> priesthood. We all have our own personal philosophical,
> social, and spiritual perspectives. We have varying degrees of
> commitment to our values. We have, in effect, our respective
> "religions." However, the poor come to us sometimes clothed
> only with their ethnicity, culture, and spirituality. It is not for
> us to dress them with our apparel.
> —HARRY APONTE (1994, p. 246; emphasis his)

A journey of migration to a new land and language involves many losses
and the challenge not merely to adapt but to reinvent a life. The process
of reinventing oneself challenges immigrants to compose a new life by ab-
sorbing novel elements without forfeiting old ones. Established religious,
spiritual, and folk practices are not only extremely hard to replace with
the values and beliefs of the dominant host culture but, with the power of
tradition, they also help resurrect the life immigrants left behind and engender the comfort of continuity and familiarity. Those practices are not
driven by mere cultural nostalgia. They are based on useful systems of belief that diminish the sense of strangeness and disenfranchisement by calling upon familiar values and legitimate resources to cope with change.

Psychotherapists trained in the Euro-American cultural set need to become sensitive to the enduring presence of religion, spirituality, and folk beliefs and develop respectful curiosity as to the possible uses of those resources in psychotherapeutic work rather than privileging only dominant, First World cultural views. This chapter addresses two interconnected, key sets of belief systems that are specially relevant to psychotherapy with immigrants and particularly with Latinos. These are the constellation of beliefs about health and illness and about religion and spirituality.

During cultural, developmental, and other life cycle transitions, immigrant families turn more intensely to the comfort and continuity of past traditions such as prayer and folk medicines. The human tendency to find comfort and stable meanings in the midst of change by revisiting cultural beliefs and rituals has been called "ideological ethnicity" (Harwood, 1981). This draw toward one's primary ethnicity can be used as a therapeutic resource to help immigrant families discover practices that enhance continuity and belonging, thereby propelling life forward while reaffirming past ties.

Even acculturated Latinos, particularly those who are normally doubtful of traditional folk practices or magical beliefs, may tend to tap into their ancestors' core beliefs when times are especially stressful. Once a therapeutic alliance is firmly established, clinicians may be able to explore this realm of cultural beliefs and practices to examine if and how clients view their potential use as supportive resources.

Beliefs about health and illness and traditional folk healing are discussed below first, followed by a consideration of religious and spiritual practices, some of which are based on magical beliefs. Although the generalizations that follow are drawn from work with Latinos, it is possible that many ethnic groups share systems of belief based on religion, magic, and folk traditions, however varied the particular contents and practices may be.

FOLK HEALTH: ILLNESS BELIEFS

Most of the pertinent literature portrays Latinos as maintaining a dual system of beliefs and practices concerning physical and mental problems—mainstream medical treatment and psychotherapy, on the one hand, and traditional folk-oriented approaches, on the other. Rather than viewing them as unconventional alternatives, I consider the folk approaches as having their own wisdom, effectiveness, and spiritual meaning and as playing a complementary part alongside conventional methods.

The health beliefs of Latinos can be grouped into two categories: beliefs in traditional or natural folk illnesses; and beliefs in the supernatural, magic, or bewitchment (witchcraft).

Traditional or Natural Folk Illnesses

A "folk illness" refers to the layperson's conception of a physical or an emotional problem. These problems are identified with nonmedical labels that summarize observed clusters of symptoms, and they derive from knowledge that is passed on informally from generation to generation. Beliefs in traditional folk illnesses are unrelated to religious beliefs, and even to social class, though they are more prevalent among poorer and less educated Latinos who have limited access to mainstream medical diagnosis and treatment.

Folk syndromes are sufficiently different from the conventional diagnostic classifications that the fourth edition of the *Diagnostic and Statistical Manual of Mental Disorders* (DSM-IV; American Psychiatric Association, 1994) includes in its appendix a glossary of culture-bound syndromes, with several that are specifically relevant to Latinos. The descriptions help clinicians make a differential diagnosis between folk syndromes and conventional categories of illness such as anxiety or depression. This formal recognition of culture-bound syndromes also legitimizes the therapist's exploration of folk illnesses and corresponding beliefs of causation and folk approaches to cure.

The most common folk illnesses are *mal de ojo* (evil eye), *susto* or *espanto* (fright), *empacho* (indigestion), *nervios* (nerves), and *ataques de nervios* (nervous attacks) (Harwood, 1981). Underlying folk illnesses are beliefs in the power of strong emotions—one's own or another's envy, anger, fear, and frustration—to influence bodily health.

Susto or *espanto* (fright) is a syndrome that can affect people of either sex and of all ages: a parent may bring a child to a clinic after a fall from a bicycle, saying that the child has lost his appetite or the gleam in his eye; a woman says that she feels out of control after she was frightened by her husband's threats to harm her. The underlying explanation of *susto* or *espanto* is that these people were deeply frightened by a traumatic experience. This explains their symptoms of restlessness, listlessness, diarrhea, vomiting, weight loss, or lack of motivation (Tseng & McDermott, 1981). Sometimes *susto* is used to justify a passive sick role or to manipulate and control social interactions in situations where few legitimate avenues exist for avoiding acute psychological stress.

Mal de ojo (evil eye) embodies the belief that social relations contain inherent dangers to the well-being of the individual. A person with *vista fuerte* (strong vision) can exert inordinate influence on another person. His or her covert glances can produce a stronger power over weaker persons, robbing the latter of their ability to act on their own accord. The victim of *mal de ojo* may experience severe headache, uncontrollable weeping, fretfulness, insomnia, and fever. *Mal de ojo* is thought to more commonly attack women and children because they are believed to be weaker beings.

Empacho refers to a type of indigestion or gastrointestinal infection that afflicts children and adults and is thought to be caused by a complex interaction between physiological and social factors. Stomach pains are thought to be a symptom of intestinal blockage and fever that causes thirst and abdominal swelling. It is believed that the afflicted person has been forced to eat against his or her will, either by allowing another to override his or her personal autonomy or by excessive politeness in accepting food when not hungry.

Nervios (nerves) refers to a general state of distress connected to life's trials and tribulations, but it also describes a specific syndrome that includes "brain aches" or headaches, sleep difficulties, trembling, tingling, and *mareo*, a form of dizziness, or simple anxiety and nervousness. A person may be said to "suffer from nerves" (*sufre de los nervios*) or "be ill from nerves" (*está enfermo de los nervios*).

Ataque de nervios has been dubbed the "Puerto Rican syndrome"— incorrectly so, indeed, as it also appears in other Latino groups. A common feature of *ataque de nervios* is a sense of being out of control. The symptoms may include dissociative experiences, hyperkinesis, seizure-like or fainting episodes, mutism, hyperventilation, crying spells, or shouting. The victim may experience amnesia of what happened during the *ataque* (Fernández-Marina, 1961). *Ataques* appear to be more common among women and people in lower socioeconomic levels. Some *ataques* are socially acceptable responses to certain situations, such as when one has witnessed or received news of a shocking family event or has faced a dangerous situation. An *ataque* may be interpreted as a call for help or a way out of an impossible situation. Life stresses such as school, work, family pressures, love torments, and attempts to maintain interpersonal harmony by suppressing anger may all contribute to anxiety and situational frustrations that result in *ataques de nervios*.

Beliefs in Disorders of the Supernatural

Magic and Bewitchment

Mal puesto or *brujería* (bewitchment) provide explanations for prolonged disorders that cannot be accounted for by traditional folk illnesses or for which folk treatments have not worked. In spite of a declining belief in witchcraft, serious disruptions in social relations are sometimes thought to be followed by various forms of bewitchment. Among these disruptions are unrequited love, quarrels and breakups among lovers, or conflicts among close family members. Following these incidents, it is believed that one of the parties may have hired the services of a sorcerer (*brujo* or *bruja*) to bewitch or place a hex on the other party. *Mal puesto* is believed to be an explanation for infertility and various forms of mental illness or "insanity," including schizophrenia. Chronic and treatment-resistant illnesses are thus more likely to be diagnosed as the result of *brujería* or witchcraft.

There are elements of cultural syncretism here, whereby it is difficult to discern the pre-Hispanic, native influence from the later Hispanic colonization. In pre-Hispanic Mexico, natural elements were invested with god-like, supernatural qualities and magical powers. These gods (of the sun, the rain, and the like) needed to be revered, sometimes through ritual sacrifice, for the cosmos (the orderly universe) and earth to be maintained. Magic was thought to benefit human beings in individual health and group survival. But it also had its dark side—it could be used to harm enemies through poisoning, drought, plagues, fatal illnesses, or other forms of harm. This became known as "black magic" performed by "black witches," while benevolent magic was consequently dubbed "white magic." White witches were called upon to cure illnesses or to resolve life problems, whereas black witches were contacted to help one retaliate by placing hexes or bewitching someone else.

The Spanish Conquest brought a different religion, Roman Catholicism, with its own beliefs and magical practices. The cult of the saints had its own stories of miracles and its own physical sacrifices and punishments to gain favors or concessions. The devil was believed to be the cause of all malignant forces, and witches were thought to have made a pact with the devil.

White and Black Witches

Both worldviews and conceptions of magic, the indigenous and the European, operated separately at first, but over time a reciprocal blending of concepts developed. Today, white and black witches are still consulted for a wide variety of problems. White magic is called upon to ward off dangers, alleviate illnesses, locate work, bring success in a new enterprise, provide luck in romance, or recuperate a lost love. Black witches are consulted when one wishes to harm an enemy, defeat a rival, or revenge an evil hex from another person. Specific rituals are part of the armamentarium of brujos (Scheffler, 1983).

Through their wisdom about human relationships, white witches may become the equivalent of local psychotherapists in the ethnic neighborhood. Often, they manage to positively connote every person involved, reassure clients, and create a boundary and a closure to traumatic events. In turn, customers feel better and newly empowered with alternative ways of thinking and behaving.

FOLK, SPIRITUAL, AND MAGICAL HEALING

The world of white and black witches exists, but it is secret and not readily accessible in conversation. More acceptable and somewhat more public is the world of natural healers who use herbs and massages but may also prescribe tasks and even talk to spirits.

Curanderismo is the indigenous method of cure for many natural folk illnesses such as *susto, empacho,* or *mal de ojo,* but *curanderos* (or folk healers) may also be consulted for impotence, depression, or alcoholism, even by those who do not profess to believe in folk illnesses or cures. *Curanderos* are a heterogeneous group distinguished by specialties in particular disorders or by particular healing powers. They use a range of treatments: herbal remedies, inhalation, sweating, massage, incantations, and a variety of ritual cleansing treatments (Gafner & Duckett, 1992).

Curanderos, brujos, and *espiritistas* frequently perform *limpias.* These are important and widely used cleansing rituals that require branches of various plants, eggs, perfumed waters, religious images, dissected animals, and candles specific to each problem. Rituals take place next to their *altares* (altars), which are decorated with ritual objects, candles, incense, and images of saints and occasionally of the devil or of other supernatural beings.

Sometimes *curanderos* specialize in certain "Western" medical problems such as menstrual cramps or prolapsed uterus, and may have anatomic charts or other objects found in modern medical offices. Yet, *curanderos* do not see themselves in competition with medical providers, particularly with regard to serious health problems. The clients, too, see value in using a dual system of health care, alternatively or conducted together (Applewhite, 1995; Mull & Mull, 1983). Reluctance to accept conventional treatment may signify a family's concern that mainstream medicine may interfere with alternative approaches such as prayer.

These studies indicate that *curanderos* are skillful at creating a warm and intimate atmosphere and that they pay tribute to the value of family connectedness by including relatives and asking them to take an active role in decision making about treatment. They are reassuring and paternalistic (or maternalistic), exuding confidence in their ability to diagnose and cure the illness, factors that may contribute to success or satisfaction through suggestibility.

Although *curanderos* do not ask or answer many questions, they do allow for ventilation of fears and hostilities on the client's part. For example, it is believed that *susto,* if left untreated for some period of time, can lead to "soul loss," a belief that generates even more fear. The cure is a ritualized recapture of the soul and its fast reentry into the body. But close observation of a *curandero*'s healing shows that much more than a ritual is involved. Tseng and McDermott (1981) report that a female client with *susto* developed a transference-like attachment to the *curandero.* She expressed a lot of her fears to him and received plenty of reassurance both in words and medicine. In addition, she was distracted from her symptoms by a series of tasks that brought her into social contact, increased her self-worth, and gave purpose to her days. The tasks of recapturing her soul, preparing medicines, and conducting relevant ceremonies brought the network of relatives and community together in support of the client.

Again, one can reflect on the convergence of therapeutic elements of the *curandero*'s practices and conventional psychotherapy and psychopharmacology.

Yerberos, or herbalists, are especially knowledgeable of home remedies and the use of hundreds of wild and domestic plants to treat body and mind. *Yerberos* are an important and widely used health resource in Latino communities. Unlike *curanderos*, they do not use traditional rituals.

Espiritismo, or spiritualism, refers to an invisible world of good and evil spirits who can attach themselves to human beings and thus influence behavior (Delgado, 1978; Garcia-Preto, 1996). In that invisible world everyone has spirits of protection, the number of which can be increased by performing good deeds or decreased by doing evil. Beliefs in spiritualism are embedded deep in history; among some Puerto Ricans, for example, a belief in spirits has been traced to the Taino Indians, who (like virtually all Native American tribes) felt that everything in nature had a spirit. Today, the enduring spiritual presence of a loved one after death is common among Puerto Ricans, although it may vary among family members according to acculturative influences (Garcia-Preto, 1996; Shapiro, 1994).

Some interpretations of spiritualism come from a social justice perspective. Fanon (1967) suggests that colonized people live in tension, containing anger that may be released destructively or displaced into magic and spiritual systems. When political action is not possible and self-determination is limited, placing oneself under the protection of benevolent and powerful spirits may help counteract fear, powerlessness, and lack of agency (Lechner, 1992; Comas-Díaz, 1995). In this context, spiritualism is thought to act as an adaptive stress-reducing mechanism among Puerto Ricans in the United States (Pérez & Andrés, 1977).

Many Puerto Ricans and some Cubans, particularly those who come from the eastern region of the latter island, rely on *espiritistas* (spiritualists or mediums), who can communicate with the spirits and have the power of healing. In their book *Families of the Slums*, Minuchin, Montalvo, Guerney, Rosman, and Schumer (1967) describe how these indigenous agents "speak" the inner language, a kind of "spiritualese" reserved to describe psychological distress. This distress is often seen as originating from supernatural sources rather than from one's own inner life. The locus of control is external, and motivation for change may come in the form of a visit by God, hearing a voice from beyond, or seeing a ghost who summons a person to return home or to stop drinking. These compelling spiritual experiences may be invoked to "save face," that is, to bring on necessary change without requiring clients to openly acknowledge responsibility or remorse, or to give in to family pressure.

In one situation, a couple couched the wife's infidelity in terms of possession by the spirit of a prostitute. With the problem framed this way, the spouses were freed of responsibility and joined together in going to an *espiritista.* The spiritualist, working within a cultural framework that endorsed externalization, accepted their explanation. He assigned them a "task" to bring the estranged husband and wife together cooperatively: they were to take a long trip to dispose of a chicken leg stuck with a nail in order to exorcise the spirit of the prostitute. Minuchin et al. (1967) comment that a middle-class psychotherapist would have directed the couple to reinternalize and personalize their problem. While this frame might be much more congruent with the therapist's own cultural set, it could have rendered the problem unsolvable for the couple. Ways to bridge mainstream therapy and *espiritismo* are offered in an enlightening clinical article by Comas-Díaz (1981).

Santería is a religion prevalent among Cubans, some Puerto Ricans, and other Caribbeans, and it appears to be widely practiced among Cuban Americans in southern Florida (Martínez & Wetli, 1982). It combines deities of the Yoruban or Orichas (Africans from southern Nigeria) with Catholic saints (Sandoval, 1977). In Cuba this religion is known as *lucumi,* and in Brazil it is called *macumba.*

No specific religion predominates in Cuba now, but there has been a significant increase in both religiosity and religious observance since the January 1998 visit of Pope John Paul II, perhaps as a spiritual refuge from recent economic hardship. Cubans are adept at blending beliefs and practices, and they do not insist on theological consistency. It is not uncommon for a person to believe in the Catholicism of Spain, in the African cults combined with Haitian voodoo, and in European spiritism with a touch of American Protestantism. Variations on these blends are great: one individual may rely mostly on Catholic practices that offer peace and hope after death, while another may regularly turn to a *santero* for help.

Santeros are priests or priestesses who function as healers, diviners, and directors of rituals. *Santeros* are very practical and will try to resolve concrete problems here on earth as well as predicting through divination the immediate future. They treat *bilingo,* or hex and spirit possession. A *santero*'s "diagnosis" of possession and a client's experience and report of the same condition may complicate differential diagnosis for psychotherapy practitioners, who may think the client is psychotic (Alonso & Jeffrey, 1988; González-Wippler, 1996). Some *santeros* operate *botánicas,* stores where herbs, candles, and other ritual objects may be purchased (Boswell & Curtis, 1984; Bernal & Gutiérrez, 1988; Comas-Díaz, 1989). For herbal aspects of *santería* see Brandon (1991).

It may be apparent by now that health for many Latinos involves a complex interaction of physical, psychological, social, and spiritual factors. It is difficult to distinguish discrete causation between psychological and somatic disorders and between naturalistic and spiritual or magical elements. Often, these elements combine and influence each other, and include the significant role played by Roman Catholicism.

RELIGIOUS BELIEFS

The impact of religious beliefs and spiritual practices in illness and healing are receiving increased attention by health professionals (Bergin, 1991; Dossey, 1993; Wright, Watson, & Bell, 1996; see also Walsh, Chapter 1, this volume). Roman Catholicism provides a common denominator of beliefs and values for all Latinos. Differences in specific content and blends of native religions vary considerable from country to country, group to group. Religions other than Catholicism are increasingly present in Latino communities, partly because of exposure to new faiths in the United States. Further, a large number of missionaries proselytize to individuals and communities in Latin American countries. They include various branches of Protestant, Pentecostal, Jehovah's Witness, and numerous evangelical and fundamentalist faiths. A number of Latinos are Jewish.

Roman Catholic beliefs shape many interpretations and attitudes toward physical and mental illness. These are primarily Christian beliefs in God as the Supreme Being, in life after death, and in the existence of a soul. Beliefs about heaven and hell, sin, guilt, and shame also play a role in meaning-making and in attributions of responsibility.

Catholicism also encompasses some magical thinking, beliefs in miracles, propitiatory rituals, promises (*promesas*), and prayers. While small altars to saints are everywhere in the streets of Latin America, immigrants may create home altars with flowers, crucifixes, bottles of holy water, and saints depicted in plastic statuettes or postcards. These practices are neither causal nor gratuitous—they often emphatically demonstrate Latinos readiness to endure suffering and deny the self in exchange for needed favors.

Devotional offerings, daily prayers, masses at home, vows of penance, and even pilgrimages to shrines may be offered to special saints in return for their intercession and commendation. Numerous prayers are offered to the Virgin of Guadalupe, the patron saint of Mexico, who is also revered in Puerto Rico and other parts of Latin America. This object of veneration offers enormous psychological protection to people and unifies them in their devotion. Her portrait, a most powerful icon, hangs in living rooms, dangles over automobile dashboards and from key chains from Mexico to East Los Angeles and to many cities in Texas or New Mexico. She is a perfect fusion of indigenous Aztec and Catholic European elements, the only brown-skinned Catholic Virgin who validates the promise of Catholicism for indigenous people. In fact, the Virgin of Guadalupe has many Indian names in Mexico and elsewhere. The most common is Tonantzín, and the legend of her miraculous appearance on Mexican soil in 1531 to a poor priest, Juan Diego, is lovingly retold by children and adults alike. A most interesting book edited by the Chicana writer Ana Castillo (1996) titled *Goddess of the Americas–La diosa de las Américas: Writ-*

ings on the Virgin of Guadalupe demonstrates the widespread multiplicity of popular meanings and symbols, and the profound love bestowed upon this Virgin by gang youth, feminists, social justice activists, and even by writers concerned with identity construction. The emotional significance of the Virgin of Guadalupe for immigrants is eloquently expressed in the following quote from that book:

> And so *la Virgen [de Guadalupe]* is called upon to cure ills north and south for loved ones or for anyone else who suffers. This gathering in L.A. [to celebrate the day of the Virgin of Guadalupe] might not be as monumental as the festival in Mexico City. But there is an intensity here that matches or maybe even surpasses the devotion back home. Perhaps it is the yearning to remain rooted in a rootless time where one's address can't be changed by twists of the economy or the border patrol. (Martínez, 1996, p. 111)

In spite of the widespread importance of religion and spirituality for Latinos, very little has been written about the interaction of religion and psychotherapy for this population. Churches and church life provide support and a sense of community. They are an important part of a client's ecological niche and often a great resource for families in therapy. Immigrants sometimes attend church in the United States because it provides a place of belonging, a way to meet other immigrants, and a socializing and educational setting for their children and themselves. A priest, pastor, or rabbi may become a key figure in times of stress. Sending children to parochial schools and getting involved with church activities and needs can provide an avenue for self-expression and status for men and women who have little opportunity for stimulation or acknowledgment through their jobs or life situations.

Adherence to church doctrine, regular church attendance, and the roles played by priests and organized religion vary in the various Latino groups. Mexicans are a devout group to which churchgoing and observance of religious holidays and rituals is considered vital. For older Mexicans, the church provides spiritual support in the form of hope or by helping individuals face pain and accept suffering. Religious leaders may be important auxiliaries to the treatment process. Therapists should ask if the client finds spiritual solace or any form of support through church attendance. For many Puerto Ricans, the church is a place for communions, weddings, or funerals. Going to church is not considered necessary, however, to reach God or the supernatural. Puerto Ricans have a special relationship with saints, whom they believe can be personal emissaries to God (Garcia-Preto, 1996). Cubans partake of Catholic values and rituals but perhaps with less vigor. Exposure to other religions has led to the incorporation of other beliefs and rituals for a considerable number of Cuban Americans.

The Interweaving of Religion, Spirituality, and Folk Traditions

The intertwining of religion and folk traditions among many Latino groups is particularly apparent during such transitions as death and bereavement. Mexicans, for example, do not ignore or avoid the subject of death, as is typical among most Anglo-American traditions. The "Day of the Dead" is an annual public fiesta in which folklore, religious litanies, sugar candy skulls, and tissue paper skeletons poke fun at death. Jokes and sayings about astute tricks and maneuverings that confuse and defeat death are common. The Day of the Dead includes a ritual of grieving that takes place each year for 4 years after the death of a family member. The family erects at home a portable altar with a photograph of the dead person, some favorite objects surrounded by *zimpazuchis* (deep yellow and purple flowers—the only ones that can be used for this ritual) and the deceased's favorite foods. After a day's vigil at their open home, the family transports the altar with its hanging objects, foods, and covers of beautifully embroidered clothes to the cemetery. Family and friends light tall candles and sit around the grave chanting and swaying. Close family members, particularly women and children, sleep next to the grave until the following morning, to "keep company with our poor dead ones" ("*a nuestros pobrecitos muertos*"). This ritual offers emotional release, and some household variant might well be used as a natural therapeutic resource if the ritual has ever been or has remained meaningful to the particular client family—although it would be hard to contemplate an American cemetery as a place to spend the night with deceased relatives.

Less lavishly, Puerto Ricans and Cubans also celebrate the Day of the Dead. Always, their funerals, processions, or street caravans to accompany the dead are very expressive, especially for a child's funeral (Santiago, 1994). Gasping for breath, heart palpitations, or chest pains *(piquetes)* in the deeply bereaved are accepted as natural expressions of grief; emotional states are not conceived as separate from bodily reactions in most Latino cultures. For Anglo-Americans who adhere to a mind–body dichotomy, these reactions may be pejoratively labeled as "somatizations." Although at first glance many of these practices appear to be more conspicuous among the poorer socioeconomic classes, there are elements of these beliefs that exist among subgroups of middle- and upper-class Latinos.

Hallucinations of the deceased, including "visitations" of spirits and ghosts, may occur for several years following a loved one's death, especially among Puerto Ricans who practice *santería* and Cubans who engage in *macombe* (an Afro-Caribbean religion). Shapiro (1994) provides an example of bereavement therapy for a Puerto Rican client who felt the ghost of her dead mother lingering. Thus, as many Latino cultures offer a blending of religion, spiritualism, and folklore, therapy may blend these elements into mainstream modalities to fashion more meaningful and culturally congruent treatment.

LOCUS OF CONTROL AND STYLES
OF COPING WITH ADVERSITY

Most Latinos share a core belief that is absolutely critical for therapists to understand: when illness or troubles strike, the cause is often attributed to sources outside or beyond the victim's influence or control. It is not unusual to attribute physical or emotional problems to external trauma with its ensuing internal reactions and interpersonal tensions. Many Latinos will automatically add *"si Dios quiere"* or *"Dios mediante"* ("God willing") when speaking of their plans for the near or distant future. These statements transmit a recognition that their lives are not under their control, as well as a belief that their lives are governed by a higher power (Muslims similarly use the phrase "Allah willing"; see Walsh, Chapter 1, this volume). The Chicana writer Sandra Cisneros (1997) sees the relatively infrequent use of this linguistic expression among Anglo-Americans as evidence that they must feel "in audacious control of their own destiny." For many Latinos, fate, destiny, or God is in charge: *"el destino, o Dios, así lo ha querido"* ("destiny, or God, has willed it").

Fatalism

The notion that little in life is under one's direct control is a worldview ascribed more frequently to minority groups. But it is important to distinguish various meanings of externality, particularly when working with culturally diverse clients. Sue and Sue (1990) note that "high externality may be due to (a) chance–luck, (b) cultural dictates viewed as benevolent, and (c) a political force (racism and discrimination) that represents malevolent but realistic obstacles" (p. 143).

"Fatalismo," a cognitive orientation or belief system (Rotter, 1966; Garza & Ames, 1972; Comas-Díaz, 1989), may resemble some of these aspects of externality. While many studies have attributed fatalism to the Latino culture, others have found it more a function of social class. Fatalism is thought to be more prevalent among poor people because they learn through recurrent experiences that powerful others and unpredictable forces control their lives. Limited opportunities to get ahead and change life circumstances fuel feelings of helplessness, a sense of failure, and futility about pursuing an active orientation. This fatalistic outlook increases psychological distress (Ross, Mirowsky, & Cockerham, 1983). It is important for therapists to distinguish between this "deficit-oriented" theory of *fatalism* and a more "resource-oriented" perspective on this construct. The ecology of lower socioeconomic status can indeed disempower individuals and limit their hopeful outlook, a situation that requires the use of empowering therapeutic approaches to compensate for such deficits. On the other hand, selective coping by trying to accept losses that are beyond one's control (aging, an incurable disease, or an unexpected death) may be a strong resource

based on a different philosophical or spiritual orientation than American instrumentalism. Employing either of the above options or both in conversation with Latinos about how they conceptualize their control over problems and solutions is probably the most respectful and helpful approach.

At first glance, it appears that belief in an external locus of control would "fit" with externalizations used by narrative therapists (White, 1989), who purposely separate a client's symptom from the client as an avenue to stimulate personal agency or choice. In fact, Wright, Watson, and Bell (1996) suggest that externalization techniques in which the illness, rather than the victim, is accused are similar to those employed by witch doctors. On closer examination, however, externalizing conversations are often based on talking about a problem as if it can eventually be defeated or evaded, and so conversations about struggle, conflict, and control prevail. This type of language use is very different from a worldview that encourages acceptance, resignation, and coexistence by making peace with an externally induced problem and belief in a higher spiritual power. Tomm, Suzuki, and Suzuki (1990) distinguish between an *outer externalization*, in which the problem is placed outside of the person and is confronted and struggled against, and an *inner externalization*, whereby the problem will remain internal and must be accepted, though perhaps not allowed to take over the person's life. (The Japanese call this latter process *Kan-No-Mushi*.) This differentiation can be helpful if we consider that an outer externalization appeals to instrumentalism, or the capacity to control and prevail. On the other hand, cultural inclinations to see problems as the result of fate, luck, or God's will reveal several internal coping mechanisms—*aguantar* (to endure), *controlarse* (to control oneself), *no pensar* (not to think), or *sobreponerse* (to overcome)—that may be supported or reinforced by inner circumscription. These types of inner externalization are more syntonic with the Latino worldview than the usual "true" externalization based on individual instrumentalism.

Self-Control *(Controlarse)*

While many Latinos hold that individuals are not usually responsible for bringing about their own problems, various degrees of self-control are possible. *Controlarse* or control of the self is a dynamic theme of Latinos, a central cognitive and behavioral mechanism for mastering the challenges of life by controlling one's moods and emotions, particularly anger, anxiety, and depression (Cohen, 1980; Castro, Furth, & Karlow, 1984). The concept of *controlarse* includes the following ideas: *aguantarse* (endurance), or the ability to withstand stress in times of adversity; *no pensar* (don't think of the problem), or avoidance of focusing on disturbing thoughts and feelings; *resignarse* (resignation), or the passive acceptance of one's fate; and *sobreponerse* (to overcome), a more active cognitive coping that allows one to work through or overcome adversity.

For example, in a rather typical Latino manner of coping with severe mental illness, the family draws together and keeps the mental illness of a young adult child within its private realm. Such a shared attitude of family members provides a good illustration of an external locus of control. Mental illness—emotional and psychological problems and solutions—are seen as the result of luck, fate, or powers beyond the control of the individual or the fault of the parents. Sometimes, mental illness is perceived as God's test; other times, it is simply God's will. Quiet acceptance and resignation in the face of an incurable illness could represent a form of sensible, humble realism that contrasts sharply with the Western optimism about endless possibilities for change.

Somatization: The Mind-Body Connection

Another form of coping related to the locus of control lies in somatization, those medically unexplained physical symptoms that commonly denote emotional distress. Depression is correlated with somatization (Barsky & Kleiman, 1983). To explain the tendency to somatize rather than "psychologize," Canino, Rubio-Stipec, Canino, and Escobar (1992) argue that Anglo-Americans may be more likely to postulate a mind–body Cartesian dichotomy than are other cultural groups, which are more likely to integrate mind–body experiences and express them somatically. Ambivalent judgments toward mental illness may make it more socially acceptable to express psychological distress through physical complaints. Also, among the poor, health care is more readily available for medical than for psychological complaints. These reasons may also explain why somatization has been frequently found among immigrants and refugees. The connection between posttraumatic stress disorder and somatization also remains largely unexplored (R. Castillo, Waitzkin, Ramirez, & Escobar, 1995).

As therapists we need to be aware that physical complaints for which medical causes cannot be found may have a number of symbolic meanings or emotional explanations. These meanings can be readily accessed by asking Latino clients if they have any suggestions or guesses as to the emotional or spiritual sources of their physical symptoms.

CONCLUSION

Beliefs are enduring aspects of people's collective and personal cultures. Understanding and respecting immigrant clients' beliefs and traditional practices connected to family health, illness, and healing enhance the successful engagement and unfolding of psychotherapy. Similarly, with Latino clients, accepting the "complementary"—a better term than "alternative"—nature of folk healing resources in the community, such as *curanderos, yerberos, santeros,* and *espiritistas,* can lead to open and mutual discussion and even fruitful collaboration between clients and therapists as opposed to the clients' parallel, guarded use of these services. For this conversation to take place, therapists need to conceive their exploration of clients' beliefs systems as a form of tapping the ancient healing mechanisms that their cultures provide, rather than as a form of feeding useless magic and superstition.

Mainstream religious practices such as regular church attendance, praying, and confession are important sources of comfort, solace, and moral guidance for many Latinos and may coexist with other practices based on indigenous magical beliefs.

I find myself often having to discover creative approaches in my quest to understand Latino meaning systems as they pertain to religion, spirituality, and healing practices. A growing awareness of cultural preferences in coping styles that stress quiet acceptance and internal endurance has raised questions for me about the universality of instrumental theories of therapeutic change, especially with clients who may already have their own cultural strengths. In the end, what has helped me in my work is to envision a holistic mind–body connection that allows for emotions to manifest themselves in bodily expressions and for problems to reside in the mysteries of relational sin and revenge, thus entering the poetic realm of human drama. Solutions lie somewhere amid the alchemy of religion, magic, and tradition and their integration with modern cultural empowering practices, all of which combined are charged with the power of enduring or healing emotions and offer an openness to new perspectives for immigrant clients.

ACKNOWLEDGMENT

This chapter is a revised version of Chapter 8 in *Latino Families in Therapy: A Guide to Multicultural Practice* by Celia Jaes Falicov (New York: Guilford Press, 1998). Copyright 1998 by The Guilford Press. Adapted by permission.

REFERENCES

Alonso, L., & Jeffrey, W. D. (1988). Mental illness complicated by the *santería* belief in spirit possession. *Hospital and Community Psychiatry, 39*(11), 1188–1191.

American Psychiatric Association. (1994). *Diagnostic and statistical manual of mental disorders* (4th ed.). Washington, DC: Author.

Aponte, H. J. (1994). *Bread and spirit: Therapy with the new poor.* New York: Norton.

Applewhite, S. L. (1995). *Curanderismo:* Demystifying the health beliefs and practices of elderly Mexican Americans. *Health and Social Work, 20*(4), 247–253.

Barsky, A. J., & Kleiman, G. I. (1983). Hypochondriasis, bodily complaints and somatic styles. *American Journal of Psychiatry, 140,* 273–283.

Bergin, A. E. (1991). Values and religious issues in psychotherapy and mental health. *American Psychologist, 46,* 394–403.

Bernal, G., & Gutiérrez, M. (1988). Cubans. In L. Comas-Díaz & E. H. Griffith (Eds.), *Clinical guidelines in cross-cultural mental health.* New York: Wiley.

Boswell, T. D., & Curtis, J. R. (1984). *The Cuban–American experience: Culture, images, and perspectives.* Totowa, NJ: Rowman & Allanhel.

Brandon, G. (1991). The uses of plants in healing in an Afro-Cuban religion: Santería. *Journal of Black Studies, 22*(1), 55–76.

Canino, I. A., Rubio-Stipec, M., Canino, G., & Escobar, J. I. (1992). Functional somatic symptoms: A cross-ethnic comparison. *American Journal of Orthopsychiatry, 62*(4), 605–612.

Castillo, A. (Ed.). (1996). *Goddess of the Americas–La diosa de las Américas: Writings on the Virgin of Guadalupe.* New York: Riverhead Books.

Castillo, R., Waitzkin, H., Ramírez, Y., & Escobar, J. I. (1995). Somatization in primary care, with a focus on immigrants and refugees. *Archives of Family Medicine, 4,* 637–646.

Castro, F. G., Furth, P., & Karlow, H. (1984). The health beliefs of Mexican, Mexican American and Anglo American women. *Hispanic Journal of Behavioral Sciences, 6*(4), 365–383.

Cisneros, S. (1997, Fall/Winter). In two humors. *Sí Magazine, 1,* 68–70.

Cohen (1980). Stress and coping among Latin American women immigrants. In G. V. Coelho & P. I. Ahmed (Eds.), *Uprooting and development: Dilemmas of coping with modernization.* New York: Plenum Press.

Comas-Díaz, L. (1981). Puerto Rican *espiritismo* and psychotherapy. *American Journal of Orthopsychiatry, 51*(4), 636–645.

Comas-Díaz, L. (1989). Culturally relevant issues and treatment implications for Hispanics. In D. R. Koslow & E. Salett (Eds.), *Crossing cultures in mental health.* Washington, DC: Society for International Education Training and Research (SIETAR).

Comas-Díaz, L. (1995). Puerto Ricans and sexual child abuse. In L. Aronson Fontes (Ed.), *Sexual abuse in nine North American cultures: Treatment and prevention.* Thousand Oaks, CA: Sage.

Delgado, M. (1978). Folk medicine in Puerto Rican culture. *International Social Work, 21*(2), 46–54.

Dossey, L. (1993). *Healing words: The power of prayer and the practice of medicine.* San Francisco: Harper.

Fanon, F. (1967). *Black skin, White masks.* New York: Grove Press.

Fernández-Marina, R. (1961). The Puerto Rican syndrome: Its dynamics and cultural determinants. *Psychiatry, 24,* 79–82.

Gafner, G., & Duckett, S. (1992). Treating the sequelae of a curse in elderly Mexican Americans. *Clinical Gerontologist, 11*(3/4), 145–153.

Garcia-Preto, N. (1996). Puerto Rican families. In M. McGoldrick, J. Giordano, & J. K. Pearce (Eds.), *Ethnicity and family therapy* (2nd ed.). New York: Guilford Press.

Garza, R. T., & Ames, R. E. (1972). A comparison of Anglo and Mexican American college students on locus of control. *Journal of Consulting and Clinical Psychology, 42,* 919–922.

González-Wippler, M. (1996). *Santería: The religion.* St. Paul, MN: Llewellyn.

Harwood, A. (1981). *Ethnicity and medical care.* Cambridge, MA: Harvard University Press.

Lechner, N. (1992). Some people die of fear: Fear as a political problem. In J. E. Corradi, P. W. Fagen, & M. Garretón (Eds.), *Fear at the edge: State terror and resistance in Latin America.* Berkeley: University of California Press.

Martínez, R. (1996). The undocumented virgin. In A. Castillo (Ed.), *Goddess of the Americas–La diosa de las Américas: Writings on the Virgin of Guadalupe.* New York: Riverhead Books.

Martínez, R., & Wetli, C. V. (1982). Santería: A magico-religious system of Afro-Cuban origin. *American Journal of Social Psychiatry, 2*(3), 32–38.

Minuchin, S., Montalvo, B., Guerney, B., Rosman, B., & Schumer, F. (1967). *Families of the slums: An exploration of their structure and treatment.* New York: Basic Books.

Mull, J. D., & Mull, D. S. (1983, November). Cross-cultural medicine: A visit with a *curandero. Western Journal of Medicine, 139*(5), 728–736.

Pérez, M., & Andrés, I. (1977). Spiritualism as an adaptive mechanism among Puerto Ricans in the United States. *Cornell Journal of Social Relations, 12*(2), 125–136.

Ross, C. E., Mirowsky, J., & Cockerham, W. C. (1983). Social class, Mexican culture and fatalism: Their effects on psychological distress. *American Journal of Community Psychology, 11,* 383–399.

Rotter, J. B. (1966). Generalized expectancies for internal versus external control of reinforcement. *Psychological Monographs, 80*(1, Whole No. 609).

Sandoval, M. (1977). *Santería:* Afro-Cuban concepts of disease and its treatment in Miami. *Journal of Operational Psychiatry, 8,* 52–63.

Santiago, M. (1994). *A Puerto Rican view of death and dying.* Presentation at the quadrennial meeting of the *Family Process* Journal, San Juan, PR.

Scheffler, L. (1983). *Magia y brujería en México.* Mexico City: Panorama Editorial.

Shapiro, E. R. (1994). *Grief as a family process: A developmental approach to clinical practice.* New York: Guilford Press.

Sue, D. W., & Sue, D. (1990). *Counseling the culturally different: Theory and practice.* New York: Wiley.

Tomm, K., Suzuki, K., & Suzuki, K. (1990). The *Kan-No-Mushi:* An inner externalization that enables compromise? *Australian and New Zealand Journal of Family Therapy, 11*(2), 104–107.

Tseng, W. S., & McDermott, J. F., Jr. (1981). *Culture, mind and therapy: An introduction to cultural psychiatry.* New York: Brunner/Mazel.

White, M. (1989). Externalizing of the problem and re-authoring of lives and relationships. *Dulwich Centre Newsletter,* pp. 3–21.

Wright, L. M., Watson, W. L., & Bell, J. M. (1996). *Beliefs: The heart of healing in families and illness.* New York: Basic Books.

CHAPTER 7

Three Spiritual Perspectives on Resilience

Buddhism, Christianity, and Judaism

STEVEN J. WOLIN

with

WAYNE MULLER
FRED TAYLOR
SYBIL WOLIN

Joseph Campbell, the noted teacher and commentator on symbols, myths, rituals, and religions, once noted that "however the mystic traditions differ, they are in accord in this respect. They call men and women to a deeper awareness of the very act of living itself, and they guide us through trials and traumas from birth to death" (Campbell & Moyers, 1988). I was attracted to Campbell's remark for the perspective it put on my work as a therapist. It was a clear and important reminder that psychotherapy's roots in the past are relatively shallow and that its scope of influence is narrow. Since ancient times and in places of the world untouched by professional therapy, spiritual teachings, writings, and practices have existed to help people with life's struggles. That many of these live on is testimony to their power and their relevance.

Having devoted the past 10 years of my life to exploring the topic of resilience (S. Wolin & Wolin, 1995a, 1995b, 1997; S. J. Wolin & Wolin, 1993), I also liked the assumptions that Campbell's remark implied. Spiritual traditions, he seemed to be saying, are optimistic. They share the belief that there is a way through "trials and traumas" and that people are capable of finding it. For me, this affirmation of the human capacity for resilience was a welcome contrast to the prevalent concern in therapy with people's vulnerability and psychological damage.

Over time, I found myself wondering what the traditions to which Campbell referred could teach me and what guidance, if any, they could offer to my colleagues. Because the question persisted in my mind longer than most, I decided to pursue it. I approached adherents of three of the world's great religions—Buddhism, Christianity, and Judaism and asked them to participate with me in a panel presented at the annual meeting of the Association for Marriage and Family Therapy in 1996 in Toronto. I asked each to describe how their respective religion viewed the question of resilience. I expressly requested that they limit their remarks to the written texts of their religions and to leave the search for applications to the therapists who attended. My goal was to respect a boundary between religion and therapy while encouraging a dialogue on how the one could enrich the other.

The panel was held over two sessions. The first session was opened by Wayne Muller, representing Buddhism. He views resilience as the Buddha-nature which is in every person. A nameless quality of wholeness, it can contain or bear the weight of whatever one is given. Fred Taylor, representing Christianity, sees the personification of resilience in Jesus, who suffered dreadful pain, isolation, betrayal, and abandonment but who never lost the capacity to extend himself in love to others. A core belief of Christianity, Taylor proposes, is that people have the same potential as Jesus and that they can prevail in overpowering conditions by actualizing it. Sybil Wolin, representing Judaism, focuses on the Exodus, the biblical account of the Jews' liberation from slavery in Egypt and their journey to Sinai where, at the foot of the mountain, they assemble and receive a divine revelation. She suggests that the Jewish experience in Egypt is meant as a universal symbol of adversity and that the injunction to live with justice and compassion that comes from Mount Sinai is their blueprint for resilience.

In the second panel session, the therapists in attendance were invited to reflect on the three talks and to discuss the relevance and applicability of the material that was presented to their own work. This chapter distills the major themes that emerged in these conversations and concludes with my own reflections.

BUDDHISM (by Wayne Muller)

For the past 22 years, I've spent most of my life in the company of people who suffer. I started by working with teenage runaways and drug addicts in New York. Then I worked with alcoholics, juvenile delinquents, gang members, and people in housing projects. I've also worked with people with AIDS and cancer, and with adults who were abused as children in some painful and intimate way.

As I reflect on my work with the varieties of human suffering, I find it is not the suffering per se that has captured my attention but rather the grace that seems to be embedded in the sorrow, loss, and grief that life deals us. If we attend with mindful curiosity and deep compassion to the way in which sorrow has been given to each of us, we inevitably begin to probe the nature of sorrow itself—and then we also uncover what may be born out of that sorrow. We are both broken down and broken open by the unexpected anguish in our life.

One of the things I appreciate about the Buddha is his courage. The story of the Buddha's enlightenment is mythic and told in much the same way we usually tell the story of Jesus' birth. The young Siddhartha, after being raised living in a palace, shielded by his protective parents from the outside world, one day took a journey beyond the palace walls. There he encountered an old man, then a sick man, then a corpse, and finally a monk. It was at that moment that Siddhartha realized that suffering is an inevitable part of the human world. He decided to undertake a long process of meditation in order to explore the true nature of this suffering. He vowed to continue his exploration of this truth, whatever the cost, until it was fully revealed to him. Finally, after years of pilgrimage, fasting and meditation, Siddhartha sat under the Bodhi tree and, as the first star of morning rose in the sky, he became the Buddha—the one who is awake.

After his enlightenment, the Buddha began teaching what he described as the Four Noble Truths. And the first of these is this: the world is filled with suffering. Essentially what he is saying is, of course, that if we take birth as a human being, then a certain measure of pain and sorrow will be our legacy. Things that we love will die. Things we hold as precious will be taken from us. People we love and trust will, from time to time, bring us harm, intentionally or unintentionally. Things we believe are permanent and inviolable will dissolve, or rust, or fall away. And this is the nature, he said, of all things.

Thus, to be born and to be given sorrow is not a mistake; it is not an injustice; it is not necessarily even a trauma that will induce some subsequent pathology. Sorrow is, in fact, simply one of the legacies of having taken birth as a human being. It is not to be avoided, but rather expected.

The Buddha said that, in any given lifetime, we would be given ten thousand joys and ten thousand sorrows. What that means is that sorrow comes in myriad forms—sometimes in the form of hunger or poverty; sometimes in the form of warfare or pestilence, drought or racism, family violence or Nazism, or the apartheid system in South Africa. The ways that pain and grief can enter our lives are infinite but unavoidable, even necessary. They are "necessary" not in the sense that they are good for us, not as in "if a little suffering is good for you, a lot of suffering must be *really* good for you"; rather, suffering and joy are like the expansion and contraction of our heart and lungs, like the rhythms of the earth itself, as it moves through the seasons, a natural part of what it means to be alive and awake. Joy and sorrow, in this continual rhythm, are necessary and intimate companions for us.

And so it means that for those growing up in an alcoholic family, or for those who are abused or neglected or hurt as children, it was not solely the fault of the abusive family that the child experienced suffering. This particular child may not have been given war, or pestilence, or famine, or poverty, or leukemia; this child received his or her portion of sorrow in the form of family abuse. According to the Buddha, it is because we have taken birth as a human being that we are given pain. The family simply put their peculiar, intimate stamp on the form of that pain. The forms of our sorrow can change; the fact of our sorrow cannot.

The Buddha made a very important and useful distinction that I think, as therapists, we miss sometimes in our practice. And that is the distinction between pain and suffering. The Buddha said that pain is inevitable. Pain is part of the deal. The Buddha said that suffering, however, arises from our relationship to the pain that we are given. If I am given some form of harm by my parents when I am quite small, that is pain. Suffering occurs if I believe that I'm maimed and handicapped and defective and broken because I didn't know what to do with the pain I was given when they were so big and I was so small, or if I feel that my trust was betrayed and I conclude that from now on I'll never trust anyone or anything again.

But, at the same time, the Buddha also says this: "You are all Buddhas." Each one of us has within us *Buddha-nature:* a nature that is fundamentally perfect and unblemished. There is a light—as in Christianity—an inner light of innate, natural perfection that it not wholly dissimilar from the light Jesus spoke of when he exhorted his followers: *You are the light of the world.* When the Buddha says we each have Buddha-nature, it means we have an inextinguishable fragment of the divine fire which burns in us, regardless of circumstance. Regardless of what we are given, regardless of how it is for us, regardless of how much difficulty and sorrow we experience, there is something reliable, resilient, and true embedded within us, something that will rise up to bear the weight of whatever we are given.

And it is this Buddha-nature—this Kingdom of God, this still, small voice, this inner light—that is a nameless quality of wholeness upon which we build our inner home. This inner self, this true nature doesn't break simply because we are given suffering. If that were true, the human race would have expired thousands of years ago, because people have been afflicted with war and famine and pestilence for as long as human beings have been on the earth. And so, clearly, there is within us all a capacity that remains faithfully capable of transcending unspeakable levels of pain and sorrow. I would like to suggest that as therapists, as clinicians, as healers, as people who are in the company of those who suffer, the alliance we make when we begin a therapeutic relationship is with that capacity, that *unbroken spark of fundamental spirit and divinity.* That is our deepest alliance.

Sometimes we mistakenly make our alliance with a diagnosis. I would like to talk about this error for a moment because I think it's fundamental to our understanding of the nature of suffering and the nature of healing.

The first question many of us ask when we are given sorrow at any time in our life is "Why me? Why me?" Sorrow is the only experience about which we ask this question. If we win the lottery, we don't ask, "Oh, why me? What did *I* do to deserve all this money?" Or if we are tired or happy, we don't go into terribly painful introspection to try to understand why this happiness came to us; or why we feel so tired: "Look at those people over there, they don't look tired. What did I do to deserve it?" The question seems foolish on the surface.

But suffering seems to be something quite different. We take it very personally, as if it has something to do with us. Where do we get this idea? It is relatively simple to discover developmentally. One of the first things we notice about the world when we're quite small and we're on our changing table is that when we are wet, somebody comes and changes our diaper. And then we notice that whenever we cry, somebody shows up to see what's wrong. And then when we smile and make a funny little face, some big person makes a funny little face right back at us. Further, when we take our bottle and carom it off the dresser, somebody hands it right back to us. This is pretty cool. The lesson we take from this is simple: "Basically, I'm in charge of the galaxy as I know it."

This, of course, is how a sense of grandiosity is born. I do *A* and the world does *B*. I smile, they smile. I cry, they show up. I'm wet, they change my diaper. I'm pretty much running the show here. The galaxy responds to my every thought, my every move. This is terrific!

But the real problem arises when, years later, having made this relatively exquisite observation about the nature of all things, just how do I think and feel and behave when someone rapes me? Or what happens when they hit me, or when they get drunk and leave me alone for hours at a time, or shout at each other, or bring me great harm? Well, then, I have to figure out: "What did I do that made *that* happen? I understand the nature of all things—I do *A* and the world does *B;* I smile, they smile; I'm wet, they change my diaper. Now, I do *X* and they hit me. I do *Y* and they violate me in some intimate, unspeakable way."

So now I try to figure out what is wrong with me that brought this suffering? What bad thought did I have that brought this upon me? Or what toxicity, what handicap, what brokenness, what pathology do I have in my body that invited or created this suffering? This could become a pilgrimage for the rest of my life—to discover, diagnose, and eradicate whatever I carry in me that makes suffering come to me. But the Buddha says, "Actually, you know, it has nothing to do with you." Even Jesus said, "In the world, you shall have tribulation." Hurt is part of the deal. Perhaps the harm they inflict had more to do with their ignorance and clumsiness than anything we said, or were, or weren't, or did. Perhaps this is simply one way that sorrow will come to us in this lifetime.

But if I remain fundamentally convinced that it *is* about me, then I'll spend my life trying to figure out why it happened to me and what is wrong with me because of it. And then I'll write a book about it—the DSM-IV. Now, the DSM-IV was written by people, many of them psychologists, many of them raised in families like these, who have now figured out just about every conceivable thing that can go wrong with us, which in and of itself is very impressive. But I would like to suggest that it's fundamentally, unintentionally, and insidiously violent to name someone by what's wrong with them.

You are the light of the world. You are saturated with Buddha-nature. There is a natural, fundamental, innate perfection, a spark of the divine that lies embedded within you that will not be extinguished by your sorrow. And your sorrows are not necessarily pathological.

We don't find "Light of the world" anywhere in the DSM-IV. But how wonderful it would be if the book were large enough to contain both our sorrows and our joys, our pain and our resilience. How wonderful it would be if we didn't have to keep stamping 309.28 in order for therapists to get paid. Because the whole system is driven by diagnosis which, fundamentally, says, "No one gets paid until someone figures out what's wrong with you." I would like to suggest that this system is fundamentally as abusive as the original trauma that caused the necessity for this healing relationship.

The Buddha said that the mind is naturally pure and radiant. In the Dzogchen tradition of Buddhism, there is a place called Rigpa, a natural perfection into which we sink. If we watch the sky and we watch the clouds, we can see that, as the clouds pass by through the sky, we don't mistake the sky for the clouds. The clouds simply rise and fall away, like all things, like the ten thousand joys and the ten thousand sorrows. Although they may at times obscure our clear perception of the sky, the sky is in no way diminished by the clouds that pass in front of it. In the same way, this relentless Buddha-nature, this luminosity, is in no way diminished or damaged by the painful circumstances of our lives.

Sometimes diagnostic names make us smaller. We need to name ourselves with a name that's large enough to hold both the ten thousand joys and the ten thousand sorrows, to hold this fundamental luminosity. And we need to ally ourselves with the deepest name, one that reflects the true nature of that person who is in our company.

There is a Buddhist parable that says, "If you take a tablespoon full of salt and put it into a glass of water and stir it and drink it, the water will taste quite bitter because of the salt. But if you take the same tablespoon of salt and stir it into a large, clear, pure mountain lake and then take a handful of that water and drink it, you won't taste the salt at all." The point of the parable, of course, is that the suffering is not caused by the salt but by the smallness of the container.

What Buddhism and, I would argue, the best of Christianity and Judaism propose is that everything we do in healing should help to make the container larger so that we can hold so much more of the ten thousand joys and the ten thousand sorrows that the Buddha speaks about.

CHRISTIANITY (by Fred Taylor)

I feel privileged to be a member of this interfaith panel probing how three great religious traditions support the capacity of the human spirit to repair from hardship and suffering. Suffering poses a critical test for theology as well as for psychotherapy. How can men, women, and children today affirm the existence and power of God and their own capacity to receive spiritual empowerment both from God and other people when they find themselves beset and stricken by powers that twist, violate, sicken, and destroy? How do we in the helping professions expand people's resilience—their capacity to endure and grow from suffering.

I have been stimulated both theologically and psychologically by the topic of resilience, as the director of an inner city social service agency. My organization, For Love of Children (FLOC), works with families, children, and neighborhoods that are typically viewed by mainstream society as "damaged." I find this a troubling diagnosis.

Negatively laden terms such as "dysfunctional," "at risk," and the like blur the connections between family and the social systems surrounding them. Such terms obscure both the possibilities and the problems in these connections. They set up a permanent, uncrossable distance such as the one observed by the traditional philanthropist who, in his self-sufficiency, gives to others and dominates them in the giving. His superiority rests on his freedom from neediness. I can see myself and FLOC, my organization, and our social workers and therapists in that position to the extent that we operate from a perspective of people that emphasizes their deficits, shortcomings, problems, and weaknesses. This perspective supports the paradigm of dividing folks into the damaged and the fixers.

The concept of resilience opens the possibility of a more level playing field, which is far more consistent with my religious tradition. We are all sinners. We are all challenged. We are all needy. We are all "in recovery" and never leave our vulnerabilities behind.

At the same time, we all have within us the capacity for resilience. The proverbial question, whether applied to the individual, the family, or the community, is whether the glass is half empty or half full. A damage mindset takes one perspective. A resilience mindset, like the great religious traditions, answers the other way.

Within all the great religious traditions, human beings are characterized by neediness. We are vulnerable to conditions, structures, and forces that threaten us. Response to our neediness can take two basic forms. In the first instance, we can attempt to protect ourselves against vulnerability by establishing a circle of possessions that support and protect us from threat. The Bible warns us against this strategy: "The love of money is the root of all evil" (1 Timothy 6:10).

Evil in this instance is not money per se. The threat is the powerful temptation to withhold and hoard our material blessings until we attain a level of security that makes us feel safe. The temptation is fed by the illusion that it is possible to free ourselves from domination by hardship and suffering by dominating our environment. We can never do so perfectly, of course, because we remain vulnerable and hostage to the blows of disease, accident, loss, and death. Paradoxically, chronically withholding people find themselves possessed both by their possessions and by those conditions and powers that threaten to dispossess them. This is the strategy of the closed self which increases suffering even while it would seek to escape it.

In the second instance, the self may conceivably open out toward others in self-giving, self-expanding love and generosity. This is the response of the open self—openhanded rather than tight fisted. Such an identity is not an abstraction. The Christian tradition is grounded in the story of how Jesus, preeminently and unconditionally, lived out this self-giving identity under concrete conditions in which people find themselves buffeted by destructive conditions and forces. He suffered dreadful pain, isolation, betrayal, abandonment, and death, but his identity with self-expanding love never broke. This is the identity which is at the heart of Christian worship and piety, an identity that has inspired incredible resiliency over the ages in inhuman conditions.

Christian piety vests power in the relationship between the believer and a creative, nurturant, and preservative God, a relationship that becomes accessible and believable through the story of Jesus' self-giving life, death, and God's response of resurrection. The story, which Christians refer to as the "Gospel" or "Good News," affirms, celebrates, and evokes in those grasped by faith a radical kind of power that liberates human beings to be who we are meant to be regardless of what has been done to us or what we have done to others.

A powerful exposition of this message is the recent movie *Dead Man Walking*. The protagonist of this true story is a Catholic nun, Sister Helen Prejean, who takes on a pastoral relationship with a convicted murderer on death row. Two threads run through the story. One is Sister Helen's patient, persistent effort to engage the tightly self-defended "macho" criminal in preparing for his own impending death. The other is Sister Helen's stressful relationship with the two sets of parents of the teenage couple whom the prisoner and his partner brutally murdered and sexually abused. The parents can neither understand nor accept Sister Helen's commitment to minister to their children's murderer. They see her actions as a violation of their children's memory and their own grief.

Both relationships—one with the prisoner, Matthew, and the other with the victim's parents—push Sister Helen to her psychological and spiritual limits. She is against the death penalty, a position that puts her at odds with the world around her. And Matthew, while welcoming the human contact she offers, resists facing the truth about himself. Only when his final appeal for a stay of execution is denied does his facade begin to crack. He then can no longer push away this servant of God. Step by step, she leads him to acknowledge his brutal deed, not to confirm his condemnation but to free him to accept God's forgiveness.

As the hour of Matthew's death approaches and he has not yet come close to facing this truth, Sister Helen probes his religious understanding. They talk about Jesus, who died on the cross for sinners. Matthew says that he knows and believes that Jesus died for him, that Jesus will cleanse him of guilt for sinning. Sister Helen replies, "Yes, Matthew, but you have to participate!" Her statement jolts Matthew, and slowly he lets go of his defenses. As he does, a new person emerges, one who is liberated to feel remorse for what he has done with his life and the pain he has caused the victims and their loved ones. Now he is ready to die and to face what he will face beyond death.

This movie, in my judgment, is an ultimate portrayal of the resilience expressed in the familiar Christian revival hymn, "Just as I am, without one plea, O Lamb of God, I come."

The Christian faith, like other great religions, is far too rich to be encapsulated by any number of words, much less a few paragraphs. Nonetheless, there is an authentic congruence between the therapeutic discipline of being as attentive to the surfacing of strengths alongside the surfacing of pain and distress and of holding human sin and God's grace together with grace, not sin, as the last word.

JUDAISM (by Sybil Wolin)

The topic of resilience, spirituality, and Judaism brings to mind Roger Kamenetz's (1994) recent book, *The Jew in the Lotus*. In it, he reports an encounter between the Dalai Lama and a group of Jews of varied persuasions, from Orthodox to secular. Students of the Tibetan Buddhist leader had arranged the meeting in response to his interest in Jewish history. Exiled from his homeland in Tibet and witness to the destruction of ancient Buddhist holy temples and lamaseries by the Chinese, the Dalai Lama wanted to know the secret of Jewish resilience. How, he asked, have Jews preserved their religion for centuries since the heart of their religion, the temple in Jerusalem, was destroyed? How have the Jewish people and Judaism spread to the four corners of the world, finding homes in different countries and diverse cultures, yet maintaining a common identity and core of belief and practices?

As a Jew, I found the book compelling because it served as a mirror that reflected our enduring capacity for resilience more sharply than our eternal history of victimization. As a psychologist, it gripped me equally for its conceptualization of resilience as a self-conscious achievement that could be reflected upon, understood, taught, and replicated.

Expectably, the Jewish respondents to the Dalai Lama did not offer a single answer or clear prescription for overcoming hardship. Jewish writings suggest many answers, and for each there are many interpretations. What follows is a commentary on the topic through one pair of Jewish eyes. It is based on the Hebrew Bible, the Haggadah (the text for the Passover service), and bits of personal experience.

The connection between Jewish spirituality and resilience first occurred to me at a wedding when, at the end of the ceremony, the officiating rabbi placed a glass on the floor and the groom, as tradition directs, crushed it under his heel. The shattering noise of the glass is meant to interrupt the mood of celebration and to introduce a sober yet reassuring observation. On the one hand, the symbolic crushing of the glass conveys that we cannot expect the joys of life to continue endlessly. Even in our moments of greatest happiness, we must not forget that life is not all pleasure but that shattering experiences also inevitably occur. On the other hand, we are reminded that we can prevail. Just as the groom symbolically crushes the glass, Judaism believes that an individual has the capacity to break the debilitating hold that hardship imposes. The timing (after the marriage vows have been exchanged) suggests the understanding and the wish that marriage will be a way for bride and groom to sustain that capacity.

The place reserved for hardship in the Jewish wedding ceremony (and, as we will see later, woven into other rituals such as the Passover seder), also permeates the Hebrew Bible and other Hebrew texts. From its opening pages, with the expulsion of Adam and Eve from the Garden of Eden, the murder of Abel by Cain, and God's near-destruction of the world by flood, to its close, with the agonies and protestations of Job, the cynicism of Ecclesiastes, and the sacking of Jerusalem and destruction of the Temple according to the prophesy of Jeremiah, the Hebrew Bible is a book of sighs and lamentations. It portrays in vivid detail every imaginable form of human suffering side by side with our enduring capacity to repair.

As Elie Wiesel (in Rosenblatt, 1995) reflects on the expulsion of Adam and Eve from Eden, "Rejected by God [Adam] drew closer to Eve. Never were the two so united. . . . Expelled from paradise, they did not give in to resignation. In the face of death, they decide to fight by giving life, by conferring a meaning on life."

Naomi A. Rosenblatt (1995), in her recent book *Wrestling with Angels*, picks up on Wiesel:

Our hearts go out to Adam and Eve for their primal loss . . . but they also earn our admiration. As they leave the Garden arm in arm, we see a couple bound together by adversity. . . . [This] is a far cry from the tearful scene depicted in Renaissance paintings. They don't apologize or despair. Their perseverance defies the pessimistic "fall of man" interpretation of their expulsion from the Garden. With their departure, we witness instead the "rise of man" as the first man and woman forge a covenant of love and interdependence dedicated to their mutual survival and growth. (p. 44)

Among the tales of suffering and repair narrated in the Bible, the Exodus stands out as a determining experience in Jewish history, practice, and worship. It seems to me that the story also conveys a characteristic view of resilience in Judaism. By the Exodus, I do not mean the second book of the Bible per se but rather the account of the Jewish journey from slavery in Egypt through the desert and to the foot of Mount Sinai, where the people receive a divine revelation which many live by to this day. Its importance to Jews, I believe, derives from the power of the story to represent the claim of hardship on our lives and in the words of Joseph Campbell in his long multipart conversation with Bill Moyers (1988), to serve as a "guide through trials and traumas from birth to death" (p. 8).

The Exodus drama begins with Joseph, one of Jacob's 12 sons. Joseph, distinguished by having been given a coat of many colors by his father, was his father's favorite. His brothers, who were envious, resentful, and angry at Joseph for his privileges, conspire to kill him. But one of the brothers, Reuben, calls a halt to the plan, and instead they sell Joseph to a band of traders who are en route to Egypt.

In time, Joseph prospers in Egypt and in time his descendants become numerous. Eventually, Pharaoh perceives their growing numbers as a threat and secures his own power by enslaving them. What ensues is a degrading, misery-laden, and life-threatening experience: "The Egyptians ruthlessly imposed upon the Israelites. . . . Ruthlessly they made life bitter for them with harsh labor at mortar and bricks and with all sorts of tasks in the field" (Exodus 1:13–14; quoted in Hertz, 1990, p. 208).

The low point is reached when Pharaoh threatens the continuation of Jewish life by decreeing that all firstborn sons of Jewish families be drowned in the Nile. Moses, who is born under this decree, is saved from that fate by his sister Miriam, who rescues him from the Nile and arranges to have him brought up in the Egyptian court.

As a young man, Moses witnesses an Egyptian taskmaster beating an old Jewish man and is driven to murder. He flees to Midian to save himself, and there he becomes an instrument of God, as the appointed leader who challenges Pharaoh's power and takes his people from bondage. With his brother Aaron, Moses leads the people, now a multitude, through the Red Sea and on a journey through the desert. The story culminates when the people reach the foot of Mount Sinai, where in thunder and smoke they receive the word of God, which consists of the Ten Commandments and the law that will govern them henceforth. The Exodus story ends as the people are about to enter the land of Canaan and establish themselves as a nation with a purpose, a clear identity, and a commitment to live by the law they had been given in the desert.

Yearly, in the spring, Jews gather together at Passover for a Seder celebration which revolves around retelling this story. Like the breaking of the glass at Jewish weddings, the Seder instructs us about the place of hardship in our individual and collective lives and the necessity and means of overcoming it. The idea finds expression in many symbols that mingle the dark and the light, the bitter and the sweet, hardship and resilience.

For instance, the matzah (unleavened bread) is the central symbol of the seder ceremony. Indeed, an alternate name for Passover is the Festival of Matzah. An unleavened flat bread without yeast, matzah is the food the Jews prepared in haste when they fled from Egypt because they could not afford the time waiting for dough to rise. Bringing together hardship and resilience, it represents at once the poor man's bread, the bread of affliction, and the bread of freedom, hope, and redemption. The Seder plate displays an egg, a symbol of rebirth and of mourning for the destroyed Temple in Jerusalem. The plate also contains bitter herbs, to remind us of the bitterness our ancestors suffered; parsley, which recalls spring and life; and salt water for dipping, which recalls the people's tears. The entire event recalls an event laden with terror and promise, destruction and creation, life and death.

A key passage in the Seder service instills participants with a sense of their own resilience and the necessity of exercising it while providing an opportunity to rehearse symbolically: "In each generation, each one of us is to regard ourselves as if we personally had gone out of Egypt." In Hebrew, Egypt is called *Mitzrayim*. *Tzr*, the root of *Mitzrayim*, which translates as narrow, constrained, and inhibited, suggests a meaning that transcends the particularity of Egypt. Everyone, it suggests, in all generations, will labor under the burden of one form of slavery or the other. Everyone must struggle to break free, to wander in the desert, and strive to reach physical, spiritual, and emotional independence. Each year the Seder ritual defines the eternal nature of the journey, charts the route, and holds out the hope and promise that we are capable of traveling it. As the Haggadah states, the celebration moves us—

> ... from slavery to freedom
> from despair to joy
> from mourning to celebration
> from darkness to light
> from enslavement to redemption ...

Our means of progressing from one end of the journey to the other is outlined in Exodus. After leaving Egypt, the Jews wander in the desert under Moses' leadership. After 40 years, they arrive at Mount Sinai. Assembled at the foot of the mountain, amid thunder and smoke, they receive a blueprint for living life unfettered from their taskmasters in Egypt and from the anger, desire for revenge, sense of entitlement, debilitation, demoralization, and all the other internal taskmasters that might have accompanied them on their long journey to the promised land and might well take up permanent residence with them once they get there.

In unmistakable terms, they are told how to live down the past, how to shed a slave mentality, and how to forge a new identity as a free people. The message takes form in a body of legislation. Rich in the language of "thou shalts," it rests firmly on a foundation of choice, duty, action, accountability, responsibility, and social and personal conscience.

Clearly this vocabulary has not been a preferred terminology for therapeutic discourse and practice. If heard at all, it is usually at the margins. Perhaps this seminar can be an occasion to ask, in the same spirit as of the Dalai Lama, whether it might be worth renewed consideration.

The legislation delivered at Sinai flows backward into its source. It is a paradox of Judaism that while the law and way of life that Moses brought down from the mountain aimed at liberating the people from a slave mentality, it relies upon the Egyptian experience as its primary rationale. In receiving the law, the people learn that slavery will be indelibly etched in the conscience but from then on is to be filtered through the lens of understanding and given new meaning: "Because you were slaves in Egypt, you know the heart of the stranger." So primary is the idea that it is repeated in varying forms 36 times in the Torah, more than any other single thought, defining the Jewish people's identity and naming its purpose.

Biblical law is designed to help keep us from the most likely consequence of our bitter experience—repeating the past and perpetuating its ravages from one generation to the next. The alternative it spells out is to take the experience of Egypt and to turn it inside out. It teaches that we do not need to re-create Egypt wherever we go, that we can learn from our suffering instead. It is a far-reaching moral vision of how to stop the suffering of others: how to be compassionate, to do justice, to treat one another with fairness and dignity, to respect the environment, to honor the dead, to give charity, never to seek revenge or hold a grudge, to love your neighbor, to bless your children, to care for the widow and orphan, to remember that we were made in the divine image and to act accordingly, to create and not to destroy. In this context, resilience can be defined as a partnership with the divine to wipe out all forms of slavery and to create a sanctuary on earth where everyone can be safe and everyone can thrive.

Jewish spirituality does not transport us away from life's troubles. Rather, its wisdom is that is that we are shaped by our troubles, that over and over again we will return to Egypt, but for each time we return, the real possibility of an Exodus exists. Judaism tells us that we are all holy and that all of us are capable of achieving freedom. The religion places a heavy burden on the individual by making resilience a moral obligation, locating its source in the will, and naming action as the channel through which it is expressed. The task is formidable, and the choice is ours. In the words of the Deuteronomist (30:19), "See, I set before you this day life and prosperity, death and adversity. . . . Choose life that you and your seed may live" (Hertz, 1990, pp. 882–883).

CONCLUSION

Following the three talks presented above, the floor was turned over to the therapists who attended. They were asked to take the opportunity to discuss with each other and with the panelists the relevance and applicability of each paper to their own practice. I had asked the panelists to think of themselves as consultants and to facilitate this discussion rather than to guide it in any particular direction. The majority of the remarks, both in content and tone, highlighted the need for continued discussion of the place of religion and spirituality in therapy. Overwhelmingly, those who spoke expressed gratitude and appreciation that such a seminar had been included on the conference program.

In this regard, I must acknowledge that the audience was self-selected. For the most part, those attending were people who have found meaning in religion and whose lives are significantly influenced by it. They described the tension they feel at practicing in a profession which they perceive to be hostile to an essential part of themselves and their experience. Many expressed frustration at having to exclude religion from their work, especially because it had been so helpful to them personally. Their expressions of gratitude and appreciation were related to feeling legitimized by the "official" sanction given to the topic by its inclusion on the program.

For my own part, the interfaith nature of the seminar and the discussion following were particularly gratifying. Accustomed to thinking of religion as divisive to the point of untold bloodshed, I was pleased to be in a setting where the theme of healing was the focus and the points of commonality could emerge. The experience satisfied a human need in me that far surpassed my interest as a therapist.

As I had expected, all three religions represented were rich in insights about resilience. Each acknowledged and respected the capacity for resilience as basic to human nature. This is not to say that any saw people as invulnerable—able to escape the hurtful and harmful aftereffects of hardship. On the contrary, Buddhism, Christianity, and Judaism all know and portray in their writings the full extent of human frailty and susceptibility to sorrow:

the Buddha said that in any given lifetime we would be given ten thousand joys and ten thousand sorrows; the resurrection of Jesus is inextricably connected to his trials; and all Jews carry the indelible scars of slavery.

The issue for all three religions is not how to avoid hardship and pain (each accepts the impossibility of that) but how to live with meaning, joy, gratitude, and awe while knowing the irrevocable claim that sorrow makes on our lives. Appreciating how diffuse discussions of spirituality can become, I was surprised that the three talks converged so powerfully on this point but, at the same time, that they were so sharply distinguished from one another. I saw the differences along cognitive, emotional, and behavioral lines.

Speaking for Buddhism, Wayne Muller viewed resilience as an "inner light," or Buddha-nature, which we come to know through a process of enlightenment exemplified and taught by the Buddha. Fred Taylor suggested that in Christian terms, resilience is emotional, the capacity to extend the self in love to others. And for Sybil Wolin, who spoke about Judaism, resilience emanates from the will and is expressed in action.

Perhaps the variations in these worldviews support the idea of individual schools of therapy. Certainly therapies have been classified in cognitive, emotional, and behavioral categories. However, I believe that the uniform respect for people's resilience described here across religions is far more essential than their distinctions. I hope that this perspective will transcend the boundaries between therapeutic schools and will be accepted as a fundamental premise in the field as a whole.

ACKNOWLEDGMENT

This chapter was originally presented at the annual meeting of the American Association for Marriage and Family Therapy, Toronto, Canada, October 19, 1996.

REFERENCES

Campbell, J., with Moyers, B. (1988). *The power of myth: Program I. The hero's adventure* [Video]. (Distributed by Mystic Fire Video, New York, and Doubleday, New York.)

Hertz, J. H. (Ed.). (1990). *The Pentateuch and Haftorahs.* London: Soncino Press.

Kamenetz, R. (1994). *The Jew in the lotus.* San Francisco: Harper.

Rosenblatt, N. H. (1995). *Wrestling with angels.* New York: Delacorte Press.

Wolin, S., & Wolin, S. J. (1995a). Morality in COA's: Revisiting the syndrome of over-responsibility. In S. Abbott (Ed.), *Children of alcoholics: Selected readings.* Rockville, MD: National Association for Children of Alcoholics.

Wolin, S., & Wolin, S. J. (1995b). Resilience among youth growing up in substance-abusing families. *Pediatric Clinics of North America, 42*(2), 415–429.

Wolin, S., & Wolin, S. J. (1997). Shifting paradigms: Taking a paradoxical approach. *Resiliency in Action, 2*(4), 23–28.

Wolin, S. J., & Wolin, S. (1993). *The resilient self: How survivors of troubled families rise above adversity.* New York: Villard Books.

CHAPTER 8

"Honor Thy Father and Thy Mother"

Intergenerational Spirituality and Jewish Tradition

MONA DeKOVEN FISHBANE

At the heart of the Jewish tradition, and at the center of the Ten Commandments, is the fifth commandment: "Honor your father and your mother, that your days may be long upon the land which the Lord your God gives you" (Exodus 20:12). According to rabbinic sources, this commandment belongs both to the first four commandments, which refer to acceptance of and obedience to God, and to the last five commandments, which deal with human relations. The fifth commandment is considered the link between divine and human realms.

This chapter will consider the command to honor parents within the context of the Jewish tradition. It will examine the nexus of values within which honoring parents is embedded: the values of tradition itself; of multigenerational continuity; of parents' obligations to pass on the tradition to their children; and of the role of the divine in relations between parents and children. Some of the laws and stories which exemplify the often difficult challenge of honoring mother and father will be explored. These traditions of filial piety and "family values" will be considered as they affect and are affected by the modern American context. Finally, broader implications for families and family therapy will be discussed, especially around intergenerational conflicts and reconciliation.

A DELICATE BALANCE

In setting out to explore classical Jewish wisdom around intergenerational connection and filial piety, I am aware that we confront these texts with modern sensibilities and concerns. Classical Judaism, like other world religions, has been traditionally patriarchal. The major voices and authors have been male, as has the imagery and language describing God. There are significant exceptions, especially in the mystical tradition; for example, the Shekhina is the feminine aspect of God, and refers to the divine indwelling on earth. Likewise, there have been some notable examples of women heroines and scholars in the classical texts. Modern feminists and liberal Jews have worked to reclaim the tradition for themselves, seeking and developing narratives about women in the Bible and postbiblical texts, and altering prayer language to a gender-neutral form. Perhaps most importantly, in recent years more and more women have taken on the central spiritual task in Judaism of study of sacred texts—an opportunity not generally available to women historically. This study affords both a way into the richness of the tradition and a way to achieve the authority and power that accrue to scholars in this religion. Within contemporary feminist Orthodox and liberal circles, women are attaining high levels of learning and scholarly and spiritual leadership.

Many of the classical texts cited in this chapter refer to fathers and sons as the prototypical intergenerational relationship, reflecting the patriarchal bias of the authors of these texts. I have chosen to cite these examples despite my discomfort with that bias, because I believe there is much spiritual value in these ancient voices. This tension between classical and modern sensibilities can be a source not only of discomfort, but also of creative integration. In my own language in this chapter, where possible I use gender-neutral or inclusive terms, referring for example to "parents" rather than "fathers," and "children" rather than "sons." However, when citing actual texts, I present them as written.

TRADITION AND NARRATIVE

Judaism is a religion of memory and narrative. The earliest and most central text, the Torah (the five books of Moses), tells of the formation of the ancient Israelite nation and its complex relationship with God. The high points of this narrative are the Exodus from Egypt and the Revelation at Mount Sinai, in which the Ten Commandments and, according to tradition, the entire Torah was given by God to Moses on behalf of the people. The Torah is the foundation text, the core of a rich and varied tradition which extends from the ancient period to the present. Interpretation and study are key spiritual activities in Judaism; almost nothing is more highly valued than sacred learning (which includes study of the Torah as well as the commentaries on it, such as the Talmud and Midrash).[1] The study of older narratives, as well as the reworking of older narratives into newer ones, allows the religion to evolve while staying attached to its roots. Through learning, prayer, and ritual, the emphasis on memory and on making present the past is reinforced constantly. The Torah is read in synagogue throughout the year, and each year at specific holidays the nodal historical events are celebrated.

Spirituality and study in the Jewish tradition are not solo tasks; Judaism is not a religion that generally encourages isolated spiritual quests. Rather, one's own journey takes place in the context of a fellowship of seekers, of worshippers, of students. Prayer is preferably conducted in a group, with a minimum of 10 worshippers. One is warned, "do not distance yourself from the community." Traditionally, study occurs with a partner, a *havruta*. The dialogue with ancient texts is conducted through a dialogue with one's fellow student, and with one's teacher. Study is a collaborative and relational process.[2]

In passing on the tradition, there is a double vision about one's relationship to past generations. The sages are constantly interpreting and adjudicating legal and moral issues; the religion evolves and responds to the demands of the present historical period. At the same time, there is a reverence for the past and for the greatness of past scholars. The rabbinic phrase "the generations have grown smaller" conveys a sense that earlier sages, closer to Sinai, had a greater wisdom; and that the current generation is lesser and must lean on the wisdom of the elders. This notion reinforces the connection with and respect for the past and for the great rabbis of earlier generations. It encourages a spiritual humility; one looks back as one moves forward.

MULTIGENERATIONAL CONTINUITY

The Jewish God is referred to in many ways. One of the most common epithets in the Bible is "the God of Abraham, Isaac, and Jacob."[3] The original covenant was made between God and Abraham, in which Abraham, in return for embracing this God, was promised descendents who would become the nation Israel, later known as the Jewish people. The nodal event of the covenant with the biblical patriarchs, then, is the promise of multigenerational continuity. Subsequently, the complicated relationship between God and the Israelites revolves around the inconstancy and infidelity of the people, and divine threats to destroy or cut off the people in response. This is accompanied by the contrasting promise of divine blessing—in the form of the flourishing of generations of descendents and of abundance in the land—if the people are faithful to God.

The survival of the nation and of one's family through descendents is a theme which echoes throughout the biblical narratives. There is a deep anxiety which surfaces around childlessness, around the prospect of one's name not being continued through one's children. Filial succession is another central motif, especially in the Genesis narratives. Sibling rivalry and hatred abound, as brothers vie for parental blessings (e.g., Isaac and

Ishmael; Jacob and Esau; Joseph and his brothers). Jacob's machinations to wrest both the birthright and the blessing of the firstborn from his brother Esau, and Jacob's deception of his father Isaac in the process, poignantly convey the intense struggles around multigenerational legacies and blessings in the Bible.

The identification of oneself multigenerationally, as the child of the parent, continues in the rabbinic period. In the Talmud and other classical texts, rabbis are identified by their familial line, for example, "Rabbi Joshua the son of Levi." Likewise, a rabbi will frequently locate himself in his spiritual lineage, by referring to his teacher: for example, "Rabbi Safra said on the authority of Rabbi Joshua the son of Hanania." In a world in which respect for parents and teachers is central, an individual's contribution to the rabbinic discussion is framed by the multigenerational context—both biological and spiritual—from which he or she speaks. Credit, respect, and even reverence for parents and teachers characterize the rabbinic discourse.

"AND YOU SHALL TEACH YOUR CHILDREN DILIGENTLY"

Multigenerational continuity is ensured in Judaism by the parent teaching the child. In the Bible, the parent is admonished: "And you shall teach [the laws] diligently to your children, and shall talk of them when you sit in your house, and when you walk on the way, and when you lie down, and when you rise up" (Deuteronomy 6:7). The teaching of Torah and its values is an ongoing, constant process; through modeling, through one's daily behavior, one is always teaching one's children.

The same chapter in Deuteronomy further instructs the parent that when the child asks, "What are these commandments?," the parent should respond, "We were slaves in Egypt . . . and God brought us out of Egypt . . . and God commanded us to do these laws, to revere God" (6:20–24). This parent–child dialogue is woven into the Passover Haggadah,[4] which is recited at the Seder. The Haggadah is a supreme moment of ritual retelling, of multigenerational questions and answers. The Haggadah poses the drama of four sons, each of whom is facing the tradition in a different way. The parent is told to answer the child in a manner appropriate to the child's nature and capacity; each child is responded to differently. The wise child seeks to understand; the evil child distances himself from the community and the tradition; the simple child says, "What's this?"; and the child who can't even formulate a question also merits a response: "You shall open him up," so he will be ready to ask. The yearly drama of the Passover Seder is an invitation to ask, discuss, and wrestle with the tradition. The curiosity of the child is to be welcomed; and the dynamics of questioning and teaching are cherished.

The value of passing on the tradition and of intergenerational dialogue is reiterated in the Talmud: "Whoever teaches his son Torah, Scripture ascribes merit to him as if he had taught him, his son, and his son's son until the end of the all the generations!" (BT, *Kiddushin*, 30a).[5] Embedded in this statement is the understanding that passing on the tradition happens one generation at a time, yet affects all subsequent generations. The same Talmudic discussion goes on to ask whether a grandfather is required to teach Torah to his grandson. Although it is not obligatory, it does result in great reward: "Rabbi Joshua the son of Levi said: 'Whoever teaches his grandson Torah, Scripture attributes merit to him as if he had received the Torah [directly] from Mt. Sinai.' " In this formulation the reward for passing on the tradition to the next generations is that one is in direct contact with prior generations; specifically, one is present at Sinai. The Talmud goes on to explain that other rabbis, upon hearing this teaching, made sure that they taught their grandchildren or brought them to school before they themselves would taste any meat at breakfast! This anecdote vividly illustrates how personally the scholars were affected by each other and by the interpretation of text.

THE DIVINE PRESENCE WITHIN THE FAMILY

The parent's obligation to teach the child is mirrored by the child's obligation to honor the parent, to which we turn in a moment. The tradition connects honoring one's parent with honoring God. The respect of parents is spiritualized, linked both to maintaining the tradition and revering God:

> When man recognizes his creatureliness before his parent, he recognizes the ultimate creatureliness, and the ultimate Creator, as well. For by acknowledging parents, man admits that he is not the source of his own being. . . . The issue of origins, then, is paradigmatic of the choice between radical self-centeredness and acknowledgment of the Other. (Blidstein, 1975, p. 5)

This acknowledgment of origins, of creatureliness, stands in marked contrast with the American ideal of the "self-made" individual. There is no "self-made" person in traditional Judaism; the individual is urged daily to acknowledge that he or she is a part of the created world.

A remarkable passage in the Talmud describes God as a partner with the parents in the creation of a person, and links honoring parents with divine presence in the family: "There are three partners in a person: The Holy One, blessed be He, the father, and the mother. When a person honors father and mother, the Holy One, blessed be He, says, 'I ascribe [merit] to them as though I had dwelt among them and they had honored Me' " (BT, *Kiddushin*, 30b). The merit does not go just to the individual person who honors parents; it goes to the person *and* their parents. It is a relational merit. The Hebrew word rendered here "among them" can also be translated "between them." We can read this in Buber's (1965) sense of the "between," the relational space between persons when they are in genuine dialogue—in the realm of I and Thou. Thus, when a person honors parents, a "between" is created which is sacred; a space in which the divine presence dwells.

Reciprocally, when a person dishonors parents, we are told that the divine presence shrinks from dwelling among them. The Talmud comments: "When a person causes pain to mother or father, the Holy One, Blessed be He says, 'It is good that I am not dwelling among them; for if I had dwelled among them, I would be pained' " (BT, *Kiddushin*, 31a).

"HONOR YOUR FATHER AND YOUR MOTHER"

The Jewish tradition expands on the fifth commandment through a web of norms and instructive narratives. Honoring parents is defined in concrete, and rather terse, terms in the Talmud; it entails giving parents "food and drink, clothing and covering, leading them in and out" (BT, *Kiddushin*, 31b). Honor is behavioral and service oriented; it is related to the need of the parent. Honoring parents is required of both sons and daughters. In addition to honor, reverence is also commanded in the Bible (Leviticus 19:3). The Talmud defines reverence of parents in somewhat more psychological terms. Thus reverence entails not standing or sitting in the parents' place, not contradicting their words, and not shaming them (BT, *Kiddushin*, 31b).

Beyond these pithy definitions, the challenges and at times the difficulties involved in honoring parents are fleshed out in the Talmud through exemplary narratives, anecdotes of adult children acting respectfully toward their elderly parents.[6] As elsewhere in traditional Jewish texts, the anecdotes center around men, and the rabbis having the discussions were male. However, daughters as well as sons are obligated to honor parents. Some flexibility is accorded married daughters with children, since it is assumed that their care for their family of procreation may take precedence over care for parents. The stories quoted here, while addressing sons, generally include expectations of daughters as well. Likewise, both mother and father are to be honored and revered.

In the Talmudic narratives around honoring parents, "the son or daughter does not, ideally, respond to demands made of him or her but is responsible for a pattern and process of *kibbud* [honoring parents]. The temper is active, not submissive" (Blidstein, 1975, p. xii). The narratives exemplify the spiritual centeredness of the son or daughter in attempting to relate respectfully to the parent, even under difficult circumstances.

One of the most celebrated stories of honoring parents concerns a pagan, Dama from Ashkelon:

> They asked Rabbi Eliezer: "How far must one go in honoring father and mother?" He told them: "Go and look what a certain gentile did for his father in Ashkelon, and Dama the son of Netina is his name. The sages sought from him precious stones for the priestly breastplate, at a price of sixty thousand . . . and the key [to the jewelbox] was under his father's pillow, and he did not disturb him. The next year the Holy One Blessed be He gave him his reward; a red heifer was born in his flock.[7] The sages of Israel came to him [to buy the heifer] and he said to them: 'I know that if I ask of you all the wealth in the world you would give it to me; but I don't want from you anything more than the money that I lost in honoring my father.' " (BT, *Kiddushin*, 31a)

The rabbis considered Dama's behavior exemplary of the "mitzvah" (commandment; good deed) to honor parents. Dama's comportment is all the more laudatory since he did not seek personal gain as a reward. It is instructive to contrast this story with a very different, modern narrative, from Robert Bly's *Iron John* (1990). In that story, a boy in the process of attaining manhood has to steal a key from under his mother's pillow! The core values underlying these two very different stories result in different "morals of the stories." In the Talmudic story, it is a virtue to restrain one's own desire for gain for the sake of honoring the father. In Bly's tale, the boy's freedom and masculinity depend on his stealing something valuable from his mother. It presumes a rejection of the mother as part of the individual's journey. Such a developmental trajectory could not be further from the traditional Jewish view.

Another well-known tale of filial care in the Talmud is told of Rabbi Avimi. His father, Rabbi Abbahu, says that Avimi has fulfilled the commandment of honoring parents. Abbahu explains that Avimi (a grown man with five adult sons) would himself run to open the door when Abbahu would come to visit. Abbahu relates that one day he asked his son Avimi for a drink of water. When Avimi returned with the water, his father had fallen asleep. Avimi bent and stood over his father with the water until Abbahu awoke. As his reward for such filial piety, Avimi was given insight into a biblical verse which until then had eluded him. A key point in this story is that Avimi not only behaved with respect toward his father, he did so without resentment. This aspect of honoring parents—taking care of them with tenderness and without anger or resentment—is important in the Talmudic view.

Rabbi Avimi is presented as a person with a keen understanding of the complex motivations involved in caring for parents. He offers the following somewhat puzzling observation: "A person can feed his father pheasant, and still be driven from the world [in punishment]; whereas another can make [his father] grind at a mill, and this brings him to the life of the world to come [the ultimate reward]." This pithy saying is unpacked by other commentators, who imagine the following scenario. In the first situation, the father eating the pheasant asks his son where he obtained such a delicacy; the son answers, "Old man, what's it to you? Just chew and eat, like dogs chew and eat." In the second case, imagine the commentators, the son puts his father to work grinding at the mill because the father has been called to serve the king. The son, sensing that this royal service will entail difficult and long labor, offers to go in his father's stead, and asks his father to mind his mill in his place. The son thus protects his father from greater hardship (BT, *Kiddushin*, 31a). The value expressed in these stories is that honoring parents is not simply a matter of proper behavior—the manner in which the honoring is done is just as important. Caring for parents in a derogatory, resentful manner does not, in this view, fulfill the fifth commandment.

Honor and service to parents are to be done because they are commanded, and for the welfare of the parent; they are not to be performed to puff up the ego of the pious child. The Talmud tells a story with an edge in this regard: "Rabbi Tarfon had a mother for whom, whenever she wanted to climb up to her bed, he would bend down to let her climb up [upon him]. And when she wanted to get down, she would step down upon him. He came and boasted of this in the house of study. They said to him: 'You still haven't attained half of the fulfillment of honoring parents' " (BT, *Kiddushin*, 31b). Rabbi Tarfon's behavior with his mother was exemplary, but his boasting was considered unseemly and detracted from his filial piety.

While the tradition makes it clear that love of parents cannot be legislated, the stories brought as examples of honoring parents are often infused with a sense of tenderness and care as well as respect. One of the sweetest expressions of this is very brief: "When Rabbi Joseph heard his mother's footsteps, he would say, 'Let me rise before the Shekhina [the Divine Presence] who is coming' " (BT, *Kiddushin*, 31b).

The principle of not shaming a parent is central to filial piety. The Talmud relates: "If a person's father [inadvertently] transgresses a law of the Torah, [the son] should not say to him, 'Father, you have transgressed a law of the Torah.' Rather, he should say to him, 'Father, thus it is written in the Torah' " (BT, *Kiddushin*, 32a). His correction of his father is to be indirect and gentle.

At times the challenge not to shame parents is sorely tested. Several episodes are related in which parents act irrationally and even physically attack their adult child. The child, while setting appropriate limits, is not to respond in kind, and is not to shame the parent in turn. "They asked Rabbi Eliezer, 'How far does honoring father and mother go?' He said to them, 'That [the father] would throw his wallet into the sea, and [the son] does not shame him' " (BT, *Kiddushin*, 32a). A more extreme case is told of Dama from Ashkelon: "One time he was wearing a golden robe and was sitting with the nobles of Rome; and his mother came and tore it off him, and hit him on the head, and spit in his face. Yet he did not shame her" (BT, *Kiddushin*, 31a).

Even when a child sets limits on disturbed parental behavior, this is to be done gently and without rage or humiliation of the parent. These vignettes convey the complex and at times painful choices adult children may face in dealing with parents. Balancing self-regard and self-protection with care and respect for parents is especially difficult when parents are unstable or abusive.

The tradition makes clear that honoring parents is not equivalent to blindly obeying arbitrary or outrageous parental requests. If the parent is frivolous and demands obedience in matters not based on the parent's genuine need, or if the parent is mentally disturbed and inappropriate in a request, the child is not required to obey the parent. Indeed, Moses Maimonides, the influential medieval philosopher and codifier of Jewish law, wrote:

> A person whose father or mother is mentally disturbed should try to behave with them as their mental state requires, until God takes pity on them. And if it is impossible for him to tolerate because they are so extremely mentally disturbed, he should be allowed to leave and to have other people take care of [his parents] as they require. (*Hilkhot Mamrim*, 6:10)

Here Maimonides excuses the adult child from the obligation to provide direct service to parents; the concern for the child's welfare in this case takes precedence. The child is not free to leave the parents unattended, however; he or she must find substitute caregivers for the parents.

The spiritual and psychological self-control evidenced in the Talmudic anecdotes around honoring parents is remarkable. Indeed, these examples of filial self-restraint go much further than we would expect of an adult child in our culture. But honoring parents in classical Judaism is not limitless either. There are limiting conditions or competing circumstances which mitigate the obligation to honor parents even within that culture so devoted to filial piety. The limit cases reveal conflicting values, some of which override filial service and care.

One of the values which overrides honoring parents is honoring the Torah. Thus, if a parent demands that the adult child act in a manner which violates religious law or encourages wicked behavior, the child is to disobey the parent. Even here, however, the parent is not to be shamed or unnecessarily rejected; disobedience should not result in discarding the misguided parent.

The adult child's spiritual and scholarly pursuits may take precedence over a parent's desire. Thus, study of Torah, choosing a teacher, finding one's own place of worship, or going to Israel all may override the parent's plan for the child. Religious study is so central a value that honoring one's teacher or spiritual master can take precedence over honoring one's parents. The tradition is careful to point out, however, that honoring teacher over parent does not absolve the adult child from filial piety altogether; he or she is still obliged to care for the parent. But care for the teacher comes first if there is a conflict.

The rabbis were attentive as well to the complex family dynamics around marital choice. There was disagreement among rabbis over the centuries as to whether persons could choose their own mates, especially if the parents objected. One view held that the child should bend to the parent's will, that marriage required parental consent. Indeed, arranged marriages were common in traditional Jewish families. Other rabbis held that love and marital choice were divinely inspired, that an individual could follow this divine command of the heart. If the parents objected to the match—assuming the proposed spouse was a decent individual—the child was allowed to disobey the parent. This view emphasized the spiritual dimension in love and marriage, seeing little virtue in an obedient, but unhappily married, son or daughter.

The cost to the adult child in caring for parents is addressed at the literal level: who should pay for the parents' care, the child or the parents? There is considerable controversy over this issue. But even those who rule that the parent pays contend that if the parent is destitute, the child must provide for him or her economically out of a sense of general charity; in this sense, charity begins at home. Thus in either case the child must ensure that the parent is sheltered and clothed, but the extent of filial financial obligation is unresolved. There is, however, a general social and ethical distaste expressed for the adult child who does not adequately care for the parent financially within the child's means.

The manner in which the Talmud addresses honoring parents in the above cases conveys the complexity involved in intergenerational relationships. Rather than simply preaching the value of fulfilling the fifth commandment, the rabbis discuss difficult questions and cases which exemplify the daily dilemmas and tensions inherent in parent–child interactions. Loyalty conflicts between the child's personal commitments and needs on the one hand, and obligations to care for parents on the other, are conveyed in these anecdotes. Fulfilling the fifth commandment is no simple task in the rabbinic view; it is composed of many moments of confusion and choice.

With all the difficulties involved, in the traditional Jewish perspective one is obligated to honor parents whether or not they have been "good parents." The obligation is not based on their merit or on the spontaneous love of the adult child for the parent. Furthermore, Jewish law addresses the obligations and responsibilities of the individual rather than the rights of the individual. In this regard it is radically different from the American system, which is fundamentally based on the notion of individual rights and freedoms. Filial piety in the Jewish tradition is considered a debt of the adult child, not an optional choice. In this regard the classical Jewish view is remarkably close to the contextual theory of Ivan

Boszormenyi-Nagy and his colleagues (Boszormenyi-Nagy, Grunebaum, & Ulrich, 1991; Boszormenyi-Nagy & Ulrich, 1981). In the contextual view, filial loyalty and filial debt are facts of life; if one does not find a way to care for and express positive loyalty to parents, one may become mired in invisible loyalty—negative and self-destructive ties to parents (Boszormenyi-Nagy & Spark, 1973). This calls to mind the reward stated in the fifth commandment for honoring parents: "that your days may be long upon the land"; and in the version given in Deuteronomy (5:16): "that it may go well for you." In both the Jewish and the contextual belief systems, honoring parents is inextricably linked with consequences for one's own life.

MODERN DILEMMAS: A CLASH OF BELIEF SYSTEMS

The values discussed above reflect the highly regulated worldview of traditional Judaism. To many modern American Jews, much of the material discussed in this chapter may seem foreign. The values and beliefs presented rest on a complex set of assumptions that are no longer widely shared among non-Orthodox Jews. Orthodox Jews adhere to the world of the rabbis, of authority, of law. The Talmud and subsequent rabbinic writings serve as their guide in their daily lives. Non-Orthodox Jews approach the tradition more optionally, as a focus of study or inspiration. In liberal Jewish American circles, creativity and personal authenticity tend to be more highly valued than strict adherence to religious law.

Furthermore, the notion of the person in traditional Judaism is very different from the notion of the person in the modern American world. The United States is the land of individualism, of freedom of choice. The traditional Jewish view of the person is much more relational, tied to family, community, and God. Whereas the trajectory of development in the American context is to become more and more independent (a life course informed by the Freudian story of development), within traditional Judaism personal development is seen in terms of learning, maintaining values, and teaching future generations. In the traditional Jewish world, the individual is accountable to the past and the future; and, in the present, to the community. There is no notion of individuality separated from all these entanglements. Obligation and duty are highly prized. Personal happiness is a by-product of an ethical life, not a goal in itself. Intergenerational loyalty and respect for parents are, as we have seen, core values. By contrast, popular psychology in the United States has made relationships with parents optional; growing away from or beyond parents is an acceptable normative development in this culture. In this view the good of the individual is paramount, and the person is accountable primarily to self (Bellah, Madsen, Sullivan, Swidler, & Tipton, 1985).

Many modern American Jews, raised on the Freudian and American narratives, are caught between two worlds. They have imbibed the ethic of the individual; yet they may also be recipients of familial messages of obligation, guilt, and multigenerational accountability. These messages, characterized—and caricatured—by the guilt-inducing Jewish mother, can be seen as echoes of the Jewish belief system, attenuated and decontextualized from the larger Jewish tradition. Jewish parents who implore their adult children to marry Jews or produce grandchildren to bring *nachas* (Yiddish: "joy") to the parents, seem strangely out of place and are pathologized in the American context. Yet such parental claims are consonant with and natural within a more traditional Jewish world. The American Jewish children receiving such messages may assume that their parents are being neurotic, and may pull even farther away to distance themselves from such intrusive messages.

The clash of values is especially poignant around the issue of intermarriage. There is a deep concern within the American Jewish community, related to the statistic from the 1990 National Jewish Population Survey indicating an average recent intermarriage rate among American Jews of over 50% (Kosmin et al., 1990). This statistic, coupled with the companion finding that most of these intermarriages result in children not being raised as Jews, raises the prospect of the attenuation of non-Orthodox Jewry in America. In light of both the value of multigenerational continuity within Judaism and the legacy of the Holocaust, the prospect of the Jewish people shrinking or disappearing strikes at the heart of the community. Intermarrying children are often puzzled by their parents' negative responses to their choice, especially if the household was not particularly religious. From the young adult's perspective, individual happiness is central, and their parents' reaction may seem excessive and intrusive. To outside observers, a Jewish family's response to the specter of intermarriage may appear intolerant; it may be seen as violating multicultural open-mindedness. Families struggling with this dilemma are caught between two competing value systems: Jewish continuity on the one hand, and American self-determination and open-mindedness on the other.

This clash of belief systems is at the heart of a serious rift within the Jewish community. In a manner unprecedented in modern history, the assumptions and practices of Orthodox and liberal Jews are so alienated from each other that some see a fracturing into two fundamentally separate religious communities. The underlying difference around adherence to rabbinic law which has characterized Orthodox Jews on the one hand, and Conservative and Reform Jews on the other, is now painfully exacerbated by the specter of intermarriage. Orthodox Jews are unable to tolerate their children marrying liberal Jews who, because of intermarriage, may not be regarded as Jewish according to traditional rabbinic law. Dialogue has broken down between the two groups, and the debate is characterized by bitterness and mutual rejection. While several religious splits have occurred previously in Jewish history, the current crisis is deeply troubling to many who value the capacity to maintain dialogue and to work creatively with difference.

While Jews struggle with these competing belief systems in this unique historical context, the tension between individual choice and intergenerational loyalty is by no means simply a Jewish dilemma; it is a common phenomenon within families of many backgrounds. Indeed, the fifth commandment is a shared foundation text for Christianity and Islam as well as Judaism. Finding a balance between filial piety and personal autonomy is a challenge in many different cultures.

CLINICAL IMPLICATIONS: INTERGENERATIONAL CONFLICT, LOYALTY, AND RECONCILIATION

Honoring one's mother and father is often a confusing prospect in contemporary life. Ethnic subcultures vary in the emphasis placed on maintaining intergenerational connection. For many in the dominant culture in the United States, filial piety is no longer integrated into a coherent worldview in which the self is defined in its intergenerational context. The values of loyalty, obligation, and embeddedness in family and community that characterize many traditional cultures do not easily hold in modern American life. These intergenerational values are often at odds with the more self-focused orientation prevalent in our culture, and increasingly in other parts of the world. They are also at odds with some therapeutic approaches which encourage personal liberation from the claims of the family of origin.

The values of honoring parents and maintaining a calm, nonreactive position with one's family of origin are, however, quite consonant with intergenerational family therapy theory. Working toward intergenerational connection and reconciliation is central to multigenerational family therapy (Boszormenyi-Nagy et al., 1991; Bowen, 1978; Carter & McGoldrick, 1989; Framo, 1976; Grunebaum, 1987; Hargrave, 1994; Karpel, 1986; Lerner, 1985; McGoldrick, 1995; Roberto, 1992; Rolland, 1994; Walsh, 1998). The contextual approach of Boszormeny-Nagy and colleagues (1991) most explicitly deals with filial obligation and family loyalty, emphasizing honoring parents as a central task of adult development. The language of obligation and debt which characterizes contextual theory comes closest to the traditional Jewish values discussed in this chapter. While other intergenerational approaches do not use the language of obligation, they still carry the implicit assumption that the individual is not free to cast away or cut off from the family of origin without paying an enormous personal price. Differentiation of self is, ultimately, a relational process, forged in ongoing interactions with family as well as other relational partners. It is not a solo journey. The self is seen in its relational, multigenerational context.

The relational view of the self implicit in intergenerational family theory is emerging in other theories as well. In the fields of human development, gender studies, and therapy a relational view of the person is being formulated, challenging the emphasis on individualism which has dominated psychology as well as American culture in general. These relational theories highlight interpersonal embeddedness and interdependence throughout the life cycle (Galatzer-Levy & Cohler, 1993; Jordan, Kaplan, Miller, Stiver, & Surrey, 1991; Mirkin, 1994; Offer & Sabshin, 1984; Stern, 1985; Stolorow & Atwood, 1992). This shift to the relational dovetails with many of the classical Jewish values discussed above. The traditional Jewish view of the person as embedded in relationships and accountability to others, the emphasis on filial loyalty and obligations, and the relational approach to study with a companion through the *havruta* system, all resonate with the more relational narrative of the self emerging in current developmental theories.

A relational/intergenerational view informs my own clinical perspective. In working with couples or adults and their families of origin, I see the negative impact of the individualistic, competitive story on their lives. Inviting clients to consider their dilemmas from a relational perspective, and helping them create a dialogue with their significant others, is at the heart of my work (Fishbane, 1997a, 1998). In particular, informed by intergenerational theory, I try to help clients balance filial loyalty with personal authenticity, boundaries, and self-respect—to honor their parents while still respecting themselves. In this view, honoring parents does not imply giving up self; rather, it entails appreciating personal autonomy within its relational context. This may include helping a client find ways to respectfully invite parents to a more mutually caring relationship (Fishbane, 1997b). When this is done without blame or criticism, parents are often enthusiastic in response, feeling connected with their adult child and feeling respected at the same time. In this context, it is much easier for the adult child to set limits, make requests, and be authentic in the relationship.

The challenge for the client is to have a voice and hold his or her own position while staying connected with parents (Carter, 1996; Lerner, 1985; McGoldrick, 1995). Holding one's own intergenerationally—balancing autonomy with loyalty and respect for parents—is a complex relational skill. It includes learning to make a relational claim in a way that honors both self and other. Parents are often able to respond with a reciprocal respect when approached in this manner. As this process unfolds, respect tends to beget respect, generating a "virtuous" rather than a vicious cycle between the generations. If the parent is unable to respond positively, the adult child has at least acted with integrity and generosity and, as in the above examples from the Talmud, has not responded to the parent with rage or humiliation. I find, with Boszormenyi-Nagy and Spark (1973), that when an individual has found a way to be constructively loyal to his or her parents and is not stuck in blame or resentment with them, that person may be freer to live his or her own life without carrying burdens of resentment into other relationships.

The following clinical example illustrates this approach:[8]

> Diana, a single woman in her 30s, comes to therapy because she is perennially disappointed in her relationships with both men and women. She describes a pattern in which she overaccomodates to others, becoming resentful and articulating her needs only when she is at the boiling point. As we explore her family of origin, she tells me that she is chronically angry with her widowed mother, feeling controlled and guilt-tripped by her. Before her father died in Diana's adolescence, the mother was disappointed in her relationship with her husband and looked to Diana, her only child, to meet her needs. After his death Diana felt even more burdened by her mother's sadness.
>
> As a child, Diana complied and tried to please her mother; as an adult, she is so resentful over this pattern that she has contemplated a cutoff with her mother. Diana holds back a great deal from her mother, feeling she will be endangered if she doesn't protect herself from maternal expectations with massive walls. She tells me, "I can't be a daughter the way my mother wants me to be; therefore I can't be my mother's daughter at all." Diana stakes her mental health on not being her mother's daughter as she believes her mother defines it, and she sees no alternative other than stepping out of relation with her mother altogether. As Diana sees it, she has a choice: She can either honor her mother, by doing exactly what her mother wants, thus giving up self; or she can honor herself, by distancing from and dismissing her mother. I suggest to Diana that she might find a way to honor her mother while honoring herself. I ask her, "How do *you* want to be your mother's daughter? What kind of daughter do you want to be?" Diana considers how she might honor her mother while staying authentic in the relationship and sensitive to her own needs. We discuss ways she can approach her mother that would facilitate dialogue and mutual respect.
>
> Diana's mother, Sarah, joins us for a session. She shares with her daughter for the first time stories of her own father's alcoholic rages, and of her mother's depression and unavailability. Sarah had determined that when she became a mother, she would never replicate the abuse and abandonment she experienced as a child. She would devote herself totally to her daughter. Furthermore, she had decided not to tell her young daughter about her own childhood, in order to protect Diana from experiencing Sarah's pain. While raising her daughter, Sarah had felt isolated; she was disappointed in her husband, who was nonabusive but also noninvolved. Following the societal dictates of the times, she stayed home and gave herself full-time to Diana, living through Diana's successes and seeking the closeness she craved in her daughter.

As Diana hears her mother's story, she softens. Where before she had seen only her mother's pathology and demands, now she sees her mother's pain and her attempts to protect and care for Diana. In addition to appreciating Sarah's experience, Diana learns to articulate her own experience to her mother in a nonaccusatory, connected manner. She shares with Sarah her sense of feeling guilty and confused at times in the relationship. Diana gradually finds a way to balance honoring her mother and honoring herself. As she experiments with this "mutual honoring" with her mother, Diana is pleased with the results. Her mother is less defensive as she senses Diana rejecting her less. When she experiences her mother as controlling or guilt-tripping, Diana is now able to stay centered. Diana responds to her mother firmly yet respectfully, giving clear feedback and setting limits in a nondefensive manner. They develop a shared commitment to both conveying their experience in the relationship. Thus when Diana tells her mother she feels controlled or guilt-tripped, Sarah no longer feels like the enemy; she is part of their joint project to have a better relationship. They even develop some humor around their old tendencies when they emerge.

In reevaluating her view of her mother, Diana allows herself to feel appreciation of her mother's strengths and gratitude for all her mother has done for her. She finds ways to express this appreciation to her mother directly. Diana's ability to feel and express this gratitude reflects her growing capacity to honor her mother and the relationship. Sarah, concerned with her own worth and the meaning of her life as she ages, is deeply moved by Diana's acknowledgment of her strengths as a mother. Diana's warmth is met with a reciprocal warmth and ease on Sarah's part. It is important to note that Diana is not simply reverting to her childhood role of serving her mother's needs. Rather, she is able to be aware of her mother as a whole person, with strengths as well as flaws.

Diana considers ways she can care for her mother as she ages without feeling overburdened, and examines her old reactivity around Sarah's complaints. Diana struggles with the balance of caring for her mother and respecting her own needs and boundaries. Perhaps most importantly, as Diana confronts these moments of choice with her mother, she no longer feels resentful and victimized in the process. Diana begins to see honoring as a positive opportunity, not just a burden. She talks with excitement of a plan to organize a celebration of her mother's 70th birthday.

In this work, Diana has achieved a spiritual centeredness; she is no longer dominated by resentment and suspicion of her mother. Diana's spiritual focus and her ability to honor her mother have ramifications beyond their relationship. Diana finds that she has more flexibility and choice in her other relationships as well; she feels less caught in her old pattern of either overaccomodating or asserting her needs angrily. She finds that "mutual honoring" works for her more generally in her relational life.

There are clinical situations in which the parent is not as responsive as Diana's mother, in which the irritable or even abusive behavior of the parent is not affected by the adult child's attempt at "mutual honoring." In such cases, it is still in the interest of the child to maintain a nonreactive, respectful stance with the parent even while setting firm limits and protecting the self from abusive or unsafe interactions. Even if abusive parental behavior requires limited contact, this need not result in a cutoff or in chronically angry reactivity in the adult child. As contextual theorists have suggested, when the adult child carries a burden of resentment and victimization, that individual is likely to victimize others through the "revolving slate of vindictive behavior" (Boszormenyi-Nagy & Ulrich, 1981, p. 167), or to assume a lifelong role as victim. Maintaining a nonreactive position with the parent, and not becoming abusive in kind, contributes to the adult child's own well-being, and to the well-being of subsequent generations.

Respecting parents in this view—as in the rabbinic view—is not contingent on whether the parent is a "good parent"; rather, it is a position that the adult child adopts out of his or her own personal and spiritual centeredness. Such a filial position is characterized by differentiation of self (Bowen, 1978); the child is not a victim of the parent, but rather is the author of his or her own behavior. Clients experience such a position as empowering, and they report a sense of freedom and relief when they are able to resist getting hooked in reactivity with their parents. This is a relational and spiritual empowerment. The adult child is not caught up in "power over" thinking with parents—thinking in which either the parent prevails or the child prevails. Rather, the child adopts a "power to" or "power with" position (Goodrich, 1991; Surrey, 1991), maintaining a focus and a clarity of purpose in the context of generosity and respect for the parent.

In the "power over" mode, the adult child is stuck in a *hierarchical* relationship with the parent. Shifting to a "power with" mode allows for the development of a *generational* view of the parent–child relationship. Whereas in the hierarchical view the parent has power over the child, which the child is likely to resist, in a generational view the parent is seen in terms of his or her own life journey. The parent who thus emerges is a three-dimensional person, and is not perceived only as a good or bad parent. This process allows for the "Thou" (Buber, 1970) of the parent to be present to the child; the adult child is then in a better position to honor parents as they are, flaws and all. Williamson (1991) proposes that shifting from a hierarchical relationship with parents in adulthood involves terminating the special parent–child relationship of obligation. By contrast, the shift I describe here affirms a stance of ongoing filial loyalty and care. The transformation from a hierarchical to a generational relationship with parents is characterized by greater differentiation, thoughtfulness, and choice on the part of the adult child. Yet it is still a unique relationship; the adult continues to be the parent's child, even as the relationship continuously evolves.

The shift to a generational view of parents may entail some grieving, as the child lets go of the project of shaping parents up and lets go of some of the disappointments and hopes of the past (Framo, 1976). On the other side of this sadness, clients often report a sense of peace. In acknowledging and accepting parents as they are today, the adult child can "wake from the spell of childhood" (Fishbane, 1998) and become an equal partner in the process of intergenerational healing. This is facilitated when the adult child focuses on changing his or her own position in the relationship rather than on changing the parent (Bowen, 1978; Lerner, 1985). A clinical paradox often emerges in this process. As the child stops trying to change the parent, the parent indeed often changes. This can be seen as an artifact of the shift in the parent–child relationship away from adversarial, mutually mistrustful, "power over" interactions to a more collaborative, relaxed "power with" tone. When the adult child genuinely gives up the project of changing the parent and becomes more accepting and respectful of that parent, the parent often feels freer to respond generously as well.

CONTINUING THE NARRATIVE: PERSONAL REFLECTIONS

Engaging with the layers of tradition and contemporary challenges around honoring parents has personal resonance for me as a clinician, as a daughter, and as a Jew. As a therapist, I have witnessed the profound shifts clients often experience when they find a way to balance honoring parents with respecting self, and are relieved of burdens of resentment and victimization. As I see it, the consequence of the fifth commandment, "that it may go well with you," is not just a moral reward, but flows from the very nature of being one-who-honors, rather than one-who-does-not-honor. In the intergenerational view, and in the traditional Jewish view honoring parents benefits the adult child as much as it benefits the parents.

Writing this chapter has also afforded me an opportunity to articulate my own relationship to the Jewish tradition and to contemporary tensions within the Jewish community. Much of the current struggle between Orthodox and liberal Jews revolves around the balance between being rooted in tradition and being open to change. The balance is delicate; if we give birth to ourselves, invent ourselves, by cutting ourselves off from our heritage, from our sources, we die spiritually because our life breath is cut off. On the other hand, if we just repeat the old text, if we are constrained by it without reinvigorating it with new interpretations and creativity, we die spiritually by suffocation. In recent years feminists have brought new challenges and life to traditional Judaism, addressing the tradition both from within the Orthodox world and from more liberal positions (Fishman, 1993). I believe these voices are crucial for the survival and enrichment of the religion. These voices create new texts and new possibilities. For the multigenerational spiritual transmission process to continue, it must be renewed by the voices of each generation. I personally seek ways to integrate my commitment to egalitarian principles on the one hand, and my deep respect for the spiritual richness of my religious tradition on the other. I walk a fine line, honoring and challenging the tradition at the same time.

The topic of this chapter is very close to home for me. As an adult I have worked at honoring my own parents, my mother-in-law, and other elders. My parents, now in their 80s, are moving to live closer to me, and they sometimes turn to me for guidance and support. It is both a pleasure and a personal challenge to perform the mitzvah of the fifth commandment. I work at being calm, patient, and respectful with my parents; I do not always succeed. Studying the classical texts and preparing for this chapter have helped me think through my own journey toward filial piety. Balancing personal needs and parental needs will be an ongoing, daily challenge. My young adult sons have watched me as I try to take care of my elders. They have told me they hope to do the same for me and their father as we age. I am grateful to be embedded in this complex multigenerational story.

In the open culture in which we live, with values in flux, I find the narratives of the Jewish tradition around intergenerational connection to be resources of wisdom. Although the contemporary context is very different from that in which the laws and expectations around honoring parents evolved, many of the principles and difficulties involved in the fifth commandment remain relevant today. As we wrestle with intergenerational tensions and loyalty conflicts, it is helpful to consider how prior generations and traditions have dealt with these issues. Engaging in a cultural dialogue with the past can, I believe, inform our present and future.

NOTES

1. The Talmud, a central text in Judaism, is a collection of legal and ethical discussions of the rabbis during the first five centuries of the common era. Classical Midrash consists of ancient and early medieval rabbinic Bible interpretation, found in various collections and volumes. Midrash continues as an ongoing process of textual interpretation and creative narrativization into the present.
2. My *havruta*, my study partner for this chapter, has been my husband, Michael Fishbane. I am grateful to him for our text study together, as well as our many dialogues on the topic. I am indebted as well to Marsha P. Mirkin and Don-David Lusterman for their feedback on an earlier draft of this chapter.
3. Some contemporary worshippers add "the God of Sarah, Rebekah, Rachel, and Leah," the four matriarchs.
4. The Haggadah is a rabbinic text from the early medieval period.

5. The citations from the Talmud are from a traditional edition of the Babylonian Talmud (BT) redacted in the 5th century C.E. All translations are my own.
6. These stories were collected and included in *Kiddushin*, a section of the BT that deals with issues of marriage and the family. This section has become a central part of traditional Jewish learning and has been excerpted as well in subsequent ethical guidebooks. Thus the laws of filial piety have become part of the guiding norms of the culture.
7. A pure red heifer was especially valuable in ancient Israel, as its ashes were used in ritual practices in the Temple.
8. The case is a composite, reflecting a relational/intergenerational approach to clinical dilemmas in honoring parents.

REFERENCES

Babylonian Talmud (BT). Tractate *Kiddushin*, traditional ed. (First redacted 5th century C.E.)

Bellah, R. N., Madsen, R., Sullivan, W. M., Swidler, A., & Tipton, S. M. (1985). *Habits of the heart: Individualism and commitment in American life.* Berkeley: University of California Press.

Blidstein, G. (1975). *Honor thy father and mother: Filial responsibility in Jewish law and ethics.* New York: Ktav.

Bly, R. (1990). *Iron John.* Reading, MA: Addison-Wesley.

Boszormenyi-Nagy, I., Grunebaum, J., & Ulrich, D. (1991). Contextual family therapy. In A. S. Gurman & D. P. Kniskern (Eds.), *Handbook of family therapy* (Vol. 2). New York: Brunner/Mazel.

Boszormenyi-Nagy, I., & Spark, G. (1973). *Invisible loyalties: Reciprocity in intergenerational family therapy.* New York: Harper & Row.

Boszormenyi-Nagy, I., & Ulrich, D. (1981). Contextual family therapy. In A. S. Gurman & D. P. Kniskern (Eds.), *Handbook of family therapy* (Vol. 1). New York: Brunner/Mazel.

Bowen, M. (1978). *Family therapy in clinical practice.* New York: Aronson.

Buber, M. (1965). *The knowledge of man.* New York: Harper & Row.

Buber, M. (1970). *I and thou* (Kaufmann translation). New York: Charles Scribner's Sons. (Ger. 1921)

Carter, B. (1996). *Love, honor, and negotiate: Making your marriage work.* New York: Pocket Books.

Carter, B., & McGoldrick, M. (Eds.). (1989). *The changing family life cycle: A framework for family therapy.* Boston: Allyn & Bacon.

Fishbane, M. D. (1997a). *Autonomous and relational narratives of the self: Ethical and clinical implications.* Paper presented at a conference, "The Autonomous Person—A European Invention?" Internationales Wissenschaftsforum, Heidelberg, Germany.

Fishbane, M. D. (1997b). *The loving update: A dialogical challenge in intergenerational relationships.* Unpublished manuscript.

Fishbane, M. D. (1998). I, thou and we: A dialogical approach to couples therapy. *Journal of Marital and Family Therapy, 24,* 41–58.

Fishman, S. B. (1993). *A breath of life: Feminism in the American Jewish community.* New York: Free Press/Macmillan.

Framo, J. (1976). Family of origin as a therapeutic resource for adults in marital and family therapy: You can and should go home again. *Family Process, 15,* 193–210.

Galatzer-Levy, R. M., & Cohler, B. J. (1993). *The essential other: A developmental psychology of the self.* New York: Basic Books.

Goodrich, T. J. (1991). Women, power, and family therapy: What's wrong with this picture? In T. J. Goodrich (Ed.), *Women and power: Perspectives for family therapy.* New York: Norton.

Grunebaum, J. (1987). Multidirected partiality and the "parental imperative." *Psychotherapy, 24,* 646–655.

Hargrave, T. (1994). *Families and forgiveness: Healing wounds in the intergenerational family.* New York: Brunner/Mazel.

Jordan, J. V., Kaplan, A. G., Miller, J. B., Stiver, I. P., & Surrey, J. L. (1991). *Women's growth in connection: Writings from the Stone Center.* New York: Guilford Press.

Karpel, M. (Ed.). (1986). *Family resources: The hidden partner in family therapy.* New York: Guilford Press.

Kosmin, B. A., Goldstein, S., Waksberg, J., Lerer, N., Keysar, A., & Scheckner, J. (1990). *Highlights of the CJF 1990 National Jewish Population Survey.* New York: Council of Jewish Federations.

Lerner, H. G. (1985). *The dance of anger.* New York: Harper & Row.

Maimonides, M. *Hilkhot Mamrim, Shoftim, Mishna Torah,* traditional ed., 12th century C.E.

McGoldrick, M. (1995). *You can go home again: Reconnecting with your family.* New York: Norton.

Mirkin, M. P. (1994). Female adolescence revisited: Understanding girls in their sociocultural contexts. In M. P. Mirkin (Ed.), *Women in context: Toward a feminist reconstruction of psychotherapy.* New York: Guilford Press.

Offer, D., & Sabshin, M. (Eds.). (1984). *Normality and the life cycle: A critical integration.* New York: Basic Books.

Roberto, L. G. (1992). *Transgenerational family theories.* New York: Guilford Press.

Rolland, J. (1994). *Families, illness and disability: An integrative treatment model.* New York: Basic Books.

Stern, D. N. (1985). *The interpersonal world of the infant: A view from psychoanalysis and developmental psychology.* New York: Basic Books.

Stolorow, R. D., & Atwood, G. E. (1992). *Contexts of being: The intersubjective foundations of psychological life.* Hillsdale, NJ: Analytic Press.

Surrey, J. L. (1991). Relationship and empowerment. In J. V. Jordan, A. G. Kaplan, J. B. Miller, I. P. Stiver, & J. L. Surrey, *Women's growth in connection: Writings from the Stone Center.* New York: Guilford Press.

Walsh, F. (1998). *Strengthening family resilience.* New York: Guilford Press.

Williamson, D. S. (1991). *The intimacy paradox: Personal authority in the family system.* New York: Guilford Press.

CHAPTER 9

Feet Planted Firmly in Midair
A Spirituality for Family Living

HERBERT ANDERSON

Human beings are meaning-making creatures. Through story and ritual we seek to order our lives in meaningful ways. Spirituality is the experience of making meaning informed by a relationship with the transcendent or divine in life. In this general sense, spirituality is *a way of living and a way of seeing life,* the commonplace attitude that influences how individuals and communities act and react habitually throughout life. Because spirituality is not linked to dogma, it cannot be limited to a particular religious tradition. Moreover, because spirituality is about authentic living as well as meaning-making, it is a highly personal reality. Tibetan monks and Christian mystics and Sufi mullahs each have their own spiritualities. So do joggers and potters and weavers and birdwatchers and breadbakers and elementary school teachers. From a Christian perspective, spirituality is about accepting the complicated and muddled bundle of human experience as the theater for God's creative and transforming work. Despite this diversity of perspectives, the general aim of spirituality is constant: to be open to the transcendent dimension of life that is present in ordinary, everyday activity.

When there is an openness to transcendence, spirituality is fashioned by the urgings of spirit, both human and divine, that move us toward wholeness and community. We often identify spirit as the fundamental dynamic or energy in life that penetrates thought, feeling, and action. It is in the "spirit," we might say, that we experience ultimate reality. Spirituality is about living and praying in that spirit with honest passion. Max Jacob, the 20th-century French, Jewish-Christian mystic, once said it this way: "You must live things, not define them." Theology and psychology depend on definitions; spirituality does not. Seeing life through spiritual eyes enables one to link the fullness of being human to a relationship with the di-

157

vine, with others, and with the world of creation. Understood in this way, spirituality is an embodied experience of the transcendent in ordinary, physical, communal activities. Conversely, ordinary human experience is a window to the divine. Because the starting place for spirituality is the human story, there is a spirituality for the marketplace, for sexuality, and for marriage and family living.

This emphasis on embodied spirituality is important today lest our present interest in spirituality invite a return to earlier forms of spiritualistic dualism that rendered bodies evil and souls good. Moreover, spirituality that is not rooted in the concrete life of communities is in danger of drifting toward disembodied vagueness or general religiosity or unrestrained individualism. The ancient Hebrews were clear that spirituality was an earthy matter. They linked spirit and body in wonderfully paradoxical ways. Because the human being is a unity, soul or liver or kidney or spirit may refer to the individual as a whole. So, for example, the literal translation of Proverbs 23:16 is that "my kidneys will rejoice when your lips speak what is right." Souls yearn and flesh cries out. Thomas Moore (1992) has suggested that care of soul, attending to human genuineness and depth and mystery, includes knowing that "a piece of sky and a chunk of the earth lie lodged in the heart of every human being, and if we are going to care for that heart, we will have to know the sky and earth as well as human behavior" (p. 20). Because embodied spirituality links earth and sky, it often feels like living with both feet planted firmly in midair.

THE RECOVERY OF SOUL

The renewal of spirituality embodied in ordinary life prompts us to examine the metaphors we use to think about the human person. The *self* has been and still is a clear image for thinking about the human dimension of becoming a person, but the self is more readily understood as a social construction than it is a gift from God. Images of the person linked with *spirit, ego,* or *psyche* also identify specific dimensions of the human person, but none has the capacity of the image of *soul* to hold earth and sky together. The human person is a bio-psycho-social-spiritual unity. No metaphor reflects that unity more profoundly than *soul*. The recovery of soul is therefore at the same time a retrieval of both the earthy and the transcendent in human life. *Soul* enables us to embody that spiritual quest in ordinary, everyday activities like family living.

We have our life from the earth and from God. That is a mystery. The care of soul begins, as Moore observes, with "an appreciation of the paradoxical mysteries that blend light and darkness into the grandeur of what human life and culture can be" (Moore, 1992, p. xix). The language of soul is therefore not technical or scientific. Soul language is poetry and song. Imagination is also the expression of soul. The sacred work of soul care is therefore art as well as science because it is the application of poetics to everyday life. That is the first and most obvious consequence of introducing the perspective of spirituality into family therapy. We will need to learn a language of soul not found in the *Diagnostic and Statistical Manual of Mental Disorders* (American Psychiatric Association, 1994) and learn the art of soul care not always available through therapeutic textbooks. What we know about the care of soul in its essence is drawn from what a soul does.

1. *Soul is the making of meaningful memory.* It is soul, as James Ashbrook (1991) has observed, that expresses meaning, and making meaning depends on memory. It is memory that makes our lives personally meaningful by linking the past and the present. When we do not take the time to remember the many facets of our lives or when we have lost our memory, we have also lost our soul. We also remember so that we do not outrun the soul. When we lose ourselves in a multiplicity of activities and concerns, we endanger the soul. Both rest and activity are necessary for soul making. Restoration has its beginning in telling the deep myths of the soul. The sacred work of care restores the soul when we listen to a story in order to make a meaningful memory. When people cannot remember, we are held in the memory of the community. And if the community forgets, we are still held in the memory of God. Soul care is both remembering and being remembered.

2. *Soul is being vulnerable.* The great enemy of soul is pretense and deception. We endanger the soul when we obscure human vulnerability with glittering images or glamorous powers. By vulnerability I mean simply our susceptibility to being wounded. Being a soul is like being a trapeze artist swinging about the earth with her feet planted firmly in midair. What is certain in being a soul is ambiguity and uncertainty. We are always in danger of losing our soul when we seek to plant our feet on concrete or eliminate ambiguity with rationality or cover our vulnerability with pretense or power. We are free to live without pretense because we believe that the soul is ultimately hidden in God, whose graciousness transforms everything we have hated or feared in ourselves.

3. *The soul waits actively.* Since Aristotle, the metaphor of soul has been used to describe that which animates our being. The images in Hebrew scriptures are particularly graphic in ascribing significant activity to soul. "My soul longs, indeed it faints for the courts of Lord," says the writer of Psalm 84. And yet the soul is not simply action or participation. It *is* that, but more. The way of the soul is passivity. We are human when we wait as well as when we act. The soul acts and is acted upon. For that reason, what is happening is getting done. It is not just that God does it, or that I do it, but that the action of soul flows from a different place. Soul is what we call our own and what distinguishes us from all others. Yet

we do not possess our life, nor do we possess our soul. The soul is more than autonomous agency. It is from God and for God. It is soul that takes the adventures that God sends.

4. Soul, formed by waiting and remembering and walking naked in the world, is *simultaneously individual and communal.* In most Western societies, the human person is understood as a particular and uniquely bounded creature with an identity, a name, and a history. This highly privatized, highly individualized concept of human autonomy is not universal, however. Most societies of the world begin with community. Personal identity is derivative of the community. The African theologian John Mbiti has described this view of the world with the dictum "I am because we are." This approach corresponds with the anthropological assumptions behind what Mona D. Fishbane (1998), among others, has described as a "dialogical or relational approach to couples therapy." Autonomy and relational accountability are inextricably linked. Egocentric perspectives of soul cannot be separated from sociocentric or communal realities. Soul is therefore best described with the paradoxical phrase *communal autonomy.*

Human systems like families are meaning-making communities with directionality and a life of their own. From a spiritual perspective, to say that a family has a life of its own implies a communal soul. While human communities like families are fiercely committed to promoting the unique gifts and autonomous intentionality of each member, their vitality also depends on seeing how deeply they belong to each other. People who seek therapy today have often lost the capacity to "belong deeply to each other." They are lonely and disconnected souls, "weakly moored in family and community who find less and less personal meaning in their roles as consumers and citizens—the two major roles offered by the market and the state" (Doherty, 1995, p. 96).

The spiritual perspective deepens what we have come to know about human systems. The family has a soul constituted by relationships. Those relationships fashion an organism with a life of its own. *Soul is what gives a living organism like a family unity and direction, making the parts into a composite whole, uniting with others and with the divine.*

Each of these images drawn from the soul's activity points to the complexity of defining being human. In order to be a lover of souls, our own included, we need to have some appreciation for this complexity. Troubled souls often bring a longing for simplicity to a situation of care. They seek prescriptions that will eliminate emotional pain or erase ambiguity. Soul is by definition paradoxical mysteries held together in a balanced tension for the sake of life and culture. When spirituality informs our therapy with individuals and families, the aim of care is to empower people to *embrace paradox, seek justice, and glimpse the contingency of life* in order to live with both feet planted firmly in midair.

EMBRACING PARADOX: LIVING CONTRADICTIONS

The philosopher Jacob Needleman once observed that the deepest and most fundamental contradictions of existence "have been placed there not to be resolved but to be lived in full consciousness of their contradictoriness" (1982, p. 7). These contradictions are not accidental. Nor are they new. They are inherent in human nature, in human community, and most particularly in family living. I understand paradox as a seeming contradiction that may in fact *be* a contradiction: two things are true that do not seem to be true in relation to each other. From a Christian perspective, the cross is a sign of the ultimate paradox: to live we have to die. If we live the way of the cross, we will live the contradictions. The last are first, and the meek inherit the earth. If we live the way of the cross, as the Roman Catholic monk Thomas Merton once observed, we will travel toward our destiny in the belly of the paradox. Embracing paradox is not easy, however. Paradox is messy and chaotic and like ambiguity and fuzzymindedness. Embracing paradox is too much like walking a tightrope or speaking with a forked tongue or straddling two paths. We would rather believe that things are this way or that way.

Embracing paradox is, however, psychological necessity and a mark of spiritual maturity. The modern malaise of the soul stems in part from the desire to handle unmanageable ambiguity and contradiction by means of pretense and subterfuge. Religious educator James Fowler has described embracing paradox as a characteristic of *conjunctive faith*, which ordinarily occurs in early midlife and beyond. In the transition to conjunctive faith, an individual is able to embrace polarities and make peace with the reality that there are many angles of vision or perspectives to truth. Conjunctive faith "must maintain the tensions between these multiple perspectives and refuse to collapse them in one direction or another . . . [because] many truthful theological insights and models involve holding together in dialectical tension the 'coincidence of opposites' " (Fowler, 1987, p. 72). A *conjunctive* spirituality will include an epistemological humility that eschews absolutizing of any kind and is willing to wait in ambiguity in order to be part of larger movements of spirit or being.

Paradoxical Spirituality: Being Separate Together in Marriage and Family

The idea of "living the contradictions" and "embracing paradox" that is part of spirituality in general is specifically necessary for family living. Family vitality depends on embracing paradoxical living. So, for example, the family celebrates autonomy and promotes community equally. *To be totally committed to the well-being of the family as community and totally committed to the development of each person in the family is as impossible as it is necessary.* Donald S. Williamson has suggested a similar contradiction in *The Inti-*

macy Paradox. The primary psychosocial challenge for both individual and family is to achieve a healthy balance between differentiation and intimacy. "We want to be emotionally free and self-determined, but simultaneously we want to share our ideas and feelings, beliefs and values, hopes and fears, monies and homes, with significant others in intimate relationships" (Williamson, 1991, p. 3). The aim of a paradoxical spirituality for family living is always to achieve differentiation within the context of warm and intimate relationships. In *The Family Crucible,* Augustus Napier and Carl Whitaker described this paradox in a very useful way:

> We feel that the family's capacity to be intimate and caring and their capacity to be separate and divergent increase in careful synchrony. People can't risk being close unless they have the ability to be separate . . . [and] they can't risk being truly divergent and separate if they are unable to count on a residual warmth and caring to keep them together. The more forceful and independent they become, the easier it is to risk being intimate and close. The more closeness, the easier it is to risk independence. (1978, p. 93)

Marriage is sustained by holding in vital, paradoxical tension the fundamental human need for intimacy and the fundamental human need for autonomy. One manifestation of this paradox is suggested by Rainer Maria Rilke's observation that "a wonderful living side by side can grow up, if they [the couple] succeed in loving the distance between them which makes it possible for each to see the other whole and against a wide sky" (1975, p. 28). Distance makes intimacy possible, but it does not guarantee that it will happen. Nor does living side by side ensure clear seeing of the other. We often see the other in marriage as a mirror image of ourselves or as an object to be used or a project to be reformed. Couples who are able to love the distance that exists between them are more likely, however, to see clearly the uniqueness of their partner. *A spirituality that embraces paradox is particularly necessary for modern family living.*

The Paradox of Mutual Recognition

Each person in a marriage may be a fully defined self, but the recognition of that uniqueness by the other is necessary for a marriage to work. The freedom to develop one's gifts within the bonds of marriage is enhanced by the willingness of each partner to recognize that growth and those gifts in the other. In *The Bonds of Love,* Jessica Benjamin makes the following observation about paradox: "The vision of recognition between equal subjects gives rise to a new logic—the logic of paradox, of sustaining the tension between contradictory forces. Perhaps the most fateful paradox is the one posed by our simultaneous need for recognition and independence—that the other subject is outside our control and yet we need him or her" (1988, p. 221). There is no theme more necessary or more complex for a vital marriage or family than the paradox of mutual recognition of equal subjects.

The experience of being recognized is not only a prerequisite for community—it is fundamental for human growth and identity. Recognition precedes empathy and is a prelude to mutual respect. What begins in infancy in the interaction between a newborn child and its mother is a lifelong need for human folk. Marriage becomes a context for growth if two people are able to see one another "whole and against a wide sky." When each partner is able to see the particular gifts of his or her spouse, domination is diminished and the possibility of equality is increased. In order to increase the possibility of equality for women and men in marriage and at work, husbands need to practice recognizing their wives in order to see them "whole and against a wide sky." That kind of seeing is necessary so that the distinctive gifts and abilities of women can be recognized. Once recognized, they can be actualized and honored both at home and in the marketplace.

Remembering Babylon, a novel by David Malouf (1993), is about the unexpected visit of Gemmy, a shipwrecked British cabin boy raised by Aboriginal people, to a British settlement in northern Australia in the mid-19th century. To the people of the settlement, Gemmy was not a Black person but he was not a White person either. Rather, he was an unsettling combination of "monstrous strangeness and unwelcome likeness." One of the people most affected by Gemmy was Jock McIver. Because of his encounter with Gemmy, the tall grass that Jock walked through all the time had "tips beaded with green" he had not seen before. He saw himself more honestly, his neighbors differently, and his wife more clearly than ever before:

> He had turned his full gaze upon her—that is what she felt. He wanted to know now what her life was beyond what he saw and had taken for granted, a shift washed and shaken to make it soft, food on the table; to inquire into her affections. It was amazing to him—that is what his tentativeness suggested—that he had known so little and had not looked. (Malouf, 1993, pp. 108–109)

Even when they were first courting, Jock had not seen her so clearly, this woman he loved so dearly. Because many men resemble Jock McIver, we know little about the women we live with or work with and yet do not look or ask in order to understand more. Because men do not always see their wives "whole and against a wide sky," they easily become objects rather than subjects, people whose uniqueness is covered over by role definition and stereotypes. Recognition is a prelude to equal regard between men and women because it helps us see the gifts each brings to our common life and work together. A *conjunctive spiritu-*

ality that embraces paradox will enable marriages to endure and flour-ish "in the spirit" of mutual recognition.

Implications for Family Therapy

1. Not all paradoxes in family living or individual life are life en-hancing. Some are crazy making. Sometimes we set up contradictory ex-pectations in children or spouses from which the only escape is to get sick. When that happens, however, paradox has been distorted. In *Para-dox and the Family System*, Camillo Loriedo and Gaspare Vella describe paradox as a "systematic ambiguity capable of producing undecidability by means of an infinite reflexive oscillaton among different levels of complexity" (1992, p. 72). There is always the possibility that a series of contradictions can turn into such an "infinite reflexive oscillation" that immobilizes rather than energizes a family. If, however, ambiguity is an inevitable dimension of the mystery of human communication, then "reflexive oscillation" is in some sense unavoidable. The paradoxical na-ture of life presses us to explore deeper metaphors of living in which oscillation does not immobilize because we understand that both sides of a paradox are true.

2. The use of "paradoxical intervention" as an intermediate thera-peutic strategy needs to be reconsidered if paradox is an enduring reality in family living. The use of paradoxical directives as Jay Haley (1976) and others have devised them is useful in breaking open distorted paradoxes. The purpose of any directive, like that of therapy itself, is to influence people to change behavior. Very often, a paradoxical intervention exag-gerates one side of a contradiction in the hope that individuals or families will move in another, more desired direction. In such situations, thinking paradoxically is a tool. The therapeutic use of paradox seeks to induce change by "prescribing the symptom" or intensifying one side of a con-flict in hopes that the individual or family will see the other side. If, how-ever, paradox is not just a means but an end or a normal state of family living, the therapeutic task includes helping people live with both sides of paradox. In that sense, paradoxical intervention becomes paradoxical in-tention.

3. If the ultimate mystery of family living is paradox, then "saying the other side" becomes a therapeutic strategy that heightens contradiction in order to expand the arena of truth. Michael Eigen (1992) has illustrated Donald W. Winnicott's true-self/false-self paradigm with a fascinating in-terpretation of the biblical story of Jacob. According to Eigen, every as-pect of Jacob's life is paradoxical: he was a wholehearted, living paradox embracing divisions and deceit. Jacob is not this *or* that but a fully human mixture of love and grief, wisdom and weakness, good and bad. "People too eagerly push for a decision so as to organize themselves in one direc-tion or another. Winnicott's work says there is value in indecision, in let-

ting either side of what might have been a decision play with each other, and growing goes well enough without always taking sides" (Eigen, 1992, pp. 286–287). One mark of spirituality for family living is the ability to embrace paradox and see the other side.

Because we are emotionally wedded to our deep metaphors and preferred absolutes, we are often reluctant to acknowledge that every story has at least two sides. As long as we are able to polarize an issue in individual or family life, we will be able to avoid facing a full account of the situation. And so scapegoating families remain stuck as long as the family problem (i.e., the other side) is located in the acting-out child. "Saying the other side" not only increases the awareness of ambiguity; it also provides the therapist with opportunities for moral reflection without moralizing. The therapeutic task with conflicted families or with troubled couples is to make sure that the other side of the story is told. This paradoxical approach to therapy requires an ability to see the less obvious side of reality and appreciate its complexity. It takes moral courage on the part of the therapist to insist that there is another side. Hearing the other side will not change anything unless everyone agrees that *there is another side*. "Saying the other side" is a liberating method only if everyone agrees that the deepest truths in life are paradoxical and that learning to live with contradiction is *one* road to marital peace and spiritual transformation. It is one way for individuals and families to live toward their destiny "in the belly of paradox."

SEEKING JUSTICE: EQUAL REGARD BETWEEN WOMEN AND MEN

If our spirituality is embodied in creation and culture, then there is reciprocity between the earthiness of family living and how we live with an ongoing awareness of transcendence in ordinary life. Spirituality is about that connectedness. There is a reciprocal relationship between the interior world of the soul and the exterior worlds in which racial and economic injustice create environments not healthy for the human soul. Spirituality is both private and public. To put it simply, intimacy with God leads to passion for the world and our passion for the world leads to a longing for God. When our spirituality is understood as a passion for the world, justice becomes a second characteristic of spirituality for family living. It is one consequence of seeing *that there is another side*. Giving voice to the voiceless or powerless in families is not simply a therapeutic strategy—it is a just thing to do. In order to challenge the abuse of power in his time, the Hebrew prophet Micah (6:8) summarized faithful living with these words: "do justice, love kindness, and walk humbly with God." For us, in our time, to do justice means to work for change so that people might live more abundantly. To do justice includes a commitment to sort out what belongs to whom and return it to them.

This process of restoration (sorting out what belongs to whom and returning it to them) is at the core of justice. When families are governed by this understanding of justice, all members are also given equal respect and consideration. Power is distributed differently. Rules about hitting or interrupting or lying are applied to adults and children equally. Everyone will have the information necessary to participate in responsible decision making. "If a family is just, it will be a community in which there is mutual respect, in which expectations are explicit, in which no individual's needs or desires permanently dominate, and in which authority is not arbitrary" (H. Anderson & Johnson, 1994, p. 81). When justice is understood as part of a family's spirituality, clear boundaries will establish and maintain "what belongs to whom," cancel debts, honor particular gifts, and redistribute power.

Seeking Justice at the Core of Marriage

If we see the other in marriage clearly and if we are able to discover through "seeing the other side" the kind of transformation that enables role changes for women and men in the family, then both a commitment to love one another and a commitment to be just with one another will be at the core of the marital promise. Pauline Kleingeld (1998), in an essay entitled "Just Love? Marriage and the Question of Justice," has proposed that we reconceive of the ideal of marriage as essentially *"not only* a matter of love, *but also* of justice. On this view, married couples ideally would think of themselves as sharing at least two overarching aims: a loving marriage and a just marriage" (p. 271). What Kleingeld is proposing fundamentally changes the framework for negotiating role equality in marriage. It is not simply that two people who love one another seek to work out some arrangement regarding role responsibilities that is acceptable, beneficial, and even fair for everyone involved but that the commitment to work for justice for each partner in the relationship is part of the marital bond.

Rhona Mahony, in *Kidding Ourselves: Breadwinning, Babies, and Bargaining Power* (1995), argues persuasively that what is needed is a reformation in the sexual division of labor in the home that is negotiated by the two people who live together. It is possible for everyone to change, but it is difficult. The sad truth, Mahony observes, is that by the time the sun sets on the typical woman's wedding day, "she has already done nearly all the negotiating over chores and child care that she will ever do" (1995, p. 5). Despite her pessimistic observation, Mahony believes that practical equality between women and men is not a dream anymore. Women have to make it happen. I agree with Mahony's hopeful analysis of the current situation but not her future plan. Men today do more housework and parenting than they used to, but it is not equal and it is still described by both genders as *helping women with the housework*. Moreover, as long as the responsibility for change in the family remains with women, maintaining a marriage and parenting children will be a woman's thing to do. Women feel guiltier than men about work-related absence from the family and therefore are more likely to choose to cut back their careers. Nonetheless, justice is, or at least should be, a family issue for men and women alike.

Couples who are determined to work toward an equal division of household and parenting responsibilities often find themselves torn by the limits of time. Even when the intent is to establish equality, there is simply too much to do and not enough time in which to do it. Sometimes we are caught in tensions of our creation because we have programmed too many activities or too much enrichment for our children. In order to meet all of our appointments, children are expected to accommodate to adult schedules. Some couples run out of time because they need to work two, three, and four jobs to afford a house they never have time to enjoy. The application of cost–benefit analysis from the economy is perhaps the most pernicious factor undermining our best intentions to realign the gender distinctions between the public and private spheres and establish equality of responsibility between women and men at home as well as at work. Attending a daughter's soccer game or taking a son's Scout group to a baseball game is costed along with the benefit of meeting a new client. Even when we do not consciously ascribe economic value to human interactions, the fact that we schedule family time like work time makes it easy to confuse them and then measure them both according to cost-effective market standards.

Seeking for justice is not antithetical to loving one another. It is the *shared goal of life together.* Joel Anderson has observed that seeking to return to traditional role patterns for women and men at home and at work is not really an option in modern industrial societies:

> Aside from the fact that returning to more traditional approaches would involve unconscionably disproportionate sacrifices from women, it would not actually eliminate the need to make complex and conflict-ridden decisions. . . . When a couple picks the traditional male-breadwinner/female-homemaker pattern today, the modern understanding of mutual and just respect requires that it be a *choice* made by *equals.* (1998, pp. 370–371)

If couples make a commitment to form a just marriage, they will inevitably experience unexpected conflicts and unseen rocky shoals that will require a wide array of skills, virtues, and practices that must be developed and practiced. These practices will include recognizing the other, empathic listening, the ability to postpone gratification, clear expression of wishes, renegotiating previously agreed-to promises, and a short-term memory that does not keep score of mutual sacrifice.

This commitment to justice does not, however, eliminate the need for sacrifice. But the deeper meaning of sacrifice is not about giving up but about giving over our freedom or our preference to a larger reality. That larger reality is a marriage of *both* love *and* justice. If both partners in a marriage are committed to a just relationship, then no one person will do all the accommodating. If both the husband and the wife are committed to forming a just marriage, then the willingness to set aside one's needs for the needs of others becomes a positive expression of a common bond. Sacrifice deepens a marital bond as long as each person in a relationship is committed to justice. When one partner does all the accommodating or when the sacrifices are not evenly distributed over time, the commitment to justice is undermined and the marriage is not just. As Kleingeld (1998) argues, "if justice is to be an important aspect of marriage, it needs to be able to unite spouses instead of structurally pitting them against each other as separate individuals looking out for their own interests" (p. 273). Husbands and wives will work together toward a just division of responsibilities only if both partners *seek justice as an expression of a spirituality for family living.*

Implications for Therapy with Individuals and Families

1. The kind of changes that once marked shifting family forms and functions over time now occur within the lifetime of a marriage. Because we can regularly anticipate changes in roles and disruptions in living that will destabilize the family as a system, we need to develop an understanding of *promising again and again* in order to keep the marriage covenant alive. I understand "promising again" as an act of fidelity beyond the initial promise. "Promising again is an act of *creative fidelity* because we see and understand implications and dimensions of the initial promise we could never have anticipated when we first made it" (H. Anderson, Hogue, & McCarthy, 1995, p. 8; their emphasis). When my wife and I married, she thought she was marrying a parish pastor. For myself, I did not imagine I was marrying someone who would become a national leader in theological education. Even when the gender roles in a relationship continue to follow traditional patterns, people are less likely to stay in the same occupation for a lifetime. Changing jobs is itself a destabilizing factor for many families because new work routines disrupt established patterns of daily living.

2. Couples need to practice making promises that are time limited, situational, circumstantial, and frequently renegotiated in order to accommodate the inevitable and sometimes necessary changes that occur in postmodern marriage. Obviously, these promises build on the primary promise of love, respect, and mutual recognition that are foundational for marriage. If one parent agrees to stay home with young children so the other can invest fully in a career opportunity, that is a situational promise that need not last for the duration of a marriage. If one spouse accepts a major volunteer assignment at the local church to head up the building

fund drive, both partners agree to forego certain social activities for the length of the campaign. When one partner sets aside his regular golf schedule while the other recovers from surgery, that is a time-limited response to a particular circumstance. If modern marriages are to move toward greater and greater equality of roles and work opportunity for both partners, couples will need to develop the capacity to negotiate, modify, and then give up circumstantial, time-limited promises.

3. In order to survive the kind of fundamental changes that occur in marriage and the workplace today, we need to discover the possibility of transformation that moves beyond adaptation. Promising again and again is an intentional, relational act that defines the self and honors the other. It is an act of mutuality that rests on the willingness of two people to recognize each other as persons of worth with particular gifts to give and a unique story to live. Both mutuality and adaptability are necessary in order to live through the changes that are inevitably a part of modern family living. Adaptation, however, is not enough. Transformation is necessary. Transformation—change in a deeper and more enduring sense—is grounded in the conviction that the continuity of a family is a reflection of God's ongoing creation. The kind of change that is transformative unites the soul of a marriage with a longing for the new thing that God is doing.

4. Because conflict and disappointment and grief will be inevitable dimensions in the life of a couple who seek to establish a just marriage, men and women will need to learn how to practice reconciliation in advance. Reconciliation, as I mean it here, is more than restoring relationships broken by conflicts over contending views of what is just: it is about a way of living and thinking that seeks to promote a peaceable environment in which husbands and wives can sort out *very* complex and competing demands on their time from work and home. Peaceableness is important because it creates a safe environment in which bonds of trust are sustained or rebuilt. Such a vision of reconciliation is never a hasty peace that ignores memories of past domination or present abuse. Nor does it require amnesia about past injustice. It does require working together for the common good at home and at work. In order to see in a new way, we need to be prepared for surprise. In order to see new roles for men at home and at work, we will need to be transformed by God in order to see new possibilities. *That transformation is most likely to occur when we live gently with the contradictions of our lives.*

FAMILIES ARE CONTINGENT REALITIES

In their introduction to *Living Beyond Loss*, Froma Walsh and Monica McGoldrick suggested that "the subject of death is the last taboo in the field of family therapy" (1991, p. xv). This denial of death in family living mirrors society's inability to deal honestly with finitude and loss as human realities. Walsh and McGoldrick have introduced important themes that need to be explored about legacies of loss, the impact of death, and the complexity of any family mourning process. The fear of death, they argue, is our deepest terror, and the loss of a family member, our most profound sorrow. It is also an issue for therapists. "We need to come to terms with our own fears of death and the limits of our control in order to detoxify issues of loss so that we do not continue to deny their significance or neglect them in our theory and practice" (Walsh & McGoldrick, 1991, p. 27). I concur with both their observations and their challenge. We need to help families understand how their own legacies of loss affect their life together. And we need to learn how to mourn the loss of loved ones when that occurs. But there is more. We need to understand that all of life is framed by birth and death. *And we are most likely to discover the deeper truth about human finitude through a spiritual pilgrimage rather than a psychological exploration.*

Each human journey has a beginning and an end. This existential paradox for human folk, according to Ernest Becker, is *"individuality within finitude"* (Becker, 1973, p. 26; my emphasis). The human creature is literally split in two: aware of a splendid uniqueness that transcends creation and enables humankind to stick out of nature with a "towering majesty"; and aware at the same time, as the Eastern sages (and William Shakespeare) knew, that we are worms and food for worms. The human creature is out of nature and hopelessly in it: up in the stars and yet housed in a heart-pumping, breath-gasping body that goes back into the ground to rot and disappear forever. The human creature is a union of opposites—of self-consciousness and of physical body. The fall into consciousness is the beginning of dread: we are creatures who know we will die. Human beings get into trouble, according to Becker, because of their inability to live with finitude and death. The elaborate artifacts we fashion, the grand illusions we spin, or the vital lies we live are all designed to repress the terror of finitude. Neurosis and sin *and family pathology* are the consequence of our denial of death.

When the ancient mystics reflected on the spiritual life, death was at the center. Finitude was the frame. And freedom was always limited. The journey of the soul not only ended in death—it carried the marks of death throughout life. When the sign of the cross is made on an infant in Christian baptism, it is a mark of finitude and death. The ancient Hebrews understand better than most that human life is limited. Living with a deeper awareness of the limitations of existence sharpens paradox, deepens ambiguity, and clarifies that "reality is remorseless because gods do not walk upon the earth" (Becker, 1973, p. 281). When this spiritual agenda is translated into family living, it is clearer that loss and death are only part of the struggle. Families will flourish and grow when somehow they are able to factor finitude into their self-understanding and daily strategies.

Spirituality, which enhances the capacity for contingency, becomes a necessary dimension of individual and family living. Two illustrations of *family finitude* will have to suffice to make the point: the limits of time and the process of letting go.

Instances of Family Finitude

One of the most disturbing observations about the tension between work time and family time has come from German sociologist Ulrich Beck in a book with the translated title *Risk Society* (1992). He has observed that a free-market economic model presupposes a society without families or marriages. "The market individual is ultimately a single individual unhindered by a relationship, marriage or family. . . . [In fact] a fully realized market society is also a society without children—unless the children grow up with mobile, single-parent mothers and fathers" (Beck, 1992, p. 116). According to Beck, and I am inclined to believe that he is right, the crisis of the family today is built into the organization of modern, industrial, market-driven societies. It is not surprising, therefore, that the family is a constant juggling act of disparate, multiple ambitions, requiring maximum mobility on the one side *with* the obligations of being married and raising children on the other side. A society that rewards people for selfishness should not be surprised that it faces a crisis in families. If both women and men are equally devoted to the marketplace and its demands, children will obviously suffer. But so will the marriage, even if there are no children.

Living with limits is difficult for individuals and families to do in an economy that depends on fostering excess in order to grow. We spend huge sums of money to create a mythic wedding in the magical hope that if the wedding is perfect, the marriage might be perfect also. Mark and Priscilla had nearly a picture-perfect wedding. Only the wind marred the perfection. Since their marriage 8 years ago, they have had two sons, two hunting dogs, a heavily mortgaged house in the suburbs, two jobs far from home at different shifts, loans on the mortgage, a bankruptcy, and a divorce. The children were cared for, but the marriage was not. They had little time for one another because they were too busy working to make the money they needed to continue the myth of a picture-perfect marriage. At a deeper level, the myth was a denial of human finitude. It is not possible to "have it all" in the first 8 years—or ever, for that matter. We all know couples like Mark and Priscilla. And we all can recognize how difficult it is to help them live with less in this particular culture. Both families and the culture are contending with a deeper spiritual issue: *that human life is finite and freedom is always limited.*

The second illustration of how families struggle with finitude is equally common. It was Kahlil Gibran, the Lebanese philosopher and poet, who reminded us that our children do not belong to us. They come from us, but we do not own them. We may house their bodies but not their souls, because their souls "dwell in a place of tomorrow you [parents] cannot go, not even in your dreams" (Gibran, 1923, p. 18). There is nothing we human beings do that is more important than welcoming a child into our family and society. We love our children outrageously and protect them fiercely and discipline them carefully, but we never possess them. They are not ours. So, from the beginning of life, as we love our children, we must let them go. It is another instance of understanding finitude at the core of a spirituality for family living.

There are numerous reasons why parents have difficulty letting children go when it is time for them to leave home. The child's role may keep the family together. Leaving home may be a loss beyond the family's capacity to cope. Parents are sometimes afraid that when children leave, they may be abandoned forever. Excessive togetherness, however, is another instance of the denial of finitude. If we understand that accepting death is the birthplace of the spirit, then we also understand that loving means letting go. "For the person who has learned to let go and let be," observed the 14th-century mystic Meister Eckhart, "nothing can ever be the same." *That conviction is an extension of the promise of finite freedom that sustains every spiritual journey. The greatest gift that parents can give their children is to love them tenderly and fiercely and let them go respectfully and graciously.*

Implications for Therapy with Individuals and Families

1. Every individual and every family experiencing loss has a story to tell about how that loss has changed their experience of the world. The primary therapeutic task in such circumstances is to attend carefully to the story of loss and the pains of grief. Our grieving is an intermediate stage between life as it was before a death occurred and life as it can be again in spite of the death. When families mourn, the story is almost inevitably complexified. Neither the loss nor the grief will be the same for everyone in a family because the relationships with the deceased varied. For that reason, communal grief, such as that experienced by a family when loss occurs, requires greater attention to rituals that will legitimate and create safe environments for the process of grieving. Family members need to intend to be together so that their grief can be shared. Grief rituals in a family context need to be expansive enough to hold differing realities simultaneously and express conflicting thoughts and emotions in response to the death of a loved person.

2. Signs of finitude are everywhere present. In the face of the pervasiveness of irrational suffering and contingency everywhere, learning to lament becomes a necessary characteristic of a life-enhancing spirituality. The alternative to such lament is apathy. When people become apathetic, nothing matters. When we become apathetic, we die before we are dead.

Apathy, as a way of coping with pain and suffering by not feeling, is a common malady of our time. Children learn too easily from adults how to close down or shut out the world when the pain is more than they can bear or the presence of finitude and death engenders feelings of powerlessness. In order to live without apathy in the midst of suffering and injustice, we will need to learn to lament. Sometimes it is the only alternative. Change or restoration is not always possible. Spiritualities rooted in the earth make us even more aware of the paradoxes and tensions of human finitude. It takes courage to live with an earthy spirituality. *If we have incorporated finitude and contingency into a spirituality, however, it will be easier to practice lament and teach it to others. Therapies of the future that are attentive to human contingency and finitude will also be willing to teach lament.*

3. If we allow death to be a teacher of wisdom as well as the liberator of the soul, ordinary moments become signs of the holy. When we learn to live with finitude and contingency, there is a new urgency to living. It is no longer sufficient to promote individual health or even family well-being disconnected from larger frameworks of meaning and commitment to the common good. Preoccupation with private gain over public good ultimately ends in spiritual bankruptcy. If we believe that human life is sustained and enriched by "horizons of significance" in the midst of finitude, then the therapeutic task includes making connections between personal concerns and transcending meaning. From a spiritual perspective, the aim of health is greater service. We find ourselves to give ourselves away. We establish a life in order to lay it down. William Doherty's challenge to psychotherapy to promote moral responsibility is germaine just here: "There is no fundamental contradiction between pursuing personal needs and promoting the welfare of the community. . . . Like responsible parenting, responsible participation in activities to preserve and promote that environment is at once generous and self-serving" (1995, p. 100). We become healthier so that we can be free to engage the world more effectively and responsibly. If there is always a "so that" to health, then the vocational or service question is part of the therapeutic process. "What will you do with your life when you get better?" *When we view life through the lens of a spirituality that has glimpsed contingency and death, the aims of our therapy will be modified.*

MYTH, RITUAL, AND A SPIRITUALITY FOR FAMILY THERAPY

Not all forms of spirituality enhance human wholeness. For that reason, taking spirituality seriously means that careful distinctions will need to be made between healthy and unhealthy religious beliefs and practices. The criteria for making those distinctions are philosophical and theological as well as psychological. Modern individuals, shaped by Enlightenment values and scientific views of the world, have until recently scoffed at the notion that unseen forces like angels or spirits could affect the course of human events. What happens in the human world, the modern mind has asserted, is the result of hard work or chance or both. From that perspective, human survival depends on individual and collective responsibility for the present and the future. Interest in unseen spirits was not deemed healthy. If, however, the spiritual dimension is a part of life that is taken seriously in therapy, it will be necessary to discriminate among "spirits" and spiritualities.

Discerning between healthy and unhealthy religious practices is difficult, however, because spirituality is profoundly ambiguous. Awareness of the transcendent can be simultaneously terrifying and empowering, a paradoxical mixture that Rudolf Otto once described as *mysterium tremendum et fascinans.* Hence the title of this chapter: feet planted firmly in midair. Ordinary categories that measure health and well-being are insufficiently ambiguous to capture the deeper truths that are almost always carried by paradox. The language of ambiguity is narrative and ritual more than carefully delineated, statistically verified diagnostic categories. As I am using it here, ambiguity refers to the multiple meanings, contradictions, and mystery in human life at its depth. In that sense, paradox is the window to the holy.

If the deepest spiritual truths are most likely to be expressed in paradox, then living with ambiguity and incomprehensibility is a mark of spiritual maturity. The ideal in human life is to be capable of being engaged in mysteries, uncertainties, and doubts without any irritable insisting on fact or reason. The inability to live with ambiguity will lead to arbitrary and rigid absolutes. The most appropriate response to life's incomprehensibility is wonder. As Alfred Margulies has described it, "the holding of a searching attitude of simultaneously knowing and not-knowing, of finding pattern and breaking apart, goes against the grain of our organizing mind, but is intrinsic to the creativity of introspection, art, and empathy" (1989, p. xii). If our aim as therapists is to help individuals and families deepen their spirituality by living in wonder, then symbol and ritual must be a regular part of our work.

CONCLUSION

Living with both feet planted firmly in midair is hard work. In order to develop a spirituality that embraces paradox, seeks justice, and acknowledges contingency, we need to be people of courage. We will also need frameworks for living that will hold our souls firmly in midair. "The ability of rituals to link time, hold contradictions, and work with relationship shifts in action offers us particular tools to work with and hold the incongruities between the actual and the ideal" (Imber-Black, Roberts,

& Whiting, 1988, p. 12). Rituals are necessary to hold both sides of a contradiction at the same time. Ritual has therapeutic value not only because it provides a container for paradox and attributes symbolic meaning to experience; in the midst of life's discontinuities, rituals also become a dependable source of security and comfort. Rituals provide a way for families to define boundaries and confirm identity. They give tangible shape to dreams and provide a framework weaving our stories into a narrative that has transcendent meaning (H. Anderson & Foley, 1998).

Attending to *soul* will add new dimensions to the therapeutic task. Our aim is not simply to help people know their story in order to reframe it. Understanding therapy from a spiritual perspective means that *one* aim is to enable individuals and families to fashion narratives that weave together human and divine realities in a single fabric. Divine stories may have their origins in the memory of a religious tradition, or they may be a particular experience of transcendence that confirms our belief that there is *something more* in human living. Weaving together the human and the divine enables people to hear their own stories retold with clarity and new possibility. When human stories are retold with transcendence in view, lives are transformed in the telling. And when lives are transformed, it is possible that both individuals and families are liberated from confining worldviews, confirmed their sense of belonging in the world, and strengthened to live responsibly for the common good of the world.

REFERENCES

American Psychiatric Association. (1994). *Diagnostic and statistical manual of mental disorders* (4th ed.). Washington, DC: Author.

Anderson, H., & Foley, E. (1998). *Mighty stories, dangerous rituals: Weaving together the human and the divine.* San Francisco: Jossey-Bass.

Anderson, H., Hogue, D., & McCarthy, M. (1995). *Promising again.* Louisville, KY: Westminster/John Knox Press.

Anderson, H., & Johnson, S. (1994). *Regarding children: A new respect for childhood and families.* Louisville, KY: Westminster/John Knox Press.

Anderson, J. (1998). Is equality tearing families apart? In L. May, S. Sharratt, & K. Wong (Eds.), *Applied ethics: A multicultural approach* (2nd ed.). Upper Saddle River, NJ: Prentice-Hall.

Ashbrook, J. (1991). Soul: Its meaning and its making. *Journal of Pastoral Care, 45*(2), 159–168.

Beck, U. (1992). *The risk society: Towards a new modernity.* Newbury Park, CA: Sage.

Becker, E. (1973). *The denial of death.* New York: Free Press.

Benjamin, J. (1988). *The bonds of love: Psychoanalysis, feminism, and the problem of domination.* New York: Pantheon Books.

Doherty, W. (1995). *Soul searching: Why psychotherapy must promote moral responsibility.* New York: Basic Books.

Eigen, M. (1992). The fire that never goes out. *Psychoanalytic Review, 79*(2), 271–287.

Fishbane, M. D. (1998). I, thou, and we: A dialogical approach to couples therapy. *Journal of Marital and Family Therapy, 24*(1), 41–58.

Fowler, J. (1987). *Faith development and pastoral care.* Philadelphia: Fortress Press.

Gibran, K. (1923). *The prophet.* New York: Knopf.

Haley, J. (1976). *Problem solving therapy.* San Francisco: Jossey-Bass.

PART III

Spirituality
and Family Therapy
Bridging the Divide

CHAPTER 10

Morality and Spirituality
in Therapy

WILLIAM J. DOHERTY

Now that spirituality is out of the closet in the therapy world, it risks becoming so conceptually diffuse that it will subsume all psychological and family healing. Historical claims of religious faiths to encompass universal truth about human nature have led many therapists to avoid the spiritual domain entirely in their work. The challenge now is to embrace a legitimate role for spiritual issues in therapy without losing the distinction between the domain of spirituality and the domains of behavioral science and clinical practice. This chapter describes a model for using clinical, moral, and spiritual language in therapy in an integrated way that does justice to all three domains but does not collapse one domain into the others. The chapter begins with my own religious context, then critiques the current literature on spirituality and therapy. Subsequent sections make conceptual distinctions between the domains of spirituality, morality, and mental health, and offer specific clinical guidelines for how to use spiritual language in therapy.

MY PERSONAL RELIGIOUS CONTEXT

In reading the literature on spirituality and therapy, I have been struck by the silence of most authors about their own religious backgrounds and current context. For example, unless I missed it, nowhere in the 21 chapters of the comprehensive edited volume *Religion and the Clinical Practice of Psychology* (Shafranske, 1996) did an author declare his or her own religious or spiritual beliefs and affiliations. And journal articles on the topic rarely give the author's religious or spiritual context. Exceptions are noteworthy: Dorothy Becvar (1996) elaborates her own spiritual journey in her book *Soul Healing*.

179

I was raised an Irish Catholic in the 1950s and early 1960s, spent 7 years in a Catholic Paulist Fathers seminary, left the seminary in 1970 amid the turmoil of that era, remained a Catholic until 1975, was "unchurched" for a couple of years, and then became a Unitarian-Universalist in 1977. Along this spiritual and religious path, I moved from belief in a traditional Christian God and an afterlife to being a religious humanist. As a religious humanist and Unitarian-Universalist, I believe in the power and importance of religious and spiritual issues and questions. I believe that religious beliefs and spiritual practices are potentially positive influences on individuals, families, and communities, as well as potential sources of pathology and destructiveness. Where I differ from religious theists is that I believe that religion and spirituality are human creations in the context of a broader natural universe, rather than containing revelations from a supernatural personal God. Where I differ from secular humanists is that I value, in certain contexts, traditional religious terms such as God, grace, and salvation, which I see as potentially powerful metaphors for the source of creative transformation in human life (Wieman, 1995). And I believe that religious communities can be a source of healing and community for many people.

PROBLEMS WITH THE LITERATURE
ON SPIRITUALITY AND THERAPY

Having never written professionally on the topic of spirituality and therapy, I set about sampling the burgeoning professional literature in this area. Nearly every author, following the lead of pioneer psychologist Allen Bergin (1980), criticizes (to some degree) the field of psychotherapy for avoiding dealing with spirituality and religion. And nearly every author distinguishes between "religion"—a set of organizational beliefs, structures, and practices—and "spirituality"—a more personal set of sensibilities about the meaning of life and one's relationship to transcendent reality (Becvar, 1996; Stander, Piercy, MacKinnon, & Helmeke, 1994). And most authors stress the importance of following the client's lead in the spiritual domain and not coercing the client into a spiritual or religious discussion (Tan, 1996). While much of this literature is valuable and enlightening, I see five problems with how spirituality is dealt with in contemporary professional literature.

First, sometimes the definition of spirituality becomes so large as to encompass most of the mental health domain as well, as Elkins (1990) does in defining spirituality in terms such as realism, idealism, ultimate satisfaction, and altruism. A term that means too much soon means nothing—and risks become everything.

Second, the emphasis is primarily individualistic. Religion, with its corporate, community nature, is frequently disparaged in contrast to spirituality as a fundamentally personal phenomenon. The image is that of the individual searcher for meaning, free to choose or discard whatever beliefs make sense at the time, and not anchored in a faith tradition.

Third, there is too little attention to spiritual beliefs and practices in families. Although there is a large literature on interfaith marriages, there is relatively little discussion of intrafamilial differences in spirituality. What happens to a couple when one partner becomes focused on New Age spirituality while the other continues to be a traditional Presbyterian? Or when religious and spiritual paths of parents and children diverge? Similarly, there is insufficient attention to spirituality as a resource for couples and families.

Fourth, spirituality is often disconnected from the moral realm of interpersonal responsibilities and obligations. At its worst, the literature treats the individual as an unencumbered spiritual self, free to grow and explore meaning with little attention to the contextual responsibilities to family, friends, and community. Some authors seem to imply that spiritual enlightenment automatically guarantees morally sensitive behavior, a position out of keeping with the historical fact that most spiritual leaders throughout history supported, or at least did not protest, the institution of slavery.

Fifth, there is too little discussion of how to use spiritual language in clinical practice. Therapy being a conversational healing medium, how do we engage in spiritual discourse with clients? Much of the literature stays at a fairly high level of abstraction and lacks guidance about how to talk about these issues in a therapy session.

The rest of this chapter will address some of these problems in the professional literature on spirituality and therapy. It will distinguish the language of the spiritual domain from those of the moral domain and the clinical domain. It will address how to use the language of spiritual dialogue in therapy; and it will touch on ways to incorporate a family systems perspective in working on spiritual issues.

THREE DOMAINS OF LANGUAGE AND MEANING

My prior related work has been in the area of morality and psychotherapy, culminating in the book *Soul Searching: Why Psychotherapy Must Promote Moral Responsibility* (Doherty, 1995). In that work, I deliberately focused only on the moral realm and not on the religious or spiritual realms. I maintained that the moral realm is conceptually distinct from the spiritual/religious realm, as seen in the difference between philosophical ethics and moral theology. And I believed that in therapy one could deal with issues of morality (defined as the domain of where one's actions have good or bad consequences for the welfare of others) without explicitly discussing spiritual and religious issues. For example, a newly divorced father's decision about cutting off from his children and starting a new life can be dealt with at the clinical and moral levels without explicitly moving into the spiritual realm unless the client brings in these perspectives.

Having limited myself to the moral domain, I nonetheless titled my book *Soul Searching* in order to convey the internal dialogue that we all have about our responsibilities to self and others (and, to be honest, my publisher thought the book would sell better with the term "soul" in the title). However, many potential readers and workshop participants were attracted to the term "soul" and expected me to discuss spiritual issues in therapy. I was able to clarify my focus and fend off these requests until August 1995, when I did a week-long intensive workshop for 15 experienced therapists, two-thirds of whom wanted to discuss spirituality in therapy along with morality in therapy. My solution was to split the workshop into two-thirds presentation of my work on morality and therapy, and one-third peer interaction on spirituality and therapy. Here I was co-learner more than teacher.

When I made the conceptual distinction between morality, spirituality, and clinical practice in our discussions, several workshop participants could not go along with me. They said that for them the religious/spiritual/theological domain was all encompassing, that it subsumed the moral and clinical domains. Another participant took the opposite stance: he saw the clinical domain as dominant in his work and said it subsumed the spiritual domain. When asked for an example, he talked about a client whose main relationship was with God. As a good systems therapist, this man treated the relationship between his client and God. But this therapist did not view the spiritual/religious/theological realm as having any independent existence; all were tools for clinical work. How could such diverse people engage in dialogue without the conversation collapsing around differences on fundamental assumptions? In particular, how could the autonomy of the clinical domain be maintained for therapists whose faith teaches them that God is the mover in all human interactions, the ultimate healer of human problems?

I remember how one participant put her thinking in a way that I could not effectively respond to: she said that, for her, just as the mind and body are one, spirituality, clinical work, and morality are one. Making hard distinctions, she believed, was akin to dividing up the mind and body into totally separate aspects of the human person. As someone who had spent a good portion of my career trying to break down the mind–body/family–community dichotomies, I did not know how to respond to her metaphorical argument.

Later that day and evening I engaged in some soul searching of my own about the profound issues raised in the group. I knew I did not want to invalidate the strong religious beliefs of several group members, and yet I was troubled with their subsuming all of therapy into the spiritual domain. It felt like theological imperialism, the flip side of Freud reducing all of religion to unresolved psychological conflicts. And how would we hold one another accountable as therapists if we saw the world differently on a theological level?

The upshot of this pondering was the following set of distinctions. The first distinction is between one's ultimate worldview, or ontology, and one's cultural and professional traditions of language and meaning, which are a kind of epistemology. At the ontological worldview level, two ends of the spectrum were represented in the group. For some participants, the theological realm was the "big circle" that subsumed all other realities, including the clinical and moral domains. Practicing therapy was a way to enact one's religious mission in the world, and all psychological healing was at heart a form of spiritual healing. For other participants, the main reality was the empirical world of behavioral science and systems theory. This was the big circle that subsumed the spiritual and moral domains, which would be dealt with as they came up in a basically clinical worldview. Other participants held middle-range views between these extremes.

I told the group that I had no wish to challenge anyone's ultimate worldview and that assertions of the primacy of the religious or scientific worldviews were impossible to prove. However, I noted that when we discuss the spiritual, moral, and clinical domains of practice, we inevitably must use the language traditions that we have inherited—and the language we use does make distinctions among those domains. My breakthrough came from the mind–body metaphor. I said that although I believe at the philosophical level that body and mind are one, I cannot avoid using terms that have been developed separately to describe the mind and the body. Thus, we do not refer to a "depressed liver" or to "sclerosis of the feelings." To do so would collapse any attempt at clear meaning because it would transpose terms from one domain of understanding to another, from one level of abstraction to another.

In the same way, the domains of clinical work/behavioral science, morality, and spirituality have evolved in their own language traditions which cannot be reduced to one another. To use an obvious example, I may believe that God created all the laws of nature, but theological study will not get me to the law of gravity. Similarly, I may believe that God created the moral law, or I may believe in the Gaia principle governing the workings of the earth and its people, but the morality of contraception and abortion will require additional ethical exploration beyond what is written in sacred texts or is evident in a meta-level theory such as Gaia. Indeed, in a pluralistic society, complex issues such as contraception and abortion are generally worked through in nontheological terms such as the right to autonomy and the right to life. With regard to the spiritual/clinical connection, witness the televangelist Jimmy Swaggart declining psychotherapy after the public exposure of his compulsive sexual acting-out behavior, in favor of a strictly theological cure through prayer to cast out the devil. He chose an either/or approach to something that many believers would see as both/and: *both* therapy *and* prayer.

In Figure 10.1, I have outlined three domains of language and meaning in therapy: the clinical world of mental health, the moral realm of obligations, and the spiritual realm of transcendent meaning. I argue that these domains should be kept distinct both for purposes of clarity and so that one does not "trump" the others. Trumping occurs when the distinctive meanings of one domain become appropriated by another, as with Freud's subsuming of religion into psychoanalytical theory. To repeat, the three domains have different modes of language and knowledge generation, different epistemologies and standards of evidence. They represent different traditions and cultures, and cannot be subsumed into one another.

Figure 10.1 gives examples of language that is specific to each domain. In examining the figure, pay attention first to the circles that reflect the language specific to the clinical domain, the moral domain, and the spiritual domain. Clinical-only terms include *personality, mental illness, self-differentiation,* and *boundaries,* terms that reflect the language and scholarly tradition of mental health professionals. Moral-only terms include *right and wrong, should,* and *obligation,* terms that have historically not been central to the discourse of therapy. I am not suggesting that therapists never use these terms, but rather that when they do so they are clearly borrowing language from the moral domain. Spiritual-only terms include *God's will, calling, faith,* and *prayer,* terms that have historically been used within religious traditions.

Before moving on to the overlap areas among the domains, I want to make the point that it is important to respect the conceptual and linguistic autonomy of terms that are specific to each domain. When the idea of a "calling" is reduced to the idea of a "need" or a "sublimation" in the psychological domain, conceptual imperialism has occurred. Similarly, when ancient biblical texts are used to justify harsh parenting practices in contemporary society, imperialism is evident. And when the morality of sexual abuse is obfuscated in clinical language of "poor boundaries," both the moral domain and the clinical domain are impoverished.

After developing this model, I came upon a similar exposition in the work of Don S. Browning (1987), a professor of religious ethics and the social sciences at the University of Chicago. Browning argues that the domains of ultimate metaphors (theology), obligation (ethics), and psychology are categorically distinct, although they have implications for one another. Beyond this basic set of distinctions, however, things get more complicated. Browning argues that all psychological theories have implicit metaphors that concern ultimate meaning in life, along with an implicit ethic about human obligations. For their own part, theologies and ethical models have implicit theories of psychological and family func-

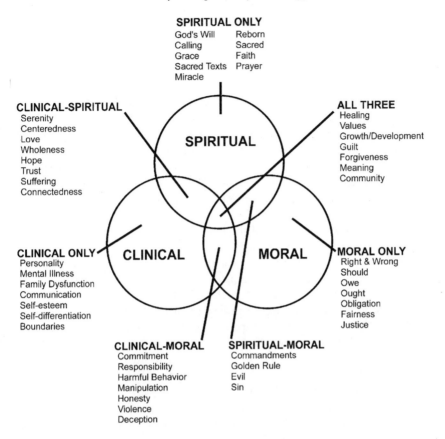

SPIRITUAL ONLY
God's Will   Reborn
Calling   Sacred
Grace   Faith
Sacred Texts   Prayer
Miracle

CLINICAL-SPIRITUAL
Serenity
Centeredness
Love
Wholeness
Hope
Trust
Suffering
Connectedness

SPIRITUAL

ALL THREE
Healing
Values
Growth/Development
Guilt
Forgiveness
Meaning
Community

CLINICAL ONLY
Personality
Mental Illness
Family Dysfunction
Communication
Self-esteem
Self-differentiation
Boundaries

CLINICAL   **MORAL**

MORAL ONLY
Right & Wrong
Should
Owe
Ought
Obligation
Fairness
Justice

CLINICAL-MORAL
Commitment
Responsibility
Harmful Behavior
Manipulation
Honesty
Violence
Deception

SPIRITUAL-MORAL
Commandments
Golden Rule
Evil
Sin

FIGURE 10.1. Three domains of language and meaning.

tioning. Thus, there is resonance across the categorically separate domains of spirituality, morality, and clinical care.

Figure 10.1 illustrates this resonance by showing overlap areas in which certain words and phrases carry meanings in two or even three domains. The clinical–spiritual overlap can be seen in terms such as *serenity, wholeness, hope,* and *trust.* The clinical–moral overlap can be seen in terms such as *commitment, honesty, responsibility,* and *violence.* Examples would be the Ten Commandments, sin, and the Golden Rule. Finally, in the center of the figure is the zone of overlap among all three domains, evident in terms such as *healing, values, guilt,* and *forgiveness.* These words resonate across spirituality, morality, and therapy. I do not defend the placement of every specific term in the model, but rather my aim is to illustrate the kinds of words that convey different kinds of spiritual, moral, and clinical meaning in contemporary U.S. society. I also note that historically clinical language has been the most recent entry into human discourse, and the most individualistic.

CLINICAL USE OF THE THREE-DOMAINS MODEL

Since it deals with the language of spirituality, morality, and clinical care, the three domains model has several implications for how therapists can approach spiritual issues in clinical practice. This discussion is intended for therapists working in secular settings where a common religious affiliation and spiritual orientation cannot be assumed or readily called upon.

First, without knowledge of the client's spiritual beliefs and preferred spiritual language, the therapist is advised to avoid introducing terms in the "spiritual-only" domain in exploring the client's experience. It would generally be a mistake for a therapist to ask the client if he or she is praying about his or her problem unless the client had already opened up this spiritual domain by referring to prayer or at least a belief in a personal God. Similarly, the secular therapist ought not to refer to the Bible without a prior understanding that the client gives allegiance to the Bible. This first implication reflects a clear consensus in the spirituality and therapy literature about therapists' following the client's lead rather than taking the lead (Becvar, 1996; Tan, 1996).

Second, therapists should be wary about self-disclosing their own spiritual beliefs and practices without establishing that the client shares them in some way or wishes to hear about the therapist's orientation. Wulff (1996) makes the incisive point that every religious claim implicitly asks for the listener's assent. For me to tell a depressed client that I know God loves her is more than a statement of my faith. It is a statement that asks for agreement and appropriation by the client, and it could be a misuse of my position of power and responsibility in the therapeutic conversation unless I am confident that the client shares my belief in a loving God. Self-disclosure that follows the client's lead, on the other hand, can sometimes be quite therapeutic if the timing is right.

Third, if the therapist is familiar with the client's spiritual language and faith tradition, and if the client is interested in using this language and calling on this faith tradition, then the therapist can serve as a spiritual consultant and coexplorer. An example is a man who had worked hard in individual and marital therapy to deal with the aftermath of his extramarital affair. But in a marital therapy session he said he was planning to attend a Catholic retreat (he had just converted to Catholicism) and seek forgiveness in Confession. When his wife objected, saying that she thought they both had put the issue behind them, he said he couldn't explain it better than to say he needed to go beyond himself and their relationship. I then said the following: "It sounds like you believe your affair offended a higher moral order than just you and your wife, and that you want to seek forgiveness from God, now that you have been forgiven by your wife." He affirmed that I had got it right, and his wife understood for the first time that he was not trying to dig up an old, settled issue but was seeking spiritual and moral healing. This case is also an illustration of the power of relational therapy in dealing with spiritual issues and moral issues, because his wife at first could not support him on the last leg of his journey of reconciliation.

Martha had finally decided to divorce her emotionally abusive husband. It was an overdue decision, I believed, because he had shown no willingness to look at his own destructive behavior, and Martha and the children were suffering with the ambiguity of whether her husband was going to move back home or whether the couple were divorcing. Martha, who had been her husband's emotional caretaker for many years, was tormented by the thought of not being able to help him now that he was facing this rejection and the possibility of relapsing into alcoholism. She said, "But there is nothing I can do for him, is there?" I replied, "Not without making things worse; others will have to look out for him now." After a pause, and pondering her strong religious faith, I added, "But you can pray for him." She sat up straight for the first time in the session and said, "Thanks for saying that. I do pray for him every day, and I'll continue to. That is the one thing I can do without confusing him and me and the kids about this divorce." I introduced this spiritual term because I was confident she would relate to it and find it helpful.

Fourth, if the therapist does not know the client's spiritual beliefs, then spiritual issues can be broached implicitly through the language of the overlap areas. The famous serenity prayer can be used without the "God grant me" introduction. A woman was struggling courageously against her breast cancer but did not believe in God; she said that she would keep fighting although she knew that the outcome was out of her control. I introduced the term "serenity" as one that resonates across the clinical and spiritual domains: it goes deeper than the term "acceptance" and connotes for many people a surrender to a broader reality than our own. Similarly, like many other therapists I make a distinction with clients between "optimism," which denotes a rational process of assessing likely outcomes, and "hope," which runs deeper and is connected by some people with spirituality. Terms such as "suffering" instead of "pain" also resonate across the clinical and spiritual domains in a safe way that does not risk alienating the client but does deepen the therapeutic conversation.

Fifth, when the therapist senses that a religious client is using spiritual-only language in a rote or empty way, introducing clinical/spiritual or clinical/moral/spiritual overlap language can enhance the client's experience. For example, should the client use the term "reborn" with little emotional resonance or conviction, the therapist could inquire about the ways in which God's love has brought growth and healing to the client. Or a couple who are considering rejecting their son because he is gay, based on statements of Christian doctrine and biblical texts, might be offered the chance to pursue the other side of the Christian story about love and faithfulness. It is important not to pit the overlap language against the client's core spiritual beliefs, but rather to create the possibility of an expanded conversation and an altered spiritual narrative when the current one seems to be compromising personal or family health.

Sixth, when a family is in conflict over different spiritual beliefs or religious tradition, the therapist can use the overlap areas to search for core beliefs and values that are shared across the family. A fundamentalist Christian and an atheist can both believe in the importance of moral responsibility and of constructive guilt when we transgress our responsibilities, but they might well agree to disagree about whether the moral order originates with God or humanity. In other words, family members can meet at the level of values, which connect the clinical, moral, and spiritual domains, rather than stay stuck with their theological differences. In one family therapy session, both the conservative Catholic father and the gay, agnostic son were surprised that they held similar desires to make the world a better place through their lives.

In sum, an appreciation of the language differences and points of connection among the clinical, moral, and spiritual domains can serve as a guide for therapists through these waters. Since therapy is basically a form of conversation, the appropriate role of spirituality in therapy will have to be played out in terms of the language we learn to use with our clients and the language they use with us. In the next section, I will apply to spiritual consultation a model I originally developed to map different degrees of intensity of moral language in therapy.

DEGREES OF INTENSITY OF SPIRITUAL CONSULTATION IN THERAPY

When authors write about their use of spirituality in therapy, they often describe their most dramatic cases and outstanding interventions. This can suggest to readers who are tentative about this area that spiritual "interventions" are generally intense, and therefore risky. I have dealt with a related concern about moral consultation in therapy: many therapists tend to view their role as (preferably) keeping quiet about moral issues or (if all else fails) telling the clients that their behavior is wrong—the *a* or *z* approach. I have developed a model of graduated levels of intensity for moral consultation, with the advice that therapists mostly stay in the low-intensity zone of affirming and asking questions (Doherty, 1995). For example, the quintessential moral "intervention" is the simple question about how the client believes his or her behavior might affect the welfare of another person or group of persons, say, "How do you think moving to another state after the divorce would affect your children?" Only occasionally is the therapist called upon to increase the intensity by direct moral challenge, as I did when I challenged a father who was about to leave town and not see his children again. Following is my adaptation of this model for the use of spiritual language in therapy. Therapist statements are arranged in order from less to more intense.

1. *Acknowledge the client's spontaneous statements of spiritual beliefs.* This may seem obvious, but many therapists historically have kept silent and seemed uncomfortable when clients uttered spiritual statements. When I asked a married woman about where she got her courage to keep trying to salvage her marriage, she replied that, although she knew that divorce was a possibility, "The heart of God would be sad if I ended this marriage right now." I told her I was moved by what she said, thereby acknowledging and validating her spiritual sensibility.

2. *Inquire about the client's spiritual beliefs and practices.* The therapist can ask clients at the start of therapy and later in the therapy whether religion and spirituality are important in their lives, or important in their thinking about their problems and how to get past them. For example, I asked a Turkish man if his religious beliefs were a resource for him during his years of intense back pain. He responded "No, I am not a religious person." No harm was done, and I had directly checked out this potential resource in his life. But I do not routinely ask every new client this kind of question in the first session; mostly I let the topic unfold.

3. *Inquire about how the client connects the spiritual, clinical, and moral dimensions of his or her life or problems.* Here the therapist explores clients' beliefs about how their spiritual beliefs ought to shape the rest of their lives. A therapist might ask a woman who is a caregiver for her demented husband what role her faith plays in her decision to keep her husband at home as long as possible. The goal would to help her connect the strands of her moral commitment, her spiritual beliefs, and her everyday behavior with her husband.

4. *Express agreement with the client's spiritual beliefs or sensibilities when such self-disclosure could be therapeutic.* Here the therapist increases the intensity of the encounter by affirming and agreeing with the client on a spiritual matter. If a guilt-ridden client says, weakly, that God loves her no matter what, the therapist can reply, with stronger words and more emotion, "I agree that God loves you more than you will ever know." A therapist who believes in an afterlife can assent when the grieving father says that his son is with God now. Of course, the therapist must be able to agree authentically with the client. Without such commonality of belief, the therapist can sensitively ask the client to explore the meaning and power of a belief, say, in the possibility of a miracle from God to save a loved one's life, without appearing to hold the same belief.

5. *Articulate the client's dilemma without giving your own position.* With the parents of the gay son who are considering rejecting him permanently (discussed earlier), this kind of statement could be made: "I can appreciate the terrible dilemma you are in. On the one hand, you have your strong religious beliefs that homosexuality is wrong and you wonder if you can be true to your beliefs and keep your son in your life. On the other hand, you clearly have a powerful love for your son and want to be there for him as long as you live. And that love is based on your religious values a well. I'm sure this is a heartbreaking situation for you." This kind of statement can be an intervention designed to highlight the second part of the dilemma—their commitment to their son—if that part of the dilemma was not explicit in their prior statements.

6. *Point out the contradictions between the client's spiritual beliefs, or between spiritual beliefs and clinical realities or moral issues.* For the above couple with the gay son, the therapist could observe that the parents will have to choose between two of God's teachings: how they see God's law on sexual behavior, and how they see God's law on parental commitment to their children. This statement goes beyond laying out the dilemma; it suggests that the parents will have to decide which of their competing spiritual beliefs will take priority. Or consider a born-again Christian woman who could not refuse to be involved with her ex-husband who had become a Christian partly to keep her in his life. He told her that a real Christian would not turn her back on a man who cared for her. Although she disagreed with him, she could not cut off contact because he did not see the situation her way; he saw her as being selfish and un-Christian. I asked her to think about Jesus throwing the money changers out of the temple. Did she think that the money changers at that moment believed he was doing the right thing out of love? She immediately saw the point and proceeded to disconnect from her toxic ex-husband.

7. *Challenge the client's way of handling spiritual beliefs on the basis of your own spiritual beliefs, your moral beliefs, or your clinical beliefs.* The key is to do this with a respectful yet firm "I" statement. For example, before ending the consultation with the parents who are heading toward rejecting their gay son and who want the therapist to change their son's sexual orientation, the therapist could say, "I appreciate how painful this dilemma is for you, and I am not living in your shoes. But before we finish this conversation, and since this may be the last time we meet, I want to give you a sense of how I feel about this kind of decision. Again, I cannot make the decision for you, but my own belief is that the highest calling we have from God is to be faithful to our children, even when they do things we believe are wrong. My religious beliefs almost always lead me to come down on the side of maintaining family commitments rather than severing them." A therapist who does not have an explicit spiritual orientation could deliver the same message by staying at the moral level: that the right thing is never to reject one's child permanently. The strictly clinical level

would not be strong enough for this kind of challenge, although mentioning the psychological and family toll of the decision on the adult son and the rest of the family might inform the moral and spiritual discussion.

The most intense forms of spiritual discourse are best reserved for extreme cases and require a good degree of empathic connection beforehand. Most of the time, the spiritually sensitive therapist will stay with acknowledging and exploring the client's spiritual meanings and faith community and how they connect to the clinical problem. Occasionally the therapist will self-disclose or summarize dilemmas. Even less frequently will the therapist set up the issues as requiring choice of one spiritual belief over another, and more rarely still will the therapist flat out challenge the way the client is resolving a spiritual/moral/clinical issue. But just as challenges are sometimes necessary in the clinical and moral realms, they can be necessary in the spiritual realm if we are to do our job as consultants and healers.

CONCLUSION

As the healing art we call psychotherapy enters its second century, its frontiers lie in tying together the disconnected threads of the human life: the genetic language of our bodies, the psychological language of our minds, the family systems language of our intimate bonds, the community language of our wider associations, the moral language of our personal and social obligations, and the spiritual language of our deepest connections and essential beliefs about the meaning and purpose of our common journey. Therapy that neglects any of these threads truncates the human personality. But just as we still have much to learn about human behavior in the clinical domain, we are in the early phases of exploring the work of the spirit in our consultation rooms and our communities.

REFERENCES

Becvar, D. S. (1996). *Soul healing: A spiritual orientation in counseling and therapy*. New York: Basic Books.

Bergin, A. E. (1980). Psychotherapy and religious values. *Journal of Consulting and Clinical Psychology, 48,* 95–105.

Browning, D. S. (1987). *Religious thought and the modern psychologies*. Philadelphia: Fortress Press.

Doherty, W. J. (1995). *Soul searching: Why psychotherapy must promote moral responsibility*. New York: Basic Books.

Elkins, D. (1990, June). On being spiritual without necessary being religion. *Association for Humanistic Psychology Perspective,* pp. 4–6.

Shafranske, E. P. (Ed.). (1996). *Religion in the clinical practice of psychology*. Washington, DC: American Psychological Association.

Stander, V., Piercy, F. P., MacKinnon, D., & Helmeke, K. (1994). Spirituality, religion and the family: Competing or complementary worlds? *American Journal of Family Therapy, 22*, 27–41.

Tan, S. Y. (1996). Religion in clinical practice: Implicit and explicit integration. In E. P. Shafranske (Ed.), *Religion in the clinical practice of psychology.* Washington, DC: American Psychological Association.

Wieman, H. N. (1995). *The source of human good.* Atlanta, GA: Scholars Press. (Originally published in 1946)

Wulff, D.M. (1996). The psychology of religion: An overview. In E. P. Shafranske (Ed.), *Religion in the clinical practice of psychology.* Washington, DC: American Psychological Association.

CHAPTER 11

Healing from Trauma
The Quest for Spirituality

MARY JO BARRETT

Trauma interrupts emotional, psychological, spiritual, sexual, and/or intellectual development and chronically or acutely impinges on a person's ability to cope or function. Most of the clients that I work with have been traumatized by physical and/or sexual violations. For the first 10 years of my work in the field of violence, I focused on helping them heal from these physical/sexual violations and from their debilitating symptoms, developing specific interventions to interrupt dysfunctional sociopolitical, familial, and intrapsychic patterns. In 1992, we began doing exit and follow-up interviews with our clients. As they left the program, we asked them what they believed had changed in their lives and to what did they attribute this change. We then followed up 6 months and 1 year later, again asking whether they had maintained their changes and, if so, to what did they attribute their changes in retrospect. We have fortunately been able to interview some clients as long as 15 years after they left the program. What they told us has changed my life and my treatment of trauma.

LOVE AND KNOWLEDGE

A Soul met an angel and asked: "By which path shall I reach heaven quickest—the path of knowledge or the path of love?" The angel looked wonderingly and said, "Are not both paths one?"

—OLIVE SCHREINER (in Keen, 1994, p. 93)

The stories our clients told us about what they believed created the change in their lives revolved around two themes: love and knowledge. First, they believed that their own desire, will, and internal spirit created the change. Generally, they reported that in their soul they had made the following discoveries: "in the depth of my bones ... [I felt that] I had [changed] and that I could change"; "Therapy was a process of getting myself back, not changing who I am but reconnecting with my spirit"; "I learned to love myself again"; "I came to remember that I deserved to be happy"; "I started to value myself and other people around me." They had tapped into a reservoir of self-love.

They also told us that the meaning of the world and what they believed about people, had changed—especially finding out that everything was not black or white, good or evil.

The clients told us of the following personal discoveries:

"I began to see that the whole world and everybody in it were not dangerous."

"We began to treat members in our families like we were being treated in the program, with respect and care."

"We learned that there were good people out there who wanted and could help."

"I started to see more beauty where there used to be only gray."

"Everyone was not good or evil; there is a middle ground."

"The therapy renewed my faith in mankind. I just kept meeting more and more people who cared and took the time for me."

"There was a time when I thought everyone would hate me for what I did. What I learned is that they hated what I did but not me."

What they told us is that by being in a treatment program they changed their view of the world and the people in it.

People want ways to bring meaning into their lives to provide access to the world of faith and meaning. A time to experience awe. Awe helps us to find the faith to move forward. (Hammerschlag & Silverman, 1997, p. 8)

The second theme of change was knowledge. Clients felt that they had become aware of their recurrent patterns and had discovered new methods of coping, functioning, and interacting. It was clear that many aspects of therapy—from the practical insights to psychoeducational processes—gave them new knowledge about how to deal with the world. They reported that they learned communication skills, how to create safe boundaries, and how to relieve their anxieties or struggle with their addictions. At the same time many clients said that they were changing on a deeper level. They felt that they were regaining the essence of who they were. As they were learning skills, methods of communicating, ways of coping with their pain and rage, they were simultaneously discovering new meaning about their world and the individuals in it.

The Buddha says that clinging is the cause of pain and that ignorance is the cause of clinging. (Dick Olney, in R. Moore, 1996, p. 24)

So, the first step in seeking happiness is learning. We first have to learn how negative emotions and behaviors are harmful to us and how positive emotions are helpful. And we must realize how these negative emotions are not only very bad and harmful to one personally but harmful to society and the future of the whole world as well. That kind of realization enhances our determination to face and overcome them. (The Dalai Lama, in the Dalai Lama & Cutler, 1998, p. 38)

As the clients learned more about people, patterns, and self they clung less to damaging old beliefs about themselves and the world around them. It became clear that the process of change had tapped a divine spark in the majority of clients we interviewed. They had realized a source of goodness and caring that moved them to act on principle, to do what is right for themselves and for others. The clients had learned through the psychoeducational techniques and their healing relationships with the therapists, their family members, and others in their groups that the negative self-judgment was hurting themselves and others both physically and spiritually. We spent many conscious moments helping clients see how hurting others was also damaging to themselves. Christianity, Judaism, and Islam all teach that each of us is created in the divine image. What we helped clients learn was that when evil thoughts, feelings, and/or behaviors present themselves to us, this becomes an opportunity to behave "Godlike." We have the opportunity to be a "creator" instead of a "reactor." This does not necessitate a belief in God. It necessitates a desire to feel and be something and someone different. Treatment had enabled the clients to envision the world and themselves differently.

The more open I was to the clients the more I heard. The change of spirit was happening simultaneously as their behaviors changed. But as they talked and I listened it became clear that this change of spirit came from the meaning and value they experienced in relationship to the treatment teams. The healing from trauma is a quest for spirituality. This quest reflects a deep need for meaning and value.

I began to look at the work I and my colleagues did through a different filter. By no means did we throw out the vast base of knowledge we had accumulated through the years. Nor did we abandon our bag of tools. We began to add a new perspective. We added the belief system that becoming spiritually aware of ourselves would invite in an energy that would help our clients resist their usual hurtful behavior. After talking with more than 200 clients, we began to overtly introduce a spiritual discipline into our day-to-day practice. As with any other body or mind faculties, the spiritual sense is a faculty that must be developed and maintained. I realized I had to focus regularly on these spiritual moments in both my professional and personal life. I approached this shift as I approach anything else: the clients told us that therapy provided meaning and human value and connection; then I set out to discover how this happened so that I and all the therapist I train could provide meaning and value more consistently.

INTEGRATING SPIRITUAL MEANING
AND VALUE INTO TREATMENT

When someone is abused, whether a child or an adult, by someone who is in a position of power over him or her and to whom he or she is attached, the result is a traumatic interruption on many levels but particularly on the level of spirit. Each story is different, but all clients report that the abuse has forever changed them and how they see the world. When individuals are abused they experience a loss of trust, a loss of innocence, a loss of peacefulness. They begin to see the world as dangerous, and there is a heightened awareness of the presence of evil inclination. They become acutely aware of their vulnerability in the universe and they no longer feel powerful. They have split into judge and the judged. They have lost their sense of self determination. They are burdened with a sense that what they do or who they are does not have much value or influence in their world.

The Dalai Lama states, "True spirituality is a mental attitude that you can practice at any time" (The Dalai Lama & Cutler, 1998, p. 300). When we view spirituality as the Dalai Lama does, we see that when the spirit is violated then the mental attitude that is practiced after the violation is one of fear, anger, pain, self-judgment, and/or self-blame. Our job then becomes helping clients practice a spiritual attitude of self-acceptance, helping them "wake up from the bad dream that they are incomplete or insufficient or lacking something" (Olney, in R. Moore, 1994, p. 4).

It was no accident that at the same time that I was involved in the follow-up study I was in the midst of my own professional crisis. I had come to realize that I had been vicariously traumatized. I had not been damaged physically or sexually, and not by family members. Yet, I had a damaged spirit. My happy, optimistic, energetic, divine spirit was gone. Rabbi Alan Miller describes internal spirituality as a Godliness, "The term God is rather the name we give to the interpersonal process of growth and creativity that takes place naturally among men and women striving towards authentic fulfillment" (quoted in Hirsh, 1994, p. 4). I had found in my life that I was no longer moving toward this process of growth and creativity. I had lost many of my essential beliefs that had brought me to this profession and to my specialty in trauma. My view of the world had changed. I no longer believed that people were basically good. Rather, I had become afraid of the evil inclination. I was feeling more certain that the evil inclination was more powerful than the human desire to be good. I was no longer as clear about the meaning of life. As a clinician I could view this as depression, but I knew in my soul that it was a crisis of spirit. An existential crisis is very different than a situational depression. Day after day, moment after moment, my work with survivors and offenders had taken me down the road of the most evil and painful human experiences. Just like the clients I work with, I had been changed forever—changed through the process of listening to them and being compassionately there for them in their most painful narratives. Of course, having a dying spirit made me more empathetic to my clients' stories about their loss of spirit, but it was destroying me and my family. I came to the realization that something must change radically for me. Like any good clinician, I made an assessment and tried to determine the symptoms and how they functioned.

At the same time that I was becoming increasingly aware of my painful loss of spirit, I was also hearing, through the interviews, stories of renewal. It was serendipitous: the path of renewal for my clients would also become the path of renewal for myself.

CONSCIOUS SPIRITUALITY

The task before me was how to rebuild my spirit so that I would be spiritually available to my clients. The next step would be how to teach others the importance of conscious spirituality. The clients need us to communicate with a vocabulary that offers hope, inspiration, and comfort. How does one develop hope and inspiration and then convey this to others?

I believe that change happens in stages. The model that we have developed in working with trauma is a three-stage model (Trepper & Barrett, 1990). Moving the unconscious knowledge to the conscious also happens in stages. Because it has proved helpful for me to organize my treatment in these stages, it was helpful for me to think about these three stages when organizing my renewal.

Stage 1: Creating a Context for Change

> There is an interesting story about P. D. Ouspensky, who was a student of the great Middle Eastern mystic L. I. Gurdjieff. Ouspensky had several turbulent nights in a row. He was taking a mind-altering drug each evening, then spending intense hours trying to unravel the mystery of the meaning of life. He would sometimes think that he had found the answer, but in the morning he was unable to remember it.
>
> On this particular night, he had the idea of writing down what occurred to him. Sure enough, when he woke up in the morning, no matter how hard he tried, his nighttime revelations eluded him. When he remembered that he had

written the answer down, his excitement was palpable. You can probably imagine his anticipation as he opened his notebook. Expecting to read a long and complicated explanation, what he found were these four words: THINK IN OTHER CATEGORIES.

—DICK OLNEY (in R. Moore, 1996, p. 3)

This was the first stage of spiritual renewal for me. I had to begin to "think in other categories." I had to become aware of what was constraining me from experiencing myself and the world around me at any given moment. The first steps were to slow down, step back, and observe. My life, personal and professional, like so many others, had become so busy and filled with routine that I had lost much of my sense of awe and the time to discover beauty. I had to create a context where there would be opportunity for spiritual growth. The Buddhists speak of "practice." I needed to create space in my life where I could practice a new attitude toward life, toward the world, and toward self.

First, I formally acknowledged the need for a shift in my spirit. I began to discuss with the important people in my life the changes necessary to rekindle my passion for humanity.

I knew I needed love and knowledge to be able to change. I asked for help. I asked colleagues, friends, and loved ones to support me on this journey and to participate in any ways that they found comfortable. Many people close to me had commented on numerous occasions that I was different, that I had lost my spirit. It appeared that I was the last to discover my dwindling spark. They were all quite supportive of this quest. They shared their own stories and offered support. I realized I needed knowledge, and so I began to read and take courses. I read about different cultures' paths toward spirituality. I explored Native American traditions, as well as Zen and Kabbalistic philosophies of spirituality and meditation (e.g., Berg, 1993). I also read outside the field of family therapy, delving into the disciplines outside of our own that have struggled for decades with the issue of spirituality. There was much literature to read. I only skimmed the surface. Once I got over the shame of my narrow lenses and my ignorance of the fields of transpersonal psychology and humanistic psychology, I gleefully feasted on newfound sources of knowledge. The work of Ken Wilbur and Dick Olney were particularly great influences. Wilbur helped me make sense of the role of mysticism in psychology and how consciousness works on a continuum. His writings on the Eastern and Western views of personal growth truly began the integration process for me. Wilbur (1991) writes in *Grace and Grit*:

According to the mystics, when we go beyond or transcend our separate-self sense, our limited ego, we discover instead a Supreme Identity, an identity with the All, with universal Spirit, infinite and all pervading, eternal and unchanging. As Albert Einstein explains: "A human being is part of the whole, called by us Universe; a part limited in time and space. He experiences himself, his thoughts and feelings as something separated from the rest—a kind of optical delusion of his consciousness. This delusion is a kind of prison for us, restricting us to our personal desires and to affection for a few persons nearest us. Our task must be to free ourselves from this prison." . . . Indeed, the whole point of meditation or contemplation is to free ourselves from the "optical delusion" that we are merely separate egos set apart from each other [and] from eternal Spirit, and to discover instead that, once released from the prison of individuality we are with all manifestation, in a perfectly timeless and eternal fashion. (p. 18)

Through my consultations with Olney, I came to recognize the importance of experiencing one's own sense of beauty. Olney's *self-acceptance training* is simply defined as "experiencing myself as I am without the inhibitions of self-judgement, self-criticism, or self-evaluation. It is not a goal, but an attitude toward life which one can come back to again and again" (R. Moore, 1996).

Dick Olney often said:

You are not your body. You are not your name. You are not your thoughts. You are not your emotions. You are not your memories. You are not the content of your consciousness. You are the unspeakable. That which cannot be named. If you name it you turn it into one more concept. A better question than "Who am I?" is "What am I?" What you are is life! You are carrying the gift of life. You are a fire that has been burning for millions of years. You are your ancestors. (in R. Moore, 1996, pp. 28–29)

As I studied it became clear to me that I had become deeply imprisoned in my own "optical delusions" and what I needed was to be on the path to freeing myself. I discovered that my journey had to involve vehicles to the unconscious. This meant providing an environment for meditation, peaceful sleep, celebration of life, and prayer.

Everyone's context for spiritual renewal is unique, but there might be some common elements. Years after I had begun renewed spiritual practice I was having a conversation with my rabbi, Brant Rosen, about spirituality and psychotherapy. He gave me an article that discussed the different needs that can be met through prayer and attempted to answer the question, "Why do people pray?" In an article entitled, "How Can Reconstructionist Pray?" I discovered that what I was doing in my office according to this article was a form of prayer. Prayer is not necessarily an appeal to God, nor is it merely asking another source to do something for us. It is an opportunity to go inside ourselves, alone or in community, and call upon our own desire and resources to create change. It is the time to look inward and draw upon our own creative, moral energy to create this positive force outside of ourselves. Prayer is a vehicle to "think in other categories" (R. Moore, 1996, p. 4) in order to unravel the mystery of life. Much of the work that was necessary to rekindle my spirit and free me from the prison I had built around myself came through different forms of prayer. It can be a form of meditation, a form of appreciation, a form of awareness of our universal membership in humanity.

I had successfully changed my environment to include the elements of prayer in my life on a regular basis. These elements seemed to summarize how spirituality works in the treatment of trauma. In fact, my own personal work and our treatment had incorporated all these elements:

- *Spiritual discipline.* We need to discipline ourselves to focus regularly on creative, beautiful, and sacred encounters, developing and maintaining a regular practice of stepping back and noticing spiritual moments as they occur—or remembering those moments.
- *Meditation.* We all live at a very rapid pace. We can learn to welcome the opportunity to slow down to remember what has deeper meaning beyond our daily distractions.
- *Connection.* This is an opportunity to leave our spiritual isolation. Through either connection with others or connection with our own sense of value and power we can focus on and perhaps express what is really important to us.
- *Celebration.* Moments of celebration, like laughter, can transport us beyond ourselves, beyond ego, beyond self-judgment.
- *Support.* Renewal is enhanced by the support of a caring group. There is often a tangible power when the energy of a group is focused in a mutual direction.
- *Rededication.* It is easy to lose perspective, to miss the forest for the trees. We all get so wound up in a situation that we lose sight of who we are and what we stand for. We need a method to draw us out of ourselves and restore the larger picture.
- *Acknowledgment of need.* Most of us are raised to think that we have control of our lives and therefore that we are responsible for what happens to us—both good and bad. It is necessary to acknowledge our vulnerability. Removing our defenses can move us to the honest self-awareness we require to get past our personal obstacles.

It also became clear to me that what the clients had been saying to us in our interviews was that therapy and their relationships with us had been part of their getting out of prison. We had incorporated these elements into our therapy. By defining prayer this way, we had been praying for 25 years with clients and not even realizing it. By having meaningful connections with others, the clients had experienced themselves as part of the greater universe, not just seeing themselves as their body, name, thoughts, memories, consciousness but something more.

Stage 1 of the model revolves around three primary goals:

1. To provide safety for the client, both in treatment and in relation to the team and moving toward safety in their lives.
2. To provide an environment where clients can begin to tell their story about all aspects of their lives, through family, individual, and group modalities.
3. To acknowledge their clients' need for change and to commit to the program.

When consciously integrating spirituality into trauma treatment we keep these same three goals. First, it is essential to provide an environment where it is safe and accepted for clients to discuss their need and desire for spiritual and moral behavior, as well as their views of it. Next we want to hear their current beliefs about people, good and evil, meaning, and relationships; what role religion currently plays in their lives; and what they think the future holds for them. Finally, how do they see therapy being helpful in this domain? Are there specific behaviors or topics about spirituality they want to integrate in their program?

In my own life, Stage 1 consisted of learning about spirituality, defining it, and then creating a plan for spiritual practice. It became clear to me that this practice is an essential part of healing from trauma. This awareness developed during the interviews, and I decided to introduce this element of connection and spirituality more overtly into stage 1 of the treatment program.

All therapists at our Center have made a conscious effort to create a physical environment that is more conducive to spiritual discipline. We have the capabilities for appropriate music, aromatherapy, as well as candles, footstools, headrests, pillows, etc. This allows the client to design his or her own context for spiritual awareness. We share with them from the beginning that we have discovered from talking with our clients that there are elements of spirituality that have been helpful to integrate into treatment such as rededication, celebration, or meditation. We discuss with them their definitions of spirituality and morality and how it may feel for them to integrate this into their treatment program. It is common for us to integrate their use of prayer or their religion into sessions. As might be expected, there are questions and discussions about our view of spirituality. Our answers are direct. We share the information we have received from past clients, refer them to literature, and discuss the personal nature of each person's journey. We are available to guide them but not direct them or instruct them on how to be spiritual. Simply put, "We are here to guide you, through the sharing of information and by example, how to transform your negative reactivity to positive proactivity toward self and one another." Many of the offenders we work with "have found God" in jail. We see this not as an answer—that they are "saved" and "cured"—but instead as part of the puzzle for understanding their abusive behavior and stopping future abuse. In other words, how do they really live a God-filled life?

We introduce language that helps them begin to understand, identify, and discuss the internal conflict of good and evil. Clients who have been traumatized understand this language instinctually. They have often already identified this conflict. We will use their language for identifying this struggle: evil inclination, Satan, the dark side, or the evil part; or we might help them by introducing the Parts Model to them (see Schwartz, Chapter 13, this volume). Stage 1 is the introduction to the concepts of spirituality and the acknowledgment of need for spiritual connection within ourselves and between people. Stage 2 is the active integration of these ideas into the program and into their lives.

Stage 2: Challenging Patterns and Expanding Realities

Stage 2 is learning the patterns that constrain us from creating harmony in our lives; it also entails practicing new methods of being proactive that will produce expanded realities. On one level this means considering the following questions: What are the patterns in my life that produce violent behavior or behaviors that are self-abusive? What are the patterns that keep me in an abusive relationship or keep me reacting to the world as a victim? What are the constraints that stop me from changing these patterns? Then together, in family, individual, and/or group modalities, we explore alternative behaviors, cognitions, and feeling patterns that help the clients expand their repertoire beyond victim/perpetrator, from negatively reactive to positively proactive.

We have discovered that the absence of spiritual connection is a variable that allows people to abuse themselves and others. During stage 2 we introduce active alternatives for bringing spiritual connection into clients' lives.

In my own quest, this meant utilizing the knowledge I had acquired in stage 1 and applying this knowledge into a conscious program of practice. It meant interrupting daily patterns of disconnection and expanding practices of connection. In practical terms, it can be understood in terms of input and output. I tried to find a balance between putting out positive and negative energy into the environment, and also between putting out too much positive energy and not putting in enough positive energy into my body. I had to practice changing patterns in every realm of my life. I began an active ritual of meditations; I gave up caffeine in order to sleep uninterrupted. I began, with my colleague, the Self-Care Exchange, a weekend retreat at a spa for professionals. I began asking for help and support on a regular basis. I tried to change on every level: how I treated my soul, my body, my friends, my family, my colleagues, strangers. It takes a great deal of energy to be mindful. When I had been living a life that had ignored my spirit, most of my energy had been sapped. Using energy to replenish energy made more sense than using energy to deplete or maintain the status quo.

I look at this quest as a training program for myself. Dick Olney named his treatment model "Self-Acceptance Training," which "includes the word training because you constantly have to be . . . [doing so] to accept yourself, moment by moment. You can never do it once and for all" (in R. Moore, 1996, p. 5). I have found that training oneself to be mindful of one's spirit, in and out of therapy, is also a moment-by-moment endeavor. The Dalai Lama and many of his followers involve themselves in rigorous training to reach virtuous states of mind—compassion, tolerance, caring, and so forth.

> So, engaging in training or a method of bringing about inner discipline within one's mind is the essence of spiritual life, an inner discipline that has the purpose of cultivating these positive mental states. Thus, whether one leads a spiritual life depends on whether one has been successful in bringing about that disciplined, tamed state of mind, and translating that state of mind into one's daily actions. (The Dalai Lama & Cutler, 1998, p. 309)

In Stage 2 of treatment, we actively teach methods to discipline the mind to bring about positive mental states towards oneself and one another. It is imperative that the clinician be practicing his or her own discipline and communicating this value system moment by moment in the therapy room. This practice comes easily to us family therapists. We are strength oriented, relational, discipline minded, solution focused, and strategic, all concepts necessary for spiritual practice. Another strength of family therapists is our action-oriented and involved approach to our clients. This stance allows the clients to experience us as human beings and puts us in the position of collaborators. Consequently, if we are involved in spiritual practice then our clients will experience us as spiritual beings and hopefully allow us to be collaborators in their spiritual quest. In their book *Healing Ceremonies,* Hammerschlag and Silverman (1997) discuss the importance of genuine human contact in the process of healing:

> True healing only occurs when both participants (physician and patient) are connected in pursuing the common goal of healing. This connection promotes healing and should be expressed. This partnership also works both ways and affords the physician with the opportunity to grow and to become reenergized. (p. 13)

Albert Schweitzer commented "patients carry their own doctor inside. They come to us not knowing that truth. We are at our best when we give the physician who resides within each patient a chance to go to work" (in Hammerschlag & Silverman, 1997, p. 16). Indeed, this is stage 2, giving that healer inside the chance to go to work. By providing the context, the supportive relationships, the mentor, and techniques, individuals, families, and groups of people can practice spiritual healing. Being the mentor for spiritual practice is an essential ingredient:

> "I watched how my therapists handled everybody and everything. How they talked to the judge, how they talked to the attorneys and how they talked to each other. They were always the same, firm but respectful. I learned a lot from watching them."

> "We had some pretty good fights during therapy but I knew he [the therapist] still liked me. I guess I learned how to fight fair during those times."

> "I always felt special, not like I was the favorite but more like I was a good person."

> "Everyone I met at the Center, and I met a lot, were all good people. I really learned a lot about how to treat people from them—particularly in group."

Teaching clients to experience liberation from negative judgment through expressive techniques such as art, movement, poetry, music, and/or journaling can help create the sense of comfort and help them behold the wonder of their lives. Helping them practice prayer, meditation, self-hypnosis, and creative imagery can provide relief from their emotional, spiritual, or physical pain. Once they experience some relief in the office they will desire that relief and want to practice on their own. People are involved daily in altering their consciousness through hurtful and addictive patterns by abusing food, alcohol, drugs, sex, and power. I want to help people alter their consciousness in nonabusive ways. I do believe that we can become addicted to balance in our lives. It becomes a natural form of altering our consciousness.

As Dick Olney pointed out,

> Every time you experience liberation from your self-image you will feel a lack of tension, a wonderful sense of open space. You can just rest in that sense of comfort and ease. Each time you feel that way it becomes easier for you to recall. You have had an experience that can give you some comfort, even when you slip back in to the bad dream. (in R. Moore, 1996, p. 28)

I want to help provide our clients with literal relief from their traumas. During our interviews over 80% commented on the relief they experienced during the sessions:

> "I knew there would be times when we would all be fighting and hating each other but I could also count on the times we would remember why we had all stayed together through all of this shit."

"Sometimes, my therapy sessions would be the only time I would feel good all week."

"I use to feel like such a loser because of all the things I did to my wife and kids. It was amazing the first time I ever saw the light in my soul."

"I remember the first time I saw my evil side; I was scared but I knew it was it. While I was doing the imagery I was aware for the first time that I could fight him with another side of me. I remember I left the office smiling."

"I remember the first time I learned to meditate and I saw Susie; she was always the friend who could make me smile. I still bring up Susie's image while I am mediating, and it is 5 years later."

"In one session I literally felt my heart break when I was talking about the abuse; I learned an imaging exercise to put it back together. I have mended that damn thing more times than I'd like to remember."

The techniques that we teach are borrowed from many practices. The clients try out different alternatives and practice what fits them. We want our clients to feel the power of their spirit. These are people who have felt powerless, disconnected, and out of control in their lives. We want part of the treatment to be their sense of power: "When you believe yourself to be powerless in determining your destiny, you fail to thrive. Choice makes a difference. . . . Choice is the greatest power you have. Believing you can influence your destiny makes a difference at every level of your being" (Hammerschlag & Silverman, 1997, p. 16). It is important to remember that the clients I am speaking of are all victims and/or perpetrators of trauma, many court mandated, many on probation, crossing all racial, religious, and ethnic groups and from different socioeconomic and educational backgrounds. Spirituality is universal and it helps us be aware of our unity.

Stage 3: Consolidation

Stage 3 of the treatment model is when we consolidate the changes the clients have made through the program, design relapse prevention, and ritualize through ceremony and celebration the changes they have made. We also celebrate the relationships they have made within and outside the program.

When I refer to consolidation of my spiritual journey it is something entirely different. The journey is never ending; it is constantly evolving. Our clients' change is constantly evolving also; it does not stop once they leave therapy.

There is a form of consolidation each and every time you practice. One can end a spiritual experience with a ritual whether that is a mindful awareness of feeling good or noticing beauty or summarizing in our mind what opportunities are available to continue spiritual practices. Noticing these opportunities is a constant rededication to the commitment to living a moral and spiritual life.

I am constantly rededicating my professional life to finding ways to provide opportunities for spiritual growth with my clients. I agree with Hammerschlag and Silverman (1997): "People want ways to bring meaning into their lives to provide access to the world of faith and meaning. A time to experience awe. Awe helps us to find the faith to move forward. Ceremonies can help provide a way to get in touch with courage and inspiration in order to find healing" (p. 3). In the consolidation stage of working with clients' spiritual quest, we acknowledge all that we have learned about meaning. We commit ourselves to trying to use those moment-by-moment opportunities presented to us to live a moral and spiritual life. Through ritual and ceremony we rededicate ourselves to the process of this quest. We bring ceremony into the sessions. We celebrate the hard work of healing. We celebrate the existential shifts that have been made from violence to nonviolence, from victim-survivor to beyond survivor. We celebrate the behavioral changes as well as the deep changes within each person's heart. By stage 3 of treatment the clients are committed to a way of life that integrates behaviors that lead to healing and not further suffering. Clients remembered some of their consolidating rituals:

> "During one of the last sessions we looked into a crystal ball and everyone in our family looked [into it] for ways that we could possibly hurt each other again. Then we imagined alternatives to help each other get out of the angry places. When some of those times came up sometimes we would start laughing because we remembered the crystal ball."

> "In one of the last sessions, I was about 18, and I remember imagining what it would feel like when I fell in love and was safe. I carried that image with me for almost ten years. When it happened, I knew it because I had felt it once before."

> "We always ended the group with music and a special affirmation. I started doing that with my kids, a peaceful bedtime ritual."

> "My parents renewed their vows after therapy ended. We took pictures, I remember feeling like I had a new beginning."

> "It was unbelievably sad to say goodbye. It was like leaving an entire group of best friends, but I felt free at the same time. I knew I would always be connected to them and that I could always get help when I needed it."

Lise, who had been in treatment as a teenager, wrote this poem when asked about her experience.

My Life's Renewal

I spun out of control
Losing sight of all hope
My family turned away
And my soul bent over in pain
Feeling neglected and betrayed
My mind overflowed with rage
My behavior became unpredictable
The ability to dream, now fictional
Saturated with anger
I put myself in danger
Behaving shamelessly
Ignoring any authority
I had collapsed
I thought no one was watching until someone caught me
They helped me to see
That I could become free
With some dedication
And spiritual application
I learned to grow
Away from the pain I had known
Able to appreciate life
With more positive insight

When I hear these lines I know that they are about spirituality. The quest for spirituality is an ongoing process, but when you experience a spiritual moment you have no doubt that your spirit has been touched:

> That is what I call basic spirituality—basic human qualities of goodness, kindness, compassion, caring. Whether we are believers or nonbelievers, this kind of spirituality is essential. As long as we are human beings, as long as we are members of the human family, all of us need these basic spiritual values. We must still find a way to try to improve life for the majority of the people. Ways to help them become good human beings, moral people, without any religion. Education is crucial. Instilling in people a sense that compassion, kindness are basic good qualities. (The Dalai Lama, in the Dalai Lama & Cutler, 1998, p. 307)

The spiritual quest during the recovery of trauma happens in stages: First, is acknowledgment, in a safe environment, how the trauma has impacted your spirit; acknowledging how you have changed and rekindling the desire to spiritually reconnect with self and other. Next, designing the personal training program that will re-create the proactive energy which lies within all of us. During this stage comes the spiritual practice that will take our personal vibrations and continue to build energy. Finally, we have the commitment to ongoing spiritual practice—commitment to continue doing something different building on compassion, morality, and kindness toward self and humanity.

To conclude, I share this meditation with you. Our clients agreed that it was helpful to punctuate endings with ritual. It can be useful to end sessions, stages of treatment, supervision sessions, or staff meetings with such a ritual. As you read each line, pause, breath, and reflect on its meaning to you:

> May I be at peace
> May I come to know the beauty of my own true nature
> May my heart remain open
> May I be whole and healed.
> And may we all bring healing into the world for the highest good
> Whatever that may be.
>
> —UNKNOWN

REFERENCES

Berg, P. (1993). *Kabbalah for the layman* (Vol. 1). New York: Kabbalah Learning Center.

[The] Dalai Lama & Cutler, H. (1998). *The art of happiness.* New York: Riverhead Books.

Hammerschlag, C., & Silverman, H. (1997). *Healing ceremonies.* New York: Perigee Books.

Hirsh, R. (1994, Spring). Spirituality and the language of prayer. *The Reconstructionist,* pp. 1–6.

Keen, S. (1994). *Hymns to an unknown God.* New York: Bantam Books.

Moore, R. (Ed.). (1996). *Walking in beauty: A collection of psychological insights and spiritual wisdom of Dick Olney.* Mendocino, CA: DO Publishing.

Trepper, T., & Barrett, M. J. (1990). *Systemic treatment of incest: A clinical handbook.* Bristol, PA: Taylor & Francis.

Wilbur, K. (1991). *Grace and grit.* Boston: Shambhala.

SUGGESTED READING

Das, S. (1997). *Awakening the Buddha within.* New York: Broadway Books.

Levoy, G. (1997). *Callings: Finding and following an authentic life.* New York: Three Rivers Press.

Miller, A. (1990). *Banished knowledge.* New York: Anchor Books.

Moore, T. (1996). *The education of the heart.* New York: HarperCollins.

Moore, T. (1994). *Soul mates.* New York: Harper Perennial Library.

Redfield, J. (1993). *The Celestine prophecy.* New York: Warner Books.

Staub, J. (1996). *Connecting prayer and spirituality.* Wyncote, PA: Reconstructionist Press.

Weil, A. (1997). *8 weeks to optimum health.* New York: Knopf.

Wolin, S. J., & Wolin, S. (1993). *The resilient self.* New York: Villard Books.

CHAPTER 12

Opening Therapy to Conversations with a Personal God

MELISSA ELLIOTT GRIFFITH

There is no completely open conversational space in therapy just as there is no totally neutral therapist. Therapist and client are always opening and closing the doors to new places together, looking for that which has not been seen, listening for that which has not been heard, negotiating together the limits and the possibilities. My partner, James Griffith, and I are attempting to make the therapy space open enough for the most significant conversations to be heard and understood, and for the most significant others to be included in the construction of meaning, even when that significant other may be the Other, who is known by many names, whom some call God (J. L. Griffith, 1986; M. E. Griffith & J. L. Griffith, 1992; J. L. Griffith & M. E. Griffith, in press). If discourse is, as Bakhtin (1981) says, basically political, if story is made from many voices competing for space, then power is having space in the discourse. Justice, then, is when clients can tell their stories as they experience them, the only just censorship being that of protecting others from harm.

The space that this justice would create for clients to speak of their experiences with a personal God can be limited both by *proscriptive constraints*—that this God-talk is not to be spoken of here, and by *prescriptive constraints*—that God can and should be spoken of here, but only in a certain way. The secular psychotherapy culture may influence a therapist to impose proscriptive constraints inadvertently, while the religious counseling culture may influence a therapist to impose prescriptive constraints inadvertently.

This is not to say that a therapist's choice to limit spiritual talk is always inadvertent. Occasionally, therapists say that they intentionally avoid

209

discussing any religious topics with their clients: "That is the business of the priest, not the psychotherapist." And some clients say, "I prefer to deal with God's business in God's house."

However, most therapists recognize the significance of their clients' spiritual experiences and wish their clients could talk freely about them. This has been evident in many conversations with secular psychotherapists, pastoral counselors, and the multitude of therapists who, like myself, are influenced by both these cultures. Clients and persons who have participated in our research[1] have told us that they want to reflect on their spiritual experiences in therapy and that they feel fragmented by attempting to delegate psychological, relational issues to conversations with their therapist and spiritual issues to conversations with their priest or pastor. As one working within a psychotherapy culture nestled within the Deep South in the Bible Belt, this is a relevant concern for almost every person I work with in therapy, since almost every person has, has had, or feels that he or she should have had a relationship with a personal God.

So why don't conversations about this relationship happen in therapy? Given that therapists, counselors, and clients want these conversations to occur, what underlying assumptions lead us, unawares, to constrain them?

THE ENTRAPMENT OF KNOWING

I had last seen Susan 2 years ago when I had met with her and her mother in my role as family therapy consultant to a panic disorders treatment program. Now she said, "I'm in trouble again. I didn't want to go back to the panic disorders specialist, because he would not ever meet with me and my mama, but I knew that you would. I guess he thought I was too old for that, but what he doesn't understand is that Mama is the best support that I have, the only one who really knows. Anyway, I get the feeling he thinks I should see less of my mama, not more, but my getting well really matters almost as much to her as it does to me."

Of course, she did not want to lock her mother out at a time like this, and why should she have to? I began to privately simmer with indignation. I could say that the steam of my indignation rose from my commitment to systemic family therapy or to the notion that it is the client's privilege to bring whom she wants to her therapy. But, honestly, the fire that made my pot boil was my own experience in mothering and, parenthetically, my own experiences as a mother accompanying a child to a psychologist. I was thinking, "Where does this guy get off, deciding that Susan's mother would be bad for her, that she is overdependent, and assuming that only he knows best about who should be involved in her treatment? Susan and her mother have solved many problems before he came along. Good for her that she has decided to forego the expert and keep her relationship with her mother!"

Susan interrupted my thoughts: "I brought you something." She pulled a book from her purse, something like *The Christian Answer to Anxiety*. I squirmed, not wanting to dishonor her but not wanting to be programmed by ideas I might find hard to swallow.

"So when I realized that I could not go to the specialist, I started reading this wonderful book that Mama got for me. I read and I prayed, and I decided to come to you. I don't know if you will agree with this man's methods, but he has some good sound Christian ideas. If I'm going to get over this, I will need all the support I can get—Mama, you, and God."

I hesitated, fearing I could not satisfy Susan and remain true to myself. I thought of a perfect solution. I would refer her to a reputable local seminary-based counseling program that I thought might parallel the ideas of her book. "I don't know that I could learn and employ his methods, but since you find this to be so valuable, would you like me to connect you with a counselor who might have more expertise with this approach?"

"No, I don't want to do that. In fact, I called the author of this book in Oregon and asked him what I should do. He told me to come back to see you because I said I was comfortable with you. He even said that we didn't have to use his methods, that we could just take what we want to use and leave the rest. I'm pretty sure that we can work it out. I just know that I need to depend upon the Lord and that I can't do it alone."

Susan was asking me to include her God, not to be programmed by her book. She just wanted me to be interested. This was really not so different than her asking the panic disorder specialist to include her mother. It made sense. So, what made me so hesitant? The same kind of kneejerk thinking, I am embarrassed to say, that gave the specialist pause. When I saw the book title, I thought I *knew* about the God with whom she related. I *knew* that this was going to be an authoritative, inflexible, totally male God who would want not only Susan but me as well to be unquestioning and to submit to his authority. Because of what I thought I knew, I almost lost this opportunity to work with Susan, her mother, and her God, who actually turned out to be concerned, calming, and the One whose quiet, gentle voice she could hear the most clearly, calling her to self-acceptance and health.

This and many other cases repeatedly teach me that if "I think I know" the basic story of someone's experience with God, I am probably beginning to close off therapeutic possibilities. I then risk joining those forces of cultural oppression that would instruct and censor what could be spoken. Resistance to these forces is possible only to the extent that I can discover and depart from my own certainties.

My partner, James, and I have been interested in the process of discovering "stories of certainty" that lure us into "already knowingness," away from curiosity and creativity. We hope to open these certainties to the refreshing breezes of wonder, in which multiple realities can coexist and relationships can evolve. Both our clinical work and our research work (Tingle et al., 1993) have helped us to move from certainty to curiosity. Surely we have only begun to discover the "stories of certainty" that intrude into, oppress, and constrain the possibilities for conversations with God in therapy. Surely, other readers may still see certainties we continue to employ that we are unable to see. Or perhaps the reader may discover certainties of her or his own.

FROM CERTAINTY TO WONDER

I will offer some "certainties" we are beginning to recognize that we have held in our work and will then offer ways that we are finding to introduce curiosity.

Certainty 1: I know what God is like for you because I know your religious denomination.

When Southerners meet one another for the first time, each person's denominational affiliation is often part of the initial exchange of information. This classification cues us into the worship style and behavioral code of that group. This established, one would be more likely, say, to invite the Episcopalian and not the Southern Baptist over for daiquiris. Of course, it could be that the Episcopalian was a member of Alcoholics Anonymous (AA) and that the Southern Baptist enjoyed daiquiris, but a stranger would be more likely to learn this than a fellow Southerner.[2]

Likewise, we are cued into images of what God is like for that group. One is likely to imagine the God of the Southern Baptist to be a close but strict father, while the God of the Episcopalian might well be thought to be a remote, more lenient parent. These assumptions are often as false as the assumption about who enjoys daiquiris.

Our research has born out the shallowness of these assumptions. For example, we could not find a correlation between measures of religious fundamentalism and the extent to which the God portrayed by the individual showed qualities of acceptance or flexibility (Tingle et al., 1993).

In therapy, stated beliefs or denominational group beliefs are also poor predictors of a person's experience of God. When I first met Thomas, I wondered if his religious doctrine would ever allow him to feel forgiveness. As he told me his story, I found myself wishing he were an Episcopalian so that he might have a lenient God—but he wasn't. He was a loyal member of a Reformed Presbyterian Church. Members of this group believe in sanctification and obedience to a strict moral code. They are known to be as clean and honest in appearance as in behavior.[3] Thomas felt unclean because of a past affair with a married woman. His secrecy about it had separated him from his faith community and his God. According to his stated beliefs, he could not approach God until he was clean because "God cannot look upon sin." Yet he could not change his ways without God's help.

"I am in quicksand," he said, "and I did this to myself. There were warning signs all around—DANGER—DO NOT ENTER—but I went into the swamp anyway, willfully. Now I am stuck in the quicksand. The more I try to get out by my own efforts the deeper I get. It is a toxic place, too poisonous for any person to enter, and too filthy for God to even look on." As time went on we talked about his dilemma from many perspectives, all along wondering what God's perspective might be. Actually, he said, he knew the Lord would rescue him. He had before. It's just that he had seen such disappointment and weariness in the Lord's face. He couldn't ask him to make the sacrifice of coming to this vile place to save him. I could not see a way out of his bind.

Then one day he described an experience like a very real daydream. In truth, his vision was as surprising to me as it was to him. He saw the Lord walking toward him, past the danger signs, boldly, into the swamp, to the muddy, smelly quicksand, bending down and lifting him up, carrying him in his arms to a cool, clear stream where he dipped and cleansed him, then carrying him out, with words of comfort, not of reproof.

"And what of the mud and the filth in that place? Did the Lord walk through it with disgust or did he walk above it, untouched by it?" I asked.

He paused to reflect. "He was in the midst of it, not above it, but it didn't seem to be a problem. I couldn't see him react to it at all because his eyes were on me."

"And did he look disappointed and weary?"

"No, he honestly just looked peaceful, genuinely happy to find me and to cleanse me and to give me rest."

The wonderful surprise to Thomas was not that his Lord would help in time of need but that the Lord would come through the filth without disgust. With this new knowledge, he could reconnect with members of his faith community. He started by forming one new friendship there that was neither dominated by a need to confess nor to hide. More recently, he has informed me that there are many trusting friendships that are now possible because he knows the grace of his Lord. With the new knowledge Thomas has given me, I can connect more creatively with other persons from conservative denominations, expecting to be surprised rather than stifled.

Certainty 2: I know what God is like for you because I know what your language about God means.

As we gather in churches to worship, we speak together the words of a liturgy, the common words that bind us together. Many persons in our city utter, "Our Father who art in Heaven," to begin the Lord's Prayer on

Sunday morning. When asked what God is like, they might say "like a kind heavenly father," and we might then think that we know about their experience.

Our[4] research conversations suggest, however, that these words, though not false, are more like a door, and though the doors to different persons' hearts may look the same, the insides are wonderfully different. These are a few of the descriptions we have heard from people we have talked with in research and in therapy (J. L. Griffith et al., 1992). Most people had started their descriptions with "God is like a kind father," but when we asked further, we heard a wide range of images spoken in quite different languages. We found this question helpful in moving from certainty to curiosity: "In those moments when God is most real to you, when you know you are with God, what do you hear or see or feel that tells you what God is like?" The responses:

> "Like a warm cocoon, enclosing me as the world falls in around me."

> "Like an exasperated mother whom I have disappointed and been ungrateful to too often."

> "Like an Olympic coach who does not model my task for me, but delights in my potential and pushes me to it."

> "Like a nourishing, flowing river that comes to me, the parched dry riverbed, and gives me life."

> "Like a strict old grandfather, angry with my continual wrongdoing, who has finally turned his back on me."

> "Like the silence in a deep, waterless cavern where I finally arrive after swimming down through a troubled lake."

> "Like a nursing mama who is happy to be close to me and always has plenty of milk. As I lay my head on her breast, I feel her breathing and hear her heartbeat and I am calmed."

When we asked, "What human relationship in your life most reminds you of the one you have described with God?," some who had begun with a description of a kind father God did, indeed, recall their own kind fathers or grandfathers. Others who related to a kind father God associated to relationships with women:

> "My mother, who kept calm and kept things in perspective."

> "Our housekeeper, who taught me about love that lasted through hard situations."

> "My grandmama, who always had a lap available."

> "My women friends who are closer than family, who confront me, encourage me, and support me no matter what."

"My other mama, my Irish Catholic neighbor lady, who always had room at her table for one more, whose house was liberatingly messy and filled with laughter, who, when she gave of herself, became more, not less, of herself."

We have also become aware that there is no language that therapists can employ—including the word "God"—which is free from oppressive connotations. One research participant, Priscilla, said, "I don't use the word God when I can avoid it. That's the word I used for the old 'Thou-shalt-not' God who stifled me for so many years. That word almost makes me sit up straight at attention, be careful, not talk, and *certainly* not laugh. That word has nothing to do with the Spirit I know now, the Spirit inside me and surrounding me who invites me to open, to love, to create, and to laugh."

"But," she smiled, "if you really need me to, I'll say 'God' with you. Just remember that it's shorthand, not the real thing." It was not necessary for me to use it, though. Now we could find new language together.

I could not ever have known what the word "God" was like for her, nor any other word by knowing its dictionary definition, or even its common cultural usage. Language, as the hermeneutic philosophers have taught, is a way of being present with another person, a way of touching the other (Heidegger, 1971; Gadamer, 1976). To Priscilla, to say the word "God" was to touch her with a hard, cold thing, but to learn and to say her words—"Spirit" and "Light"—was to touch her with a strong, enveloping goodness; for her, "the real thing."

Certainty 3: I know what God is like for you because your image of God is a reflection of your early attachment figures.

Object relations theorists propose that the God-image is a synthesis of parts of parental images (Rizzuto, 1979). We earlier described a feedback cycle that explained how such an image of God, drawn from early life sources, could remain stable over time (J. L. Griffith & M. E. Griffith, 1992). These ideas could guide the therapist to maintain a story of certainty wherein the character of a person's God cannot transcend its resemblance to the character of the person's parents.

What interests us now, however, are not explanations for the stability, but rather the transformations, differences, and unique outcomes that could never be predicted by these theories. These latter elements deconstruct our certainty, and questions based on these elements free us to be curious.

Carol came to therapy for help with extreme anxiety symptoms. She was a brave and determined woman, working three jobs to support herself and her daughter. I often privately wondered whether I could offer her anything in an hour that would be more helpful than the nap she appeared to need. "Must you work this hard? Could family or maybe bank loans help?"

"No, there is no help, and, yes, I am physically exhausted, but I can handle it."

As we talked more it seemed that this philosophy had served her well through a difficult life. Her inner talk seemed to go something like: "This is tough, but I'm tough too, and I can handle it"; or "If I can handle it, then I should handle it."

I wondered if, given a choice, this was a philosophy she would select to guide her life. Carol thought she would prefer in the future when making decisions to ask, "Am I comfortable with this?" and "Is it worth my time and effort?" But she felt it would be very difficult to change, since she received so much praise for her stamina. I began to wonder who in her imaginal dialogues (Watkins, 1986) might encourage her to seek a more comfortable life and who might bind her more into the "If I can, then I should, handle it" lifestyle. As she reflected on these questions, I asked where God might be in this debate. I knew Carol to be a spiritual person who was a sensitive, comfort-giving woman to her daughter and friends. I expected her to say that God would want her to stop suffering and to have rest and comfort.

Her reply jolted me: "Well, this must be how God wants it or he would change it. He would get some money to me, but obviously he doesn't want it to be any easier for now."

"So he wants it this way?"

"Yes, I think he could change it. I see him somehow getting money to my friends. But there are no family checks coming to me. There is no let up. I am suffering, and so is my daughter. It's like he's saying, 'I know you can work very hard, harder than most people, so I know you can do this.' "

I asked, "What is it like to hear these words from God? Do you tell him you're suffering?"

"It's lonely. I don't feel very close to him. I don't tell him anything. I'm not even sure he hears me."

"What do you sense from him, as he urges you to work hard? A tone of voice, a face, a posture? Could you show me?"

"I can't see his face, because his face is turned away. I can only see the side of it, like this," she demonstrated, standing erect, embodying a God with arms crossed, stonefaced, head turned away.

"What does that face mean?" I wondered with her.

"I'm not sure—either anger or disappointment. He doesn't tell what it means, but it feels awful to me."

We paused. I asked, "Has there been a human relationship in which you had this feeling of a face turned away, not knowing what it meant, but feeling awful?"

Her gaze drifted away. "Well, maybe with my grandfather. He was strict and very religious, but he was really good to me in lots of ways, the steadiest person in my life. I hated when he was angry with my cousins, though. He wouldn't say he was angry. He would just ignore them, not acknowledge them. Sometimes he would have gifts for the rest of us but not for the ones he disapproved of. That was awful."

I did not say a word. In a flash, Carol was aware of the parallels. "Wow," she said, "that's pretty similar. I mean, intellectually, I believe this is not all there is to God, but that's sure how he is for me right now, way out there, not very concerned about me, but he has gifts for those others."

This was a point where I could have asked her what she believed, what she knew intellectually that was different than her experience, but she had already said she *knew* this did not tell the whole story of God, yet still this was her experience. I was interested, not so much in what she knew, but how she knew that "This is not all there is to God." As with any relationship, one could assume that Carol's experiences with God were broader and more varied than could be captured by any single story, including the one about her grandfather. I asked then not about similarities to the grandfather story, which seemed to be so limiting, but about times when her experiences with God were unlike those with her grandfather.

"Carol, has there ever been a time when you experienced God being with you in a different kind of way, a time when God surprised you?"

"Oh, yes, I can remember a time very clearly years ago. It was after I had stopped drinking, not long after I became a Christian. I was facing so much, sinking deep into depression without the relief I once had from getting drunk. One night I decided I had to go drink. I couldn't take feeling this bad anymore. I got dressed to go. I knew that the Lord would be disapproving of me, maybe angry with me for doing this wrong thing, so I didn't want to think about him. But I sat down before I left and turned, and there was Jesus sitting beside me . . . weeping . . . not weeping in a way to make me feel guilty . . . just sad for me, deeply sad that I was about to do something to hurt myself and that I was hurting. He just didn't want me to hurt. It was like he took my hands and we wept together. I didn't need to go drink then. In fact, it was then that I first was able to ask for help for the depression and got some therapy which did help."

I wondered what was possible in the presence of the Lord who wept with her that was not possible in the presence of the God who turned a face away. I also asked her, "If Jesus were here with you now, weeping, knowing your suffering, how would he talk with you about your life, your hurting now?"

"I'm not sure, but it's enough to just have him near now. I haven't felt that presence in a long time."

Now, whether a person's description of God is generous or stingy, kind or cruel, like or unlike early attachment figures, I always ask, "Is there any other way you have experienced God, any way that surprised you?" Almost always there is. If the person would like to be more with God in this way, then this can be a point of curiosity, or time to delight in, to historicize, and to expand this alternative and desired story (White & Epston, 1989).

It is still quite useful to hear the stories that people often relate about similarities between experiences with God and experiences with early attachment figures. But if such a story is unwelcome, it can become less constraining when known as only one of many stories of the person's relationship with God.

Certainty 4: I know what God is like, and you need to know God as I do.

All of the stories I have written here end with a person describing an encounter with a loving and accepting God, a God of grace. I remember these stories because I love them.

I must then always ask myself if I am imposing rather than co-creating these endings: I hope not, for a God of grace imposed is still imposed. I learned this many years ago from Mary.

Mary was in serious danger of death from self-starvation, entrapped in a vicious binge–purge cycle. She knew that she needed inpatient treatment but refused to consider it—not because she didn't want it, but because she felt she didn't deserve it and that she didn't deserve to upset and worry and cost her parents more than she already had.

Mary mentioned that she had attended a church that was known in our city for its acceptance, although she had always sat in the back row. I hoped that going to that church might show her a God who deemed her acceptable and worthy of living.

I asked, "Do you ever talk with God about your dilemma about going to treatment?"

"Of course not. It's no use."

"Why? What would happen if you did?"

"God," she said with a bitter tone of sarcasm, "isn't talking to me these days."

I asked her if she could show me what that was like. She showed me Mary, seated on the floor, head down, eyes looking down, and God, high up and far away, back turned completely to her, speaking these words grimly: "I have given you chances to change before, and you have failed. You have been selfish and stubborn. I have tried and tried to help you, but I have grown tired of you. You don't really want to get well, and you have used up your chances with me." Her God never flinched, never considered turning to look at her. On questioning, she was very sure that was how God was and that any other experiences of God were now invalid. It was understandable, after all, since she was unlovable and unbearable.

I was horrified. I felt my body stiffen and recoil. I could not let her go on. I interrupted her: "No, Mary, that's not God! I know it's not! Don't you see?" I began to explain.

She turned me off with a bored cold stare and left the room. I don't know if she said with her eyes or her lips, "I didn't come here for preaching," but I knew I had betrayed her and been untrue to what I had promised the therapy would be about.

After that I listened and tried to understand. We didn't stop talking about God, but our talk changed. I asked Mary with genuine curiosity what it was like sitting in the back row listening to descriptions of a God who would always forgive, yet finding a God who had become fed up and turned his back. "It's like a thick piece of glass is between me and the rest of the church, not sound-proof but feeling-proof glass. It gets thicker every week."

Then one day she came into our appointment with light in her face. "I'm ready to go inpatient. I need to take care of myself. I want to live. Lots of other people want me to live, too, even God wants me to live." I was happy but stunned: "What happened? How can this be?"

"On the elevator coming up here, I ran into a little girl. Well, she's a big girl now . . . but she was little when I took care of her. I used to babysit her every day. I was so surprised to see her. It's been years."

"And what did she say?"

"Nothing, really. She just hugged me. She was so happy to see me. She loved me. She always loved me. I suddenly knew I was lovable. Somehow, I knew God loved me too and that I must get well."

Mary did get well. I'm not sure how to understand the role of the therapy as a part of it all, but she tells me it helped her get ready and that what helped was that I did not get scared and did not take charge of her life. She didn't remember how close I came to trying that, but I do. If my fear and knowingness had guided me to take charge of her life by preaching my own God, Mary likely would have been forced either to falsely acquiesce to get me off her back or to leave the therapy.

*   *   *

It would not be true to feminist values to omit my own context that gives births to, delights in, and struggles with this work. For me, this cannot be only therapy. It must be congruently connected with my own experience with God. When I hear experiences and descriptions that I feel could not be God, I want to defend and correct, as if someone were to have misunderstood my sister. I would have to defend her—to say, "No, you're wrong. She's not like that. She's kind and good." So will I not do for God as much as I would do for my sister?

The way I reconcile this dilemma is that, while my sister needs my defense and I also need to defend her to strengthen and protect our relationship, the God I know does not need my defense. In the act of defending or silencing the attack of my client, I decrease possibilities for that person's intimacy with his or her God and intimacy in the therapy.

CONCLUSION

Undoubtedly, I will again become seduced into certainties, attempting in therapy to provide, rather than to co-create, the meaning of an experience with a personal God. The hope is that it is in the very acknowledgment of these breaches and their repair that intimate interaction can occur (Weingarten, 1992). Indeed, after I wrote this paper I offered my telling of their stories back to "Thomas," "Priscilla," "Carol," and "Mary," for repair and their revision. Each of them gave me a re-vision, a new way of seeing the story, an expanded understanding of his or her evolving relationship with God, and the part our therapy and research conversations played in that evolution. Each has changed not only how I see therapy but also how I see God.

It is in this context of these intimate interactions that a person continues to co-create an evolving story with God that is uniquely his or her own, not dominated by my story, nor a psychological story, nor even the story of his or her particular religious doctrines. Though these other stories may compete for space in the discourse, and may influence and contribute to the evolving narrative, primacy must be given to that person's story as the individual describes his or her experiences, with the words and the meanings the person teaches us, and the possibilities and surprises that are encountered.

My tradition says, "The Holy One's name is Surprise." If one is too certain of her specifications of God, she will miss God. A rabbi told me that the Israelites could not wholly name God. They said "Yahweh," which meant "I am who I am, and I will be who I will be." Movement and mystery. Still, just as I sometimes get peace confused with safety,[5] I get faith confused with certainty. I do believe, though, that to search for the one is to lose the other.

APPENDIX

The Conversations with God Research Project in the Department of Psychiatry at the University of Mississippi School of Medicine is studying characteristics of intrapersonal dialogues with a personal God that may suggest how these dialogues can best be employed as a resource in individual and family therapies. Thus far, 30 community volunteers have been studied, each of whom considers his or her relationship with a personal God to be a vital relationship. In one aspect of the study, subjects supply a variety of self-report data on theological orientation, degree of fundamentalism, personality characteristics, characteristics of family of origin, and characteristics of self–God relationship. In a second aspect of the study, subjects enact a videotaped psychodramatic role-play of a moment or situation in which the presence of God was intensely experienced. Subjects are interviewed to determine relationships between particular narratives of personal experience and specific expressions, metaphors, and nonverbal gestures used in communications with God during the psychodramatic interview. The videotapes are analyzed utilizing Structural Analysis of Social Behavior, a coding system for interpersonal communications.

Among the preliminary findings: (1) All expressed images of God contained both maternal and paternal characteristics, with descriptions of God by persons who identified themselves as fundamentalists being the more paternal. (2) Fundamentalists and nonfundamentalists did not differ on measures of authoritarianism, self-esteem, locus of control, social support, or family environment scales, except that nonfundamentalists showed greater family participation in active recreational activities. (3) Although nearly all participants consistently referred to God as "He," about half associated specific attributes of God to particular memories of a mother or grandmother. (4) Most participants showed an evolution of relationship between self and their personal God that occurred primarily in adult life through discontinuous, transformational changes prompted by major losses and crises. This shift in relationship typically was a movement away from an emotionally distant or controlling self–God relationship that strongly resembled the childhood relationship with one or both parents to an intensely affiliative, intimate self–God relationship relatively free of dimensions of control and lacking characteristics of the early life relationship with parental figures (J. L. Griffith et al., 1992; Tingle et al., 1993).

ACKNOWLEDGMENTS

This chapter originally appeared as one of a group of articles on therapy as resistance to cultural oppression, a special edition of the *Journal of Feminist Family Therapy* (The Haworth Press, Inc.), 7(1/2), 123–142 (1995). It was simultaneously copublished in *Cultural Resistance: Challenging Beliefs about Men, Women, and Therapy* (Kathy Weingarten, Ed.), pp. 123–142. Harrington Park Press, an imprint of The Haworth Press, Inc., Binghamton, NY, 1995. Copyright 1995 by The Haworth Press. Reprinted by permission.

The ideas and work offered here are the fruit of the encouragement and close collaboration with my partner, James L. Griffith. I am indebted in this work to many other conversational partners, notably, Sallyann Roth, Gloria Martin, and Julie Propst, and to the generosity of the persons who allowed their stories to be told here. I am especially grateful to Kathy Weingarten not only for her thoughtful editing but also for helping me to understand this work as resistance to cultural oppression.

NOTES

1. Our Conversations with a Personal God Research Project is conducted in the Department of Psychiatry at the University of Mississippi School of Medicine. Characteristics of intrapersonal dialogues with a personal God are studied in order to learn how these dialogues can best be employed as a resource in individual and family therapies. For further information on the project, please write the author.
2. I hope these stereotyping views are not offensive. I decided to choose the Episcopalians and the Southern Baptists since I have personal affiliations with both groups and have and still do benefit from both these associations.
3. Members of this denomination collaborated with me to construct this description.
4. Though most of the clinical and research work refers to persons who are Protestant Christians, the research team at work on our Conversations with a Personal God Project includes persons who are of the Catholic, Hindu, and Greek Orthodox traditions. The members of this team have been Alexis Polles, Jeanetta Rains, Carol Tingle, Dinesh Mittal, Nancy Krejmas, James L. Griffith, and myself.
5. Dietrich Bonhoeffer (executed at Flossenburg Concentration Camp in 1945), a pastor invloved in the resistance to Hitler, in addressing the Christian churches in Germany, implored them to realize that the quest for their personal safety was not the quest for peace. In fact, the actions that might ensure their safety would be the very actions that would destroy God's peace, which could only come with justice (Glazener, 1992).

222   SPIRITUALITY AND FAMILY THERAPY

REFERENCES

Bakhtin, M. M. (1981). *The dialogic imagination* (M. Holquist, Ed.). Austin: University of Texas Press.
Gadamer, H. G. (1976). *Philosophical hermeneutics.* Berkeley: University of California Press.
Glazener, M. (1992). *The cup of wrath: The story of Dietrich Bonhoeffer's resistance to Hitler.* Savannah, GA: Beil.
Griffith, J. L. (1986). Employing the God–family relationship in therapy with religious families. *Family Process, 25,* 609–618.
Griffith, J. L., & Griffith, M. E. (1992). Therapeutic change in religious families: Working with the God-construct. In L. Burton (Ed.), *Religion and the family.* Binghamton, NY: Haworth Press.
Griffith, J. L., & Griffith, M. E. (in press). *Sacred encounters: Including spiritual and religious experience in psychotherapy.* New York: Guilford Press.
Griffith, J. L., Griffith, M. E., Rains, J., Tingle, C., Krejmas, N., Mittal, D., & Polles, A. (1992, November). *Quality of relationship between self and a personal God: Its narrative history and relationship to individual and family variables.* Paper presented at the American Family Therapy Academy/George Washington University Research Conference at Captiva Island, FL.
Griffith, M. E., & Griffith, J. L. (1992, October). *Including relationships with God in therapy with religious families.* Workshop presented at the 50th Annual Conference of the American Association for Marriage and Family Therapy, Miami, FL.
Heidegger, M. (1971). *On the way to language.* New York: Harper & Row.
Rizzuto, A. M. (1979). *The birth of the living God.* Chicago: University of Chicago Press.
Tingle, C. V., Griffith, J. L., Griffith, M. E., Rains, J., Mittal, D., & Krejmas, N. (1993, May). *God–person relationships: Their character and relation to individual and family system variables.* Paper presented at the 146th Annual Meeting of the American Psychiatric Association, San Francisco, CA.
Watkins, M. (1986). *Invisible guests: The development of imaginal dialogues.* Hillsdale, NJ: Erlbaum.
Weingarten, K. (1992). A consideration of intimate and nonintimate interactions in therapy. *Family Process, 31,* 45–59.
White, M., & Epston, D. (1989). *Literate means to therapeutic ends.* Adelaide, South Australia: Dulwich Centre Publications.

CHAPTER 13

Releasing the Soul

Psychotherapy as a Spiritual Practice

RICHARD C. SCHWARTZ

What is the nature of the psychotherapeutic enterprise? What am I, as a therapist, trying to do when I offer to help clients? I've asked myself these questions repeatedly over the past 20 years and have noticed a gradual yet dramatic shift in the answer. Despite my nonreligious socialization and scientific training, I've been led by my clients to increasingly spiritual answers.

This has not been an easy or smooth journey from my original focus on finding ways to help people solve their problems as quickly and efficiently as possible to my current interest in helping people gain more access to spiritual wisdom and energy within and around them. A brief history of this journey, which is the development of the internal family systems (IFS) model, will provide some context for understanding how therapy can become a spiritual practice.

THE INTERNAL FAMILY SYSTEMS MODEL

The IFS model (Schwartz, 1987, 1988, 1992, 1995, 1997; Goulding & Schwartz, 1995; Nichols & Schwartz, 1997; Breunlin, Schwartz, & Mac Kune-Karrer, 1992) represents a new synthesis of two already existing paradigms: systems thinking and the multiplicity of the mind. It brings concepts and methods from the structural, strategic, narrative, and Bowen schools of family therapy to the world of subpersonalities.

Parts

This synthesis was the natural outcome when I, as a young, fervent family therapist, began hearing from clients about their inner lives. After I was able to set aside my preconceived notions about therapy and the mind, and began to listen to what my clients were saying, what I heard over and over were descriptions of what they often called their "parts"–the conflicted voices or subpersonalities residing within them. Although it was very new and strange to me, this was not a new discovery. Many other theorists have described a similar inner phenomenon, beginning with Sigmund Freud's id, ego, and superego, and more recently the object relations conceptions of internal objects. It is also at the core of less mainstream approaches like transactional analysis ("ego states"), psychosynthesis ("subpersonalities"), and now manifested in cognitive-behavioral approaches under the term "schemata." I was intrigued with how these inner entities functioned together as a system.

Since my family therapy background left me steeped in systems thinking, it was second nature to begin tracking sequences of internal interaction in the same way I had tracked interactions among family members. I learned that, across people, parts take on common roles and common inner relationships. I also learned that these inner roles and relationships were not static and could be changed by intervening carefully and respectfully. I began conceiving of the mind as an inner family and experimenting with techniques I had used as a family therapist.

The IFS model, then, sees a person as containing an "ecological system" of relatively discrete subminds, each one intrinsically valuable and seeking a positive role within. Life experiences force these subminds or parts out of their valuable roles, however, which can reorganize the internal system in unhealthy ways. This process is similar to the way, in an alcoholic family, children are forced into protective and stereotypical roles by the extreme dynamics of their family. While therapists have noticed that siblings in alcoholic families often find themselves in one of several rigid roles (e.g., the scapegoat, mascot, or lost child; Wegscheider-Cruse, 1985), those roles do not represent the *essence* of those children. Instead, each child is unique and, once released from his or her role by intervention, can find interests and talents separate from the demands of his or her chaotic family. The same process holds for internal families–parts are forced into extreme roles by external circumstances and, once it seems safe, gladly transform into valuable members.

What circumstances force these parts into extreme and sometimes destructive roles? Trauma is one factor, such as the effects of childhood sexual abuse (Goulding & Schwartz, 1995). But more often, the values and interaction patterns of a person's family create internal polarizations that escalate over time and are played out in other relationships. As these internal patterns and their parallels to family patterns became clearer, it seemed possible to understand all levels of human organization–intrapsychic, family and culture–with the same systemic principles and to intervene at each level with the same ecological techniques.

Managers, Exiles, and Firefighters

Are there common roles for parts across people? After I had worked with a large number of clients, some patterns began to appear. Most clients had parts focused on keeping them functional and safe—parts that tried to maintain control of their inner and outer environments by, for example, keeping them from getting too close or dependent on others, criticizing their appearance or performance to make them look or act better, or focusing on taking care of others rather than on their own needs to ensure acceptance. These parts seemed to be in protective, managerial roles, so they are called the *managers*.

Where a person has been hurt, humiliated, frightened, or shamed in the past, he or she will have young parts that carry the emotions, memories, and sensations from those experiences. We've all experienced at times child-like fears of aloneness, shame, vulnerability, or pain. Managers often want to keep those feelings out of consciousness and consequently, try to keep these vulnerable and needy parts locked in inner closets. Those incarcerated parts are known as the *exiles*.

The third and final group includes those parts that go into action whenever a young exiled part floods the person with extreme feelings or makes the person vulnerable to being hurt again. When that is the case, this third group tries to put out the inner flames of feeling as quickly as possible, so they are called the *firefighters*. They tend to be highly impulsive and seek stimulation that will override or dissociate the person from the exile's feelings. Bingeing on drugs, alcohol, food, sex, or work are common firefighter activities.

THE SELF

I entered this world of parts in the same frame of mind that had led me into family therapy—striving to find the best ways to help people solve problems. If my clients could reorganize their inner relations, maybe that would loosen the knots of their external lives. While this world of parts seemed bizarre and fascinating, there wasn't anything particularly spiritual about it. It wasn't until I encountered people's Selves that I began to get inklings that my clients and I were on a spiritual journey.

Who are we at our core? Each model of family therapy has had a different answer to that question, and the answer has defined much of the therapy. The most popular answer in family therapy now comes from the constructivist movement and informs the many versions of narrative therapy. This answer is that there is no core self: Who we are is dependent on our relational, conversational context, and consequently is highly fluid and plastic. We are sponge-like in our ability to internalize discourses from our culture and our families, and it is a myth that there is an entity within us that transcends those discourses and keeps an independent moral compass (Gergen, 1985, 1991; White, 1991). With this version of the self, narrative therapists are understandably interested in engaging clients in conversations that co-create new, more empowering views of themselves, rather than trying to help clients look inside for those views (White, 1995; Freedman & Combs, 1996).

The Self of the IFS model is the inner state that the constructivists claim doesn't exist. In this sense, what I am calling the Self is analogous to the soul, as described in many different spiritual and religious traditions. My beliefs about the Self's existence in that sense don't come from theory. I came to an awareness of its existence accidentally and have achieved a deep conviction in its existence in everyone only after years of experimenting.

Encountering the Self

As I struggled to understand and map clients' networks of parts, I began using the technique of boundary making, borrowed from structural family therapy (Minuchin, 1974). That is, for example, if a woman felt extremely angry at her son, I might ask her to find that angry part and, in her mind, ask it to separate from her temporarily—to create more of a boundary around it so we could get to know it better. Or, if she felt afraid of her husband, I'd ask her to separate that part too. As I helped many clients separate parts, I was amazed to find that when they succeeded, they universally shifted in demeanor and perspective toward qualities that made for harmonious internal and external relating; qualities like compassion and love, acceptance and confidence, curiosity and patience.

Upon separating some parts, one client of therapist John Carney (1996) exclaimed, "I can't describe what an experience this is for me. . . . All of a sudden I feel like I have a solid place to stand. . . . It is like I am the center of a May-pole and all these parts and problems revolve around me . . . but they're not me . . . me, who I am, deep down. . . . I feel like 'I' [placing hand over heart] can deal with these problems now and not feel like I am the problem" (p. 248).

When I asked people what part of them was there when they were in a similar state, they would say things like "That's not a part, that's my Self; that's my core or true Self; that's who I really am." I found that if I could convince clients' protective manager and firefighter parts to let them stay in the state of Self-leadership they knew just how to heal themselves and their relationships.

It was a big surprise to find this kind of Self in some of my clients who had been severely abused by their parents. From developmental psychology, I had been led to believe that such a strong and competent ego could only develop through having had at least adequate parenting during crucial childhood periods. The emphasis on internalization from developmental and psychoanalytic psychologies has led many therapists to believe that this kind of ego does not preexist, but rather is an internalization of a good parent. That is, it is thought to be imported into the person through a loving relationship. Some of my clients' parenting not only was inadequate, they had been tortured and betrayed systematically and daily. If one subscribed to developmental or neoanalytic theories (or constructivist, for that matter[1]), the kind of Self I was encountering in them should not exist. Indeed, the job of the therapist for models based on those views is to help the client internalize new messages or stories.

To account for what I was observing, I had to deconstruct my developmental assumptions and consider the possibility that this Self was not derived from parenting but came from somewhere else. At first the only plausible explanation seemed to be that human beings, like all organisms, have the innate ability to heal themselves emotionally, as well as physically, and that the Self was the embodiment of that healing capacity. From that perspective, the Self was like the immune system—inherent in our genetic programing, and, if not suppressed, maintaining of our health.

As my clients and I became more acquainted with the nature of the Self, that highly materialistic explanation seemed inadequate. As they released their Selves more fully, my clients were having experiences that could only be classified as spiritual. Not only were they able to go to their pain and unload it, they were also feeling a pulsating, warm energy flow through their bodies, sometimes feeling blissful or rapturous and other times feeling oceanic and boundaryless. They sensed that their lives had meaning and sometimes received clear messages about what they were here to do. Some clients even began to be visited by images or light that seemed different from their parts and had a comforting, soothing effect—making them feel less alone and occasionally giving direct advice or facilitating the work with their parts.

Because these observations contradicted my cosmology and made me fear being seen as yet another New Age dabbler, I fought their logical conclusion for years. But over time the evidence became overwhelming and I began to conceptualize the Self as the soul of the person—the place in them that was God, or through which God-like energy could flow. The more I read about the soul and how it has been conceived by different cultures, the more this definition fit, and the more ironic it seemed that so many spiritual or religious traditions knew about and helped people access the soul while so few psychotherapies did.

This split between the psychotherapeutic and the sacred has not always been there. Historians of psychotherapy acknowledge priests and shamans as the first to heal the psyche (Deikman, 1982). In the nineteenth century, medical and emotional treatment was arrogated by scientific medicine, and Freud's project for a "scientific psychology" increased the split by deeming religious phenomena as neurotic and conveying a picture of human nature as a cauldron of base instinctual impulses (Grof, 1985). Jung (1932) broke with Freud and maintained spiritual elements, including a transcendent higher self, in his psychology, but was marginalized for decades precisely because of those spiritual elements (Vaughn, 1991).

The humanistic movement in psychology of the 1960s and 1970s, while not overtly linked to the spiritual, tried to counter Freud's pessimistic picture of people by emphasizing the upside of human potential (Rogers, 1961, 1980; Maslow, 1971; Gendlin, 1981; May, 1961). They intuited the existence of the Self. For example, consider this passage from Abraham Maslow (1962):

> We have, each of us, an essential biologically based inner nature, which is to some degree "natural," intrinsic, given, and, in a certain limited sense, unchangeable, or, at least, unchanging. . . . [It] seems not to be intrinsically evil, but rather either neutral or positively "good." What we call evil behavior appears most often to be a secondary reaction to frustration of this intrinsic nature. . . . If it is permitted to guide our life, we grow healthy, fruitful and happy. (p. 3)

Other writers embraced much of humanistic psychology but also took the leap into spiritual realms by suggesting that humanity's great potential is rooted in our mystical nature. These transpersonal psychologists incorporated meditation and other techniques designed to produce spiritual experiences (Assagioli, 1973; Grof, 1985; Tart, 1986; Vaughan, 1991; Wilber, 1980). Despite these efforts, mainstream psychology was untouched by spiritual considerations and remains so today. Ironically psychology, which comes from the Greek "study of the soul," stopped studying the soul in this century (Carney, 1996).

With the exception of Virginia Satir, family therapy, in its struggle for credibility, followed the lead of psychology in ignoring the transpersonal and humanistic movements. Satir herself was marginalized within mainstream family therapy in part because she was seen as too interested in creating loving, soulful connections between people, rather than getting them in control of one another. In her later work she was openly moving toward spiritual issues, as illustrated by this statement: "We are devine in our origins. . . . I believe we have a pipeline to universal intelligence and wisdom" (Satir, 1988, p. 338).

In the 1990s family therapy moved away from control and toward collaboration, with much more attention paid to making warm, respectful connections with clients. Yet Satir's groundbreaking contributions (and, through her, the humanistic movement and Carl Rogers) are virtually ignored by narrative and solution-focused schools who are rediscovering the importance of the therapist/client relationship (Nichols & Schwartz, 1997).

The Self as Witness

With the foregoing as background, let us ask again, "What is the Self?" The more parts my clients were able to separate from whatever was left, the more they experienced the sense of well-being and pure awareness described above, and the more they knew just what to do to heal. I devised an exercise, for example, in which a client imagines herself at the base of a mountain and asks her parts to remain at the base while she journeys up the mountain. She doesn't see herself on the mountain; instead, I ask her to be on the path, such that she sees her surroundings but not herself. Periodically I ask her to see if she's having any thoughts and, if so, to find the parts giving them to her and send them back to the base. As she does so, she increasingly becomes pure awareness and will experience the Self in the ways I've been describing. Exercises like these lead to the conclusion that the Self is the pure awareness that exists when one steps away from the stream of thoughts and emotions we usually identify as ourselves. While I stumbled onto this conceptualization of the Self as the emptiness or awareness that is there when one separates from one's thoughts, fantasies, and emotions (many Eastern philosophies refer to these conscious elements of personality as the ego, as opposed to Freud's more specific definition of ego), this conception of it is central to many spiritual traditions.

For example, in Zen Buddhist meditation the practitioner is to simply observe his or her thoughts, fantasies, and emotions as they enter consciousness, and then let them leave without judging or trying to change them. In doing so, the meditator becomes disidentified with— nonattached to—his or her ego because it becomes clear that those thoughts or emotions are not who he or she really is. Who is it that is doing the observing? Who are we behind our thoughts, actions, bodies— behind anything we can observe or identify? Ken Wilber (1996) provides the clearest answer to that question I have found:

All those objects in your awareness are precisely not your observing Self. All those things that you know about yourself are precisely not the real Self. Those are not the Seer; those are simply things that can be *seen*. . . . This deeply inward Self is witnessing the world out there, and its is witnessing all your interior thoughts as well. This Seer sees the ego, and sees the body, and sees the natural world. All of those parade by "in front" of this Seer. But the Seer itself cannot be seen. If you see anything, those are just more objects. Those objects are precisely what the Seer is not, what the Witness is not. . . . You are the vast expanse of freedom through which all of these objects come and go. You are an opening, a clearing, an emptiness, a vast spaciousness, in which all these objects come and go. . . . So when you rest in this pure Seer, in the pure Witness, you are invisible. You cannot be seen. . . . You are the pure source of awareness, and not anything that arises in that awareness. (pp. 221–223)

Since we cannot see our Selves but we see and hear from our parts all the time, we tend to identify with parts—with our extreme desires, thoughts, and emotions. It's no wonder so many of us have poor self-esteem. It's too bad so few of us know who we really are.

When people are able to convince their parts that it is safe to separate from their core, they gradually sense their defenses dropping and their hearts opening. They report feeling increasing equanimity, compassion and perspective. They sense a warm energy flowing through their bodies, and their awareness is increasingly present oriented—uncluttered by the usual stream of thoughts or fantasies. This is what I am calling the true or core Self.

Self = Soul

So in the IFS model, Self and soul are synonymous. As several writers (Campbell & Moyers, 1988; Smith, 1982; Vaughan, 1991) have pointed out, equating Self and soul is in accord with the tenets of all the world's great religions. The Greek Delphic oracle advised, *"Gnothi seauton"*—"Know thyself." Lao Tzu taught that to know others is wisdom, but to truly know yourself brings enlightenment. Sidhartha directed followers to look inside themselves and realize that "Thou art the Buddha." Jesus said the Kingdom of God was within each of us and that we each contain the light of the world. Mohammed taught that he who knows himself knows his Lord (Carney, 1996). Contemporary author Deepak Chopra (1997) recently echoed this perennial wisdom:

> Self and spirit are the same. Asking "What is spirit?" is just a way of asking "Who am I?" There isn't spirit outside you; you are it. . . . The "I" that is truly you is made of pure awareness, pure creativity, pure spirit. . . . What is important here is that the Self is a real experience. It is not an ideal far removed from reality—which is how most of us think of the soul—but is as close to you as breath. The Self is love's source, and therefore, it is more real than the things that block love—anger, fear, egotism, insecurity and mistrust. (pp. 33, 14)

To make this equating of Self and soul work, however, we need to clarify the term Self. The equation makes no sense if, like most of Western thought (including psychology), we consider Self to be the total person, complete with all manner of thoughts and emotions. We all think and feel things that are not very soulful. The equation does make sense if we think of Self as our core that lies beyond the banal chatter of our parts. The IFS model's separation of parts and Self seems an important step toward bringing spirituality into psychotherapy. Huston Smith (1976), a preeminent religious scholar, describes the soul this way:

Situated as it were behind the senses, it sees through the eyes without being seen, hears with the ears without itself being heard. Similarly, it lies deeper than mind. If we equate mind with the stream of consciousness, the soul is the source of this stream; it is also its witness while never itself appearing within the stream as datum to be observed. (p. 74)

In other words, the Self/soul lies behind and is not the parts or the senses.

Parts as Constraining Self-Awareness

Peoples' protective parts are the ones that carry extreme emotions and beliefs—anger, fear, egotism, insecurity, mistrust, and many others—that keep them from leading their lives with their Selves. These parts do not trust that it is safe to allow the Self to lead a person's life because of how much he or she has been hurt, rejected, humiliated, or abused in the past. These parts try to protect this inner core of love and compassion by burying it under extreme emotions or obscuring it behind the inner voices that shout "danger" or fantasize revenge. These parts will not release their grip of the Self until they are certain that it will not result in further damage.

Thus, many people have little or no awareness of their Selves. They might have vague inklings of the love that exists within them but spend their lives trying to get love from Mr. or Ms. Right, or give up the search and withdraw within the safe, lonely fortress their parts provide, keeping away from anyone who might stir the love within them. I believe that the desire for connection with another's Self is innate and very strong, but it can be overridden by fear that creates walls of separation.

A person who is leading with the Self is easy to identify. Others describe such a Self-led person as open, confident, and accepting. They feel immediately at ease in a Self-led person's presence, as their parts sense that it is safe to relax and release their own Selves. They sense in the person's eyes, voice, body language, and energy that they are with a person who is "real," solid, and unpretentious.

Self as Leader

The nonattached, nonjudging, nondual Seer or Witness—the state of pure awareness or emptiness—is the most common description of the Self in the spiritual literature and accurately captures what I encountered with my clients when they separated from their parts. But their Selves were not merely passive witnesses. While in this Seer or Witness state, they wanted to interact with their parts in compassionate ways and began to do so. They could remain openhearted even in the presence of parts they had previously hated or feared, and those parts sensed that it was safe to drop their guards and reveal their real motives and desires. The differentiated Self seemed to know just what to say to parts to reassure them, or how to hold them so they would trust that they were in safe hands. Thus, the Self was not only the Seer who wasn't swimming in the melodrama of the parts, but it could also be a compassionate, competent leader.

This leadership aspect of the Self is what the IFS model has explored extensively. Many other psychotherapies encourage clients to observe, rather than be overwhelmed by, their extreme cognitions or emotions. This kind of witnessing is an aspect of cognitive-behavioral, Gestalt, Bowen, and psychoanalytic therapies. Narrative approaches help people step back from and examine the taken-for-granted stories that govern their lives and "externalize" their feelings or problems. From the IFS perspective this is similar to asking someone to separate from their parts.

Helping people separate from and observe their feelings, fantasies, delusions, narratives, interpretations, body sensations, and the influence of other people—turning down the inner noise such that they can taste the Self—*will* produce greater perspective and equanimity. Some spiritual traditions believe that achieving this kind of nonattachment is the essence of spiritual practice and that trying to change rather than simply to observe is a mistake. They encourage people to remain in the passive observing/accepting Self state.

But that process alone will not transform or heal the extreme emotions and beliefs that generate all the noise. In other words, one may experience relief from being overwhelmed by pain or shame, but the parts carrying the pain and shame remain and continually try to overwhelm. To produce lasting harmony, these parts must be helped to unload the feelings and beliefs they accumulated from past events (what the IFS model calls burdens), so they can leave their extreme roles and take valuable ones.

Self as a Compassionate Witness

What does it take for these parts to unburden and transform? I have found that the primary requirement is for a person's Self to fully witness the story of how a part got its burden. For example, when my client Julie was able to convince her manager parts it was safe to separate from her Self she felt ready to approach a child-like exile part that she knew was in pain. (In describing this process, she wouldn't say that she saw her Self approach the child because then who would it be that was seeing her Self? Remember, the Self is the Seer, so as she approached, she saw the child getting closer but she didn't see her Self, she was just there with the child.)

After Julie (as her Self) was able to hold and comfort the child and the child trusted that Julie cared for her, Julie asked the child to show her what she wanted Julie to know about the past. Julie then began to silently witness scenes from her childhood in which she had been ridiculed by her peers for being fat. While these were not new memories, Julie later said that she had no idea those events had been so devastating for her. Once the child part believed that Julie now understood what had happened and appreciated how bad it was, the child was able to take "a black substance" out of the child's heart that contained the shame of those events (she unburdened). The child immediately felt lighter and more playful, and Julie's depression lifted. Here, Julie's Self was an active leader who negotiated with her managers, nurtured her exile, and compassionately witnessed her past.

I don't know exactly why this Self-witnessing process works so well, except that parts, just like people, seem to need to know that what happened to them has been recognized by someone who is significant to them. In many cases, that is all they have been waiting for, and they can immediately unload their extreme feelings and beliefs after being witnessed.

REALIZING WHO WE ARE

I have considered another, more spiritual explanation for the effectiveness of this process. Many spiritual traditions suggest that life is a training ground in which we are presented with challenging lessons about being less fearful and more compassionate. As we learn these lessons, we come closer to recognizing who we really are—that we are God. Wilber (1997) provides a clear description of this position:

> The realization of the Nondual traditions is uncompromising: there is only Spirit, there is only God, there is only Emptiness in all its radiant wonder. . . . [T]hese sages universally maintain that absolute reality and the relative world are "not-two" (which is the meaning of "nondual"), much as a mirror and its reflections are not separate, or an ocean is one with its many waves. So the "other world" of Spirit and "this world" of separate phenomena are deeply and profoundly "not-two." . . . This becomes your constant realization, through all changes of state, very naturally, just so. (pp. 281, 283–284)

Could it be that these lessons are contained in the burdens the parts carry? Could the burdens carry what has been called Karma?

That is, as we go through life, we accumulate from interactions with our families and our culture, or from traumatic events, beliefs and emotions (burdens) that influence the parts that carry them to cloud our experience of the compassion and well-being of the Self. These burdens keep us from knowing who we really are. When people are able to finally witness the scenes that led to the accumulation of these burdens, they often feel as though they suddenly see the world differently, as if a great learning has taken place. Usually that learning involves greater love or compassion for a person or for themselves (i.e., for the part of themselves that had carried the burden), or a greater awareness of how the world operates.

In addition, once an unburdening has taken place, people experience an increased ability to access their Selves and the spiritual energy that it generates or runs through it. This energy has been given different names by different traditions, including the life force, *Ki, Chi, Sakti, prana,* and the Holy Ghost. After an unburdening, it is as if a clearing has occurred. Something that was obstructing the flow of that energy or its entrance into the system has been removed.

THE SELF-TO-SELF CONNECTION

While it is fulfilling for one person to experience Self-leadership, it is even more so to experience a Self-to-Self connection with another person—when each person's Self is present and their energy intermingles. When two people experience the Self-to-Self connection, they reach, at least temporarily, across the walls separating them and touch, perhaps unconsciously, the awareness that all human beings are the same at some level—that we all are spirit. This awareness comforts and nourishes both people: they sense the love and compassion that exists in each other's hearts; they have a glimpse of who they really are behind their protective masks. The tone of their interactions reflects that awareness, and they desire each other's company.

The paradox of life in families is that family members often desire this connection with each other more than with anyone else, but also are more afraid to try to get it from each other than from anyone else. Consequently, they circle around one another hoping for the connection to happen, and feeling chronically hurt and disappointed that it doesn't. I believe that innumerable family arguments and impasses have this disappointment at their base. It follows, then, that if one can simply increase the Self-to-Self connections among family members, many of their problems will diminish in importance or vanish entirely.[2]

Breaking the Self-to-Self Connection

I believe that Self-to-Self relating is the natural state of human beings. If two people were raised in ideally nurturing environments, they would not have to work at being intimate in this sense, it would just happen effortlessly. Few of us have been so fortunate, however. Each hurtful interaction we had as a child convinced some parts of us that Self-leadership is dangerous. Like parental children, those parts arrogated from the Self responsibility for dealing with the world and increasingly boxed in the Self's exuberance and openness. Even when those inner managers allow some of our Self's energy to flow in a relationship, they can rapidly whisk us back within walls of anger or fear at the first sign of danger. It is as if they have formed a castle within which they keep our Self and our other vulnerable parts (the exiles). Like sentries they constantly scan the environment for threats, particularly during times when they have allowed us to become vulnerable by dropping the drawbridge and releasing our Self. When the alarm sounds, they reel in our love and compassion, bolt the door, and ready our inner army for battle.

Some of these protective managers are so effective that our internal experience shifts dramatically. Even with people we love a great deal, at times when they hurt us we can immediately lose that love and feel nothing but disdain or anger toward them. The Self-to-Self connection is broken as each of us retreats behind the walls of our respective castles.

INTERNAL FAMILY SYSTEMS FAMILY THERAPY

It is these protective parts that often create and maintain the interpersonal problems that bring families into our offices. When family members trust that it is safe to come out from behind their protective masks, suddenly they seem less menacing to one another and their problems less daunting. They can truly listen without feeling that they are losing face or the struggle for control. They can once again detect the love that they thought had disappeared, and they become more willing to compromise.

The challenge of therapy then becomes finding ways to help family members trust that it is safe to release their Selves and to make Self-to-Self connections with one another. This is a different endeavor than co-authoring new narratives; directing solution-oriented conversations; coming up with rituals, tasks, or directives; or making interpretations. It is different because the therapist is not leading clients toward a particular view of their problem or toward a new set of behaviors. Instead, the therapist is simply trying to increase the amount of Self-leadership in the room and then trusting that whatever happens next will be healing.

Trusting that process does not come easily even for therapists who believe in the existence of the Self. For therapists who do not know about the Self or subscribe to theories that preclude its existence, therapy is effortful. They struggle to give clients something they believe the clients lack, whether that something is information, insight, empowering narratives, a solution focus, medication, ego strength, or self-esteem. Clients sometimes resist these gifts precisely because they are gifts—they came from the therapist's efforts rather than from within themselves or their interactions with other family members.

When therapists trust that each family member has a Self, they become less interventive and strategic. They can become truly collaborative because they have faith that the system they are working with—whether an individual, couple, family, or company—knows how to heal itself. The only thing it lacks is trust in its Self and the Self-to-Self connection with other systems. The role of the therapist is to increase that trust such that those resources are released.

THE THERAPIST–CLIENT CONNECTION

This is only possible, however, when the therapist can maintain Self-leadership, thereby forming Self-to-Self connections with clients. When clients sense the presence of the therapist's Self, their protective parts relax and begin to allow the client's Self to emerge. Once the energy of a Self-to-Self connection has flowed between therapist and client, the healing process is activated. John Carney (1996) provides an excellent description of this experience:

> There is a distinct quality to this type of collaborative work between the Selves of the therapist and client. Although hard to articulate, this writer can sense it deeply when fully engaged with a client. Besides warmth and compassion, there is an additional sense of awe and relatedness to the client that transcends the boundaries of either of our psyches. This writer loses track of the physical space around us. It is experienced as the Self of the client and my Self being "there," in the moment. In a sense, it feels like sharing a meditative state with another. (p. 213)

After this connection has been made, the therapist's primary job is to monitor it and foster similar connections between the client and his or her parts, on the one hand, and his or her family members, on the other.

This is simple, but often it is also extremely difficult. Therapy, especially IFS therapy because of the level of client vulnerability involved, is highly provocative of protective parts of both client and therapist. Therapists are often unaware that parts of them are reacting and breaking the connection. Many client's have acutely sensitive parts detectors that can tell immediately when that has happened. Usually they will react in kind, becoming protective themselves, which can easily lead to an escalating distance or power struggle between the therapist and the client.

To prevent this, we as therapists need two things: first, we need to become more aware of and work with our own parts that are triggered by this process; second, we need to use our clients' parts detectors to help us identify times when our parts take over. Giving permission to clients to comment when they sense the absence of the therapist's Self is growthful for the therapist and empowering for the client, especially those clients whose perceptions were disqualified in their families. It is not easy to encourage clients to challenge us this way, however. We have been trained to maintain the comfortable expert stance by deflecting such comments with questions like "What's going on in you that makes you think I'm not here?" Once we trust that the Self-to-Self connection with clients, not our perceived expertise, is the key to healing, we are better able to get our expert parts to step back and let our clients help us maintain the connection.

THERAPY AS A SPIRITUAL PRACTICE

As therapists we are fortunate to have a set of daily Self-leadership[3] practice periods, otherwise known as sessions. My sessions are times when I deliberately concentrate on practicing Self-leadership, and my clients' parts provide a variety of challenges and provocations. Before a client arrives I will try to feel the energy of the Self and will try to keep that energy flowing through the whole session. I'm also frequently asking my parts to step back and trust my Self, trust that energy. With some clients' parts this is very difficult, and my parts still take over at times. But it becomes easier with practice and, when I'm successful, it makes doing therapy a pleasure.

To maintain Self-leadership in the face of provocation, our parts must be able to trust our Selves enough to quickly step back and let our Selves handle the situation, despite the fact that they're still upset. When this works, I will feel upset inside but will not be overwhelmed by the upset parts and will remain the "I" in the storm—dealing calmly, confidently, and even compassionately with the situation, while sensing parts that are seething or cowering inside.

The Self may want to speak for some of those parts so they feel acknowledged but not have the parts take the driver's seat. When my parts take over and express their feelings, it often has the effect of activating parts in the other and of distorting my perceptions as the speaker. In contrast, my Self can say the same words that a part would say and yet my clients can hear it because they hear the caring behind it. Their connection to me is not broken, whereas it often is broken when parts take over.

After the storm has cleared and I have some time, I will go to my parts and help them with their reactions. These situations are always fertile. When parts are activated, their burdens are more evident and I can help them unburden. When they trust my Self to lead in a tense situation and then my Self cares for them afterward, they feel safe and can further relax into the comfort of Self-leadership.

Some people think that Self-leadership means always being warm, open, and nurturing, so they are reluctant to trust their Self in situations that call for assertiveness. This is a misconception. The Self can be forcefully protective or assertive. The energy of the Self is both nurturing and strong—yin and yang. Thus, it is possible and preferable to let the Self handle occasions where you have to set limits or defend yourself with clients as well as times when you are in a nurturing role. Much of the martial arts is about the practice of Self-leadership.

To conclude, I have come to view therapy as a spiritual experience for my clients and for myself. When everyone involved is in the embrace of the Self-to-Self connection and the energy of the Self fills the office, the work is effortless and I feel blessed to participate. I now feel refreshed and alive at the end of eight-session days, rather than the thorough depletion I felt when I had to make things happen. In addition, many of my clients are quite expressive of their gratitude for helping them feel more connected to one another and to spiritual energies or experiences. They report the feeling that their lives have more meaning; they are changing their lives in ways that are more aligned with their deeper intuitions; they do not have to engage in huge inner battles to create these changes; and they are better able to remain the "I" in the storms that rage around them. Gradually, I am catching up to them.

NOTE

1. In this sense, the constructivist (and, hence, narrative) and developmental psychological views of the self are similar. Both see it as constructed by internalizing external interactions.
2. Murray Bowen (1976) similarly emphasized the desire and fear of Self-to-Self connections in families but had a less spiritual view of Self.
3. Because of the power-over connotations of the word "leadership," I want to clarify that by Self-leadership I mean releasing my Self such that my compassion can flow to my parts and my clients. It does not mean trying to control them or my clients. The leadership of the Self is never coercive.

REFERENCES

Assagioli, R. (1973). *The act of will.* Baltimore, MD: Penguin.
Bowen, M. (1976). Theory in the practice of psychotherapy. In P. Guerin (Ed.), *Family therapy: Theory and practice.* New York: Gardner Press.
Breunlin, D., Schwartz, C. R., & Mac Kune-Karrer, B. (1992). *Metaframeworks: Transcending the models of family therapy.* San Francisco: Jossey Bass.
Campbell, S., & Moyers, W. (1988). *The power of myth.* New York: Doubleday.
Carney, J. (1996). *Beyond a "positive gay identity": An integrative humanistic–transpersonal–internal family systems therapy approach to affirming self-discovery, holistic health and psychospiritual growth in gay, lesbian, and ambisexual clients.* Clinical research project for the Illinois School of Professional Psychology, Chicago.
Chopra, D. (1997). *The path to love.* New York: Harmony Books.
Cooper, G., & Kahn, L. (1997). Truth and reconciliation: Healing the wounds of apartheid. *Family Therapy Networker, 21*(3), 13–14.
Deikman, A. (1982). *The observing self: Mysticism and psychotherapy.* Boston: Beacon Press.
Freedman, J., & Combs, G. (1996). *Narrative therapy.* New York: Norton.

Gendlin, E. (1981). *Focusing.* New York: Bantam New Age Books.

Gergen, K. (1985). The social constructionist movement in modern psychology. *American Psychologist, 40,* 266–275.

Gergen, K. (1991). *The saturated self.* New York: Basic Books.

Goulding, R., & Schwartz, R. C. (1995). *Mosaic mind: Empowering the tormented selves of childhood sexual abuse survivors.* New York: Norton.

Grof, S. (1985). *Beyond the brain: Birth, death, and transcendence in psychotherapy.* Albany, NY: State University of New York Press.

Jung, C. G. (1932). Psychotherapists or the clergy? In *Collected works of Carl Jung* (Vol. II). Princeton, NJ: Princeton University Press.

Maslow, A. (1962). *Toward a psychology of being.* New York: Van Nostrand.

Maslow, A. (1971). *The farther reaches of human nature.* New York: Viking.

May, R. (1961). *Existential psychology.* New York: Random House.

Minuchin, S. (1974). *Families and family therapy.* Cambridge, MA: Harvard University Press.

Nichols, M., & Schwartz, R. C. (1997). *Family therapy: Concepts and methods* (4th ed.). Needham Heights, MA: Allyn & Bacon.

Rogers, C. (1961). *On becoming a person.* Boston: Houghton Mifflin.

Rogers, C. (1980). *A way of being.* Boston: Houghton Mifflin.

Satir, V. (1988). *The new peoplemaking.* Palo Alto, CA: Science & Behavior Books.

Schwartz, R. C. (1987). Our multiple selves. *Family Therapy Networker, 11,* 24–31.

Schwartz, R. C. (1988). Know thy selves. *Family Therapy Networker, 12,* 21–29.

Schwartz, R. C. (1992, May/June). Rescuing the exiles. *Family Therapy Networker, 17,* 22–28.

Schwartz, R. C. (1995). *Internal family systems therapy.* New York: Guilford Press.

Schwartz, R. C. (1997, March/April). Don't look back. *Family Therapy Networker, 21,* 40–45.

Smith, H. (1976). *Forgotten truth: The primordial tradition.* New York: Harper & Row.

Smith, H. (1982). *Beyond the post-modern mind.* Wheaton, IL: Quest Books.

Tart, C. (1986). *Waking up: Overcoming the obstacles to human potential.* Boston: Shambhala.

Vaughan, F. (1991). Spiritual issues in psychotherapy. *Journal of Transpersonal Psychology, 23,* 105–119.

Wegscheider-Cruse, S. (1985). *Choicemaking: For co-dependents, adult children, and spirituality-seekers.* Pompano Beach, FL: Health Communications.

White, M. (1991). Deconstruction and therapy. *Dulwich Centre Newsletter, 3,* 21–40.

Wilber, K. (1980). *The atman project: A transpersonal view of human.* Wheaton, IL: Theosophical Publishing House.

Wilber, K. (1996). *A brief history of everything.* Boston: Shambhala.

Wilber, K. (1997). *The eye of spirit.* Boston: Shambhala.

White, M. (1995). *Re-authoring lives: Interviews and essays.* Adelaide, South Australia: Dulwich Centre Publications.

CHAPTER 14

Stretching to Meet What's Given
Opportunities for a Spiritual Practice

KATHY WEINGARTEN

To the oft-cited pair of difficult subjects—sex and money—I would certainly add spirituality. Mine, that is. I have no trouble listening to you tell me about your spiritual experience and practice; it is writing about mine that stops me cold. Fear: I will be casting my words, my stories, out to thousands of readers whose faces I have never seen, whose voices I have never heard, none of whom have entered into any agreements with me about how they will receive these reflections on loss and love. Curiosity: can I create in this text a prologue that will safeguard me as I write, like a net under a person walking a tightrope? This prologue/net consists of asking for a certain kind of listening stance, one in which judgment and evaluation are temporarily suspended while my tales fill the space.

I am asking from my readers what I provide my clients: asking for the reader to adopt the listening stance I have come to believe assists in creating a spiritual dimension to the work that I do. I listen for what is and can be, not just for what was and should be. Clients make much of the latter; I can assist my clients by noticing what they have not made much of yet—the still small green shoots of awareness of what they want to be so. I bring to this listening a willingness to empty myself of preconceptions, expert knowledge, and facts. I go alertly blank. At these times, I feel vastness and emptiness, terror and wonder looped together. I learned to listen this way when my mother was dying from cancer, a story I will tell below.

There are effects of listening this way. Respect and connection (terms from psychological discourse) develop. Reverence and awe (terms from a spiritual discourse) can too. These feelings form a conversational net, a matrix within which talk of pain and joy, grief and grind can proceed with some ease. Listening this way provides comfort.

Comfort, care, connection, commitment, and *compassion*—these are a few of the words in my spiritual lexicon. *Listening* and *love*—these are a few of the practices I embrace in my clinical work. I am willing to face anguish and joy with others. This, to me, is the heart of a spiritual practice.

LISTENING

Perhaps my prologue should be longer, but a story is pressing to be told now. It is a story about my mother's dying and how when my mother was dying, I listened my heart out. I will start my story on Thanksgiving Day, 1973, in the kitchen of the house I lived in as a teenager. I was 26 years old, a second-year graduate student at Harvard in clinical psychology and public practice, active in the women's health movement, a feminist, and afraid. My mother, then 58, had been telling me about vaginal bleeding she had been having for 6 months, which her internist told her was nothing. As she described it, her doctor had not taken a detailed history, had not examined her belly, nor done an internal exam. My mother, now, felt a lump on her side and, appropriately, was worried. I learned in that conversation that she had never seen a gynecologist; she was afraid to offend her internist, who had always done her annual Pap exam.

With a mix of tears and anger, I told her that I was worried too. I asked her to see a gynecologist, and she demurred. We talked for over an hour, and toward the end I pulled an ace out of my sleeve. Knowing the effect it would have on her, I told her that I only wanted one gift for Hanukkah: a card stating that she had an appointment with a gynecologist.

I got that card and a phone call after the appointment: the gynecologist had felt a mass in my mother's abdomen. She needed to be followed. One month later, the mass had grown and my mother was scheduled for a hysterectomy. She was told there was a 99% chance that the mass was benign.

While my mother had watched her side bulge, I had begun interviewing couples for my dissertation research on the influence of employment patterns on marital interaction. I was up to my eyeballs juggling a part-time clinical internship at a child guidance center, working on my dissertation, and apprenticing myself to a family therapist who practiced at Boston State Hospital. I saw two families under his direction, taping and transcribing my interviews for each hour of weekly supervision. From him I was learning the power of secrets in families, the dynamics of triangles, and the importance of direct communication. Little did I know how soon this new learning would cause pain and conflict in my own family.

February 1974: I was on the train to New York while my mother was undergoing surgery at Montefiore Hospital in the Bronx. The plan was that I would meet my father in Manhattan and we would travel together with my sister to visit my mother, who would be out of the recovery room by that time. I cried on the train and in the taxi but stopped the moment I saw my father's face. Pacing, striking his sides, and causing a one-sided jingle whenever his fist hit the coins in his right pocket, he was literally beside himself. A man was present who was ravaged by sorrow and fury. This man could not speak. Minutes went by. I did not recognize his voice. "It's everywhere." His contorted vocal cords emitted the two words, but the sounds of the letters dipped and swayed so I wasn't sure he was speaking English. It took me a couple of seconds to decode the words and then their meaning.

"Go. I can't go. You go. Don't tell her. Say nothing. She expects to see you. Go."

I left my father. My sister had not showed up. Where was she? What did she know? It was snowing heavily, and the bus ride to the Bronx was long and sickening. In retrospect, I know that I was in shock. I repeated the same question to myself over and over. How can I lie to my mother? Only days later did my thinking become more nuanced and the questions I posed more textured. What if my father cannot bear to talk with my mother about her dying and she is alone with her fears? What if we disagree as a family about what should be done, about what is right? Only years later, in my theoretical work (Weingarten, 1997), did I pose these questions: What if voice is dependent on audience? What if a person can only speak what she believes others can bear to hear?

I didn't have to lie to my mother that night. She was groggy and in pain. Happy to see me. Happy to hold my hand. Happy to let me stroke her arm and run my fingers through her hair. She dozed; I sat dazed. I suppose I did start to listen in a new way that night. There were no words per se. I listened to her breathing. I listened to my breathing. I noticed that when I breathed along with my mother's breath, my breath settled and, for a moment, I was less afraid. This was a clue.

Three days later, six of us lied to her, standing three to a side of her hospital bed, with my mother, propped up on pillows, looking expectantly from one to the other. Four of us—my 31-year-old sister, her husband, my husband, and me—believed what we were doing was wrong. Two of us, our father and my mother's newly acquired oncologist, insisted we would deprive her of hope if we told her that the cancer was widely disseminated throughout her body and that no one with her particular tumor had survived more than a year. At that bedside meeting, she was told that she had had a cancerous tumor but that it had been surgically removed. She would be followed closely, but there was no plan for treatment.

My mother survived for 2½ years. My family lied to her for the first of those years. During that year in which I was not supposed to tell her the "truth," I learned to listen. I banished what I thought I knew about her tumor and her life span in order to be fully present without hypocrisy to what she had to tell me. My few "facts"—that no one with her tumor had survived longer than a year, that they had *not* gotten it all—faded in importance compared to the rich tapestry my mother wanted to discuss. I entered her territory and navigated with her map. This way of listening, antithetical to most of my professional training which encouraged *me* to be the expert, created my mother as the expert on her life—and her dying. My "knowledge," besides being wrong, was a distraction. I was full of feeling about the "when," the time frame of which I thought I knew. Had we focused on "when," we would have lost the opportunities in the here and now to be together for much more.

And there were many opportunities. Certainly, imminent loss contextualized much of our time together. But loss was the background and pleasure in each other's company was the foreground. The kind of listening I learned to do helped make this possible for me. This listening allowed me to still my own thoughts in order to hear my mother's (Weingarten, 1998a). This kind of listening brought me in touch with a spacious calm I could tap for myself and offer to others. It helped me ride the swells of pain and loss, grief and rage, sorrow and joy which eventually taught me patience. Any down would rise up. There was always a metaphorical shore. I came to believe this. These are beliefs that are now stitched into the fabric of my awareness, and they inform my spiritual practice.

My mother and I talked a lot: in New York, in her home; in Cambridge, in mine; and on the phone, in the space between, connected by conversation and the feeling that flows through the wires.

As she got sicker, talk tapered. By chance, her final months coincided with my first pregnancy, her life waning as my body waxed full of child. In April 1976, my mother was hospitalized yet again. She had metastases in the lining of her heart and lungs for which they treated her with radium implants. I was 36 weeks pregnant, desperate to see her, but her doctor feared it was unsafe for me to visit.

It is Friday afternoon. I am sitting in the room that will be this baby's room. He will turn out to be a boy, Ben. My mother and my entire family are in New York: at the hospital, returning from the hospital, or going to the hospital. I am weeping and feeling so, so sorry for myself. What will my child have of my mother? I look at the three items she has managed to send (or have sent) to the baby: there is a piece of narrow embroidery; a pair of striped OshKosh overalls, size 2; and a teddy bear. I cannot fathom that these three items will be all that my child has of her.

Of course, they are not all that he has—and, rocking, I realize this too. "He will have me," I say to myself, "and through me he will know my mother and her love." Peace suffuses me. I feel a contentment and calm I have not experienced in months except in my mother's presence. I have that "all's right with the world" feeling I get on mountaintops and after lovemaking. I am exhausted.

I leave the house and shop for salt-free fancy foods my mother will love. I call our pediatrician-to-be and explain the situation. He encourages me to go to New

York, advising me to wear a lead apron when I am with my mother. I go. I see her.
Covered with a sickly green shield, I bend my huge body to kiss her gray cheeks. I
am luminous with hope and certainty, believing that although she will die, she
will always be with me.

And I have been right. I would not wish the death of a loved one on anyone, but I also know that the hours spent loving and listening to her, opening myself to sorrow, and finding connection in loss have stood me in better stead as a clinician and a person in the world than any professional training I have ever had.

FEAR

Both of my children were born with birth defects. Ben's, a ventricular septal defect, closed when he was 2 years old, was heard again when he was 12, and closed again when he was 14 years of age. Although the first year of adjusting to my worries about him were difficult, I know from my experiences with our daughter, Miranda, that I didn't really know the taste of fear.

Miranda was born 8 minutes after noon on the eighth day of the month, auspicious numbers. During the hours before we learned that Miranda had a rare genetic disorder from which she might die, I talked to family and friends, describing our new baby as beautiful and adorable—as any new mother would—and remarking on three features that later would become the cornerstones of a medical diagnosis. To my maternal eye, it was amazing that she was full-term size 4 weeks early; I thought that she had the cutest little creases on her earlobes; and she kept her tongue at an angle outside her mouth, like a kitten about to lick a bowl of milk. I went on and on about these features, never once imagining that my rapturous descriptions of these three observed phenomena would be redescribed by a medical language that would transform these already-beloved features from sources of joy to sources of worry (Weingarten & Worthen, 1997).

Four hours after her birth, the pediatrician who had been present at her delivery nervously walked into the hospital room and, with photocopies of three articles in his hand, informed us that our daughter had Beckwith–Wiedemann syndrome (BWS). He was sorry to have to tell us this, but he felt we should know immediately. Large percentages of children with BWS developed retardation, malignancies of the internal organs, and asymmetric growth of the limbs. Miranda, he told us, had been transferred to the special care nursery; they were uncertain that she would be able to feed and, he cautioned us, she might not live.

Postcesarean, in a morphine-induced spaciness to begin with, I couldn't believe that this already beloved child was at such risk: of death, of cancer, of deformity, and of retardation. My husband, Hilary, and I wept, and, as has become the pattern of our lives, we quickly made a plan. I worked the phones. Hilary went directly to the nursery, where he spent the next 12 hours rocking Miranda, singing to her, and working with her and a bottle until he could report to me and the staff that she was an avid, agile nurser.

Two episodes were decisive in setting our course with Miranda, a course in which we scrutinized carefully every bit of conventional wisdom, trusting only those who, like we, observed Miranda herself, with exquisite care. We learned to value what narrative therapists call "local knowledge" (White & Epston, 1989, citing Michel Foucault). The first episode concerns Miranda herself. She was examined by many doctors, and each of them found something else wrong with her. The disparity between the doctors' pleasure at discovering something else—wrong—with our daughter and our fear about caring for her was vast. On the fourth day of our hospital stay, a fellow in developmental pediatrics evaluated her. He was to have arrived an hour *after* her feeding, but because he was very late he arrived when she was hungry. I asked if I could feed her, and he insisted that it would interfere with his tests.

I saw the test; I saw his data. Nothing prepared me for his conclusion: "She is too poorly integrated to tolerate stimulation from more than one sensory channel at a time. If you are feeding her, don't talk to her. If talking to her, don't hold her. Keep her environment very simple. And by all means, don't allow her brother into the room with her. He will overwhelm her limited ability to stay organized."

Gentle Ben had already lovingly held her and sung to her. We had noticed no distress. I had seen her hyperresponses to the tests, but I knew that she was hungry and that the pediatric fellow was somewhat rough in his handling of her. Hilary and I dismissed his findings, deciding to take our cues from Miranda, who was already reassuring us by her consistent responsiveness, her avid nursing, and her easy comforting.

The second episode concerns the relationship between Miranda and me. Miranda was born at noon and whisked to intensive care within hours of her birth. I was not allowed to have her in my room until 46 hours later. Gazing into her eyes, I felt blissful with my baby despite what I knew were challenges ahead.

We had not been together very long when the pediatrician who had made the diagnosis of BWS entered my room and sat on the bed. Watching us, he made a pronouncement: "Good. I see that you will be able to bond after all." Having had no concern about bonding, I was temporarily thrown by his comment. Looking at him, looking at her, realizing that his presence was interfering with the very feeling he was concerned that I develop, I was able to dismiss his comment as not applicable.

We came to value experience-near wisdom (White, 1998, citing Clifford Geertz): our own, and those who worked closely with us and with Miranda. Those professionals who listened and observed carefully, reaching conclusions on the basis of what they saw rather than what the text said should be so, became my heroes. The day Miranda entered kindergarten, a dramatic and poignant milestone for me, I was walking on the sidewalk, tears in my eyes. Weeping as much out of relief as for joy, I thought I saw God. Startled, I looked again and realized I had caught the glimpse of the pediatric guru who, when Miranda was 3 months old, had told us he thought Miranda would live, that she was bright, and that BWS was a spectrum disorder with which she was very mildly affected.

The first 6 years of Miranda's life taught me a great deal about the vicissitudes of fear. I could chart the differences between mind-numbing panic, acute terror, and chronic, corrosive fear. Fear made me heavy; the object of that fear, Miranda herself, made me light. Being with her was like the meditation practice I learned later. It forced attention to the present, to the now, where teaching, laughing, cajoling, shepherding were as necessary as tending and ministering. It taught me to release vigilance in her presence, and it taught me humility about what I could not do.

In high school, I read all I could of the poet John Keats, including commentaries and biographies. I circled around his letter on negative capability, intuiting that I would find it apt for years to come. In this letter he writes, "*Negative Capability*, that is when man [*sic*] is capable of being in uncertainties, Mysteries, doubts, without any irritable reaching after fact & reason" (Bate, 1963, p. 249). Being with Miranda exercised my negative capability; it stretched me to live with uncertainties. This is something I can now do, and, at my best, I can do so without "irritable reaching." This quality, too, is part of my spiritual practice.

WHITE CHOCOLATE

Listening to others without my own agenda, opening myself to intense emotion, learning how to be still in the presence of uncertainty without any irritable reaching, riding out the turns of fear, and showing up in the present have all been lessons learned from life that I use daily in my clinical practice. They are what I bring to my relationships with clients that creates, I believe, a sense of spaciousness for others. In my office there is world enough and time. I, at least, have a sense of the sacred. I feel my breathing slow, my focus heighten, and an immense respect for the people who gift me with opportunities for transformative conversation. This is what I mean by a spiritual practice.

By the time Miranda was 6 years old, I was ready to work with other families whose children had life-threatening illness, and this has been a central, although numerically small, part of my clinical life for many years. Having gone to the edge of the cliff and believing I—we—would go over, I have felt a strong commitment to walk to the edge of the cliff with other mothers and fathers, knowing that the strength to go there with them comes as much from my journey back as the journey there.

Working with families whose children are dying has been both hard and beautiful. I am haunted by the image of the first small coffin I saw lowered into the ground, one fine November day. Knowing that death will come, drawing on my own experience, I have been clear that part of my work with parents whose children are dying involves the discovery of what sustains. Love or sleep, laughter or prayer, walking or biking, pasta or potatoes, there has always been something that brings a moment of relief into the sea of pain. I believe that my task is not just to be present to pain but to help others find a possibility for relief in something they already know about themselves. My hope is that I can give this preknowing mass and movement.

I do this for myself and for my family as well.

It is June 1991. A long day. I am taking Miranda, age 12, to the dentist where she will learn whether or not she needs braces. When we go home, she must quickly grab something for dinner because she has her school's spring concert this evening. The dentist seats us in an alcove and begins to tell her his conclusions. I observe that on the front of her chart, as we have requested, are the words, in capitals, "DO NOT DISCUSS BWS WITH CHILD." The dentist begins. "On a scale from 1 to 10, your mouth is an 11," he says. "You have the worst alignment of your teeth that it is possible to have, and you will most certainly need braces." Miranda is stunned. "But, I brush my teeth every day." she asserts, irrelevant to the situation, but an act of resistance nonetheless to this brutal, totalizing presentation of an opinion. "Why?" she asks. "Because you have BWS," he tells her. "Your lower jaw has grown disproportionately, and this is just one of the consequences." I am gesticulating wildly and, then, not caring if I am rude, I stand up and tell the dentist we will discuss this at another time.

By the time we reach the sidewalk of the large, urban street we are on, Miranda is howling in rage and distress. She is running down the street, with no regard for the heavy rush hour traffic alongside us. I run after her, pulling her writhing body to mine, holding her tightly in an embrace. She is pouring out questions: "Why did he say that to me? What did BWS do to me? What is happening to my body? Is it doing it all over? Is there more I don't know?" And much more.

"Look," I say to her, "this sucks. What he did to you was wrong and it's a big problem. BWS is a big problem, too. But we can't do anything about either of them right now. You have one hour to get to your concert. I know that's important to you. Your job now is to figure out what will help you pull yourself together so you can do the concert."

With some hesitation, and with her eyes doing a quick movement, suggesting that an interior search is taking place, she says, "White chocolate. White chocolate will help."

We search. We find. In the store, well-brought up as she is, she takes one bar of white chocolate. "No," I say as I take the bar from her hand and put it back on the shelf. "You have a job here, too. You have to figure out how many bars of white chocolate this event has been. How many bars of white chocolate do you need now and for later to manage what's just happened?"

Five times she reached for the large, paper-wrapped bars of white chocolate. Each time, she paused and contemplated, assessing, I imagine, the damage to her and the need for repair.

Today, I regard white chocolate as her sacrament. The image of her removing the bars is continually present for me, confirming my belief that in times of trouble, with love and support, people can access what sustains them and it can make a difference. Believing this in the face of unrelenting trouble—events and feelings that press on persons beyond what it would seem the spirit can bear—is a hard-won spin-off of my own efforts to keep faith with the possible. It allows me to feel certain that if I ask, "Is there something that provides solace which is available now?" then the direction of this inquiry, and the conviction I bring to the questioning, will construct the possibility and the actuality of solace for those in the heart of pain. This is a belief I have practiced in my own life. It is one of the ways my struggles have stretched me.

ALONENESS

I have asked myself the question I asked Miranda many times, perhaps most memorably one dark night in December 1988, several days after learning I would need chemotherapy and radiation to treat a newly diagnosed breast cancer. "What can you access now that is already available to you that will staunch this pain?" I answered, "Spirituality." I then asked myself this: "What do you understand about your spirituality? What will make it present for you now?"

My answer did not surprise me: connection. I did not invoke a connection to a God who might comfort and accompany me. Instead, I turned to people I knew, and some I did not. I called people and wrote them; people called and wrote me back. I asked certain people to be my witnesses. Everyone I asked agreed to do so. A man who owned a bed-and-breakfast I had once stayed at, after I informed him, sent me a poem every week. A Norwegian friend sent me a picture of a mountaintop that I keep in my glove compartment to this day. Friends gave me amulets and healing stones.

These connections were sustaining. They sustained hope, and they provided comfort. The relational matrix within which I did the rituals of daily life and ceremonial life mostly held terror at bay.

Mostly. Nights, that time when in the darkness of the soul, as F. Scott Fitzgerald has written, it is always four in the morning, were awful for me. Nights, connection dissolved and I faced what cancer's bottom line was for me: You die alone. Alone. For a person who has devoted herself to the care of others and for whom intimacy has been a passion, the idea of death/disconnection was intolerable.

I panicked. I obsessed. I railed against it. I also practiced meditation, breathing, and mindfulness. I exercised daily. I took hot baths. I struggled and I gradually came to live with the idea of aloneness, both my own everyday aloneness and my own Ultimate Aloneness. I confronted aloneness in the context of my own mortality. I tried to fight it and found that I could not. I did not accept it either. I learned that I would have to live with it and manage it somehow.

From this struggle, I learned what many of my clients come into therapy already knowing: There is a darkness that no love will ease (Weingarten, 1998b). I am able to sit with them, in the void that this knowledge illuminates, and talk about what can coexist with—not ease—the void. For me, connection remains the answer. I value connection, although I know that I will not always have it. Stretching to face the inevitability of my death, not just once but recurringly, forced a relationship to aloneness. Tending to this relationship is part of my spiritual practice.

INTIMACY AND COLLABORATION

For all of Miranda's life, my skills as a psychologist, child therapist, and family therapist have been invaluable. I have used what I have learned not from an expert position but from a side-by-side position, trying to make my skills visible to her so that they would transfer more quickly and easily. From the beginning, my immersion in a strength-based, nonpathologizing theoretical model stood us all in good stead. Believing that through the alchemy of love and listening, pain can transform itself into resilience, I never feared that her multiple hospitalizations, procedures, or chronic discomfort would diminish her.

In a chapter titled "On Ethics and the Spiritualities of the Surface: A Conversation with Michael White," White discusses a "form of spirituality that concerns one's personal ethics; that concerns the modes of being and thought that one enters one's life into; that is reflected in the care that one takes to attain success in a style of living. This is a transformative spirituality, in that it so often has to do with becoming other than the received version of who one is" (Hoyt & Combs, 1996, p. 36).

In many respects White's description of an active creation of the self one wants to be, rather than a passive acceptance of the self that others think one is, characterizes the way we have operated as a family and as individuals so that all of us, but Miranda especially, can be the selves we want to be. In Miranda's case, the potential limits and constraints were made visible to us immediately. Our job was to accept and transcend, and to know when to do which.

With our help, Miranda has fashioned an identity that elevates her personhood over BWS's claims on her life. The struggle to do this is often immense, for her and for us. Being her partner in this struggle has helped me in my clinical work immeasurably, especially with clients for whom trauma has a history of swamping preferred identities. With these clients, I often feel that the work we do is like the work with Miranda. It requires attention to what is desired, not what is given. It requires belief that what is desired is not only possible but always also already present.

In 1993, when Miranda was 14, BWS shifted from an intermittent to a steady presence in her life. Sadly, she is now in constant pain. Plagued by loose connective tissue, including of the blood vessels, she is prone to sudden dislocations of her joints and fainting.

To accommodate the realities of her body, I see clients and write at home, 5 minutes from Miranda's school, to ensure that I can get to her within minutes if needed. For her part, she is stoical and clear, letting us know exactly what she needs and why. Often she needs to talk. Not always about the immediacy of her current situation. Often about others who have struggled and who have made their struggles count for others. Reading first-person narratives of disabled persons, she finds in their accounts a direction and purpose for herself.

At age 17, in March 1996, Miranda dislocated both of her shoulders so severely that they couldn't be repositioned. For treatment, she was encased in a metal and plastic brace from her pelvis to her neck, with her arms kept rigidly in place by steel supports from shoulder to fingertips. She required 24-hour face-to-face care. Offered a home tutor, she insisted that she would go to school. Despite excruciating pain, despite an inability to read because the muscle relaxants and painkillers she took affected her eye muscles as well, despite having to have a personal care attendant with her at all times, Miranda went to school every day for the 6½ weeks of this ordeal. She told us, "The only way to change people's attitudes to disabled people is to expose them to us."

Concurrently, at the time that this happened to Miranda, I was working with a middle-aged woman who had become suicidal again. This time, she was able to ask for help and I told her that far from finding her phone calls intrusive, I saw them as evidence that she believed she was worthy of care and support, two experiences that had been lacking in her bleak and damaging childhood. These phone calls, in my view, were evidence that what she desired—comfort—was not only possible but also proved that her ability to secure it for herself was already present

My client, I will call her L, described herself living under a "blanket of pain." I was able to reach her there. Now, having spoken to her about this chapter, I know that she would say that in our work together a sense of possibility was present. She would also say that the space between us often felt sacred.

Having read my papers on intimacy, she would also concur with my experience that much of the time our conversations consisted of intimate interaction (Weingarten, 1991, 1992). In these papers, I propose a distinction between intimate interaction, in which meaning is co-created or shared, and nonintimate interaction, in which meaning is rejected, provided, or misunderstood. I suggest that intimate interaction between clients and therapists is therapeutic and that nonintimate interaction rarely is. However, I make clear that it is in the inevitable lapses of intimate interaction that occur between therapists and clients that there is an opportunity for profoundly meaningful collaboration.

When one is a therapist with a child with a serious medical condition which flares up erratically but suddenly, it is inevitable that one cannot always be available to clients. Intimate interaction at the level of conversation may be present, but at the level of the sessions themselves, there is always the likelihood that an appointment will have to be canceled at the last moment. A conscientious person, disciplined and reliable to a fault, I have tangled with BWS in this regard: how to care for clients when Miranda needs my attention, urgently and immediately.

Susceptible to creating those "inevitable lapses" in intimate interaction, I have honed my skills at repair so that I can continue to practice a conversational art for which I believe my life experiences have particularly prepared me. I have wanted to share what I have learned with others, even though I have known that we might be interrupted.

These interruptions were particularly difficult for L. As much as possible, I had tried to be consistent with her, letting her know with as much warning as possible when I would have to reschedule appointments. During the period that Miranda was in braces, I responded to L's between-session phone calls as quickly as I was able, but not as rapidly as I had in the past. I didn't explain, and L didn't question me about this. Ten days after Miranda's dislocations, I had to cancel an appointment with L. Depressed and despairing, L was sad and worried that she was too much for me and that I would abandon her. I told her that I had canceled because of an unplanned doctor's appointment for Miranda that I had to attend. I didn't say more. She worried out loud, as she had several times before, that I would have to leave my practice because of my personal life. I told her that I hoped that this would never happen; that it hadn't happened yet, and that I had managed to care for Miranda and care for my clients over all these years.

Pushing the point further, and bringing it close to the emotional core of her early life, L told me that she feared I would leave her for the "sicker" child. If I did, I let her know, it would never be the same as what had happened to her before because I would acknowledge her needs, I would attend to them, and I would be devastated myself.

In the beginning of April, it became clear to me that I could no longer manage the unplanned phone calls. I was seeing a few clients, people like L for whom continuity of contact was essential, and the rest of my time I cared for Miranda or attended to the bureaucratic circus that had ballooned around her. Evenings, when L usually called, I was either reading to Miranda or doing physical care. Miranda could do nothing for herself. Not scratch her nose, change position, eat, read, wash, or toilet herself. Her care took the time of two parents and an occasional friend as well.

Eventually and reluctantly the thought took form that I could no longer manage L's phone calls. Knowing that the cost to myself was too great, that the calls were not pro forma but hard-won efforts to reach out for comfort from a desperate woman who needed my concentrated presence, which I could not give, I called L's psychopharmacologist to see whether she would be able to cover phone calls for me and I talked to L's former group therapist as well to see if she would be available as backup, in case. I scheduled a session with L and her husband to tell them I could no longer take her calls, framed so positively in our work together, and that I could only meet with L for our regularly scheduled appointments.

The session was hard. Having slept very little in the previous 2½ weeks, miserable that I could not provide what my client needed and deserved, I was nonetheless clear that I had reached my limit. I explained briefly what had happened to Miranda and the requirements for round-the-clock care she now had. I explained that I would still meet with L but that I could no longer return her phone calls.

In this session, I acted on my belief that the process of being included in *meaning-making* (i.e., the sharing of meaning which creates intimate interaction) is a process that can contain terrible pain and unhappiness. It was not "natural" for me to share my daughter's troubles, but it seemed clinically necessary to create the conditions for L to manage the loss of our phone contact. I trusted that by including her in my process, she would feel respected and valued at the level of our relationship even though, at the level of my behavior, I was setting a limit on my contact with her.

That session was a turning point. It has also taught me about the sturdiness of the human soul and the will to feel strong and whole. Rather than feeling that I had abandoned her for Miranda, L felt that I cared deeply for them both. Identifying herself with Miranda, as a person I was intent on helping, she released herself to have empathy for herself as well as my daughter. I have L's permission to reproduce excerpts from a letter she wrote Miranda hours after our session.

Dear Brave Fighter:

This is for you and for me. It's a pep talk from a moment of calm to remind the courageous one inside that pain, suffering and despair pass. . . . We will survive it. And make meaning of it. It will be the texture and richness of that which fuels our passions. Our goals are made of this stuff, the stuff of surviving and surpassing. Now when things are perhaps least clear, when recovery feels agonizingly cloaked in misery, when all sorts of pain and frustration wreak havoc in as many ways as imaginable; now is the urgent time to let love and compassion from outside *and* inside be the soothing balm to tender the hurt so we can fight on.

I read Miranda the letter and called L to let her know her reactions. Miranda was touched that compassion for her had triggered L's compassion for herself. It confirmed her worldview that one person's suffering can have value to others. It made her feel useful not helpless. I felt awe that a circle of caring had created such positive effects all around.

As for L, there have been struggles since then, but she has never lost her compassionate connection to herself. She is working on making self-care and self-empathy steadfast companions. This fall, after we talked about whether I could write about this time in our joined lives, she wrote me a letter vividly describing her view of that time.

I reproduce this letter in its entirety because it is eloquent and insightful. It addresses intimacy and collaboration, those principles around which I have tried to live my life. I believe that they have stood me in good stead for the activity of "being there" for clients, for family, and—not insignificantly—for myself.

Kathy, I am trying to sort out my thoughts following our discussion of your chapter. I'm thinking that I'd like to share my understanding of what happened and how it came to be and where it led. For starters, I went back to your 1992 article on "A Consideration of Intimate and Non-Intimate Interactions in Therapy." I think that our history of shared and co-created meaning led us into the kind of intimacy that set the stage for the actions and interactions of last April. It was because I felt safe and secure, because you were reliable where boundaries were involved, that the convergence of situations could lead to openness and its profound impact on us all. For me to be in so much pain and hear you say you felt concerned about my needs in the face of your own need to be less available because of Miranda's situation made me feel at once understood (you got where I was at) and respected (you shared significant personal material) and concerned (because it brought me out of my pain and into my caring place). Knowing the seriousness of the situation and feeling great empathy for you and Miranda, I felt a yearning to respond. The parallel of seeing myself and Miranda as both suffering from uninvited troubles created movement. In empathy for her, my self-empathy expanded. Sort of like how group treatment works.

So, I'm thinking that you too, in feeling my pain, your pain, and her pain brought us into a unique intimacy where despite my not personally knowing her, I felt connected; that we all impacted each other in meaningful ways. That you as therapist centralized all this pain and in setting boundaries for managing it (availability to me, taking care of yourself, responding to your daughter) created some kind of opportunity for us all. When I wrote my letter to Miranda it was from a place of identification and deep caring of her (as another suffering person, as a child of someone I care deeply about) and of caring for myself too. It was a mutual pep talk. In talking to her, I could hear myself and really take it in.

One thing that meant a great deal to me was your phone call and subsequent sharing of the letter's impact on her. It made me feel like I was connected and helped. I think being connected and having meaning is tied in here, but at the moment, I'm not sure what to say about it. I'll consider this a reflection in progress and bring this to you in half an hour when I see you.

Another thought. I do believe that your own ability to carry your own trauma (the cancer and Miranda's health problems) created a model for me as a person and a therapist. I saw how you can bear it and go on and still be an outstanding clinician even when you have intense private concerns. I saw how it didn't have to be an either/or situation of who got attended to. Given my personal history, that had its own impact. You respected my ability to adapt to constraints, you responded to that, it was as if a sleeping part of my spirit woke up and said, "Huh? What's happening here, what can I do with it?" I have a feeling I know more than I have words for at present. To be continued.

CONCLUSION

I have no doubt that my clinical practice would have had a spiritual dimension to it independent of the influence of the events of my mother's death, my daughter's genetic disorder, and my own experiences with cancer. I believe I have always had an inclination toward a spiritual sensibility. However, I cannot imagine how I would have arrived at the particular understandings that I now have without the life events I have written about in this chapter.

These are the elements of my spiritual practice: listening without my own agenda; opening myself to sorrow; finding connection in loss; attending to the present; resting within uncertainties; accepting fear; tending my relationship to aloneness; believing that there is always something that can be sustaining; working for a preferred identity; and relating intimately and collaboratively. Squeezed together in one paragraph, they look skimpy, not robust.

But robust they have been. Each one has a tale attached, fragments of which have made their way into this chapter. Each one is a lesson I have taken from life experiences that I would never have wished on myself but from which I have become the person I am. Lessons like these accrue. They start off like drips of water during a spring thaw after a heavy snowfall, relentless and steady. And they create a substantial runoff, a flow.

So, too, my lessons have started from single moments of pain and worry and gained mass and meaning. There have been no sudden blinding revelations when I knew what to do and knew what was "right." Rather, I suffered a long time and then gradually, because I was desperate to turn sorrow into sense, I gathered ideas that sustained me.

I hope that my story—a story of suffering and sustaining practice—will be of some help to others. If it is, meaning will have sprung from sorrow.

REFERENCES

By convention one cites those books and articles that are clearly "referenced" in the text. I have done so here. However, there are other passages that have so informed, impressed, and inspired me that I have them in my very cells. These sources are immanent in the text but not visible on its surface. For these, I am profoundly grateful—and, as well, I am grateful to the reliable resource that reading has been for me.

Bate, W. J. (1963). *John Keats*. Cambridge, MA: Harvard University Press.

Hoyt, M. F., & Combs, G. (1996). On ethics and spiritualities of the surface: A conversation with Michael White. In M. F. Hoyt (Eds.), *Constructive therapies* (Vol. 2, pp. 33–59). New York: Guilford Press.

Weingarten, K. (1991). The discourses of intimacy: Adding a social constructionist and feminist view. *Family Process, 31,* 285–305.

Weingarten, K. (1992). A consideration of intimate and non-intimate interactions in therapy. *Family Process, 31,* 45–59.

Weingarten, K. (1997). *The mother's voice: Strengthening intimacy in families* (2nd ed.). New York: Guilford Press.

Weingarten, K. (1998a). The small and the ordinary: The daily practice of a postmodern narrative therapy. *Family Process, 37,* 3–15.

Weingarten, K. (1998b). Review of "The shared experience of illness: Stories of patients, families, and their therapists." *Families, Systems, and Health, 16,* 179–182.

Weingarten, K., & Worthen, M. E. W. (1997). A narrative analysis of the illness experience of a mother and daughter. *Families, Systems, and Health, 15*(1), 41–54.

White, M. (1998). *Narratives of therapists' lives*. Adelaide, South Australia: Dulwich Centre Publications.

White, M., & Epston, D. (1989). *Literate means to therapeutic ends*. Adelaide, South Australia: Dulwich Centre Publications.

CHAPTER 15

Heart and Soul
Spirituality, Religion, and Rituals
in Family Therapy Training

JANINE ROBERTS

The healing spirit will elude those who have an agenda to
impose. Men and women who want to proclaim their private
truths at the vulnerable and ill are not physicians (*or
therapists*).
—PAUL R. FLEISCHMAN (1994, p. 20; emphasis added)

I worked with a client, Yvette, when I was on internship, who
told me that when she and her husband fought, the figurines
of saints on top of the TV cabinet moved. They turned their
faces to the wall; they fell over. She interpreted this as a sign
that something was wrong in the house. I was raised
Catholic, but not Italian Catholic like Yvette. I was in a quan-
dary. Should I treat her beliefs as delusional or as a resource
in therapy?
—CHRISTINE (therapist, age 32)

One of my clients, Ron, aged forty-seven, was recently
diagnosed with colon cancer and is facing surgery and
possibly chemotherapy and/or radiation treatments. His view
of why he got it is that it is a random event—"things happen."
His wife, Alisa, has a very different take on it. She's wondering, "What is the universe trying to tell me? What lessons do
we need to learn? How is this my Karma?"
      I'm supposed to be doing couples therapy with them.
They are already in a lot of conflict. I don't know how to
manage the fact that they have such different views.
—JAMES (therapist, age 41)

BELIEFS: YOURS, MINE, AND OURS

The spiritual and religious beliefs of clients are seldom addressed directly
in family therapy training (Abbott, Berry, & Meredith, 1990; Prest &

256

Keller, 1993; Taibbi, 1990). And yet, as the preceding two vignettes show, they are often very present in the issues that people bring to therapy. Spiritual beliefs[1] can be both a tremendous resource in treatment or a constraint. Rachel and George, dealing with the loss of their only son when he was 16 in a car accident, believed that he was so perfect that God wanted him by his side. Their therapist listened carefully to their convictions and helped them to articulate these beliefs clearly, as well as find ways to share them with others. For instance, they made up photo cards of their son with a quotation about what a gift he was to God, to send to friends thanking them for their support after his death. Respect for the beliefs of Rachel and George gave them comfort and helped them with their deep grief and sorrow.

A survey of 1,225 Latina women in California, funded by the National Cancer Institute, was conducted to find out why Latina women underutilized preventive services for cervical cancer: "Nearly 25 percent of the women surveyed believe that cervical cancer is God's punishment for an immoral life-style. Among first generation Hispanic immigrants, the figure jumps to 43 percent" (*Family Therapy Networker*, May/June 1997, p. 17). In this case, beliefs act as a constraint against people having regular Pap smears or seeking out other preventive services. One of the researchers, a physician, F. Allan Hubble, noted that people who wish to inform Latinas about the need for Pap smears "may actually drive patients away, if they are not aware of the shame-laden perception" (p. 17).

If family therapists are not aware of the worldviews of clients about life's purpose, guilt, fate, afterlife or other beliefs that have a spiritual component, they may be missing key elements that impact on issues people are trying to sort through in therapy.

The spiritual beliefs of therapists are addressed even less in training or in clinical work (D. Anderson & Worthen, 1997). Reasons for this include worries about imposing ideas on clients, the secular–religious boundaries in society, and the desire in the field of psychology to be seen as "scientific."

But clinicians' spiritual beliefs can also be a constraint or a resource in treatment; if they go unexamined, the therapist does not have help identifying blind spots, nor tapping into how his or her own values may be useful in therapy. For instance, a therapist who is an agnostic may not ask about religious beliefs or church, mosque, temple, or synagogue connections, which may be a key community link for a family.

A person who is familiar with various beliefs and religious groups may be able to work with clients quite differently than someone without that information. Kevin, raised Unitarian, was having a difficult time understanding why a client, Anne, raised Irish Catholic but no longer practicing, was agonizing over whether to have an abortion. In seeking supervision on the case, Kevin talked with a Catholic colleague. She explained to him how having an abortion was still considered a sin by the Catholic church, that some factions viewed it as akin to killing someone, and that it was an affront to God as well, because it meant a woman was taking God's work into her own hands. With this information, Kevin was able to go back and ask very different kinds of questions of Anne about guilt, sin, autonomy, sexuality, pregnancy, and her beliefs in her relationship to Catholicism. As the conversation opened up, Anne felt more understood and found it easier to make a decision.

Being more cognizant of both clients' and therapists' spiritual and/ or religious beliefs can make them more available (when appropriate) as part of the therapy process. In the rest of this chapter, I will share six exercises that I have developed which can be used in training and supervision as well as clinical practice to learn more about when, where, and how to work with or not work with spiritual beliefs.

A safe arena in which to explore this aspect of life is with other trainees and colleagues. They can bring to bear on the discussion their listening, reflective, and analytical skills to examine what it means to cross boundaries into this topic. Also, generally in therapeutic work, I think it is important that therapists have some informed experience with the kinds of things they ask clients to examine. This means not only knowing a variety of techniques but personally working with them in some fashion so that therapists have empathy for the intricacy of lived experiences, as well as ideas on how to work with contradictory responses that may come up.

These six exercises are presented in a sequence in which they build upon and complement each other. They are offered as starting points for designing and adapting your own exercises to fit with your context. Each exercise is. described; directions and time needed for them are given. Ideas are also introduced about ways to adapt some of the exercises for use with clients. This is an important part of the process, as it keeps linking the experiential work done by people to therapy. The focus is thus kept on becoming better clinicians.

The first exercise, "Out in the Open," invites participants to complete unfinished sentences such as "Spiritual beliefs in my life. . . . " It is intended as a warm-up. In dyads, participants can help each other sort out and articulate their thoughts about the place of spiritual convictions in their life as well as make distinctions between what are seen as religious experiences and what are seen as spiritual ones.

The next exercise, "On the Line," brings in ideas of others in the family therapy field and is structured to facilitate a series of mini-dialogues with a number of people. This can quickly open up the discussion to a wider range of issues.

The third exercise looks at the sacred aspects of family rituals. All families have rituals. Examining spiritual beliefs and practices through looking at daily rituals such as mealtimes and bedtimes, or family traditions such as birthdays and anniversaries, can be a gentle entrance into and a different perspective on the topic.

The fourth exercise, "Through the Ages," uses a genogram as an anchor point for some guided imagery and poses questions such as, "What is your first memory of what you would call a spiritual or religious encounter?" This exercise can help participants examine familial patterns over time.

The last two exercises move closer to therapeutic practice. "Questions, Questions: Who's Got the Questions?" includes several inquiries about how to appropriately introduce ideas about spirituality into therapy. The final exercise offers suggestions about ways to structure role plays to simulate sessions.

For all of the exercises, say the phrases, questions, or ideas slowly. Repeat them a little so people can mull over them. Help people to concentrate by making a focused and contemplative atmosphere with your voice.

OUT IN THE OPEN: UNFINISHED SENTENCES

This exercise can be a good warm-up, as it helps people start to name, explore, and explicate the context for their beliefs. It is also very open-ended, which can aid people in discovering what may be important themes for them. Done in dyads, it is a safe format where disclosure is with only one other person and choices can be made easily by the partners about how much to disclose.

About 40 minutes are needed to do the exercise. For a group of people who do not know each other at all, it may be important to work through any issues of trust and boundary setting before beginning. For example, you might talk about what people need to feel safe disclosing information (such as partners will not share things with the larger group without checking it out with the other person first, or nothing will be shared outside of the workshop). There might also be some discussion about what kinds of both verbal and nonverbal responses are important so that people feel they have been heard by others and/or what helps participants to build trust. A key role for the facilitator in this discussion is modeling respect for the range of ideas which might emerge, as well as helping people to give concrete examples.

To begin the actual exercise, the facilitator says the first unfinished sentence (see Box 15.1) and asks each member of the dyad to finish it with the first thing that comes to mind. Ask people not to edit or think about their response too much. Then, give the dyads 3–4 minutes to talk with each other about why they completed the sentence in that way.

People may want to write down their initial responses to be able to go back to them after they listen to their partner. This can free them to be better listeners. The important thing is to keep and support the energy that can get generated between two people interacting. If people are looking down and writing too much, this can detract from dynamic inter-

---

BOX 15.1. Out in the Open: Unfinished Sentences

1. Spiritual beliefs in my life (as a child, adolescent, young adult—choose different time frames) . . .

2. Learning about spirituality . . .

3. Therapy and spirituality . . .

4. Religious beliefs in my life . . .

5. My mother's (or the person who took on this role) religious life . . .
   My father's (or the person who took on this role) religious life . . .
   My grandparents' religious life . . .

6. The spiritual beliefs of my clients . . .

7. The role of my spiritual and/or religious beliefs in therapy . . .

---

action with their partner. Having the unfinished sentences up on an overhead can support those who have a visual learning style. Giving participants a handout of the sentences afterward can make them less concerned about writing things down exactly.

Sophie completed the first sentence as follows: "Spiritual beliefs in my life as a child were unsettled, and as an adolescent, even more unsettled." Her partner, Brad, completed the same sentence with "Spiritual beliefs in my life as a teenager were sunk in guilt." They then went on to discuss what they had said with each other. Sophie commented, "My family was Jewish, but I didn't feel as if they practiced Judaism because it meant particular things to them and it helped them know how to lead their lives. Rather, it was because they were supposed to do it because 'that's what good Jews did.' I heard that phrase a lot. On the one hand, I had the words that these were important spiritual practices; on the other hand, I watched the behaviors, which were quite different. It was very unsettling."

"That clicks with what I experienced," said Brad. "I was raised Episcopalian, but it was like we went to church out of guilt—because that's what it meant to be a good person. If you didn't go, you were bad. But it was not as if my parents believed in the church because it comforted them. It was more because it made them virtuous."

Have participants go through all the sentences as in the example above. If you wish, you can add an eighth sentence to complete this exercise: "Doing this exercise was. . . . " This can help to provide closure to doing the sentences as well as help the partners in the dyad to see their own experience against the backdrop of someone else's. The juxtaposition of different people's reflections can help each participant to notice new things about their experience, flesh it out more, and make more detailed distinctions. For example, Sophie got clearer about why her experience was so unsettling by hearing Brad talk about how his family did not seem to take pleasure in churchgoing. "We had too many 'shoulds,' too," said Sophie. "We had to dress up, sit for hours in the synagogue. We weren't allowed to drive or use any mechanical things. It was a tense time in the family."

When the dyads have completed the exercise, ask the partners to give each other any affirmations and appreciations for things they have shared. This can be another way to provide closure for the exercise.

To get some group interchange going, you can ask people to come back together and see if there are several dyads who are comfortable sharing both what it was like to do the exercise and what issues came up for them that seemed particularly knotty, juicy, or useful to explore more. It can also be productive to ask people how they might adapt this exercise to use with clients as a way to keep making links between their own experience and clinical practice. For instance, Hwei Ling was fascinated by how her spiritual and religious ideas had shifted over her life. She said, "I think it would be useful to have clients finish off with each other four or five sentences about their beliefs and experiences at different time periods. It would give them a structure to reflect back on and have a sense of how they came to their current views. I think I would add another phrase, too: 'My spiritual beliefs in the future. . . . ' This could help people clarify aspects they might want to be moving toward."

Abdul commented, "I think I would, for some clients, use phrases that separate out religious practices and spiritual beliefs. I think these can be quite distinct and contradictions and tension points between them might be important for family members to understand."

ON THE LINE: VIEWS AND VOICES.

This second exercise is intended to open up the dialogue more broadly and move beyond personal experiences and ideas. What theorists and clinicians have said about the role(s) of spirituality and religion in family therapy is introduced and people are invited to react to these statements by placing themselves on an imaginary line depending on whether they agree or disagree with the statement. People then take a few minutes to discuss with others on the line why they put themselves there.

This is a good exercise to do after the unfinished sentences; it is more contemplative and lays a foundation for understanding the context of individual beliefs. "On the Line" provides a format for people to move out with their beliefs into a wider arena of ideas in a relatively short period of time that makes for a vibrant interchange (see Box 15.2).

Clear space in the room you are in and ask people to pretend there is a line across it from one corner to another. Tell the participants that you will read a statement and that they are then to put themselves on the line

---

BOX 15.2. On the Line: Voices and Views

1. All persons, even those who consider themselves agnostic or atheistic, are spiritual, whether or not they choose to express their spirituality through religious language or practice. (p. 4)

2. Spirituality is defined as subjective engagement with a fourth, transcendent dimension of human experience. (p. 3)

3. Three basic assumptions of spiritually based therapy are the following:
   (A) God (or a Divine Being) exists.
   (B) Human beings have an innate yearning for connection with this Divine Being.
   (C) This Divine Being takes an active interest in human beings and acts upon their relationships to promote beneficial change. (p. 3)

4. Hart (1994, p. 48) suggests that the therapist's deepest vocation may be to serve as an embodiment of divine love, in effect, as an "incarnation of God." (p. 11)

Note. All quotes are from D. Anderson and Worthen (1997).

---

based on whether they agree or disagree with it. The closer they stand to one corner (identified as the "agree" corner), the more it means they agree with the statement, and vice versa. After people have placed themselves, give them 3 or 4 minutes to talk with others in dyads or triads about why they placed themselves where they did. Encourage people at opposite ends of the line to talk to each other. These are often some of the liveliest discussions and help people to gain different perspectives. Some 30–40 minutes are needed to do this exercise in its entirety.

The statements that I have chosen to have people react to are from a recent article in a family therapy journal on spirituality by D. Anderson and Worthen (1997), two pastoral counselors. It was the lead article in the *Journal of Marital and Family Therapy.* Let people know where the statements are from. Read the first statement several times, and encourage people to move onto the "line." You can also have the statements on an overhead, showing each one as you say it out loud.

Doing this exercise with one group, a lively discussion was generated about the differences between spirituality and religion. "The third statement was the most provocative one for me," said Eunice. "I felt like it was way too narrow of a definition. Those assumptions to me were religious tenets for Christian-based therapy, not spiritual tenets."

"I reacted to them, too," said Manuel. "They did not reflect different cultural or spiritual beliefs from around the world."

"Many of the ideas in the quotes felt imposed, like prayer in the schools. Like in #2, I don't think you have to be in some fourth plane to have a spiritual experience. It might be as simple as a walk in the woods," added Andrea. "To me spirituality is more open than a lot of the ideas expressed."

Other statements can be chosen for this exercise and used with the same format. People in a class or training group can be asked to bring in possible quotes. What is important is that they are not personal statements from anyone in the group, as this would affect the group dynamics and participants' freedom to openly agree and disagree.

This exercise generates a lot of ideas quickly. As Andrea said, "Being able to talk to so many people in such a brief period of time opened up a lot of new perspectives for me." Guillermo commented, "Each statement gave me a holding point to examine, move around, and go off from. Having to explain to others where I put myself helped me to clarify what my responses and ideas were."

In order to adapt this exercise for use with clients, some changes need to be made. First, rather than using quotes from professional literature, statements need to be more generic and open-ended, and drawn from typical family experience (e.g., "Many things in life are predetermined by fate and there is not much you can do about them." "An important part of healing for me is my spiritual beliefs." "Within a family there should be room for different religious and spiritual ideas."). Second, this should only be done with clients where the intent is to open up dialogue, not to stir up contentious debate. Thus, there needs to be basic tolerance and trust within the family.

Finally, because the family you are working with will probably always be smaller than a training or supervision group and part of the potency of this exercise depends on having a number of people articulate different views, you may need to ask clients to imagine where others that are close to them or others in their community might place themselves. Discussion can then ensue about how those other perspectives make them feel about their own beliefs.

RITUALS: A LOW IMPACT INTRODUCTION

A low-key entrance into the theme of spirituality can be via a look at family rituals. All families have rituals: they provide a window into central values and beliefs and often express what families consider as sacred. Many exercises have already been developed to help people understand the role of ritual in their lives (Imber-Black & Roberts, 1998; Roberts, 1999). These can be easily adapted to focus more primarily on rituals with a spiritual component. The only exercise that will be presented here is one to help people scan and identify across the four different types of family rituals—day-to-day rituals, family traditions, holiday celebrations, and life cycle rituals—where spiritual aspects were central.

About a half hour is needed for this exercise. Ask people to get com-

fortable and do whatever will help them to focus on their memory and interior experience (rather than the noises and stimuli around them). This
might mean removing things from their lap, breathing more slowly, putting feet flat on the floor—or perhaps closing their eyes or just focusing on
one place in the room. Once people have begun to relax, here are some
suggestions for how you might guide them through their memories.

RITUAL REMEMBERING

I am going to ask you to scan across different types of rituals both in your life
as a child and currently and to think about what spiritual and/or religious aspects of them have been or are important to you. I would first like to ask you
to think about daily rituals like mealtimes, bedtimes, how you say hello and
goodbye. You may have a meditation in the morning when you wake up, or
practice yoga in some way—or have a moment of silence at meals, prayers at
night time. How have these been important to you in your life? Who are others who join you or do not join you in these practices? What impact does that
have on your relationship? Are there aspects of these rituals that feel obligatory or hollow? What changes might make them more meaningful?

The second kind of ritual I would like to ask you to think about is family
traditions. This includes events like birthdays, anniversaries, vacations, and
reunions. Where do spiritual expressions come into play in them? Perhaps a
family prayer at a reunion, or a remembrance of family members who have
died. Or some way in which the sacredness of life is acknowledged at birthdays, or birthing stories are told. Or perhaps it is vacationing in a place of
particular spiritual or religious significance to you. Or an anniversary
marked of an important transition in the family.

Which family traditions have more spiritual components to them—birthdays, anniversaries, reunions, vacations? Why do you think that is?

Holiday celebrations are the third type of family rituals. As I name a
range of celebrations that occur as we pass through the year, I would like to
ask you to think of any spiritual/religious practices that go along with them.
There might be special foods, music, mantras that are said, prayers, gathering with other people. Think about these elements as I name any holidays
that were and/or are important to you: New Year's Day, Three King's Day,
Chinese New Year, Ramadan, Passover, Memorial Day, Fourth of July, Rosh
Hashanah (Jewish New Year), Yom Kippur, Halloween, Divali (Hindu New
Year), Thanksgiving, Hanukkah, Christmas, Kwanza.[2]

What memories have stayed most vividly in your mind of different holiday celebrations? How are these connected or not to spiritual and/or religious practices? What is the significance of these memories to you?

The last kind of family rituals I am going to ask you to peruse are life cycle rituals—ones that take us on our journey from birth to death. These include events like engagements, showers, commitment ceremonies, weddings,
baby-naming ceremonies, adoption day parties, rituals for pregnancy loss,
leaving home, divorce, graduations, retirements, funerals, and other new rituals for today's life cycle passages. As you think about them, what spiritual aspects of them come to mind? How do these elements help transitions and
changes over the life cycle?

I would like to ask you to think back over the four different types of rituals: daily rituals, family traditions, holiday celebrations, and life cycle rituals.
In which area do you or did you have the richest examples of spiritual and/or

religious practices which were meaningful to you? Which areas were not as rich? Where might you like to amplify any practices? What might you like to change about other practices? When you are ready, please come back to this time and space.

Thinking about family rituals is a very accessible manner to explore spiritual and religious ideas, beliefs, and practices. This exercise can be a good way for people to step into that arena, as work with rituals may be something that they are already using as a resource in therapy. This exercise can also help people be more aware of spiritual aspects of rituals which they have not focused on or named as such.

THROUGH THE AGES:
RELIGION, SPIRITUALITY, AND THE GENOGRAM

This exercise will help participants look at larger patterns in their extended family over time. It uses each person's genogram as the anchor point for people to then be led into some guided imagery, and to consider some questions about spiritual beliefs and practice in their life (see Box 15.3).

You will need approximately an hour: 10–15 minutes for the introduction to it and the drawing of the genogram; 15–20 to add to the genogram as the facilitator asks participants the questions below; 15 minutes for dyads to give each other a tour; and 10–15 minutes to process the exercise overall and brainstorm on ways to use it with clients. Participants will need around 10–15 minutes first to do a basic genogram of three or four generations, so that they are then free to concentrate on the content you will present. Each person needs a large piece of paper and colored crayons, markers, or pencils. As people have their completed genograms in front of them, ask them to think about the genogram questions given in Box 15.3.

When people are done responding to the questions and suggestions of things to ponder, ask them to take a partner on a tour of their genogram. Keeping in mind the things they have been asked to consider, each member of the dyad should walk the other through their history. It can be helpful to have the prompts visible on an overhead. This can facilitate the asking of more process questions such as "Which of the questions or comments by the facilitator were the most provocative for you? Or the most disturbing? Or opened up the most things for you to consider?"

It can be instructive to ask people to hold up their genograms to share with the rest of the group or tape them up on the walls. Clinicians can learn more ways to help clients indicate patterns on genograms from the sharing of imaginative participant ideas. For example, Mara, whose

---

BOX 15.3. Genogram Questions and Guided Remembering

1. What is your first memory of what you would call a spiritual or religious encounter?

   - Where does that memory sit within you?
   - What kinds of feelings does it bring up?
   - In what ways does that memory inform you now?
   - How can you show this in some way on the genogram with color, a symbol, a phrase?

2. What was passed down through the generations to you about religious and/or spiritual beliefs?

   - By what people did?
   - By what they said?
   - By what they gave to you?
   - By religious or spiritual events you were asked to participate in or were excluded from?
   - What gender messages were embedded in these actions?

   How can you indicate some of the key things passed down to you on your genogram?

3. What rituals of life cycle changes were marked by some kind of ceremony and/or religious event (e.g., baby naming, Bar or Bat Mitzvah, Confirmation, weddings, or funerals)?

4. What were major shifts in religious/spiritual identification for various family members?

   - How can you indicate these on the genogram?
   - What was the impact on one or two key relationships with these shifts?
   - How can you show this?

5. How do various people in your extended family use or not use religious/ spiritual beliefs and practices to get them through difficult times?

   - Which of these strategies have you incorporated the most yourself into your life, or pushed against the most?
   - How can you show any of this with a word or phrase, a symbol, different colors?

---

family was predominantly Irish Catholic but with varying degrees of commitment to the church, colored in crosses to indicate strong believers, crosses that were just outlines to represent tentative believers, and crosses that were X'd out to represent those that had left the church. This enabled her to see some very interesting generational patterns, with dramatic shifts over four generations to many fewer connections to the church. Randall put in letters for the range of different groups represented in his genogram; B for Baptist, M for Muslim, L for Lutheran, and NA for New

Age. KoKwang, who had come to the United States from South Korea, indicated how he felt about being Buddhist in such a predominantly Christian society by drawing a small temple besieged by crosses.

Besides stimulating ideas on how to help clients to creatively show their history, this exercise aids people in seeing larger patterns beyond their own direct experience. Lise, whose family was a mixture of predominantly Jewish and New England Yankee Protestant, saw links she had not made before with the legacy of her English forebears fleeing England in the 1600s, looking for religious freedom, and her Jewish grandparents leaving Europe because of oppression in this century. As she said, "I've always thought of them as two very distinct heritages, but there is this thread that connects them—they both wanted freedom for their beliefs."

Joseph, an African-American man, told the story of his uncle who returned to Alabama from serving in World War II, having had a dream that he should return home and serve the community. He came back to his small town and did just that. Joseph went on to become a psychologist and also dedicated his life to helping others: "Like my uncle. I made this association for the first time today when I looked at what my relatives modeled for me about spirituality."

Therapists are more likely to inquire about and add information about spiritual and religious beliefs of clients on genograms if they see the importance of that realm in their own life. Being exposed to other people's experience can also pique their interest and inform them about other ways to think about spirituality. Having prior experience in ways to integrate it into a genogram or show it can also increase therapists' comfort level and likelihood that they will incorporate this theme into any gathering of family history.

QUESTIONS, QUESTIONS: WHO'S GOT THE QUESTIONS?

The next to last exercise is a series of questions about therapists' spiritual values as well as how they come into play or not in therapy (see Box 15.4). In training people to work with these issues, I think it is important to keep finding ways to link what people are exploring and discovering with therapeutic process. These questions should be done in small groups of two, three, or four people.[3] The size of the group will depend partly on how much time you have and partly on whether you want people to get to know others more intimately in a small group. If you have done some of the previous exercises primarily with dyads, it can be instructive to have a larger group of people sharing their responses to the questions. This provides more exposure to a variety of experiences and ideas.

A warm-up for this exercise can be a brief guided remembrance where participants are asked to recall a time or times when they felt some

---

**BOX 15.4. Spirituality and Religious Beliefs in Families
and Family Therapy**

1. Who taught you the most about spiritual/religious beliefs as a child?
   - Did you learn different things from men? From women?
   - From people inside your family? people outside your family?
   - How were your beliefs then looked upon by the larger society?
   - In what ways were social class issues reflected in membership in different religious/spiritual groups?

2. What did you learn about yourself as a boy/girl through your experiences of spirituality and/or religion?
   What has been the influence of religion and/or spirituality on major adult decisions in your life or in the lives of other key family members (e.g., abortion, choice of people to date and/or marry, circumcision, or divorce)?

3. What ways have any of the various identities you have (as a divorced person, married person, gay person, heterosexual, woman or man, person with some physical challenge, parent, etc.) been supported by religious scripture/doctrine/tradition? Or not supported?
   What has been difficult for you personally about spiritual and/or religious beliefs? What has been healing?

4. When is a time in which you think you appropriately introduced ideas (or can imagine appropriately introducing ideas) about spiritual and/or religious beliefs into the therapy process?
   What helped to make it appropriate?

5. Values, beliefs, and biases are all embedded in different spiritual and/or religious practices.
   What is a way (or ways) you check to make sure you are neither imposing nor ignoring key belief systems as either a resource or a constraint in therapy?
   Can you state this as a guideline for others?

---

kind of spiritual solace or connection. Who or what was around them? What feelings did they have? What do they carry with them now from this memory? What would be one way to express it to others with words, with a gesture, or movement?

As a way to begin, you can ask the participants to briefly share the feelings that were evoked for them with others in their group either nonverbally or verbally.

These questions are meant to be a general guide. People are encouraged to go off on other questions that they find interesting, drop ones in the exercise that do not draw their attention, and stay with ones they find more intriguing. Groups can be asked to work with the questions by letting one person at a time respond to questions under the first theme and then go onto the questions under the following themes (2–5). Or one person could go through all of the questions of interest to him or her, while the partner(s) are the listeners. A useful way to keep building a good community of listeners is to ask partners to share what resonated for them when they heard other people talk. Again, the group can be brought together as a whole to share their experience of the exercise and ideas generated.

As with the previous exercises, participants are asked to come up with links to practice as a way to keep a focus on providing good treatment. One group came up with the following guidelines for ways to appropriately introduce ideas about spirituality into therapy: (1) Do it in a frame of open inquiry about clients' beliefs, not sharing your own (which could be seen as proselytizing). (2) Ask clients if this feels like an arena they want to explore more. Take your cues from their energy and interest level. (3) Be attuned to circumstances of people's lives that might bring up and/or pull for attention to spiritual and/or religious beliefs. (4) Be sensitive to the biases of the larger culture about religious and/or spiritual beliefs. For instance, the unfounded accusations that people at first made in the Oklahoma City bombing incident that it was Muslim terrorists reflected prejudices against that religion.

ROLE PLAYS: WAY ON INTO IT

The closest proximation to actual work is to do role plays. Scenarios can be written up to act out, or people can be asked to improvise them. Often the most active role plays are ones where people just make them up, as issues they present are often at the core of things that are the most meaningful to them. Here is one scenario written out:

DENIAL HAS ITS PLACE: A ROLE PLAY

Father—early 40s, tax accountant. Works both outside home and has home office. He is spending more and more time in his home office.

Mother—late 30s. Works outside of home as monitor for the state for family day care centers. Used to run a day care center in the family home. Has been taking some leave time to be at home.

Oldest son—14, diagnosed with leukemia a year and a half ago. Avid baseball player before the illness and solid student.

Second son—13, not doing particularly well in school. Lot of conflict with older brother both before and after illness.

Youngest child—a girl, aged 5. Seems to be disoriented, not at all sure about what is going on in the family.

The therapist wants to support the hopes of the family for a remission for the oldest son. At the same time, every couple of weeks when she sees the family, the son is visibly weaker to the point where family sessions need to be moved to the home. No one talks about the possibility that he might die. The therapist is concerned about the impact this is having on all of them, especially given the father's withdrawal, the younger son's history of conflict with his brother, and how disconnected the daughter seems.

The next therapy session ends up being in the oldest son's bedroom because he is too weak to get up out of bed. While the mother is gathering the rest of the family, the oldest son makes it clear to the therapist that he thinks he is going to die.

The therapist wants to help them talk about this together and learn more about their beliefs about death, loss, life after loss, and life after death. She is afraid to upset the parents' denial about how ill their son is, as the denial certainly seems to be giving them the fortitude to get through a very difficult period.

Crucial to working with role play is building in structures to support people as they are doing it, as well as analysis and discussion of what people are learning from it. For instance, the role play can be done with a live supervision or reflecting team format (T. Anderson, 1987; Roberts, 1997) so that the therapist and family can get "phone-ins" or the benefit of ideas from the reflecting team. Also, people can be asked to observe for specific things (like issues and questions that have come up in some of the previous exercises).

Another possible format is to have reflections on the role play given by teams afterward. Rich information can also be obtained by interviewing the people who played the different roles in the role play. This is a good way to help derole people as well, an often neglected aspect of role plays. Family members can be asked to comment on their responses to things the therapist tried; the therapist and family members can share where they felt engaged and connected. Suggestions can be given for other ways to address interactions. It is important to be as attentive to how you set up this part of the role play as the actual role play itself. Good working structures for analysis and discussion will enable you to get the most out of the actual scenario.

MOVING BEYOND

These exercises are intended as starter yeast for your own ideas. Try parts of them yourself. Adapt and change ideas around to fit situations you are working in. Experiment with others; ask participants for feedback; rework the exercises based on their input. Bring in other family therapy techniques. For example, you might have people make a floor plan (Coppersmith, 1980) of a place of worship that has been important to them, or sculpt (Papp, 1976) their relationship to spiritual and/or religious beliefs over time. Enjoy!

ACKNOWLEDGMENTS

Thanks to Don Banks, EdD, Deborah Berkman, PhD, Stephen Blane, EdD, Julie Cox, MS, Rich McKeown, LICSW, Jessica Morris, PhD, Laurie Ostendorf, PsyD, and Donna Volpe, PsyD, for feedback and ideas on these exercises.

NOTES

1. Please note that I am using spiritual in a broad sense of the word here and thus subsuming religious practices under it. It is cumbersome to keep referring to "spiritual and/or religious" convictions throughout the chapter. However, there are also times when I want to highlight distinctions that may exist between spirituality and organized religion. In places where I refer to both spirituality and religion, it is in the service of helping people sort out some of these differences that are often glossed over.
2. It is important to have a range of holidays that reflects the constituency of your group.
3. You may have ongoing groups in training that you can give this exercise to. For instance, as part of a class, I have had Bowen support groups which met regularly outside of class time to look at multigenerational family history of participants. A group such as this can be given the exercise to do on their own if they wish.

REFERENCES

Abbott, D., Berry, M., & Meredith, W. H. (1990). Religious belief and practice: A potential asset in helping families. *Family Relations, 39,* 443–448.

Anderson, D., & Worthen, D. (1997). Exploring a fourth dimension: Spirituality as a resource for the couple therapist. *Journal of Marital and Family Therapy, 23,* 3–12.

Anderson, T. (1987). The reflecting team: Dialogue and meta-dialogue in clinical work. *Family Process, 26,* 415–428.

Coppersmith, E. (1980). The family floor plan: A tool for training, assessment and intervention in family therapy. *Journal of Marital and Family Therapy, 6,* 141–145.

Fleischman, P. R. (1994). *Spiritual aspects of psychiatric practice.* Cleveland, OH: Bonne Chance Press.

Imber-Black, E., & Roberts, J. (1998). *Rituals for our times: Celebrating, healing, and changing our lives and our relationships.* Northvale, NJ: Jason Aronson.

Papp, P. (1976). Family choreography. In P. J. Guerin (Ed.), *Family therapy: Theory and practice* (pp. 465–479). New York: Gardner Press.

Prest, L. A., & Keller, J. F. (1993). Spirituality and family therapy: Spiritual beliefs, myths, and metaphors. *Journal of Marital and Family Therapy, 19,* 137–148.

Roberts, J. (1997). Reflecting processes and "supervision": Looking at ourselves as we work with others. In C. Storm & T. Todd (Eds.), *The complete systemic supervisor* (pp. 334–348). Boston: Allyn & Bacon.

Roberts, J. (1999). Beyond words: The power of rituals. In D. Weiner (Ed.), *Action methods in psychotherapy: A practical guide* (pp. 55–78). Washington, DC: American Psychological Association.

Taibbi, R. (1990, July/August). The uninitiated. *Family Therapy Networker,* pp. 31–35.

CHAPTER 16

Spirituality Expressed in Community Action and Social Justice

A Therapeutic Means to Liberation and Hope

ALICE DE V. PERRY
JOHN S. ROLLAND

In the early 1980s the Yale Medical School held a conference about the effects of nuclear war on children. One of the presenters, the Harvard psychiatrist John Mack, told a story about a teacher who had asked her young students how many of them believed that there would be a world for them to grow up into. Only one hand went up. The teacher expressed curiosity about the singularity of this student's belief. He explained that he saw his mother and father out lots of nights a week working to prevent a nuclear war. His parents' concerted effort to resist and remedy the violence of nuclearism gave him a sense of confidence and a sense of a future. Their activism, a strategic intervention in the social order, generated for their child both possibility and promise. Their justice-seeking had a therapeutic and spiritual benefit; it created hope.

This chapter examines spirituality as it is expressed in and generated through social justice activism. It explores the several therapeutic benefits that such activism can engender, specifically hope, empowerment, and the healing that comes with equitable, harmonious relations. We argue for the inclusion and application of a social justice critique in the work of family therapy in order that the therapy might be socially responsible, contributing to genuine transformation not just accommodation. We recommend for therapists and families alike participation in social justice activities both as an expression of spirituality and as an intervention that can be enhancing to and amplifying of healing both within and among persons and within and among communities. Drawing from case material and from the experience of our own activism, we explore and analyze the specific therapeutic benefits of a justice-seeking spirituality, while cautioning against the potentially adverse effects of unexamined participation in and unwitting support of dominant competing spiritualities within our culture, specifically: individualism, materialism, violence, professionalism, and despair.

Over the past three decades social activism has been for the two of us a source of hope, confidence, and empowerment. We have each been involved principally in the work of peace and disarmament, and variously in the work of welfare reform, health care reform, Central American solidarity, reproductive rights, violence prevention, gender equity, and economic justice. Underlying—indeed, motivating—our activism have been feelings of empathy and anger in response to troubling and painful disorders in the social fabric.

SOMETHING AMISS:
SEEKING TRANSFORMATION, PURSUING JUSTICE

Anger, writes the feminist theologian Beverly W. Harrison, "signals something amiss in relationship" (1989, p. 220). The heartache of "something amiss," its pain keenly felt, while sometimes numbing, is invariably a mobilizer. Typically it is "something amiss" that brings individuals and families into therapy, seeking transformation. Similarly "something amiss" motivates the work of social justice, mobilizing individuals like ourselves to engage the community (local, national, and/or global) with the goal of its transformation.

Activism can take many forms: the social service work of homeless shelters or soup kitchens; the community organizing of tenant groups or neighborhood block watches; legislative advocacy on such issues as gun control, environmental justice, educational reform, or health care reform; civil rights marches, gay pride parades, antiwar demonstrations, or acts of civil disobedience. In essence activism is a strategic intervention in the larger system with the goal of changing injurious practices, of counteracting the abusive and dispiriting effects of injustice, and of creating or restoring equitable and harmonious relations. Activism's goal, in short, is the establishment of justice, which in its biblical understanding means quite literally "right relations." In addition, activism is empowering and can help to connect oneself and one's purposes to the larger realm of social good.

Woven thoroughly into the various acts of mercy, protest, organizing, imagination, and resistance that constitute expressions of activism is hope. To step out and to challenge the way things are certainly requires a vision alternative to the present order of things. But principally activism requires the hope, often in spite of the evidence, that such imagined and preferred alternatives can be made real and that that which is amiss can be set right. Hope, as the theologian Walter Brueggemann describes it, "is the refusal to accept the reading of reality which is the majority opinion" (1978, p. 67); it offers a "promissory call to a new future" (p. 66). Activism not only requires hope, it also helps to generate it. The experience of being out there, working with others toward a desired change, motivated by the heart's conviction, helps to create the confidence that, in the words of the late-14th-century mystic Julian of Norwich, "all shall be well, and all shall be well, all manner of things shall be well."

Such social justice activism is an integral and essential expression of spirituality. We believe it should not be considered either "other than" or separate from spirituality, but rather, properly understood, social justice activism is the fruition of spirituality. It is spirituality in full bloom. At the same time the realization of just relations, like a fertilizer, helps to foster and strengthen the growth of spirituality.

This intimate, organic kinship between spiritual well-being and justice is certainly recognized in many religious texts and traditions. As Pope Paul VI observed, "If you want peace, work for justice" (Larson & Micheels-Cyrus, 1986, p. 126). "Justice and peace will kiss each other," writes the Psalmist (Psalm 85:10). The word for peace in this context of Hebrew scripture is *shalom* (and in Islam, the Arabic *salaam*), which carries a meaning far more holistic and profound than the political definition: absence of war. Shalom means a sense of wholeness, connectedness, at-oneness, harmony—in short, spiritual well-being.

SPIRITUALITY: "EMBODIED IN THE NITTY-GRITTY OF LIFE"

Spirituality, as we are defining it here, involves the awareness that at the heart of things, at the heart of human existence and of all creation, there is a profound interconnectedness, an intricate interdependence. We are created dependent and interrelated. This has been well expressed thus: "I have lived inside another person, so I am a person" (Wehr & Young-Eisendrath, 1989, p. 135). The self, as we know it individually, is negotiated within the context of community. It is the interiorization of community. Bellah, Madsen, Sullivan, Swidler, and Tipton in *Habits of the Heart*, argue that we "need to remember that we did not create ourselves, that we owe what we are to the communities that formed us, and to what Paul Tillich called 'the structure of grace in history' " (1985, p. 295). Only arrogance allows humankind to believe that we stand apart or can survive alone, separate and dominating. Theologians like Paul Tillich (for one) have argued that the essence of sin is precisely such separation, whether it be from fellow human beings, from the environment, or from God. In actuality humankind is a social species: we need community and the mutuality and solidarity that expressions of love and respect sustain.

The lens of spirituality brings into focus the reality of a sacred power, energy, or life force that infuses, suffuses, and connects all that is. This power, transcendent and yet inclusive of all, is variously named in different religious traditions: God, Spirit, Chi, Divinity, Mystery, Jesus, Allah, Love. In every instance the language points towards a realm of beneficent spiritual reality, creating, connecting, and inspiring (literally, *inspiriting*) the created order and each creature within it.

Many give voice to the awareness of such spirituality, particularly writers and mystics. The novelist Alice Walker captures it when Shug in *The Color Purple* says, "I believe God is everything. . . . Everything that is or ever was or ever will be. And when you can feel that, and be happy to feel that, you've found it" (1982, p. 178). And often family members in therapy articulate this awareness as well. "When I'm plugged into the socket of God," one family member explained, "I am clearer and have more energy."

Spirituality is sometimes described as if it were only a private and interior enterprise, "me and my God," abstracted and uprooted from the socioeconomic–political context. In contrast, the spirituality that we are describing here gets its hands dirty. It is down to earth. It is the experience of spirit immersed, embodied, incarnated in the nitty-gritty of life. "All the domains of human existence—ecology, economics, health, prayer, politics, sexuality and education—are in the province of spirituality" (Brown, 1988, p. 117). Spirituality thus understood locates "divine revelation . . . in the concrete struggles of groups and communities to lay hold of the gift of life and to unloose what denies life" (Harrison, 1989, p. 214). Jesus' teaching that the "kingdom of God is at hand" (Mark 1:15) points to this concept of spirituality. Such an "at hand" spirituality invites us, in kind, to become engaged, to immerse ourselves, and to align ourselves in "right relation" with the spirit-filled world that is our home. Such immersion effectively realizes the profound interconnectedness and kinship with all creation that is the human condition. Martin Luther King, Jr., expressed his recognition of this profound interconnectedness at the heart of things when he wrote that "injustice anywhere is a threat to justice everywhere" (Washington, 1986, p. 290).

This understanding of spirituality calls into question constructs of separation and division and exclusion, the various borders, barriers, and boundaries (and conflicts over the same) that "Balkanize" our world. When people are spiritually alert and alive, they discover (recover) themselves not as fundamentally apart and isolated but as essentially connected and engaged. "The life of spirituality," writes theologian Robert McAfee Brown, "will be located in the midst of the world's turmoil, rather than in safe havens of disengagement" (1988, pp. 118–119). More than just an insight, spiritual attentiveness inspires one to action. Spirituality inclines one to engage the world with a praxis characterized by a sense of responsibility to and for the creation in all its fullness and by a commitment to live in right relation, through practices of love, compassion, caring, and mutual respect.

How is this intimate, organic kinship between spirituality and social justice activism relevant to the work of family therapy? As the opening story suggests, a family member's participation in political and social change activities can have distinctively therapeutic benefits not only for that individual but for the whole family system. Such activism can make a substantial difference to how one feels about oneself, the meaning of one's life and intimate relationships, one's vision of and possibilities for the future, and one's experience of connectedness to (and security in) community. Participation in the work of social justice can also make a substantial difference to the very nature and health of the communities to which we, therapists and families, belong. A justice-seeking spirituality, we believe, offers a critical therapeutic resource for the healing of broken spirits and broken relationships within communities, be those families, neighborhoods, workplaces, marketplaces, municipalities, or nation-states.

JUSTICE-SEEKING SPIRITUALITY:
A RESOURCE FOR HEALING AND LIBERATION

How might we understand the content of a justice-seeking spirituality? The Book of Exodus, in its early chapters, provides a paradigmatic example, one that has become the signature story for liberation theology. Liberation theology, which emerged during the late 1960s and the 1970s in developing nations, initially in Latin America and then in Asia and Africa, challenged conventional theological approaches, creating such discomfort for the Vatican that several prominent liberation theologians have been investigated. Liberation theology is threatening in large measure because of its starting point. It starts not with tradition, nor doctrine, nor the imprimaturs of the religious hierarchy, but rather with the experience of those in need, specifically with the "suffering, struggle, and hope of the poor" (Berryman, 1987, p. 6). It is a bottom-up theology, "a theology of the people . . . rather than a theology of the experts" (Gutierrez, 1984, p. vi), which privileges the voices of those most disenfranchised and oppressed by the dominant power structures (religious as well as political). Liberation theologians claim, in a phrase popularized by the Peruvian theologian Gustavo Gutierrez, that God has "a preferential option for the poor," that those who are least in the eyes of the powers-that-be are the first in God's eyes. Liberation theology combines with this perspective a sharp critique of "society and the ideologies sustaining it" (1984, p. 6). It emphasizes that release from captivity, whether to poverty (or affluence), intimidation, abusive relationships, addictions, racism, exploitative economic policies, or any such conditions which damage the human spirit, is essential for the flourishing and vitality of human persons. If, as the early church father St. Irenaeus said, "The glory of God is a human being fully alive," liberation from unjust and oppressive social structures (politics) is just as critical as liberation from intrapsychic constraints (psychology). Spiritual well-being and justice, right relations, are inextricably tied. A commitment to spirituality, the recognition of divine spirit infusing all creation, inspires activism in defense of that creation.

The Exodus story illustrates the activism of a justice-seeking spirituality. There we learn that God, Yahweh, hears the cries and suffering of God's people, the Israelites enslaved in Egypt, and then calls Moses and commissions him to lead the Israelites from the bondage of Pharaoh's oppressive and murderous rule to the promised land of freedom. From the perspective of Pharaoh the suffering of the people of Israel is not a problem. It is an intended consequence of a "justifiable" and "fiscally responsible" economic policy ensuring a cheap labor supply, much as the institution of slavery did in the United States many centuries later. But to God, the heart of compassion, the people's suffering is intolerable and requires liberating action. God's very being is connected to the well-being of the Israelites; God cannot be at peace until they are free. And such freedom can only be won through the daring activism of mobilization, organization, and public protest against unjust social structures: "Let my people go." Resistance is the order of the day. It is not an acceptable option to help people to accept, adjust to, be quiescent about, or be tranquilized to their suffering. Nor is it adequate to work on an individual, case-by-case basis to relieve or assuage suffering. Pharaoh must be confronted; unjust social structures must be challenged, in order for individuals to be free, to be whole, to be fully alive.

It is our belief that the work of family therapy needs to contend with and confront oppressive social structures if it too is to be truly liberating for people. Howard J. Clinebell has argued that "behind every personal problem is a cluster of societal problems" (1983, p. 189). As therapists we need to take seriously that behind many personal and familial problems there are often "clusters of societal problems," or—put differently—that the personal is political (even planetary, as some have suggested) and the political is personal. Intersections of the personal and the political are most obvious in the prevalence of depression among women in a sexist society, for example, or posttraumatic stress whether from warring on a battlefield or in a bedroom, or the struggles of individuals with AIDS, but evident as well in the common events of the daily round of living. Disorders in the socioeconomic and political context affect our experience of personal vitality and spiritual well-being.

THE HEALING CONNECTION OF AN ADVOCACY COMMUNITY

Betsey's story provides an example. A divorced white woman in her early 40s with a young child, Betsey felt both worn down and "bruised" not only by her ex-husband but by the legal system. With very limited resources and the primary responsibility for the care of her special needs child, she was no longer able to hire a lawyer but instead represented herself when her ex-husband filed for a downward redetermination of his already very modest child care payments. In therapy sessions Betsey voiced feelings of anger, despair, and isolation. "Am I being punished? What have I done to deserve this?" she cried. Pointing her finger upward, she asked poignantly, "Is this God's idea of a cruel joke?" She imagined God as a black-robed judge on a high bench. She felt harassed and struggled with the dispiriting feeling of being disempowered. As her therapist, I (A. de V. P.) noticed feeling somewhat disempowered myself, knowing the economic disadvantage that women often experience after a divorce, the difficulty collecting child care support, and the patriarchal bent of the legal system.

Betsey felt disempowered and isolated, but she came into a newfound strength when she connected up with a local coalition that provides advocacy and free legal counsel for women struggling with former spouses and the court system. This community of support and action helped Betsey to come to recognize her personal struggles not as isolated but systemic and shared. She felt heard and strengthened by their solidarity. Members of the coalition began to accompany her to her courtroom appearances. Not only has she been able to speak up there, but she has now become, on occasion, a spokesperson for the coalition. Participation with the coalition has been for Betsey an empowering and liberating intervention. She has felt more spirited and alive, less diminished as a person, and more hopeful about her own capacity to help others and be an advocate for those struggling as she has. She also is more inclined now to believe that God is supportive and caring rather than punitive.

INGREDIENTS OF A JUSTICE-SEEKING SPIRITUALITY: LIBERATION THERAPY

Betsey's story suggests some of the ingredients of a justice-seeking spirituality, ingredients that can be gleaned as well from the Exodus story and that can help to inform the development of what might be called "liberation therapy":

- The importance of community for the work of liberation and the restoration of justice. This is a counter to isolation and individualism.
- The use of a wide-angle lens that sees, beyond (and within) dis-

crete cases of suffering, the fuller picture of systemic, political, and societal forces. This is a counter to decontextualizing the problems of individuals and families.

- The decision to be public about suffering, to tell the story, rather than to hold it as a private anguish or internalize it as personal failure and shame. This is a counter to the personalization that can end up blaming the victim.
- A sense of identification with and honoring of pain, with the ability to say, in the words of the poet Theodore Roethke, "I believe my pain" (quoted in Macy, 1989, p. 204). This is a counter to denial.
- The recognition of mutuality—that our stories and futures interlock with those of others respecting the reality that, as the Russian monk in Dostoevsky's *The Brothers Karamazov* taught, "we are each responsible to all for all" (1880/1950, p. 356). This is a counter to divisive, exclusionary, or polarized (us/them) thinking.
- The recognition of an affinity with and empathy for those who are hurt and oppressed. This is a counter to elitism and privilege or any other such expression of disconnection.
- The commitment to be engaged, immersed, rather than to be aloof, indifferent, resigned, or impassive about injustice. This is a counter to the diminishment of our own humanity and the erosion of community or social solidarity if we stand apart.

To be sure, such justice-seeking spirituality requires an individual decision. Betsey needed to decide for herself to join up with the coalition for justice, for instance. Or, for another example, on one particular bus ride one particular person, Rosa Parks, decided not to go to the back of the bus. But activism is not a private or solitary enterprise anymore than spirituality is. To the contrary, it grows out of the awareness that we are not alone and that our sense of dignity and well-being is intricately tied to our participation in community, to the experience of working for the common good. As H. Richard Niebuhr argues, we "cannot be selves save as we are members of each other" (1978, p. 52). Our individual health is tied to the community's health. Moreover, as Larry Graham writes in his book *Care of Persons, Care of Worlds*, "The destiny of persons and the character of the world are intertwined" (1992, p. 13). Or, as Chellis Glendinning suggests, "In a kind of interplay of mutual causation, the themes we play out in our private lives mirror those we are exposed to in our society, and vice versa. Could there be a relationship between nuclear war and wife battering? Between alcoholism and toxic contamination? Between global warming and workaholism?" (1994, p. xii).

A critique one might make of therapy, including family therapy, is that its practice has sometimes been too decontextualized, without adequate attention to this "interplay of mutual causation," to the intertwining of "the destiny of persons and the character of the world." The therapeutic lens, even for family therapy which widened the angle beyond the individual, has still been more close-up than wide-angle. A number of family therapists have broadened our range of vision to the powerful influences of culture, social class, gender constraints, and social systems, such as the workplace and health care (Boyd-Franklin, 1993; Falicov, 1995; Imber-Black, 1988; McGoldrick, 1998; Mirkin, 1990; Rolland, 1997; Walsh, 1998; Waldegrave, 1990). Yet in most mainstream clinical practice, interventions still tend to focus on individual client families, while leaving out the families' larger communities, which are often communities that we as therapists share with our clients. Indeed, it is only when families join together in concerted efforts that problems affecting us all can be tackled, whether they entail neighborhood violence that destroys lives and security, or media images of beauty that contribute to eating disorders in teenage girls.

A justice-seeking spirituality, both of our clients and of therapists (in either our professional or personal capacity or both), leads to a caring and concerned engagement with the larger community. That engagement holds the promise not only of strengthening the well-being and health and fabric of the community, the "ties that bind," but also of strengthening the well-being, the sense of purpose and promise, and the hopefulness of individuals and their families (Walsh, 1998). The sense of self and family well-being emerging from and strengthened through socially active engagement with the larger community can be liberating, affirming, and salvific. Community action can most definitely be a therapeutic intervention.

THE CONVICTED, COMPASSIONATE SELF IN ACTION

A case in point is Mary Beth, a white woman, in her early 40s, wife, mother of two adolescent boys, director of a credit union in a community hospital, and a recently matriculated student at a state university. Embarrassed by her lack of a college degree, she has tended to easily get separated from her sense of competency. Despite all that she has done, feelings of inadequacy often overtake her. She has struggled with depression and anxiety, and is currently being treated for these conditions. In the context of therapy she has at times voiced self-hatred and has had fantasies of running away from all her responsibilities. Her feelings of inadequacy have been further aggravated since her 13-year-old son, Timothy, who had been acting out at school, was recently diagnosed with depression. She has tended to feel responsible for his depression.

By chance one day, early on in the therapy, I (A. de V. P.) happened to notice a letter that Mary Beth had written the editor of a local religious paper. She was protesting the decision by a diocesan authority to evict a soup kitchen from a local church. The letter was strong and impassioned, reminding the religious authorities of the scriptural mandate to serve the poor. Here, I thought, was a voice of conviction and compassion, stunningly clear and empowered, beyond anything I might have expected based on the more typically doubting and self-deprecating voice I was used to hearing in the context of therapy.

I became curious about the strength of Mary Beth's convictions and the intensity of her compassion. Might these not be resources for her to draw on and for the work of therapy to draw out? Later in therapy Mary Beth mentioned another way she has been putting her convictions into action and extending herself to others. As part of a class assignment, she had done volunteer work for an organization called Daily Bread. She had decided to continue her involvement after the class ended, inviting her son, Timothy, to join her. Together on a weekly basis, they deliver an evening hot meal and breakfast-makings for individuals of modest means recently discharged from local hospitals and recovering from or struggling with health problems (AIDS, for example). I asked Mary Beth to reflect on her commitment to this activism, its meaning for her, and its effects on her.

She invited me to accompany her and her son one day, and I did. I was immediately struck by how self-assured, engaged, and animated Mary Beth was as she delivered the meals. It was as if she had broken free of the burdens that so often oppress her spirits. Both when talking with the recipients of the meals and with me about this later, she was enthusiastic and gracious, expressive of a caring and compassionate self. Clearly she and her son enjoy this volunteer work. Timothy says he enjoys "helping other people." He adds, "I feel warmhearted and helpful." Just as clearly, they enjoy doing it together. It has been good for their relationship. Mary Beth explained that the drive home gives them an opportunity to discuss lots of issues: "It keeps an occasion open for Tim to talk about his feelings. He tends to be more focused." She is very clear that she and her son deliver not only nutritional sustenance but emotional as well. The work also provides emotional sustenance for their relationship with each other

Mary Beth does this community service, she explained to me, because she is concerned about people who fall through the cracks in our society and cares about acting on their behalf. The work has had particular meaning and benefit for her, keeping alive for her the memory of a very dedicated physician cousin who died at a young age of AIDS. Volunteering for others with health problems has been a way to heal her grief. Her cousin would be, she believes, "very proud" that she is "helping in this way" when there is still such a stigma about AIDS. "People still need to be touched; people still need to be hugged," she said. Mary Beth does both. This volunteer work also helps her to gain "perspective," reframing her own struggles and hardships. "The grass is not always greener," she said. By her participation Mary Beth experiences that her person and presence make a difference and are of value. By her participation she helps to generate the hope of a community that cares.

For me as therapist it has become important, in the context of the therapy, to recognize and reflect on the convictions that inspire Mary Beth's commitment to community work. That recognition has helped to create a fuller and more accurate picture of Mary Beth. It also has helped Mary Beth to value and develop her distinctly healing resources of passion and compassion and to value herself as someone who cares and does make a difference.

FAMILY THERAPY INTERVENTIONS FOR HEALING, EMPOWERMENT, AND HOPE

How can family therapists promote and help to develop a justice-seeking spirituality with client families? We want to highlight three important ways: (1) fostering justice-seeking connections and community for our client families; (2) fostering connections between therapists, client families, and the community; and (3) fostering connections among professional colleagues.

Fostering Justice-Seeking Connections and Community for Client Families

For Betsey and Mary Beth their justice–seeking activism has brought therapeutic benefit, in each instance opening up more room for hope, helping to strengthen a sense of empowerment and purpose, and generating the healing or sense of well-being that comes through the experience of connection and community. It is important for family therapists to be mindful of interventions that can enhance and extend the possibilities of such benefits. The most obvious intervention is what in liberation theology (and the work of the Brazilian educator Paulo Freire) is called *conscientization,* enabling "persons to hear their own voices and to perceive the dimensions of injustice contributing to their situation" (Graham, 1992, p. 107). For therapists this involves hearing the cries of the people and, rather than just trying to ease their pain, encouraging them to do the political analysis and reflection enabling them to understand the systemic causes of their pain. An intervention that follows from this first one of conscientization, or reflection, is action, prescribing for members of families justice-seeking activism (specific to their particular concerns, needs, and passions). Some examples, are participation in community or advocacy organizations like Mothers for Justice, Mothers Against Drunk Driving, or various gun control groups; issue-specific support groups like the National Family Caregivers Association, or rape or incest survivor groups, survivors of homicide victims, or AIDS support groups; or service organizations like Daily Bread or Habitat for Humanity. The goals of such activism include the creation of an empowered community and social change, working to make things more just. Such activism can, as Mary Beth and her family experienced, help to recontextualize family members' problems, changing their perspective much as widening the angle of a lens does. Moving out of and beyond oneself can be empowering, leading one to find oneself anew.[1] Such activism also can elicit, literally call forth, and help to cultivate individual and familial resources, qualities of generosity, commitment, compassion, dedication, self-giving, vulnerability, empathy, and courage, all of which are resources to draw on for healing. And such activism may well help to heal disorders and injustices in the social structures.

Our culture is biased toward stories of individual or family responsibility. By encouraging families to engage in justice–seeking activism, therapists can also help families to expand their family narratives to larger system and community narratives, thereby helping to strengthen a collective sense of responsibility and empowerment. Such a systemic narrative includes an appreciation of all levels—individual, family, community, and broader culture. As family therapists, we are ideally situated to help to promote precisely those connections with community that help rebalance scripts skewed too narrowly toward individual responsibility (and blame). The following case illustrates this approach.

One economically depressed working class neighborhood requested help from the community-based satellite clinic of a regional mental health center for problems with an adolescent gang that was disrupting and vandalizing the local library after school hours. Initially, the solution was defined in terms of intervention at the individual level with the trouble-making adolescents and their dysfunctional families; the parents were viewed as unable to provide adequate structure and control. Introducing the perspective of a wider angle lens, one clinician noted that the city had several years earlier entertained a request to develop a youth community center for this area of the city and had endorsed the idea, but it had never followed through with providing the necessary funds. This lack of follow-through had reinforced the community's view of themselves as marginal and powerless. The individual acts of violence had developed in this larger context.

As an alternative to traditional therapeutic intervention, a team of three clinicians, including myself (J. S. R.), was constituted to approach these adolescents regarding help with the city's lack of follow-through on their commitment to develop a youth center for their community. We invited the "troublemakers" to provide leadership to resurrect this idea and confront the city with honoring its commitments. This intervention worked. Gradually, the initial core group of adolescents recognized the need for a larger critical mass; they began to mobilize their own families, other adolescents and their families, local churches, and other neighborhood organizations in a community organizing effort. The connection with community went still further. Aware that annually, as a community service, the first-year students at the Yale School of Architecture would design and help build a worthy project in New Haven, I suggested a linking. Besides the enormous cost savings, I saw this as an opportunity for collaboration between parts of the larger community that were normally far apart geographically, socioeconomically, and culturally. The Yale students and the Architecture School embraced the project. Public hearings and media attention brought final approval and funding. Adolescents (including the original gang members), their siblings and parents, other members of the community, and Yale students worked alongside one another in building the youth center. In addition, adolescents were included in the advisory committee to help develop and oversee the future of the youth center.

A more traditional intervention would have located the source of the problem and the focus of intervention in the individual adolescent and/or their families. Instead, we viewed the problem behavior systemically as an expression of dysfunction at the level of this neighborhood's lack of adequate services and their marginalized, inequitable status within the city. As mental health professionals, we redefined the problem so as to facilitate the process of empowerment for the adolescents, their families, and the community at large and to enable actions toward achieving greater social justice and community well-being.

Yet another way to foster connection and community is through the use of time-limited or ongoing monthly multiple family discussion/support groups (Steinglass, 1998). They can serve as a cost-effective, powerful therapeutic approach for families facing similar life challenges such as health and mental health problems (Rolland, 1994). With psychoeducation, rather than therapy, as the stated goal these groups are more acceptable for families unaccustomed to using traditional mental health services. A major benefit of such groups is their ability to counteract isolation by establishing networks that extend well beyond the group meetings. This is particularly important for conditions such as AIDS, which are prone to patterns of secrecy and fears of stigma and discrimination that can severely isolate a family.

Sometimes, multiple-family support groups can empower families in their struggles with other systems. For example, a time-limited group (six sessions) was offered to families coping with occupationally related respiratory diseases resulting from chemical sensitivity. For many, inadequate workplace health safety precautions to toxic chemical exposure were significant in causing their conditions. Many of the cases involved discrimination and litigation with previous employers. The group meetings were empowering for participants. At the last meeting of this psychoeducational series, the group decided to form an information, advocacy, and self-help network for themselves and other similarly affected families throughout the state.

With many families, prescriptions for action may not be necessary to help them to connect with communities of support and empowerment. As therapists we may need simply to be more intentional and thorough in scoping out the activism that is sometimes already part of a family's spirituality and of their "connective tissue." That activism may be participation in a religious congregation or community of faith, or volunteering as Mary Beth and her son do for a social service organization, or working for nuclear disarmament, school reform, or some other cause. What do these engagements mean for the family members? What inspires or motivates the activism? What effects does the activism have on the family unit? How do these involvements reflect and/or effect both the belief system and the well-being of the family? Do they help to generate hope? Do they create or contribute to a sense of empowerment? Do they help to create or enhance the experience and reality of community?

Such questioning on the part of therapists opens the therapy room door to parts of the family story (and health) that all too often can be either eclipsed by the presenting problems or overlooked by the family or the therapist or both. Family members may simply take such activities for granted without fully appreciating or even recognizing their therapeutic benefit. Therapists, meanwhile, may be using such a close-up, problem-focused lens that they do not even notice, much less attend to, a client family's larger context of community involvement and spiritual activism.

Such inattention is problematic for two reasons. It overlooks potential "cotherapists," to the extent that a client family's expression of a justice-seeking spirituality through participation in community or congregational groups can generate, as we have been arguing, the therapeutic benefit of hope and empowerment and can therefore be a resource to draw on for healing. Inattention also can create a dynamic whereby as therapists we end up treating families individually and in isolation, as if abstracted from their context, rather than treating them holistically and in the context of the community where they live and where they create meaning and find purpose.

Fostering Connections between Therapists, Families, and Community

Full collaboration means active and equal partnership of various professional disciplines, client families, and the community. If we believe in socially just partnerships, as therapists we have an ethical responsibility, where possible, to challenge elitist aspects of our professional identities and the adverse spiritualities of our work systems, as evidenced particularly in hierarchical power relationships and in the resulting effects of marginalizing and subordinating families we serve.

Recent collaborative models in the family therapy field, such as the use of narrative approaches (H. Anderson, 1993; Freedman & Combs, 1996; Hoffman, 1990; M. White & Epston, 1990) are congruent with and expressive of a justice-seeking spirituality. The major focus of these models is to move the therapist away from the expert-in-charge stance toward a more egalitarian partnership with clients. The hope in this process is to empower families and transform therapy into a mutual search for new options and understanding. Development of a reflecting process and reflecting teams (T. Anderson, 1991) has helped level the therapy playing field, through open discussion between the team of professionals and client families. In this method, the reflecting team first watches a family session, then openly discusses it while the family and therapist listen, and ends with the family's reaction to the reflecting team's discussion while the team listens. This facilitates a supportive, open, more egalitarian process in which the client family feels part of a larger team and the therapist team feels more connected to the family from mutual interaction with them.

As family therapists, we can foster our own connections with wider justice-seeking communities by forming relationships with consumer advocacy organizations that serve the needs of populations related to our areas of expertise. Many such organizations have professional experts on their advisory boards. In my (J. S. R.) involvement in serving families with serious illness, I have found collaborative relationships with such consumer organizations as the National Family Caregivers Association, the Well Spouse Foundation, the National Alliance for the Mentally Ill (NAMI), and illness-specific organizations such as Y-ME (the national breast cancer organization) empowering for both families and professionals.

Many advocacy organizations have extensive experience with policy formulation and gaining access to the policy process. Many have professional lobbyists and consultants who are able to have their voices heard in a variety of circles that could benefit a coalition of professionals and consumers. As one strategy for developing socially responsible service delivery systems, we should not underestimate how the potential of alliances with consumer groups can help us. In turn, clinicians can provide the consumer advocates with the family-based research and clinical data to buttress their own experience and insights and thus help them be more effective advocates.

Fostering Connections among Professional Colleagues

The future of the profession and personal well-being of family therapists is tied to our ability to envision and translate systemic thinking into the larger society and issues related to social justice. With changes in the system of health and mental health care, we are in grave danger if we understand our professional vulnerability as family therapists to be outside the larger sociopolitical context, leading us into isolationist, competitive struggles for a shrinking turf. Worse than the old adage of "rearranging deck chairs on the sinking Titanic," we sometimes appear to be "fighting over the deck chairs." Our own professional vulnerability is isomorphic with the families we treat and in many ways a microcosm of the overall status of health care in the United States. If we are going to help our clients, we cannot afford to let our own feelings of fear and even of despair allow us to retreat into our offices. Our own empowerment and that of the families we treat is largely dependent on our seeing our need for connection to each other and communities beyond our offices.

As family therapists, we can band together to advocate for social justice concerning issues of discrimination to families. The recently formed Council on Contemporary Families (CCF) is one such initiative. The CCF is committed to promoting the strength and welfare of all families, by fostering an informed and constructive discussion of what contemporary families need and how those needs might best be met. The CCF sees a need for accurate information on which to base public policy on the problems facing diverse families today. The CCF views the national discussion as having become politicized under the rubric of "family values" characterized by simplistic diagnoses and one-size-fits-all prescriptions. This harms many people by stigmatizing and pathologizing any family that differs from the traditional, idealized norm. The CCF feels that explanations of family difficulties and promotion of family strengths must not be based on moralistic political rhetoric or nostalgia that glorifies a vanished past, but rather on systematic evidence gathered from research on the actual array of current family forms. The CCF advocates for public policies and private initiatives that promote this philosophy.

CULTURAL VALUES THAT CHALLENGE SPIRITUALITY

If our work as family therapists is to be truly liberating and collaborative, if we are to be part of the solution and not the problem, if we are to help families and individuals to be "fully alive," connected in community, we as therapists (and as citizens, too) have a responsibility to be extremely vigilant. As therapists we need to be awake and aware of our own constraints in fostering and pursuing this justice-seeking approach. Otherwise, the risk is that our practices will contribute to, reinforce, or even replicate tendencies in our society that separate people and undermine the solidarity of community and of community involvement that is at the heart of spirituality. Otherwise, the risk is that we will be healing wounds lightly, or in the words of the prophet Jeremiah, "treat[ing] the wound of . . . people carelessly."[2]

The tendencies in our society that separate and isolate people, erode community, and trivialize meaning are real and seductive; they are embedded in and intrinsic to the American culture. Individualism, to take one example of a tendency, "lies at the core of American culture," observe Bellah et al. (1985, p. 142). In recent decades loss of community and blatant cynicism about community have replaced idealistic notions of community action and the communalism of the 1960s. This demoralization accompanied the intense individualism of the "me generation" and a heightening of a competitive spirit of winners and losers. In many ways, ideas of community retreated to the level of family, with the family viewed as the basic set of connections or a safe haven that would buffer us from the cutthroat, competitive jungle of the "outside world." Another such tendency is materialism or consumerism. As the theologian Walter Brueggemann describes it, consumerism is "the seduction that getting and having and using is the main mode of humanness" (1978, p. 126). It fosters "I–it" relationships and undercuts the mutuality and collaboration that are essential to community and spirituality. It seduces us with the promise that between every need and fulfillment is a product.

Yet another tendency characterizing, indeed infecting, the American culture is violence. No less a body than the U.S. Judiciary Committee on March 12, 1991, reported that the United States "is the most violent nation on earth" (Graham, 1992, p. 244). Violence is clearly in the American grain.

Professionalism can be yet another tendency. If, as family therapists, we experience ourselves as fundamentally different from the families "we treat," then we begin a process of disconnection not only from those families but also from their existing and potential communities. We lose therapeutic effectiveness. Systemically, we become less and less available to the possible connections not only for the client families but for ourselves in connection with our clients and these communities. We jeopardize the right relations that result from working collaboratively with clients and community and relating in an egalitarian rather than hierarchical manner.

Despair is yet another tendency. It has been argued that "despair is the spirituality of empire."[3] In the current world order the United States is clearly an empire—in fact, *the* empire. Those who benefit from the current unjust distribution of power and wealth have little interest in encouraging liberation. They have a vested interest in the status quo and the immobilizing reality of despair that so often overtakes and oppresses those in our communities who are "down and out": the unemployed, the poor, often single mothers, those with addictions, the disabled. Despair serves empire because, typically, concomitant with loss of hope and loss of heart is a loss of confidence in one's own power (or motivation) to change the way things are, to make a difference, to transform the world, even one's immediate world. Thus disempowered, people often become docile and learn to tolerate the intolerable, to leave unchallenged the indefensible, to surrender to the way things are, disbelieving in the possibilities for transformation; in short, they accommodate injustice. Protest is silenced. Despair reigns.

Family therapists need to be vigilant precisely because these cultural tendencies—individualism, consumerism, violence, professionalism, despair—function like counter or competing or adverse spiritualities. Like all spiritualities, these too have their various tenets—for example, might makes right; the survival of the fittest; pulling oneself up by one's own bootstraps; money is power; there is nothing that money can't buy; it's a dog-eat-dog world; nice guys finish last. The effects of such tenets are several: competition, exploitation, commodification and objectification of persons, abuse, narcissism, separation, division. Each is obviously counter to the benefits of the justice–seeking spirituality we have been describing and recommending: connection, community, caring, compassion, and consciousness of divine spirit infusing and sacralizing all that is. These counterspiritualities all lead to the erosion of community and humanity.

These counterspiritualities are pervasive and ubiquitous in our culture, however. They are tendencies we all contend with. No one is unaffected. We inhale these tendencies, sometimes unawares. Like pollutants in the air we breathe, they can build-up in us, to toxic levels. Chellis Glendinning points to the effects of toxicity in her book, *My Name Is Chellis & I'm in Recovery from Western Civilization*. Everybody she knows, she writes, is "in recovery: recovery from personal addiction, childhood abuse, childhood deprivation, the nuclear family, sexism, racism, urban alienation, trickle-down economics, combat service in the trenches of the gender wars, the threat of extinction, linear thinking, the mind/body split, technological progress, and the mechanistic worldview" (1994, p. ix). All are exposed, creating, in Glendinning's words, "massive suffering throughout our society."

Meanwhile therapists have no corner on immunity from these counterspiritualities. Our very practice as mental health professionals is itself affected (infected). As evidence of the adverse effects on the practice of therapy, the psychologist James Hillman has identified several developments. He points to the way in which mental health has moved from being "a charity to a commerce." It has become a commercial enterprise making profits from illness. Has mental health been selling its soul? Mental health has also moved its focus from the body politic to the individual (or to the individual family), using such a close-up lens that therapists have often failed to see that, again in Hillman's words, "The sickness of the individual is the sickness of the state, or of the kingdom."[4] Given these developments (with managed care compounding and aggravating them further), as therapists we may find ourselves contributing to, complying with, or caught up by the tenets of our culture's counterspiritualities. We can be seduced, experiencing ourselves, for example, foremost as professionals and as part of the professional system and distinct from client-consumers and their communities. Although we may disdain the corporate control of health care, our identity as professionals and the fears we have of losing our increasingly precarious professional status and base of financial security lead us to cling to this ambivalent relationship. In the process, we become increasingly disconnected from our clients and communities. In the world of managed care our clients become increasingly wary of our motives. In the same way, those controlling the health care system are wary of our forging stronger connections to clients, communities, and consumer-advocacy organizations. They know that this is the one alliance that could change the current balance of power and transform the health care system in our country.

Family therapists need therefore to be vigilant. Both as professionals in our clinical practices and as individuals, we need to be engaged in the activism (the resistance) of a justice-seeking spirituality if we are to protect against the adverse yet seductive effects of our culture's constricting spiritualities. The justice-seeking spirituality that we have been describing and advocating in this chapter promises expansive therapeutic benefit. It offers an antidote to our culture's counterspiritualities. At the same time it offers a means, if not a method, for fostering the connections and community, the right relations, that are intrinsic to and vital for the liberating experiences of hope, empowerment, and healing. A justice-seeking spirituality moves people from separation to belonging, from disconnection to community, from powerlessness to empowerment, from compliance to compassion, from unjust relations to right relations, from despair to hope. A justice-seeking spirituality promises to be healing and vitalizing not only for our client families but also for ourselves as family therapists and as human beings.

NOTES

1. This represents a spiritual truth and insight, articulated in ancient Scriptures, in the teachings of Jesus for example: "Those who find their life will lose it, and those who lose their life for my sake will find it" (Matthew 10:39).

2. Jeremiah 8:11: "They have treated the wound of my people carelessly, saying 'Peace, peace,' where there is no peace."

3. This concept of despair was put forth in the first draft of the Kairos/USA (1994) document. The Kairos movement in the United States engaged more than 125 multicultural, faith-based local groups, organizations, or churches in theological reflection about the *kairos* of the Quincentennial in 1992. The document in its final version was entitled "On the Way, From Kairos to Jubilee." Three earlier *kairos* documents inspired the writing of "On the Way." In 1985 South African Christians wrote a *kairos* document challenging, from a theological perspective, the apartheid system in South Africa. In the late 1980s Central American Christians wrote a *kairos* document, reflecting theologically on their reality and time. Similarly, Christians from the Phillipines, South Korea, Namibia, South Africa, El Salvador, Nicaragua, and Guatemala wrote "The Road to Damascus: Kairos and

Conversion" (Brown, 1990). All four documents seek to name and reflect theologically on a *kairos*, a decisive time in history that invites communities of faith to respond in creative, courageous, and prophetic ways.
4. Notes from a lecture given by James Hillman at a conference on "Psychotherapy: What Is Its Future?" held at the Omega Institute, Rhinebeck, NY, 1993.

REFERENCES

Anderson, H. (1993). On a roller coaster: A collaborative language systems approach to therapy. In S. Friedman (Ed.), *The new language of change: Constructive collaboration in psychotherapy* (pp. 323–344). New York: Guilford Press.
Anderson, T. (1991). *The reflecting team.* New York: Norton.
Bellah, R. W., Madsen, R., Sullivan, W. M., Swidler, A., & Tipton, S. M. (1985). *Habits of the heart.* Berkeley: University of California Press.
Berryman, P. (1987). *Liberation theology.* Oak Park, IL: Meyer Stone Books.
Boyd-Franklin, N. (1993). Class, race, and poverty. In F. Walsh (Ed.), *Normal family processes* (2nd ed., pp. 361–376). New York: Guilford Press.
Brown, R. McA. (1988). *Spirituality and liberation.* Philadelphia: Westminster Press.
Brown, R. McA. (Ed.). (1990). *Kairos: Three prophetic challenges to the churches.* Grand Rapids, MI: Eerdmans.
Brueggemann, W. (1978). *Prophetic imagination.* Philadelphia: Fortress Press.
Clinebell, H. J. (1983). Toward envisioning the future of pastoral counseling and AAPC. *Journal of Pastoral Care, 37*(3), 180–194.
Dostoyevsky, F. (1950). *The brothers Karamazov* (C. Garnett, Trans.). New York: Modern Library. (Original work published in Russian 1880)
Falicov, C. J. (1995). Training to think culturally: A multidimensional framework. *Family Process, 34,* 373–388.
Freedman, J., & Combs, G. (1996). *Narrative therapy: The social construction of preferred realities.* New York: Norton.
Glendinning, C. (1994). *My name is Chellis & I'm in recovery from Western civilization.* Boston & London: Shambhala.
Graham, L. (1992). *Care of persons, care of worlds.* Nashville, TN: Abingdon Press.
Gutierrez, G. (1984). *The power of the poor in history.* New York: Orbis Books.
Harrison, B. W. (1989). The power of anger in the work of love. In J. Plaskow & C. Christ (Eds.), *Weaving the visions: New patterns in feminist spirituality* (pp. 214–225). San Francisco: Harper & Row.
Hoffman, L. (1990). Constructing realities: An art of lenses. *Family Process, 29,* 1–12.
Imber-Black, E. (1988). *Families and larger systems: A family therapist's guide through the labyrinth.* New York: Guilford Press.
Kairos/USA. (1994). *On the way, from kairos to jubilee.* Chicago, IL: Author.
Larson, J., & Micheels-Cyrus, M. (Eds.). (1986). *Seeds of peace: A catalogue of quotations.* Philadelphia: New Society.
Macy, J. (1989). Awakening to the ecological self. In J. Plante (Ed.), *Healing the wounds* (pp. 201–212). Philadelphia: New Society.
McGoldrick, M. (Ed.). (1998). *Re-visioning family therapy: Race, culture, and gender in clinical practice.* New York: Guilford Press.
Mirkin, M. (Ed.). (1990). *The social and political context of family therapy.* Boston: Allyn & Bacon.
Niebuhr, H. R. (1978). *The meaning of revelation.* New York: Macmillan.
Rolland, J. (1994). *Families, illness, and disability: An integrative treatment model.* New York: Basic Books.
Rolland, J. (1997). The meaning of illness and disability: Sociopolitical and ethical concerns. *Family Process, 36*(4), 437–441.

Steinglass, P. (1998). Multiple family discussion groups for patients with chronic medical illness. *Families, Systems, and Health, 16,* 55–71.

Waldegrave, C. T. (1990). Just therapy. *Dulwich Center Newsletter, 1,* 5–46.

Walker, A. (1982). *The color purple.* New York: Washington Square Press.

Walsh, F. (1998). *Strengthening family resilience.* New York: Guilford Press.

Washington, J. (Ed.). (1986). *A testament of hope: The essential writings of Martin Luther King, Jr.* San Francisco: Harper & Row.

Wehr, D., & Young-Eisendrath, P. (1989). The fallacy of individualism and reasonable violence against women. In J. Brown & C. R. Bohn (Eds.), *Christianity, patriarchy, and abuse* (pp. 117–139). New York: Pilgrim Press.

White, M., & Epston, D. (1990). *Narrative means to therapeutic ends.* New York: Norton.

Index

(*b* indicates boxed material; *f* indicates a figure)

293

295

D

Daily Bread, activist organization, 281
Dalai Lama, 129–130, 196, 203, 207
"Day of the Dead" fiesta, 114
Dead Man Walking, 128
Death, 40–41
  African American beliefs, 97
  denial of, 40, 169–170
  Native American view, 40–41, 45
Death penalty, views toward, 22
Deep breathing, 44
Deficit-oriented fatalism, 115
Deloria, Vine, Jr., 16, 22, 24, 48
Delphic oracle, on self, 230
Despair, isolating value, 288–289
Devil, belief in, 18
*Diagnostic and Statistical Manual of
  Mental Disorders* (DSM–IV)
  Latino syndromes, 106
  religious/spiritual problems, 32
Discourse, concept of, 209
Distress
  loss of loved one, 40
  spiritual sources of, xi, 38–39
Diversity, religious and cultural, 13–
  16, 22, 48
Doherty, William J., 35, 86, 173
  spiritual context, 179–180
Dossy, L., 39, 63, 64
Du Bois, W. E. B., 93

E

Eastern Orthodoxy, in United States,
  12
Eastern religions, healing in, 33
"Ecological system," IFS, 224
Eigen, Michael, 164, 165
Einstein, Albert, 32
Embodied spirituality, 158
Empacho (indigestion), 106–107
Empty chair technique, 98
Endurance, Latino coping strategy,
  116
Espanto (fright), 106
Espiritismo (spiritualism), 15, 110
Espiritistas (spiritual mediums), 109,
  110–111, 117–118
Ethical values, role of, 5–6

Ethnicity, impact on religious
  diversity, 14–16
Euthanasia, views toward, 22
"Evangelical" Christians, 13
"Evil eye," 15, 106
Evil inclination, 196, 202
Evil, nature of, 128
Exercises, spirituality, 258, 259–270,
  260*b*, 262*b*, 266*b*, 268*b*
Exodus, story of, 131–133, 277
Externalization, among Latinos, 115–
  116
"Extratherapeutic factors," 85

F

Faith
  health benefits of, 39
  nature of, 22–24, 38
Faith healers, view of, 31
Families
  beliefs about illness, 64–65
  caregiver, suffering of, 66
  diversity, 3–4
  divine presence in, 140–141
  justice within, 166
  religious practice, 9
  religious rites/ceremonies, 5
  resilience, 37–38
  religious diversity in, 48
  spiritual practices/beliefs, 181
  "underorganization" of, 77
Family assessment, spirituality review,
  35–36
Family finitude, 171–173
Family life cycle
  religion in, 10–12
Family rituals, exercises, 258, 263–265
Family therapy
  critique of, 279–280
  embracing paradox, 161–165
  justice-seeking spirituality, 282–287
  spirituality in, 3, 4, 34–35
Family values, 9, 136
Fanon, Franz, 110
Fatalism (*fatalismo*)
  among Latinos, 115–116
Feminism, on patriarchal traditions, 19
Filial loyalty, 146, 148

T

Talmud
  filial piety, 140, 141–145, 149
  multigenerational identification in, 139
Tao religion, in United States, 13
Teaching, parental role, 139
Teenagers, religious beliefs of, 11
Therapist
  constraining beliefs of, 66, 68, 74–75
  and families in poverty, 73–81
  health beliefs of, 65
  self-leadership, 236–237
  spiritual beliefs of, 50, 63, 87, 90
  as spiritual expert, 86
  spiritual focus, 79–81, 83
"Think in other categories," 198
"Through the Ages" exercise, 259, 265–267, 266b
Thurow, Lester C., 79
Tillich, Paul, 274–275
Torah
  filial piety, 140, 144
  role of, 137–138
Traditional religious beliefs, role in family system, 36–37
Transactional analysis, 224
Transpersonal psychologists, 228
Trauma
  impact of, 224
  nature of, 193
  relief from, xi, 204
  vicarious, 196–197
Treatment, concept of, 33
12-step programs, addiction, 41–42

U

Unitarian/Universalist, 13, 180
Universal spirit, belief in, 17
"Universal within," 78
"Unknown God," 77

V

"Vacation Bible school," 94
Virgin of Guadalupe, 112–113
Vista fuerte (strong vision), 106

W

Walker, Alice, 23–24, 275
Well Spouse Foundation, 286
Whitaker, Carl, 162
White, Michael, 81, 86, 249
Wiesel, Elie, 130
Wilbur, Ken, 198, 229, 233
Williamson, Donald S., 152, 161–162
Winnicott, Donald W., 164–165
Witches, Latino beliefs, 107, 108
Witness
  self as, 229–230, 232–233
  therapist role, 66, 67–68, 74

Y

Yerberos (herbalists), 110, 117–118
Y-Me, activist organization, 286
Young adults, religious practices, 12

Z

Zen meditation, 44, 229